Children, Youth, and Spirituality in a Troubling World

Children, Youth, and Spirituality in a Troubling World

Mary Elizabeth Moore
Almeda M. Wright, EDS

CHALICE
P R E S S
ST. LOUIS, MISSOURI

Bible quotations, unless otherwise noted, are from the *New Revised Standard Version Bible,* copyright 1989, Division of Christian Education of the National Council of the Churches of Christ in the United States of America. Used by permission. All rights reserved.

Scripture quotations marked (CEV) are taken from the *Contemporary English Version.* Copyright © 1991, 1992, 1995 by American Bible Society. Used by Permission.

Scripture quotations marked (ESV) are from *The Holy Bible, English Standard Version®,* copyright © 2001 by Crossway Bibles, a publishing ministry of Good News Publishers. Used by permission. All rights reserved.

Cover art: FotoSearch
Cover and interior design: Elizabeth Wright

Visit Chalice Press on the World Wide Web at
www.chalicepress.com

10 9 8 7 6 5 4 3 2   09 10 11 12 13 14

Library of Congress Cataloging–in–Publication Data

Children, youth, and spirituality in a troubling world / Mary Elizabeth Mullino Moore and Almeda Wright, co-editors.
    p. cm.
  ISBN 978-0-8272-0513-0
  1. Children–Religious life. 2. Youth–Religious life. 3. Parenting–Religious aspects–Christianity. 4. Church work with children. 5. Church work with youth. I. Moore, Mary Elizabeth, 1945- II. Wright, Almeda. III. Title.
  BV4571.3.C45 2009
  270.083–dc22

                                                        2008044099

Printed in the United States of America

Contents

Acknowledgments

This book begins with gratitude, especially to the children and youth with whom we have walked in making the book. They have been wise, vulnerable, energetic, and revelatory. They have informed and delighted us, and they have raised profound, often unnerving questions. Our gratitude also extends to the countless children and youth whom we picture as we cast hope for the book's future. We hope the volume will contribute to the flourishing of all those young people whose mentors, religious leaders, families, and friends read these pages.

We also wish to thank several particular people, beginning with the Association of Practical Theology (APT), which engaged in two extended sessions on the subject of children and youth in a troubling world in 2002, a double session connected to the American Academy of Religion, followed by the APT's biennial conference. Some chapters in this volume were presented initially in one of those gatherings. The APT discourses helped identify themes on which practical theologians have much to contribute; they also identified issues, research projects, and theoretical frameworks that have since generated further study and dialogue. One purpose of this volume is to expand and deepen that ongoing conversation, bringing practical theologians together around a common concern about which they have much to offer in insight and practical wisdom.

This volume is communal in another significant way. It was part of a three-year focus on Children in Law, Society, and Religion, sponsored by the Center for the Study of Law and Religion (CSLR, formerly Center for the Interdisciplinary Study of Religion) at Emory University. Funding was provided by The Pew Charitable Trust, Inc. Through the generosity of CSLR and Pew, we were able to sponsor a writers' conference in May 2005. In this venue, we engaged the chapters of this volume in a public panel and in small working sessions with academic and professional leaders. The working conference enhanced esprit de corps among the authors and enlarged our visions. It also helped authors deepen, refine, and integrate their work with that of others. We left the conference with a sense of the whole, together with practical guidance for our particular chapters. This contributed to the quality of the book and to the vitality of our work in integrating practical theological research on young people. For the support of CSLR, we say a particular thank you to John Witte, Anita Mann, Amy Wheeler, and April Bogle. For the conference itself, we say thank you to the authors, who worked together magnificently, and to a team of assistants and readers who engaged the early versions of chapters with astuteness and guidance. These included: Sybrina Atwaters, Julia Wallace, Jessica Davenport, Sheila Elliot, Natalya Shulgina, Sarah Poole, Pam McCurdy, Cathy Wright, Andy Webb, Michelle Holtmann, Jeannine Pope, Sharletta Green, Katie Davis, Mike Stone, and Lauren Dunkle.

We also offer thanks to the editorial teams with whom we worked in making this book. Ulrike Guthrie, a freelance editor, gave important guidance at the outset, suggesting ways to integrate a volume that has many authors. Trent Butler was very helpful to us as we worked with Chalice Press, as have been Cynthia A. Meilink, Lisa Scronce, and Gail Stobaugh. To these people, with their expertise in editing and communications, we say a hearty thanks!

Finally, we thank our readers, who will continue the dialogue sparked by this book. More important, you will continue sharing your gifts with the young, while receiving and delighting in the gifts that young people themselves are eager to share. We hope sincerely that the book will contribute to young lives and to those who love them!

Contributors

Claire Bischoff is a doctoral student in the Graduate Division of Religion at Emory University, and coeditor of *My Red Couch and Other Stories on Seeking a Feminist Faith.*

Susanne Johnson is Associate Professor of Christian Education at Perkins School of Theology, Southern Methodist University, in Dallas.

Jennie S. Knight is Assistant Professor in the Practices of Religious Education and Community Ministries at the Candler School of Theology, Emory University in Atlanta.

Joyce Ann Mercer is Professor of Practical Theology at Virginia Theological Seminary in Alexandria, Virginia, and a licensed clinical social worker. Her most recent book is *Girltalk, Godtalk: Why Faith Matters to Teenage Girls–and Their Parents.*

Veronice Miles is an ordained Baptist minister serving as the Jessie Ball DuPont Instructor of Homiletics and Christian Education at the Wake Forest University School of Divinity.

Bonnie J. Miller-McLemore is E. Rhodes and Leona B. Carpenter Professor of Pastoral Theology at the Divinity School of Vanderbilt University and author of several books on women, families, and children, including *Let the Children Come: Reimagining Childhood from a Christian Perspective* and *In the Midst of Chaos: Care of Children as Spiritual Practice.*

Mary Elizabeth Mullino Moore will become Dean of the School of Theology, Boston University, in January 2009. She is the author of several books and currently directs the Women in Theology and Ministry Program at Candler School of Theology, Emory University, where she is also Professor of Religion and Education.

Rodger Nishioka serves as Associate Professor of Christian Education at Columbia Theological Seminary in Decatur, Georgia. He served for twelve years as denominational staff in youth and young adult ministry for the Presbyterian Church (U.S.A.).

Evelyn L. Parker is Associate Professor of Christian Education at Perkins School of Theology. She is the author of several books and articles, including *Trouble Don't Last Always,* and the editor of *The Sacred Selves of Adolescent Girls.*

Luther E. Smith Jr. is Professor of Church and Community at the Candler School of Theology at Emory University in Atlanta.

Joshua Thomas is an ordained priest in the Episcopal Church and a doctoral student at Emory University, focusing on interfaith peace education with youth.

Katherine Turpin serves as Assistant Professor of Religious Education at the Iliff School of Theology in Denver.

David F. White is C. Ellis and Nancy Gribble Nelson Associate Professor of Christian Education at Austin Presbyterian Theological Seminary.

Almeda M. Wright is a doctoral candidate in Practical Theology at Emory University, where her research focuses on spirituality and race-identity development among African American youth. She currently serves as the Assistant Director and Research Coordinator of the Youth Theological Initiative at Candler School of Theology.

Karen Marie Yust is Professor of Christian Education at Union-PSCE and author of several books on spiritual formation.

INTRODUCTION

Children and Youth Choosing Life

MARY ELIZABETH MULLINO MOORE

A young man drove five of his friends on a weekend outing. As he approached a curve in the road, a bit too fast, he lost control of his car, careening off the road and into a tree. Five of the six young men in the car were killed, leaving their families and loved ones to mourn the tragic, unexpected loss, and leaving the family of the driver to mourn their son's driving error, not unlike the errors that most drivers make many times in their lives. How does one choose life when haunted by the unexpected immanence of death?

Some threats to life are more predictable than a car accident. By August 2007, the war raging in Iraq had taken more than 3,500 United States soldiers' lives, more than 65,000 Iraqi lives, and still additional ones from other countries. A large percentage of these, both soldiers and civilians, were children, youth, and young adults. Meanwhile, children die on city streets from hunger, gang violence, and drive-by shootings. Others die at the hands of their parents. Still others perish from water contamination in places where prolonged violence has destroyed infrastructures, such as refugee camps in Darfur and in Palestine. To these threats we add the destructive powers addressed in this book: the realities of "boy codes," father-loss, family abuse, racial discrimination, poverty, civil war in one's homeland, media-enhanced materialism, and the complexities of peer and adult relationships. How do we encourage children to choose life in such situations? How do we create conditions in which they can flourish and build their lives for lifelong flourishing?

The idea of choosing life challenges a world in which many young people have few choices and in which death bells ring, death tolls rise, and death threats echo. This book is about that choice. The authors have collectively committed themselves to understand the troubling realities of this world and to help build a world in which these troubles are not the last word. Our purpose is to choose life for the sake of young people, drawing upon the life-giving elements of religion and culture, and critiquing that which thwarts life.

The practical theologians who have written here address two critical questions:

- what is at stake for young people?
- what is possible?

They have drawn upon the resources of their craft to conduct research, analyze the present situation, reflect theologically and culturally, and propose future directions for life-giving ministries with and for the young. They do so with the scholarly gifts they have cultivated, as well as the illuminating discoveries and captivating prose that allow them to shine fresh light on perplexing questions. We begin by considering questions that motivate this volume; we proceed by reflecting on methods by which authors have addressed these questions and themes that have emerged in our collective work.

What Is at Stake?

What is at stake for the authors and readers of this book? More important, what is at stake for the children and youth for whom and with whom we journey? I suggest that the central issue is whether we will love life or love death. The immanence of death shapes our world, as does the love of death, or the habit of loving death. The late Grace Jantzen contrasts this habitus of death (necrophilia) with a habitus of life (natality).[1] Though Jantzen spent her own last years living with cancer, she was less frightened by her impending death than by the death-dealing ethos of Western culture. Tracing epics of Western literature and religious-political rhetoric, she described an ethos of loving death and celebrating war. In this ethos, people make war leaders into heroes, "fight" war and poverty with war language, create enemies to serve as scapegoats, and seek to resolve problems by combative politics or military force.[2] This is the world that shapes the lives of young people, and it shapes the options from which they choose.

In light of Jantzen's analysis, we in the West (and I would add many parts of the Eastern world) have deeply ingrained habits of loving death. How can we, in such a world, create habits of loving life and create conditions in which the young can love life and flourish? Indeed, people do seek to love life, but sometimes in ways that ignore or magnify the powers of destruction. Frequently, we allow tragedies and needless destruction to go unnoticed: the war toll in Iraq; injustices and fears in Israel and Palestine; destruction in Darfur and Bosnia-Herzegovina; inhumanity in family lives;

cultural materialism; and rape of water, land, and air. Jantzen's analysis, informed by Pierre Bourdieu's reflections on habitus, pushes deeper.[3] She urges us to see that we have been formed into this habitus of loving death and that we can be re-formed into another habitus. That is what is at stake: the habitus of loving and choosing life.

In particular, this volume is about loving and choosing life for and with children and youth. It is about drawing life from spirituality and religion. It is about finding and nurturing life in human culture, even in the more troubling aspects of the world in which we live. The title derives from these three dimensions: children and youth, spirituality, and the troubling world. Much more could be said about each of these, but the value of our work is the attempt to bring them together. Other books explore the history, psychology, and sociology of childhood and youth; others explore the complexities of spirituality and its relation to religion and diverse religious communities; others analyze the troubles of our current world. We need not repeat these. What we intend, instead, is to find paths of hope in the lives of young people, in their spiritual traditions and communities, and in the world as it is. What we intend is to build on those hopes for the sake of future practice.

As regards children and youth, a critical issue is how we approach young people in ways that are honest about tough realities and still life-affirming. How do we avoid temptations to idealize, victimize, problematize, theorize, and utilize the young? This is challenging because we do want to glimpse and appreciate young ideals while recognizing the realities of victimization and the problems that young people face without making overgeneralizations and oversimplifications. At the same time, we want to develop useful theories and find ways in which children and youth can be agents of their own liberation and life-making. We hope to do all of this without abstracting young people into an ethereal realm or using them for our adult aims. We cannot be completely oblivious to the dangers I have named, but we can at least acknowledge that the dangers are real and that we seek and hope to avoid them as much as possible.

As regards spirituality and religion, a critical issue—especially for practical theologians—is to draw upon the resources of spirituality and religion in a full-bodied way: rediscovering, reclaiming, critiquing, reforming, and reconstructing them. We hope to be honest about traditions without dismissing them or making glib assumptions about their problem-solving, answer-giving potential. Some chapters draw upon particular traditions in fresh ways. Some raise fundamental questions, and others suggest revisions to theological theories and religious practices for the sake of young lives.

As regards culture, a critical issue is to recognize the death-loving, death-dealing aspects of culture, while also recognizing and claiming the life-supporting aspects of culture that permeate the world. Culturally speaking, the very language that people in the United States and many other parts of the world use to describe young lives often re-inscribes the concerns that we seek to address. Such language even directs people away from hope. Language such as "youth-at-risk," for example, categorizes youth into those who are in danger of being destroyed by cultural pressures and those who are not. The very label can be destructive to those youth whose lives are haunted by harsh realities. Cultural practices that limit tolerance for children in public places further encumber young people in their search for life. Further, the association of certain kinds of dress or music with certain values is another cultural danger, thus obscuring and oversimplifying the complex expressions and longings of young people. What is needed is a way to reflect honestly on the harsh realities of the world and on the particular ways in which children and youth are vulnerable to those realities without assuming that these are purely determinative of young lives or beyond the possibility of cultural transformation.

In sum, the choice for life is at stake in this book. The authors seek to understand, advocate for, and foster life-giving practices with children and youth. We seek to nourish a life-giving spirituality that critiques, resists, and re-forms our troubling world. Such hopes seem beyond possibility; but we are committed to discern what is possible and to develop ideas, visions, and practices through which the possible becomes real.

What Is Possible?

We do not claim that everything good is possible to fit in one volume. We know, however, that a wealth of literature has recently been published on children and youth, alongside a multiplication of projects and experiments for responding more adequately to the young in schools, religious communities, social agencies, and families. We hope to build upon these efforts and to do so with the unique expertise of practical theologians with diverse specialties, experiences, and forms of research. Our desire is to move beyond the simple identification of problems and solutions, because young people are more complicated, wise, and powerful than this approach suggests. Further, we hope to move beyond abstractions and oversimplifications about young people and their religious communities and cultures. Our hope is to understand with depth and to contribute with creativity to the interrelated lives of children, youth, and the worlds in which they live.

To accomplish such high goals, we have addressed a cross section of life situations in which young people live, attending to young people of diverse social classes, ethnicities, genders, and life situations. Our intention is to discover ways by which children and youth can choose life, ways by which churches and other communities can nourish the lives of young people, and ways that children and youth can foster life in their churches and communities. These are large intentions, and we hope to uncover large visions, while simultaneously offering realistic images and practices to guide the future. We also hope that the diversity of our studies, focusing on young people within diverse contexts, complements work that has already been done with foci on particular socioeconomic or ethnic communities.[4]

We come to these challenges as practical theologians with diverse expertise and interests. Many are preachers, pastoral caregivers, religious educators, and ethicists. Some are activists, some are empirical researchers, and some are theory-builders. Most of us combine these. The divisions and subdivisions are only relevant to show the scope of our interests. We are bound together in our love of young people and in our hope that practical theologians can corporately make a contribution to their well-being.

What specifically does this mean? Practical theology can be defined in many ways. For the sake of simplicity, we offer a working definition of the field: *the study of God and the world by engaged reflection on action (past or present practice) and reflection for the sake of action (future practice)*. Practical theology, thus, originates in the world of practice, moves into engaged reflection and construction, and returns to praxis as the goal. As a field of study, practical theology is both new and old. The earliest theology of most religious communities was practical theology. In early Christian communities, for example, we find Paul's letters. Paul analyzed the contexts and practices of the communities to which he wrote; he reflected theologically on these contexts and practices; and he made proposals to the communities for action. Paul's letters were grounded in *praxis* knowing and located in the particular communities that inspired Paul to write them. Similarly in this book, we focus on the contexts and practices of living communities. We reflect on them theologically. We propose future actions for communities who care about children and youth. Our "engaged reflection" takes many forms, including reason, imagination, and aesthetic exploration (especially narrative exploration). Thus our methods vary and, we hope, complement one another.

As practical theologians, the authors of this volume are particularly concerned about how the love of life and the love of death are manifested in the world today. Thus, we have approached our various chapters with methods attuned to these large purposes and to the diverse communities we have studied. Our methods include empirical description, narrative analysis, theological and cultural analysis, reconstruction of theories and practices, and mapping of new directions for understanding and engaging with young people. Herein lies one of the distinctive contributions of this book--drawing largely on qualitative research and reflection thereon. This complements some of the more statistically oriented and issue-focused work that is currently available.[5] Statistics can give overviews of random samples, but cannot highlight the complex textures of young lives and the communities in which children and youth live. Issue-focused work can explore social and theological issues in depth and can develop significant approaches to address these issues. A book such as ours does something distinctive, bringing different issues and approaches into dialogue and thus building upon and complementing the work that is presently available. For this purpose, the range of methods, subject matter, and contexts is important, as is the dialogue with other scholars and writers who could not be present in this one book. More specifically, our methods include:

Literature review. Some authors, such as Bonnie Miller-McLemore and Veronice Miles, have focused on recent literature and the dominant understandings of children and youth in that literature.

Personal experience as case study. Others, such as Luther Smith and Katherine Turpin, have drawn upon personal experience to provide case studies, bringing their experience into dialogue with statistics, movements, and literature.

Retrospective accounts of ministry. Similarly, Karen Marie Yust, David White, and Jennie Knight have drawn upon their experiences. Their particular approaches have included the study of journals and printed ministry documents from a particular period of ministry with young people. They have created retrospective accounts of these ministries and engaged in a critical, constructive dialogue between these ministries and perspectives in the current literature.

Field observations and interviews. Another methodological genre is field observations (Almeda Wright, Susanne Johnson, and Mary Elizabeth Moore) and interviews (Evelyn Parker, Veronice Miles, Rodger Nishioka, Joshua Thomas, and Moore). Each of these proceeds differently, utilizing complex methods suited to the particular study. For example, Joshua Thomas conducted longitudinal interviews with young people in Bosnia-Herzegovina after the war that tore their land apart. Susanne Johnson combined field observations with interviews to understand the power of youth community organizing (YCO).

Action research. Finally, the method of action research is represented in this volume by Claire Bischoff, who conducted story-sharing and media-reflection groups as part of her "Stories of Gender" project. She observed the groups over a period of weeks, recorded field notes, and reflected with the young women about their individual and collective experiences.

Such a mix of methods suggests the richness of the volume and the potential for conversation within each chapter as well as among chapters. Different subject matters and different methods uncover diverse realities, issues, and visions, thus expanding the potential of the volume to deepen understanding and stir imagination for the future.

We acknowledge also what we cannot do in this volume. We cannot, in a collection such as this, explore one issue or perspective in depth, though some issues, such as poverty and violence, are explored in more than one chapter. What we can do is to discern convergent themes in the larger discourse. We turn now to these.

Emerging Themes: Building and Pushing on Current Literature

Themes in this book resonate with a global discourse. For this reason, we enter in a spirit of dialogue. Dialogue is critical to practical theology, which seeks to understand the world, to imagine what the world can be, and to project religious practices to enhance that future. Practical theology is complex, however. It includes and connects with many fields–preaching, pastoral care, constructive theology, religious education, administration and leadership, ethics, congregational studies, and others. Further, its dialogue partners include scholars in diverse areas of theology, religion, and the social sciences. Practical theologians typically bridge across worlds–between areas of study, and between scholarly discourse and living communities. The result is a wide range of genre within the field, as well as considerable pressure to write for broad audiences attracted to journalistic prose and to make credible appeals to well-known theorists in other areas of study. For these many reasons, practical theologians engage in little written dialogue among themselves, thus dampening a generative, depth-seeking discourse.[6] In the pages of this book, we hope to create such a discourse, and we hope also to engage with others who are not part of this book but are partners with us in the work. We begin the dialogue here, naming common themes in young people's lives as they are explored this volume.

Gifted

Children and youth are *gifted.* Indeed, their resources surpass what is often expected of them. Karen Marie Yust describes the creativity of adolescent girls in a residential treatment facility. Katherine Turpin describes her daughter's ability to write new endings to stories popularized by Disney and others. David White describes the creations of youth in the Youth Discipleship Project, including drama, media productions, and a community garden. Susanne Johnson describes the remarkable ability of young people to give leadership in community organizing. Evelyn Parker even recognizes "holy indignation" as a gift that can help transform communities and unjust social practices.

Emerging from the gifts named in this volume are needs, especially for self-expression and accomplishment. Karen Marie Yust portrays these needs in her vivid description of Natalie's creativity with Goth cosmetics and Gillian's passion "to knit as many hats for babies in the neonatal intensive care unit at Boston Children's Hospital as she could produce in her free time." Evelyn Parker underscores the importance of young people having constructive opportunities to express and reflect upon their rage. David White awakens readers to the eagerness of young people to create worship, media events, or a theater production on dating relationships and gender roles. These examples reveal that gifts are not only treasures for the future, but are contributions for the present moment, which youth need to share and the larger community needs to receive. Self-expression and accomplishment are natural yearnings for gifted children and youth.

Situated

Children and youth are also *situated within social contexts and personal life histories.* The authors probe many of the complexities of these situated realities. We discover in these pages, for example, that gender is complex. Rodger Nishioka interviews young men and discovers that "boy code" values and discouraging experiences, such as low achievement in school or intense judgment by teachers and peers, weigh heavily on boys. On the other hand, the boys he interviewed did not fit the theories exactly. Curtis, for example, was not at all sure that the boy code was present in his setting, and both Curtis and Nathan make good grades in school. We see here, as in other chapters, that gender pressures and influences are real, but they are not uniform. They are shaped differently in different contexts and different lives. Joyce Mercer similarly discovers that the life histories of young girls who have experienced father-loss challenge existing theories about fathers and daughters, and Claire Bischoff discovers that young women tell varied stories about what it means to be a girl in spite of dominant cultural images.

The complexities continue when we read of the experiences of young people who lived through the war in Bosnia-Herzegovina, experiences that left some determined to help rebuild their country and others eager to move on and have a comfortable life for themselves and their families. These diverse responses are understandable in light of the childhood traumas of war and the present economic and social crises of their country. The diversity reveals, however, how difficult it is to generalize or to assume simple contexts. Similarly, race plays a complex role in young people's lives–a case that Almeda Wright makes when she names the marginalization of African American youth, and Evelyn Parker makes when she describes the rage that builds up within African American young people as a result. Veronice Miles connects this marginalization with patterns in biblical texts. Jennie Knight recognizes how the pressures to conform vary among youth from diverse social classes and ethnicities. White, middle-class girls seem to experience more of this pressure than girls from other ethnic communities and lower socioeconomic backgrounds.

Being situated is more than living within a social context. Young people also have unique personal histories. Joyce Mercer describes the unique experience of father-loss for young girls and the diverse forms of such loss. Karen Marie Yust describes the journeys of young women in a treatment facility and the ways in which their unique and difficult life journeys have shaped their self-expression and longings.

Yearning

Another mark of children and youth is their *yearnings, arising from the complex interplay of their inner being, interpersonal and community experience, cultural influences, and experiences of the Transcendent.* For Katherine Turpin's daughter, the yearning was to see and shake hands with a Disney princess. It was also to be part of her church community. From the perspectives of Veronice Miles, Almeda Wright, and Evelyn Parker, the yearnings of youth are to break silence and to bear their testimonies. For young women who engaged with Claire Bischoff, the yearnings were to share their stories, hear the stories of others, and reflect together. For the young people of Bosnia-Herzegovina, the yearning that Josh Thomas heard most often was to rebuild their lives with jobs, families, and stability. For the young people Susanne Johnson interviewed, the yearning was to contribute to a more just and equitable community. Yearning and hope are the central themes of my chapter. They include yearning for the Holy, for community, to understand the world, for ethical guidance, and to make a difference in the world. Underneath these yearnings are deep passions, which need to be recognized and appreciated for the power they bear.

Isolated

A fourth mark of children and youth is that they are often isolated— *isolated from adults/mentors, from their peers, from God, from faith communities, from healthy images of adolescents, and from themselves (their true selves).* This isolation impairs their ability to imagine new futures and construct healthy identities. One early reader of these chapters, Kate Hurst Floyd, in her review describes the isolation as sad:

> I can't help but feel a kind of sadness and injustice that youth are so isolated; this is particularly tragic and ironic because they live in an ever-increasingly "connected" and globalized world. But the result seems to be that we are increasingly disconnected from actual human and divine relationships.

Almeda Wright echoes this awareness as she ponders the yearning of African American young people to be heard:

> [A]mong African American youth, the predominant issue is not that they have lost their ability to speak for themselves nor that they feel they have nothing worthwhile to say. More often, what they say is not deemed significant or credible. Therefore, when they speak, the youth sense that "no one" is really listening or caring about what they say.

Indeed, many authors in this volume have analyzed the complexities of isolation and have emphasized practices such as community-building and listening.

Young people often express a strong need to overcome their isolation, as is the case with the young girls whom Joyce Mercer describes in her narratives of father-loss. When given opportunities to engage intensely with others and develop fuller relationships, young people respond very positively, as the glowing reports in chapters by Claire Bischoff and Jennie Knight show. Young people are eager to make meaning, to speak ("live out loud"), and to travel with "co-journers," according to Veronice Miles. The multiple analyses of isolation in this volume do not lend themselves to simple descriptions of a problem and simple solutions. We are, instead, made aware that isolation is an existential reality that is not amenable to being fully overcome. On the other hand, it is ameliorated by good listening, community connections, and strong relations with mentors and peers.

Identity-shaping

A fifth mark of children and youth is the *challenge to form and re-form their identities among competing influences and claims on their lives.* Some authors place the formation of identity at the center of their work. Katherine Turpin and Claire Bischoff problematize the challenge of girls forming identity when faced with media-reinforced cultural scripts of princesses, ideal body types, and sexual appeal. For Turpin, focused on children, the challenge is to counter popular culture, permeated by Disney and other popular storytellers and image makers. For Bischoff, focused on youth, the challenge is to foster identity formation that is "enduring yet adaptable," especially in the face of media images and adult absence. Almeda Wright focuses her identity analysis on the challenges of African American young people. She is concerned with the silencing and disregarding of their words and actions. In response, she proposes that hearing and sharing testimonies may be a vital way to foster identity formation.

Imagination Seeking

One of the particularly fresh emphases of this book is on imagination— *the imaginative capacities of young people and their need to imagine and reimagine their lives.* In the early chapters, Luther Smith and Bonnie Miller-McLemore invite *readers* to imagine, re-envisioning the ways we understand and relate with children. Most authors highlight the imaginative qualities of young people themselves and awaken readers to the social functions of imagination. We see the imaginative use of cosmetics as providing a point of human connection (Yust). We see how imagination can counter dominant culture, as when Katherine Turpin invites her daughter to imagine alternative stories to the dominant Disney narratives with their happy-ever-after, rich, and beautiful endings. We see how imagination can create space to grieve father-loss (Mercer), to shape alternative visions of masculinity (Nishioka), to approach biblical stories and images of God in fresh ways (Yust and Miles), to create and live into new life narratives (Thomas and

Bischoff), and to envision and work toward more just communities and social structures (Johnson and White). For Claire Bischoff, imagination is important to youth's identity work. For Josh Thomas, it promises a way by which young people can re-envision and re-narrate their lives after living through war and socioeconomic upheaval. Imagination is thus critical for the present and future lives of young people.

Socially Endangered

Social endangerment is another mark of young lives, especially *endangerment by violence, poverty, materialism, and media formation.* Luther Smith's chapter frames the issue at the outset, focusing on social forces that threaten children and youth. He acknowledges problems of poverty, limited access to healthcare, and spiritual crisis; and he poses questions that others seek to address in later chapters. From another direction, Jennie Knight accents the alienation between youth and adults, the prevalence of stereotypes and ethnic tensions, and the pervasive problem of violence. She poses hospitality as a way forward, thus echoing Smith, who is concerned with how many churches care for their own children but disregard others. Viewed together, these two chapters underscore the potential for hospitality toward children and youth within and outside the faith communities.

To these chapters can be added features in others. Violence is addressed within domestic contexts (Yust), national contexts (Thomas), racialized contexts (Parker), and contexts of poverty and attendant injustice (Johnson). It also takes more subtle forms, as in the repeated note of young people's being ignored, unheard, and denigrated.

In Need of Public Witnesses

This theme leads directly to the eighth and final mark of children's and youth's lives—*the need for public witnesses.* This mark appears in the first two chapters of the book, thus framing the discussion that follows. Children and youth, according to Luther Smith, need advocates in all quarters of the community, including interreligious and ecumenical bodies, as well as the unique witness of each faith community. Speaking particularly to Christian churches, his own religious communion, he bemoans the tendency of churches to ignore children and to attend, at best, to "their own." He blames human culpability for the churches' failure, especially "the lack of loving attention and activist care in the public square." Building on a similar theme, Bonnie Miller-McLemore bemoans the narrow conception of children and of Christianity in public debates and the narrow conception of children in contemporary Christianity. Her hope, thus, is not only for advocacy in the public square, but also for "public conversation that incorporates children and religion" more fully and carefully, with full awareness of "the adult proclivity to misuse children and the study of children for some other purpose."

As the book unfolds, the theme of public witness expands. Some authors, such as Susanne Johnson and David White, underscore the importance of youth as *agents* in public discourse and in social problem-posing and problem-solving. The authors' combined emphasis is thus on public witness *by, with, and on behalf of* the young.

This introduction now concludes so the book can begin. Our central hope is that children and youth might treasure their lives and be treasured by others so they may choose life again and again. Treasuring the young underscores the harm that can befall them in a troubling world and the urgent need for people, young and old, to imagine and actively contribute to a healed world, marked by love and justice and peace. With this vision and hope, we begin.

PART ONE

The Young in a Troubling World

When Celebrating Children Is Not Enough

Luther E. Smith Jr.

Every church I know celebrates children and encourages its members to care for them. Their programs include religious education, designated children's Sunday worship services, children's choirs, graduation celebrations, and service projects with the poor, elderly, or disabled. A few of these churches extend their witness to the children of their community through day care, tutoring, vacation Bible school, and recreational programs.[1]

What churches do to nurture children is commendable. Still, the absence of church involvement in the lives and issues of many children is conspicuous. Millions of children linger in crises without religious care. Some children are overwhelmed by an environment of poverty; children with chronic illnesses are without healthcare. Children suffer stress, anxiety, and even death from living in communities plagued by violence. These are the young people whom The Annie E. Casey Foundation describes as "America's most disconnected youth": teens languishing in foster care, youth enmeshed in the juvenile justice system, high school dropouts, and teen parents.[2] Others express a similar concern for younger children who are forced to the social margins.[3]

Why are so few churches involved with these challenges? Is this the result of deficient theologies and ecclesiologies? Are churches intimidated by the complexities of influencing public policy? Do churches fear these children and their circumstances? The questions themselves embarrass the church. They imply that churches may be ill-prepared to fulfill their identity and mission. However, the issues that embarrass us may point us toward transformation.[4] We can begin to see transformative possibilities when we name our spiritual crises and live into our faith with ever greater clarity and resolve. The embarrassment we feel can be a prelude to more faithful discipleship.

This chapter tarries with these questions and discusses their implications for a spirituality that embraces all children. A practical theology that avoids such questions and their promise for transformation is neither worthy of being considered faithful practice nor sound theology. Even more important than the viability of a particular practical theology is the viability and vitality of children. What we speak and what we practice should foster "response-ability" for the children whom God has entrusted to us.

My reflections in this essay are informed by over thirty-five years of personal activism with children's issues; thus, my method might be described as a combination of memoir and case analysis in dialogue with data and literature about children. One caveat is worthy of note. In my engagement with children and advocacy, I have worked extensively with interfaith organizations. The challenges of caring for children are for all faith traditions; yet I feel especially answerable for the witness of my own tradition—Christianity. I am (and on a corporate level, the churches are) held accountable to its teachings and examples. This essay's focus on churches is not a dismissal of the need for all faiths to engage with children's realities; rather, the focus reflects my sense of urgency for discussion within my own family of faith.

Children in Crisis

Churches care about children. While the Christian faith teaches care for *all* children, congregations commonly focus only on their own children. This leads some church leaders to adopt the primary strategy of caring for children by increasing the number of children in their churches. If the children are seen, known, and loved by members, then they will receive the support that comes from a church family.

The accent on caring also characterizes congregations that embrace children from the community. In many churches, however, members are wary of children whose backgrounds and motivations are unknown. Thus, they offer few expressions of hospitality to community children. Carl S. Dudley's research on small churches verifies this pervasive practice. He finds that nonmembers often experience difficulty in being accepted into a small church's caring network. In these churches, interpersonal relationships formed over extended periods of time define the boundaries of care. Thus, nonmembers are considered outsiders for whom the church has no obligation.[5] Though the dynamics of large churches are more complex, they can also be places where nonmembers do not feel welcome—especially children who do not fit the majority profile.

Even when churches welcome children with open arms, their witness is still needed on behalf of the millions of children who remain in desperate circumstances. Care and nurture for these children depend more on churches finding their way to the public square than on children making a trek to the churches. As Bonnie Miller-McLemore discusses in the next chapter, the public square is the place where policies and practices determine whether or not children survive and thrive. Educational forums, letter writing, participation in legal hearings, advocacy marches, and engagement with institutions that play a major role in children's lives are public square activities. Sometimes overlooked or forgotten by the church, the public square is a crucial place for Christian witness on behalf of children.

To be clear, I am not primarily addressing Christian *individuals* in the public square–people whose jobs in agencies and government place them in that arena. Christian individuals who serve children through their jobs often express discipleship in that way and extend the church's witness; however, the witness of individuals does not replace the church's collective presence as local church, denomination, ecumenical force, and interfaith organization. Church presence in these collective forms offers a different influence on issues affecting children. When the church acts as a body, it affirms a communal identity, with collective discernment and determination. Its collective voice and resources have a distinctive influence on policymakers and the general public.

Even with this capacity to influence how children are acknowledged and embraced in the public square, the church's record is characterized by absence and silence. On major issues facing children–issues regularly considered by school boards, local governments, state legislatures, and Congress–churches are mostly missing in action. Obvious examples come to mind that challenge this conclusion. Many churches are visible and outspoken in the public square on issues of abortion and same-sex relationships. Christians are on all sides of these issues, contending with one another over whose position is more consistent with the tenets of Christian faith. Convictions are so strong and emotional expression so fierce that Christian activism is at times not only intense, but also ugly.

Abortion and same-sex relationships are important issues. They deserve vigorous civil debate and respectful strategies of persuasion. By no stretch of the imagination, however, can we argue that these are the only issues worthy of attention, especially when millions of children are in a life-and-death struggle. Ironically, unlike the disagreements over abortion and homosexuality, Christians would likely find more common ground about positions and remedies as they focused on other issues besieging children.

Do any Christians find infant mortality acceptable? And yet the United States, the world's richest nation, ranks forty-second among countries with the lowest infant mortality rates.[6] A myriad of severe and sometimes lifelong health problems accompany low birth weight–a problem affecting one in thirteen babies born in the United States.[7] What group of Christians would advocate withholding prenatal care that would improve infants' chances of healthy lives? In one year, over three million cases of child abuse and neglect were reported in the United States.[8] Even with disagreements about the efficacy of corporal punishment, one would be hard pressed to find churches endorsing child abuse and neglect. Every day in the United States eight children are killed by firearms.[9] Despite this culture's romance with guns, what Christians dare shrug when asked about ways to limit children's exposure to gun violence? Worldwide, we see trafficking in child prostitution, child soldiers, and over 100 million children who are killed, maimed, or displaced by war. Do these realities merit Christian indifference?

Human culpability is the source of most of these crises. All of these crises persist and grow from the lack of loving attention and activist care in the public square. Marian Wright Edelman, one of the most notable child advocates in the United States, places blame for what is happening to children on the failure of "people of conscience" to put forth a decent struggle on behalf of children. We react to the crises of our children with resignation rather than outrage. She writes:

> It's time to close the adult hypocrisy gap between word and deed for children. It's time to compete with those who would destroy, neglect, and lead our children astray. The soul snatchers have been busy at work turning family and child dreams into drugs and violence and greed and consumption. The budget cutters have been relentless and swift in pursuing their special interests and turning child hopes into cold despair and grinding child futures into dust. Child advocates must get better and tougher at reclaiming our children's birthright to freedom from fear and want by working together and with more disciplined messages and priorities.[10]

This is the challenge for people of faith. The "hypocrisy gap between word and deed for children"[11] is wide. How else could we hear so much in our sanctuaries about the significance of children and see so little activism in the public square on their behalf?

Understanding the reasons for this gap is crucial for reducing or eliminating it. One explanation is that churches and other institutions of high ideals are hypocritical by their very nature. The "fallen" state of humanity and the self-centeredness of institutions (prepared to jettison their ideals to survive another day) are explanations often given for this hypocrisy. These theological and sociological explanations may have elements of truth, but they are not sufficient to foreclose analysis. First, they fail to explain successful initiatives in bridging the gap between word and deed. Fallen humanity and self-centered institutions have often responded to crises with heroic effort. The church's absence from the public square and from discourse on critical issues named here is a result of choice more than nature. Second, "fallen nature" explanations of human failure do not fully explain the *extent* of the gap between word and deed. Doing very little on public policy issues is one thing. Doing nothing is a whole other matter.

Children confront health, economic, and social crises that threaten their futures. Additionally, the adults on whom they depend are in faith crises that restrain their responsiveness to the realities of children. Understanding faith crises is essential to liberating adults to advocate in the public square with the passion and compassion that God desires and God's children need.

Children on the Margin

A Georgia State legislator described to me how she and her colleagues looked with amusement upon animal rights activists who came to the state capitol to advocate for policies to protect animals. The legislators were amused because the activists' cause was not a priority on the agenda of any legislator. Then she said:

> But these people persisted. Day after day they were at the capitol pushing their cause. Outside they distributed literature to passersby. Inside they spoke with legislators about the urgency for new protections for animals. To my surprise, by the end of the legislative session, they had received most of what they wanted.

The legislator continued with a comment that stunned me: "I've been a legislator for over twenty years. And in all my years here, serving on the committees with oversight on programs affecting children, I have never experienced the tenacity for children that we experienced from the animal rights activists." I do not present this example to diminish the importance of protecting animals. The stunning aspect of the legislator's comment was the absence of a comparable effort on behalf of children. More than a description, her comment was an indictment.

Could it be that we celebrate children *instead of* advocating for them? Is it possible that our lack of activism reflects ambivalence about the worth of children? Indeed, many cultures through history have considered children of marginal significance. History is replete with societies that have treated children as cheap labor, property for arranging marriages that improve families' social standing, or soldiers in war. The inherent worth of a child as a human being who deserves protection and nurture is lost when children are primarily valued for their profitability to adults.[12]

Consider a story from the gospels (Mk. 10:13-16) in which Jesus confronts the marginality of children in his culture. Jesus was involved in the esteemed act of teaching, and people were gathered to hear holy instruction from a holy man. Traditionally, nothing superfluous should interrupt such a sacred time. Yet, into this place of holy teaching and time, people brought little children so that Jesus might bless the children. Jesus' disciples reacted to prevent the interruption of this adult event. They "spoke sternly" (10:13) to those who brought the children. This was not the time for children to occupy the attention of those involved in holy discourse. Upset that the children were blocked from his company, Jesus said, "Let the little children come to me; do not stop them; for it is to such as these that the kingdom of God belongs" (10:14). Jesus uplifted children as people who were meant for the holy. He embraced the children and blessed them.

This biblical story establishes the importance of children to all that is holy.[13] The kingdom of God entails children. They embody the very characteristics that are crucial to anyone who is pursuing God's ways. Jesus invited, esteemed, embraced, and blessed the children. They may have been interruptions to the agenda of adults, but they were not interruptions to lessons on holy striving that Jesus taught. In word and deed, Jesus transformed children's marginal status to one that is integral and instructive to the whole community of faith.

Unfortunately, after hearing the sentiments of the text, we cannot say, "case closed." Children remain on the margins of attention in churches and the public square. In light of improvements in child labor laws, mandatory public education, and social services for orphans and children in abusive homes, this statement of marginality could be challenged as an exaggeration. These three examples of public action are presented as evidence that society has progressed in caring for children. The case remains open, however, because we have failed to make sufficient progress on these very issues when they resurface in places and forms that seem distant from our original concerns.

We enforce child labor laws in the United States, but we have failed to enforce provisions against child labor in trade agreements with developing countries. Public education systems have high dropout rates among poor and ethnic minority students. State budgets are under-funded to meet the basic and special needs of children in foster care. The economics of protecting and nurturing children would appear too costly for international businesses and state and national budgets.[14]

Economics also drives the sexual exploitation of children. The network of providers, financiers, and publicizing agents is so extensive that it is called an "industry." Further, producers of video games, music, films, and toys expose children to gratuitous violence. Children are central to the economics of sexual exploitation and selling violence, and they remain marginal to Christian activism.

In state after state, legislators have decreased the age by which juveniles can be tried as adults for certain crimes. Some have even pushed to execute juveniles who previously would have avoided capital punishment by virtue of their age. The prevailing notion seems to be that adult behavior indicates readiness for adult penalties. As a culture we are quick to place upon children adult "response-ability" and to punish childhood deviance. Even juveniles who are not accused of felonies will find themselves in a judicial system that is unprepared to render needed care and rehabilitation. They are assigned lawyers who are not familiar with the juvenile codes. Juvenile detention facilities are crowded beyond intended capacity. Psychological services are absent in the detention experience of many juveniles.[15] The major voices in the public square about such problems are investigative journalists and juvenile justice advocates. They become discouraged by the absence of religious institutions in protesting what befalls children who enter the juvenile justice system. One could conclude that, as long as children behave, they are deemed worthy of Christian attention and compassion. If their behavior offends, however, they move to the margins of the churches' concerns; their lives are entrusted to the state.

Seldom acknowledged is the explanation that children's marginality occurs because they are perceived to be less important to the needs and concerns of adults. In the economic realm, until adolescence, children are not major consumers of large-ticket items, though Katherine Turpin's chapter in this volume reveals how children are increasingly targeted as consumers and how their consumption is sharply rising. Children are not yet expected to be economic producers, so they are largely invisible in the economic sphere except as objects for advertising products. One of the most commonly stated explanations about why politics and government budgets fail to be child-oriented is the fact that children cannot vote. Persons involved in the political machinery feel no indebtedness to children for their offices. Could this also explain why children sometimes lack advocacy from the church? Why are the needs of children less a priority for the church than the expectations of adults? Is this because children are not church officers or substantial financial contributors?

Sexual abuse is a vivid example because adult perpetrators often receive more support from church members than do the child victims. Victor I. Vieth, Director of the American Prosecutors Research Institute's National Center for Prosecution of Child Abuse, writes:

> In speaking at a child abuse conference, I asked the prosecutors in the room who had cross-examined a clergy-person appearing as a character witness for the accused to raise their hands. All hands went in the air. When asked how many had ever used a clergy-person as a witness for the victim, all hands dropped... In a case where the defendant was found guilty of raping a minor, a minister testified that the defendant had a good reputation in the community and that he was a truthful person. In making this claim, the minister was compelled to admit that the defendant's previous guilty plea to two counts of sexual battery, "did not in any way affect [his] opinion of the defendant."[16]

Unfortunately, Vieth's comments represent what occurs frequently with churches. This may be explained as churches wanting to avoid legal procedures. Further, most churches resist involvement in the "private" issues of families. The message for children is clear, however: you cannot rely on the church as an ally when you are a victim of sexual abuse.

Children with disabilities also have marginal status in churches. I have heard parents lament their inability to find a congregation that embraced children with disabilities. Because most congregations lack experience in caring for these children, they find it difficult to justify the expenditure of time and resources for one child when so many other children could benefit from the church's capacities. The parents of these children are often directed to a church that has developed ministries for disabled children (if such a church exists in their community). Without congregations' intimate involvement in the lives of families with disabled children, one understands why the parents of these children feel so alone when advocating for social, educational, and medical services for their children in the public square. If the followers of Jesus, who supposedly care for the most vulnerable, are reticent to be involved with disabled children in their sanctuaries, then who will stand with these children in the public square?

Perhaps the largest categories of children on the margin are the poor and ethnic minorities. They suffer the greatest physical deprivations and emotional traumas. In addition to being vulnerable to the juvenile justice system, sexual abuse, and disabilities, the high incidence of poverty exacerbates health problems, dangers to physical safety, and difficulties in utilizing education as a means to a better life. The lack of media attention to abducted and missing children from among the poor or from ethnic minorities has underscored the marginality of these children. This lack of attention to their plight and numbers has caused many to question openly whether our society perceives these children to be expendable.

In this critique of churches and their care for children, I realize that some churches are extraordinary witnesses to children on the margins; however, they are the exception. Their witness heightens awareness of how the majority of churches are not responding to God's call to care for all children. The churches that are in the public square feel the loneliness of not standing shoulder to shoulder with other faith communities. They take pride in their efforts, but they are frustrated by the surrogate role they play for those who remain on the sidelines. Further, the numbers of those involved with children on the margins and also active in the public square are disproportionately low; thus, they cannot rescue churches from this overall critique.

If the churches are in touch with the realities of children on the margins and if they are passionate about these children, where are the large numbers of persons who represent this awareness and passion? Where are the conferences to initiate prophetic activism? Where are the letter-writing campaigns bemoaning the absence of protective legislation and the threat of bad legislation? Where are the rallies to protest cuts in budgets and programs that serve children? Where is the word made flesh for children in the public square?

The Crisis Within

Why are so few churches involved with these challenges? The answers are legion, as are the issues confronting children. Naming causes can be demoralizing. Each cause has long and deep roots in church histories, cultural ethos, and personal experience. Naming, however, can help diagnose the problems in need of transformation.

The sheer number of issues confronting children overwhelms churches. Rather than marshalling energy to address what a church can accomplish, a focus on issues can lead to resignation as people perceive the enormity of effort required to protect and nurture children. Martin Luther King Jr. warned against "the paralysis of analysis" that befalls caring persons and institutions.[17] They suffer the misperception that whatever they do will not make an appreciable difference in children's lives. Consequently, no action is taken. Added to this, people find the issues of the public square, especially ones that involve public policy and legislation, to be complex and confusing. Church leaders feel unprepared to interpret issues and processes in the domain of professionals. Lacking the requisite expertise, church leaders assume they have nothing to contribute to public square debates.

The slow process by which policy and legislation come into being can also enervate church members. Attending public hearings, writing letters, organizing educational forums, and monitoring every stage of the process over a two-or-three-year period is tedious to many persons. Even if they are clear about what needs to be done, the required time and energy for issues is a sacrifice they are unwilling to make. In addition to these impediments, modern life routines make such a sacrifice of time difficult. If a child has two parents, both are likely to work outside the home. These parents are responsible for driving children to recreational events, music lessons, doctors' visits, or service organizations. School systems ask parents to assist children with homework and to be involved in school programs to enhance the educational experience of their children. Single parents feel under greater stress in their efforts to fulfill these roles. Adults who do not have primary care responsibilities for young children have busy, fatiguing schedules as well. Many rejoice when they are finally able to involve themselves in their work, hobbies, or retirement activities in ways that were impossible when they had to care for children.

The effort to care for one's own children is exhausting. To persons involved in parenting, participation in initiatives to care for other children seems praiseworthy but not possible. Decisions to enter the public square are often made on the basis of whether an issue affects "my child." This way of making decisions is understandable in light of limited time and energy, but reveals an insidious ethic that undermines a compassionate society. When people only feel responsible for their own "kind," the gap grows between diverse ethnic, racial, religious, and economic classes. This jeopardizes mutual understanding, civility, and compassion. A challenge for the churches is to find ways to bridge the gap between those whose children are well cared for and those whose children are at-risk of succumbing to deprivation, abuse, and failing social institutions.

One factor in overcoming this gap is overcoming society's increasing fear of children. Media reports on children in gangs, as perpetrators of horrendous crimes, and as challenging adult authority in schools have shifted the portrayal of children from innocents to out-of-control juveniles. The move to increase penalties for juveniles and to try them as adults is a reaction to this portrayal. The growing cultural tendency to fear children makes individuals less willing to risk interaction that involves crossing ethnic, racial, and class boundaries. People ask if these out-of-control children are worth the effort. They also wonder if they will be safe if they relate with these children. When a society distances itself from populations of its own children because it fears them, society leaves these children to exploitative elements (such as gangs, prison culture, the sex industry, and drug dealers) that are eager to claim the children as their own.

Some churches are reticent to address systemic children's issues because major "movers and shakers" in the public square are members in their pews. The administrators of agencies, school board members, politicians, juvenile justice officials, and others may be leaders or honored members of their congregations. In some of these churches, the public officials resent any involvement of their church with issues related to their public responsibility. For them, church is a refuge from the public domain. The last thing these public officials want to discuss in their congregations are issues in which they may be subjects of inquiry or protest. On the other hand, I know congregations in which such persons are invaluable resources for involving their congregations in public life. I also know public leaders who are frustrated that their churches do not make use of their expertise for moving the church toward activism for children.

Pastors are understandably uncomfortable about encouraging initiatives that could result in one group of members challenging the public responsibilities of other members. Even when the approach is issue-focused and distinguishes persons from their public offices, some public officials take criticism of their public roles as a personal affront. A church that does everything possible to avoid internal conflict is likely to avoid issues with potential to stir tension among members. Here again the question should be asked: Must the welfare of children be sacrificed to the etiquette of conflict avoidance? Is this just another instance of adults choosing to support one another at the expense of the nurture of children? Must children remain marginalized to keep the peace?

Perhaps the most fundamental reason that few churches are involved in the systemic issues of children is that most churches perceive themselves as marginal to the public square. They perceive themselves as shaping moral people to be moral decision-makers. They endeavor to make church life a meaningful experience of spiritual growth for children and civic authorities. They do not envision their church as having a direct role in shaping public life.

Does the sense of marginality result from civic leaders consigning churches to the margins of public affairs? Or is this status of marginality self-imposed by churches because of their ecclesiology or their self-assessment of incapacity for public life? Do some churches view activism in the public square as a violation of the separation of religion and state? Responses to these questions can shape a church's adopted identity of civic marginality or its decision to challenge that identity. Churches that move to the heart of public discourse experience more than a shift in social location. They experience a spiritual conversion. They hear biblical texts on social justice as narratives that inspire and define them rather than as narratives that shame them. Civic meetings and legislative hallways become places of Christian witness. With this transformation, a church need not be intimidated by or timid with public discourse on behalf of God's children.

Beyond Celebrating Children

The last section of this chapter offers recommendations for a practical theology agenda that facilitates and sustains spiritual conversion. At stake is the church's fulfilling its identity and mission. Also at stake is a more hopeful future for millions of children.

Theological diversity will always characterize the church. This diversity constitutes the church's heritage and will constitute the church's future. The agenda of practical theology is not to articulate a "one size fits all" theology as the impetus for empowering congregations to be involved in the public square. In addition to being futile, a monolithic theology would violate the different ways churches have come to know God's mission. Just as diversity in the public square is a value that must be defended, cherished, and celebrated, diversity among the churches should also be honored.

All theologies, however, are not equally responsive to the challenges of children. Theologies that define children as the property of parents justify and reinforce attitudes conducive to child abuse. Theologies that interpret the church as the only refuge from problems of a broken world reinforce disinterest in the other social institutions that shape children's lives. Theologies that are only concerned about saving children's souls inform indifference to the conditions of children. *Practical theology can help churches consider how their theology instructs and empowers them to be good news for children.*

Here are some of the questions that form and re-form theologies and ecclesiologies that are faithful to God's passion for children:

- Why should the church support initiatives that improve children's health? What initiatives can the church take to improve children's health?
- Why should the church advance efforts to protect children from abuse? What can the church do to protect children from abuse?
- Why should the church extend its outreach to children involved in the juvenile justice system? What can the church do to care for children in the juvenile justice system?
- Why should the church prepare to care for families that have children with disabilities? What can the church do to prepare to care for families that have children with disabilities?
- Why should the church be responsive to the particular needs of at-risk children? What can the church do to be responsive to the needs of at-risk children?
- Why should the church be involved with the issues that effect children locally, nationally, and globally? How is the church involved with these issues locally, nationally, and globally?

Wrestling with these questions can lead to closing gaps between official and operative theologies as well as between children and adults.

Closing Gaps between Official and Operative Theologies

A church's *operative* theology is best known through questions such as the ones I have posed above—questions that invite us to reflect on our deepest religious commitments, the mission of the church, and the actions in which we engage. This is different from a study of formal theological statements and official church doctrines. Churches can have a hundred theological convictions about caring for children; but if there are no initiatives on behalf of children, their rhetoric is but a "noisy gong or a clanging cymbal" (1 Cor. 13:1). Where a church's *official* theology expresses compassion for and commitment to children, hopefully, a church's *operative* theology reflects this as well. The Christian witness is based on the Word made flesh. Our theological beliefs depend upon the crucible of community for testing their claim upon our hearts as well as our heads. Our beliefs are also formed, in part, by the actions in which we participate.

The gap experienced in communities between official theology and the operative theology may be attributed to two theological problems. The first problem is that church members may not fully believe that God can be trusted to sustain them in the public square. Hardly anyone will admit this because it so contradicts Christian identity. Consequently, Christians will resent any implication that God fails to have their trust. But the array of excuses for noninvolvement in public life masks a deeper spiritual problem: uncertainty about God. Will God keep controversy from getting out of hand? Will God protect the church and its members from humiliation and suffering? Will God preserve the congregation's membership and financial stability? The lingering feeling is that God cannot be counted upon to answer their fears as they want God to answer them. This leads people to argue that the church's mission would be damaged by controversy, humiliation, injury, membership loss, and financial instability.

The oft-used terms "social activist" or "prophetic community" to describe a church's involvement in the public square suggest a particular orientation for bearing witness to the Gospel. Sometimes people assume that the less visibly activist or prophetic churches have chosen to bear witness through their sacred rituals and pastoral care. These are false distinctions. Prophetic activism relies upon individuals formed by ritual and caring relationships. Sacred rituals and nurturing relationships are invigorated by activism on behalf of God's call to justice and reconciliation. The failure to be involved in the public square is therefore not so much a matter of predilection for bearing witness as it is a retreat from trusting God. The realities of the public square trump convictions about God's sustenance. Here we have a spiritual crisis of great magnitude.

The second theological problem that reinforces the gap between official theology and operative theology concerns naïve conceptions. These conceptions prove dysfunctional for churches entering the public square.

One theological assertion is that committed Christians can correct *all* social problems in a community. Christians are inspired by the vision of building the realm of God on earth; however, with thoughtful analysis or involvement in community issues, communities soon learn that the world does not conform to their enthusiasm. Experiences of frustration quickly become states of despair. The public square overwhelms a congregation's sense of capacity. Churches could avoid this depleting experience by recognizing the importance of doing *something* rather than doing everything or nothing at all. With children's issues, for example, a church could devote itself to providing foster care opportunities for children. A thousand issues remain, but that one issue embraced by the church can be a path of faithful witness, transformation in the lives of children, and joy.

A second theological assertion about community assumes that problems can be fixed once and for all. I have heard preached from the pulpit: "What God fixes stays fixed." This belief is based on the conviction that the community is fixable and that doing God's work leads to *progressive* changes that continually reduce the number of community problems. Under this notion, a church may only wrestle with a few issues, but it sees itself as making an irreversible contribution to establishing the realm of God. Inevitably, a church experiences frustration with the ongoing nature of issues. Innovative programs to help juvenile offenders can have high success rates, but some children return to destructive behaviors. Legislative successes for children one year are followed by a new legislative session that threatens to reverse previous accomplishments. Churches need help in taking on issues without the illusion that they are fixing problems to the extent that they can be scratched off a "to do" list for children. Transformations made in a child's life can last for a lifetime, and transformations made in community institutions can create a more child-friendly environment. Even successes can be followed, however, by new waves of crises. A spirituality of caring and healing is a powerful witness to Christian love, even when "fixing" situations does not occur.

The final theological assertion is that community is most successfully transformed through the devoted efforts of a single congregation. Images of the lone prophetic voice inspire the conviction that community needs the intensity of a committed fellowship more than involvement from multiple community entities. Unfortunately, too many congregations believe that their most effective witness in the public square occurs when they act alone. They avoid entangling themselves in meetings with other religious groups or social agencies. Collaboration never comes to mind or is rejected. Clearly, some programs for children operate best under the auspices of a single congregation. Still, many more issues require ecumenical, interfaith, and/or social agency cooperation to make a difference. Legislative action, efforts to influence public policy, and attempts to mediate conflict between youth in different communities are examples in which collaborative action is more effective. This conviction has grown in me in years of working with the Interfaith Children's Movement of Metropolitan Atlanta (ICMma). No one congregation or religious community has access to all the information for understanding an issue, or to all the people needed to influence an issue. In addition, the increased fellowship that results from working with people outside a single congregation can be energizing. Congregations benefit from a theology of ecclesial practice that encourages collaboration.

This discussion highlights two issues for Christian churches: a spiritual crisis and an impoverished theology. If we are to offer hope for children in crisis, we need to deepen our trust in God and develop a more adequate theology of community. If any other proposals for service in the public square are to make sense, practical theology needs to begin by addressing these two issues. This does not mean that individuals must go through extensive religious education programs before entering the fray of public life. The lessons to be learned may best be received through involvement with children's issues. Whether as a prelude to involvement or as reflective discourse in the midst of action, discerning the adequacy of our faith in God and of our images of community transformation is essential to a public witness that withstands the test of reality.

Discernment never ends on the spiritual matters of trusting God and engaging the community. New realities of the public square present new challenges. Repeated discernment need not be viewed as an exasperating exercise born from inadequacy. A continual returning to the Source of our faithfulness and the reality in which we live can enliven spirit and body. Discernment is a practice born from eagerness to live in right relationship with God. It is a form of prayer, and Paul instructs the community of Thessalonica to pray without ceasing. Prayer aligns one's spirit with rejoicing and gratitude (1 Thess. 5:16–18). In that spirit, we can continually discern God's movements and question and deepen our theological convictions and actions.

Closing Gaps between Adults and Children

Just as discernment helps close gaps between word and deed, and between formal and operative theologies, the gap between adult and child must also be bridged. Fundamental to closing the gap is building relationships between adults and the children on whose behalf they witness. Children must not be reduced to statistics, issues, and problems. Such a reduction makes children an abstraction, and presenting children as an abstraction is a form of dehumanization. When adults know children by their names, faces, voices, thoughts, and feelings, children become real to adults—and caring adults become real to children. As children become real, adults experience a child's conditions of crisis as contexts for caring rather than as just regrettable circumstances.

Adults need not relate to all the children affected by a public issue, but they need to know some child's story from personal experience. This is possible with most issues. Some children's issues, such as child prostitution and child soldiers, may provide less personal accessibility to the affected children. Film documentaries, books, and articles can be used to tell these children's stories, offering intimate personal portraits. No one wants to parade children in crisis before adults and force them to describe realities that may be too painful to speak. This is an example in which collaboration with agency personnel, who work with these children on a daily basis, can help a congregation know these children. The personnel have the skills for structuring opportunities that introduce adults to the children and their stories with sensitivity and mutual respect.

Another strategy for bridging the gap between adults and children is to equip children to discern, critique, and navigate in the world created by adults. One way to do this is through programs that provide children the requisite skills to discern the cultural forces that impact their lives. Media literacy, for example, is an educational approach that teaches children how to think critically about what they see and hear. Mass media is one of the most powerful influences upon children, bombarding children with messages of consumerism, sexual intimacy, ethnic norms, personal identity, and violence. Media literacy takes seriously children's ability to acquire the requisite skills to assess and evaluate these messages.[18]

In media literacy programs, children receive insights on how media persuades. One educational technique to combat this persuasion is to place children in the roles of writers, directors, and producers of media messages. The children learn how the messages communicate a point of view by focusing the audience's attention on selected images, sounds, and words. They discuss the values being promoted, alternative ways of viewing a message, and the meanings for their own lives. Instead of being passive recipients of media, children become critical interpreters of media, and their creators.

The gap between adults and children sometimes widens when adults are in the role of telling children how to think and what to do. Children tend to rebel; they resist ceding all power and authority to adults. Media literacy acknowledges children's capacity to discern and make responsible decisions. Children involved in media literacy experience adults as facilitators of children's wisdom and authority rather than as enforcers of obedience to adult authority. Media literacy programs occur in many public education systems and some churches, but more programs are needed if children are to be analytical about the influence of media in their lives. Adults can advocate for these programs to be available in the public schools and their local churches.

Affirming the capacities of children also occurs in programs that place children in situations in which they are responsible for others. Older children can tutor and play with younger children. Children can read to senior citizens—to compensate for the senior's poor vision and/or to provide companionship. These are important ways to honor the whole child. Children do not want to be known only for their vulnerabilities and failings; they want to be noticed for their capabilities and successes. Opportunities abound for children to experience adults as sources of affirmation who proclaim their strengths.

Finally, the gap between children and adults is bridged when children are integral to the identity, mission, and work of the church. The Sunday worship service can be an indicator of the centrality of children to a church. Do children contribute to worship through reading scripture, serving as ushers and acolytes, giving announcements, and singing in a choir? Are children relegated to a "children's worship service," or do they have roles in every worship service? The adage "out of sight, out of mind" portrays what can happen when children are absent from Sunday worship. If children are not seen as contributors to worship, or if they are only present until the children's sermon, then dismissed to some location outside the sanctuary, one can understand how children are perceived as marginal to church life. If they are marginal to a church's primary time of gathering, they will also be marginal in religious thinking about the public square.

I am not arguing against church procedures that provide religious education to children while adults worship in the sanctuary. This format can be responsive to the needs of children and adults. However, the marginal status of children is reinforced when worship has no roles for children or times of presence for all children. Adults' presence with children in sacred times and places is vital if we are to see the spiritual value of being present with and for children in the public square.

Conclusion

When churches diligently involve children in their identity, mission, and work, they receive blessings from children. Such churches are also more able to extend their passion for children to the public square–a place that influences the well-being of the whole society. Practices of welcoming, embracing, and blessing children (Mk. 10:16) are essential to establishing a nurturing environment in church life and in the public square. The late William Sloane Coffin Jr. encourages people to engage the larger world with consciousness of our children. He says:

> We don't inherit the world from our parents so much as we borrow it from our children. In what shape then shall we return it: with more hunger and arms than ever before, or with less of both? And there's another question: it is not whether or not the churches could make a difference; it's whether or not they will.[19]

Coffin's words are a challenge to dominant values regarding children. In light of that challenge, we need to address several questions in the church's theological reflection and action. What will be our legacy to children? What will they cherish as examples of our prophetic witness on their behalf? What lessons will our actions teach about courage, justice, and tenacity? What stories will they tell of our bearing witness to God's power to transform the world? I pray that we so give ourselves to caring for children that we are not embarrassed to ask these questions.

Children deserve to be celebrated, but celebrating is not enough. Children require much more, and this is what we need to give. Children do not have the power to demand our attention, but they need our attention. We can reduce their marginality in church and society. We can be compassionate as we care for them in their crises and times of uncertainty. We can empower them with discernment and coping skills in a troubling world. As important as all of this, we can empower them also to care for a troubled world. We will not be able to accomplish all that our hearts desire for children, but giving ourselves fully to them is all God asks. This is enough.

2

Children and Religion in the Public Square

"Too Dangerous and Too Safe, Too Difficult and Too Silly"

BONNIE J. MILLER-MCLEMORE[1]

Children and religion have not fared well in the public realm in either modernity or postmodernity. In modernity, both were banished. Modern intellectuals pronounced the subject of children "at once too dangerous and too safe, too difficult and too silly," in art historian Anne Higonnet's words, "good only for second-rate minds and perhaps for women."[2] So children disappeared from art history and from lots of other scholarly subjects. Modern intellectuals regarded religion with similar suspicion. In postmodernity, spirituality suddenly gained new popularity, now disassociated from religion and its perceived institutional trappings of maintenance and moral mandates. Meanwhile, marketers, politicians, and academics ushered children back into view, but, more often than not, they have used them to promote some other religious or ideological agenda.

Scholars in religion have offered little help in all this shuffling and violation. So far they have not said much about the misuse of children for other ends, except in the acute case of sexual abuse. Over the last century, the subject of children has held minimal interest in the religious academy—until quite recently.

In this chapter, I join this recent attempt to put the discussion of children back on the table. I trace some of the characteristics of their public and intellectual neglect and exploitation and then offer a possible framework for reintroducing them into theological studies. I begin by examining the characterization of children in some of the current debates before turning to their (mis)representation in twentieth-century theology and to the contribution of a practical feminist theology in offering a fuller understanding. The subject matter of children, I argue, challenges the usual division between biblical, historical, systematic, and practical theology. Its reintroduction into academic study requires fresh rubrics that cross over and work among these categories.

My argument runs one step deeper, however, than a call for reorganizing theological study and raising public awareness to include children and religion. In this chapter, I do not attempt either an exhaustive portrait of the public discussion of children or an exacting outline for their inclusion in theology. Such tasks deserve more extended attention from those in the church and academy for a more disquieting reason: In many discussions of children, as my underlying argument will show, children themselves slip into the background. The very nature of children and childhood makes it incredibly hard to keep children as the central subject and to avoid using children to promote some other purpose. This is as true in academic and public circles as it is in parenting itself, and is a problem that merits Christian concern. My larger aim, therefore, is to invite public conversation that incorporates children and religion not only more fully but also more carefully, with special sensitivity to the adult proclivity to misuse children and the study of children for some other purpose.

The Narrow Conception of Children in Public Debates

Contemporary debates about children have had a strikingly narrow focus. Among the many important concerns, such as welfare reform, education, foster care, and consumerism, public discussion often gravitates back toward two issues—the controversy over the impact of day care and the reinstitutionalization of marriage as the best solution to the decline in child welfare. The latter and more recent discussion often begins with a slate of all the indices of why "our children are in trouble." These range from low standardized test scores to increased poverty and suicide to high homicide rates among fifteen-to-twenty-four–year-old males. Such statistics are cause for grave concern. However, many neo-liberal spokespersons use these data as reason to rally around marriage.

A three-part argument, first articulated by sociologist Barbara D. Whitehead in a widely discussed 1993 essay, has become a mantra of the marriage movement. It begins with these words: "Divorce and out-of-wedlock childbirth are transforming the lives of American children." Such children, it continues, "do worse than children in intact families on several measures of well-being."[3] Whitehead details the problems created by parents who pursue their own interests and by stepparents who create additional risks. Then she identifies the solution: the promotion of the intact, two-parent family. She, along with other prominent educators and politicians on the Council on Families in America at the New York–based Institute for American Values, issued a Report to the Nation on marriage in 1995, whose executive summary promoted the same three-part case.[4] The divorce revolution has failed; the failure has created terrible hardships for children; the time has come to rebuild a family culture of enduring marital relationships.

Outspoken critics on the progressive side take offense at this interpretation. Social scientists from a range of respected universities composed editorials of their own, identifying what they see as the real problems before us.[5] They organized an alternative think-tank based in Washington, D.C.–the Council on Contemporary Families. Its initial mission was to promote the "strength and welfare of all families."[6] Members of the council's original organizing committee–Judith Stacey, Arlene Skolnick, and Stacey Rosencrantz–as well as political philosopher Iris Young, worry about a monocausal analysis that blames self-centered mothers and fatherless families as the root causes of crime, poverty, violence, and drug abuse. They contend that economic and social factors, including corporate greed, low wages for women, losses in real earnings and breadwinner jobs, high-level marital conflict, and a decline in social resources, are far greater impediments to children's well-being. Poverty and the trend toward early dropping out of school are as much a cause of early childbearing as a result. Poverty, ethnicity, and many other factors shape the "plural childbearing cultures" that characterize United States society.[7] This alternative view has developed its own slogans: many factors contribute to family stress and simplistic diagnoses are problematic, if not racist, classist, sexist, and heterosexist; alternative families should not be stigmatized; and all families should be valued and supported, no matter their form.

This controversy borrows energy from an earlier, equally divisive issue–what editorialist Ellen Goodman dubs the "Thirty Year War" over childcare.[8] Study after study on the impact of institutional care has been done, without completely conclusive results. Debate arose once again around the April 2001 results of the National Institute of Child Health and Human Development's ten-year, ten-city study of over 1,100 preschool children, the most comprehensive early-childcare study conducted to date in the United States. Some people cited the finding that 17 percent of preschoolers in childcare for more than thirty hours a week are highly aggressive in kindergarten. They interpreted this finding as confirmation that mothers should stay home with their children. This was, in the words of one chief investigator, Jay Belsky, the "moral of the story."[9] Other people contended that this conclusion overlooks other interesting results, such as the increased language and thinking skills of children in childcare. More generally, the assertion that mothers should stay home distorts evidence that, on the whole, children in quality day care fare well and that two-income families are happier, healthier, and better off.[10]

These debates are uncannily reminiscent of common household arguments among spouses and partners over who is doing more housework.

In such arguments, a detailed accounting of respective workloads does not address the deeper problems. Both parties are usually doing more than either can handle, and they exaggerate their individual view to make a point. In the immediate moment, each person simply wants to be heard. Ultimately, however, what is needed is a greater sustaining vision about what children really need and what faithful parenting looks like in such a context.

Analogously, both sides in the cultural child-related debates overstate their case. Advocates for the intact family and stay-at-home mothers tend to sound moralistic and provincial; supporters of diversity and day care sound amoral and negligent. At the same time, both sides have some merit. Adults have made selfish decisions about marriage and paid work that ignore children's well-being. Sustaining marriage for children's sakes needs to be taken more seriously by society at large. Children during their first few years of life benefit from stable parental care and the steadfast attention of two parents or, indeed, of as many adult friends and relatives as people can muster. But young children also benefit from interactions with other caregivers and peers when day care is well run and kept within reasonable limits. A lone parent with sole responsibility for children, still usually the mother, is not the only or even the best way to raise children. Nor should political policy mandate that mothers on welfare leave their children to work while political ideology urges middle-income mothers to stay home. Multiple factors besides failed marriage and institutional day care make adequate care of children challenging. It is not helpful to restigmatize families that are already struggling. Lacking adequate social support and emotional and economic resources, most people are doing the best they can most of the time to care for their children.

In general, however, I am particularly troubled by a quiet change of subject in both controversies. Children's well-being does not remain at the center. These debates devolve into ideological fights over adult lifestyles that use children to support a preferred cause. Rallying for children's welfare becomes the front for other agendas, whether that of upholding a pristine vision of marriage, polishing a tarnished memory of mothers-at-home, or defending family diversity regardless of the costs. Serious consideration of children's real needs in a greatly changed world gets lost.

In 1994, parishioners of St. James Episcopal Cathedral two blocks from Chicago's affluent Magnificent Mile responded to the *Chicago Tribune*'s decision to cover the stories of all the children murdered in 1993. Sunday school teachers and children erected a Lenten cross in memory of the sixty-three dead (many from families too poor for grave markers). Over the next few years the memorial caught the public eye, moved many souls, and sparked public action. But in 1998 the weatherworn cross blew over, parts of it were moved inside, and people simply considered other uses for the plaza. The new peace marker that now stands there, as Jule

Ward and James Halstead remark, "sadly...says nothing of the children we continue to lose to violence every day of every year."[11] In the church and newsroom, people had moved on to other issues. Even where the interest seems unadulterated and directly aimed at children's well-being, sustained public attention to children is a challenge. Grappling with children's needs is difficult, especially when children cannot speak fully for themselves, when their stories no longer elicit adult interest, and when the problems surrounding their welfare seem so intractable.

The Narrow Conception of Christianity in Public Discourse

Equally troubling, efforts to carry on public discussion of children typically neglect religion. A few years ago, two books attempted to move attention to children beyond the problems of divorce and day care. Children face serious hurdles, Sylvia Hewlett and Cornel West observe in *The War Against Parents,* not because "parents are less devoted than they used to be" or "love their children less," but because "the whole world is pitted against them."[12] In a similar book, *The Assault on Parenthood,* Dana Mack admits that, despite her conservative views about marriage, in "our eagerness to blame single parenthood and divorce for the contemporary crisis of children," we overlook cultural perils.[13] Even though the authors of the two books write from divergent political positions, they agree about the problems of a poisonous popular culture. Hewlett and West want better governmental support for working parents, while Mack wants the chance for women to return home. They both see cultural forces, such as popular psychology and its so-called "parent-bashing" or the entertainment industry and its indiscriminant promotion of sex and violence, as waging a "silent war against parents."

Unfortunately, neither of their respective solutions is ultimately satisfying because of their limited understandings of religion and culture. Crammed with statistics, news items, and personal stories detailing the many facets of a family-hating culture, both books offer a common blueprint for policy change as their primary answer—tax relief, work place changes, legal support, and media and educational reform. Certainly, renewal of rights and social reforms are needed; however, lacking in their otherwise scrutinizing investigations is an exploration of religion as an essential component of culture.

Hewlett and West, for example, argue that the "key to the future" is precisely the "creation of a new political and cultural environment."[14] Yet it is hard to imagine creating new public norms or challenging a predominant public morality of materialism and big business without addressing moral and religious traditions and beliefs. Attempting the kind of cultural overhaul they desire in the value of children and the practice of parenting will not get far without more careful attention to one of the most powerful culture-shaping institutions. Many social scientists, public intellectuals, and popular writers call for just such a cultural change of heart without grasping the critical role that religion might play. This is especially surprising among spokespersons familiar with religious knowledge and symbols, such as West, from who one might expect more engagement with religion. Mack points to the largely untapped resources of religious congregations. But she ridicules efforts to critique and reform influential aspects of Christian and Jewish tradition. She thus dismisses as trivial the important efforts by religion scholars to reform the common use of religious belief to uphold the patriarchal family, female submission, and the ideal of self-sacrifice, particularly for women.

Generally speaking, people seldom expect religion to inform nonmembers or the wider society on matters related to parenting and children. With modernity's reliance on science and technology in the twentieth century, both religion and children have become private matters. Secularization and technological progress divested society of the "three most ancient and most powerful concomitants of the sacred—mystery, miracle, and magic,"[15] says Peter Berger in his well-known *The Sacred Canopy* of the 1960s. He failed to notice, however, that mystery, miracle, and magic are precisely, and not coincidentally, elements evoked by childbirth and appreciated more by children than by adults. Dismissal of religion goes hand and hand with the dismissal of children from public view and the devaluing of their care as an essential cultural and religious activity. Religious belief, children, care of children, and motherhood all fall below the ambitions of the so-called smart-thinking mature adult. In the ideal modern scientific world, real adults should get over religious confession just as they should get beyond children and far away from those who care for children. Most people today, both within and beyond religious communities, still do not see religion as a credible resource for understanding or caring for children.

The Narrow Conception of Children in Contemporary Christianity

Until the last several years, Christian theology has mirrored these problems in a paradigmatic and problematic way. "Real" theology in the last century has been extremely adult centered. The primary subject is the mature adult. It is not an exaggeration to say that, after Horace Bushnell's well-known mid-nineteenth-century theology of childhood, the door slammed shut on children as a respectable topic. During a panel on the child and moral agency at the Society of Christian Ethics several years ago, theological ethicist Cristina Traina voiced this concern. Looking back over recent and distant Christian history, she observed, "Typically children's moral agency is an afterthought, a topic introduced to complete a theological system, and so must be forced into a script written for a universal history of salvation, usually with adults in mind." What would theological discourse look like, she asked, if "reflection on sin, salvation, and moral agency began rather than ended with childhood?"[16]

Although Traina speaks here about the entire Christian corpus, the problem is most acute for twentieth-century theology. The volume behind the above panel, *The Child in Christian Thought*, edited by Marcia Bunge, reveals that premodern theologians sometimes paid surprising attention to children. In the last century, however, the topic of children, like women's work, has been, in Bunge's words, "somehow 'beneath' the job of the systematic theologians."[17] Thinking about children has been a bit like the housework of the theological school: no one wants to do it. Because of their distance from domestic care, many men in the field of religion did not regard children as a credible subject. Many women did not take up the topic because of their proximity to children and their sometimes onerous immersion in daily care. Similar to the teaching of children in the educational wing of congregations, children as a scholarly subject was pushed off to the academic wings, surfacing mostly in religious education and pastoral care.

There are exceptions in the second half of the twentieth-century, of course, prior to the recent revival of interest in childhood studies. But even these exceptions, coming from an academy still largely governed by European American men, reveal problems in assumptions about children in the wake of modernity. In the 1960s Catholic theologian Karl Rahner devoted a significant essay to children. He insists that children and childhood have "unsurpassable value" or value for the Christian life that adults cannot surpass. Childhood is "infinite openness," such that only the person who "becomes that child which he only begins to be in his own childhood" attains participation in "God's interior life."[18] Rahner issues, in short, a theological mandate to take children seriously, not only for their own sake but also for the sake of a full Christian faith in adulthood. Catholic scholar Mary Ann Hinsdale rightfully identifies this essay as a "major contribution to Catholic theology and Christian thought on the child in general."[19]

Tellingly, however, Rahner frames his remarks by making clear that, although he will address ways to think about childhood, reflection on how people should teach or raise children "cannot be the aim of a theologian." He does not explain exactly why this is the case. But he confirms Bunge's suspicion that theological reflection on the care and formation of children is beneath the job of the systematic theologian, who must instead consider, in Rahner's words, "what the divinely revealed word has to say about childhood."[20] The first line of the essay itself makes the following disclaimer: "Our purpose in offering a few ideas on the theology of childhood at this point is not, in any direct sense, to be of assistance to those who, in some way or other, whether as parents or teachers, are engaging in looking after children."

In the early 1990s, process theologian Douglas Sturm also moves off the beaten path of systematic theology to take up the cause of children's liberation. Like Rahner's brief treatment, this essay is a welcome addition to a meager discussion. The adult-child relationship, Sturm contends, exemplifies one of the last strongholds of domination, parallel to master-slave and male-female relationships of the past, and hence constitutes a final frontier for liberation theology. Children number "among the most vulnerable and most victimized of peoples."[21] Their struggles extend beyond those identified by the recent marriage movement–failed marriage and divorce–to include fallout from technology; violence; worldwide poverty; moral confusion about racism, materialism, and corporate greed; and exploitation through child labor, prostitution, adoption trafficking, and pornography. Children deserve greater recognition within a human community that promises, in his words, the "mutual self-development of all participants."[22] Yet, in Sturm's effort to support valuable steps by the United Nations to grant children equal rights to shelter, security, love, and self-determination, he barely mentions families and parents, everyday life with children, or important differences between adults and children. He ignores how children's increasingly prolonged dependency within postmodern society, coupled with a heightened exposure to adult pressures, raises particular problems for children and their caregivers. In Sturm's work, children become an ideological subject rather than a proximate, living reality.

This happens more explicitly in a recent book on marriage. We find a systematic theologian, Adrian Thatcher, speaking out for children's liberation again, but he has something different than Sturm in mind. Children need protection from a world largely designed around adult desire, particularly as manifested in choices about divorce and the suffering it causes children. As this implies, his chief concern in "putting children first" is to claim their centrality within a redefined and reinvigorated Christian marriage, his more primary project.[23] He criticizes inordinate maternal self-sacrifice and calls for greater equality between mothers and fathers–an important contribution in itself–but says remarkably little about actually living with and rearing children within such relationships. Children are secondary to his aim of reestablishing the sanctity of marriage as an institution. They are one of the "goods" of marriage; they illustrate God's blessing on the marriage and symbolize or demonstrate marital love.

Interest in children's representative value more than their literal presence characterizes a recent essay on children by Jürgen Moltmann. He identifies children as "metaphors of hope." To his credit, he begins by sketching three different angles from which to understand children–as concerned parents and teachers, as children themselves, and as adults recalling our childhood. Both the Jewish view of children as gifts and the Christian hope in the Messiah as redeemer free us from worshiping our own children and even from the obligation of childbearing itself. Every child brings the "light of hope" into the world and offers a "chance" for the "reign of peace."[24]

In using the idea of child as "metaphor" as his primary phrase and argument, however, Moltmann suggests that we see children figuratively as pointing to something else rather than as embodied persons themselves. Indeed, the complicated reality of care of children and their faith formation is not represented in this essay either. Children are "metaphors of our hopes, of that which we want, wish for and expect." They are also "metaphors of God's hope for us: God wants us, expects us, and welcomes us."[25] Moltmann's essay tends to hold real children at a distance, offering little description of their many immediate and complex needs.

What about literature in religious education, the body of scholarship many people assume offers resources on children? Oddly enough, a closer look at two of the most widely recognized twentieth-century classics, John Westerhoff's *Will Our Children Have Faith?* and James Fowler's popular *Stages of Faith*, reveals that they are centered as much on adults as on children and family life. Both these acclaimed texts are wonderful books on faith. They are not actually books on children, at least not to the extent that one would expect from title and reputation.[26] They help adults who used to be children and who work with children understand stages through which adult faith passes on its way to greater maturity. They are not books on understanding childhood anew in an increasingly complex society. As troubling, the appeal of these books to a wide readership largely overshadowed scholars in prior decades who addressed children more explicitly, such as Iris V. Cully and Sophia Lyon Fahs, and even those who have addressed them anew more recently.[27] *Will Our Children Have Faith?* does an excellent job addressing the problematic location of education in the Sunday school wing and working to move it back to the center of faith formation in the congregation as a whole. The title misleads readers, however, into thinking Westerhoff addresses children directly.[28] Instead, his governing question is more accurately, "Will the adults who care for children have faith?" Similar to Fowler's work, the primary subject is the adult looking back over life to judge where one stands and where one is going as an adult in relationship to childhood faith. The focus is not "being children today" or "raising children in faith" or "becoming children" but, as one of Fowler's books is titled, "becoming adults" in Christian faith.[29] Fowler sees faith as a "verb" or a generic way of making meaning "prior to our being religious or irreligious."[30] Consequently, children's faith is disconnected from the formative habits, practices, and rituals so important to their development and to families and congregations in general.

In this sampling, focused primarily on white men who have had power in the academy, I am not being completely fair to the richness of the texts. Each one does make worthy contributions. Nor am I including significant developments in the last few years among scholars in religious education and other areas of theological study. As I have argued elsewhere, books in religious education by Elizabeth Caldwell, Brad Wigger, Karen Marie Yust, Catherine Stonehouse, and Jerome Berryman have done a great deal to turn around the problem I identify.[31] Those in other fields, such as David Jensen and Marcia Bunge in systematic theology; Margaret Bendroth in Christian history; independent religion scholar Kristin Herzog; Susan Ridgely Bales and Christian Smith in sociology of religion; John Wall in ethics; O.M. Bakke in biblical studies; and Don Browning, Pamela Couture, and myself in practical theology have also called for religious understandings that more fully include children's perspectives.[32] In fact, this growing body of literature in childhood studies in religion, including this book itself, partly proves my point by demonstrating by sheer contrast what was so missing in much of twentieth-century theology.[33]

My purpose here is to note how easily children as a central subject has slipped (and can slip) into the background, certainly in systematic theology, a field dominated by men until recent decades, but also in classic texts in practical theology. As happens in the wider public sphere, deliberation on children can subtly and too easily become a means to some other–equally important and certainly related, but still primarily adult–agenda. As early as 1985, pastoral theologian Andrew Lester had already commented on this problem. In a book on caring for children in crisis, he notes how few theological books actually grapple with the realities of children.[34] This neglect is intimately connected to a pastoral neglect of children as people with genuine needs in periods of crises *and* in periods of well-being. It is high time, argues another pastoral theologian, Herbert Anderson, and his co-author, pastor Susan B.W. Johnson, in 1994, that theological "definitions of what it means to be human" incorporate childhood.[35] A richer portrait of the complex needs of children is needed to enliven an academic theology that, in its erudite deliberations, has lost touch with the lively unpredictability of life with children.

Studying Children: A Practical Feminist Theological Approach

Making children a central theological concern challenges the generally accepted categories of study in theology–what has been called the "theological encyclopedia" or the nineteenth-century organization of the study of religion into the four self-defined areas of biblical, historical, systematic, and practical reflection. This schema goes back to Friedrich Schleiermacher's efforts to secure a home for religion in the modern European university in the early nineteenth century. Theologians who inherited this framework assigned practical theology a circumscribed role. It concerned professional acts of congregational ministry as performed by either clergy or laity. As such, it was primarily the application of theoretical truths discovered in biblical, historical, and doctrinal theology to concrete church situations. Despite practical theological efforts to challenge this view in recent decades, many theologians still bracket practical theology as peripheral to the "more important" theoretical work of biblical, historical, and systematic theology.[36] The sheer matter of institutional and curricular organization in theological schools makes it hard not to misperceive systematic, historical, and biblical theology as the "real work" of theology, and practical theology as simply the application of this work to acts of ministry. Studying children, however, necessarily challenges these traditional categories.

Taking children seriously as a theological subject requires a movement across the conventionally separate disciplines in the study of religion. It requires a circular hermeneutical movement—from an exploration of dilemmas, to an investigation of religious resources, back to renewed practice. This movement includes moments of serious social scientific, historical, biblical, and constructive religious and theological exploration as part of a larger practical theological effort in the public arena. In short, the best way to study moral and religious dilemmas of children and child rearing is from the perspective of practical theology fundamentally redefined.

Other practical theologians have called for such redefinition. Don Browning has stood at the forefront, arguing that the theological encyclopedia ought to be radically reconceived. He describes the entire enterprise as "fundamental practical theology," with four "submoments": descriptive, historical, systematic, and strategic practical theology.[37] Practical theology does not just focus on personal and pastoral problems. A critical task of practical theology is to interpret modern culture and to articulate a social ethic and public norms that are derived from religious tradition in dialogue with public problems. In a word, a practical theology of children has the role of mediating between powerful religious symbol systems and the wider society.[38] It tries to bridge the gap that sometimes arises between the efforts of systematic theologians to shape a religious worldview and the daily practices that actually form such a world. As a rule, systematic theologians are better at shaping overarching worldviews and formal doctrines than at monitoring the way people practice their faith and actually live out these ideas on a daily basis within society. A practical theology of childhood takes this additional step. In dealing with religious texts, the final aim is distinct from systematic, biblical, and historical theology. The aim is to understand what is going on so as to effect change in a situation, in the theological ideas that define it, and in the broader public sphere.[39]

The particular subject matter of children requires just such a movement across the divergent areas of study in religion and an orientation to the wider public. It also requires an orientation toward practice. Childhood is not a purely theoretical concern, although children can certainly be studied in theory. Raising children is, at heart, a practice that engages and embodies a rich variety of developed and undeveloped theories. Religious practices with children do not come after theory or understanding. Practice guides understanding from the beginning and is also the end toward which theory moves.[40] Practical theological knowledge about children involves an investigation of what pastoral theologian Rodney Hunter calls the "wisdom of experience," or what I would describe as the thought or wisdom that develops from the practices of being a child and of raising children. Hunter uses the phrase to talk about "a form of practical knowledge" distinct from descriptive knowledge of "what is" and normative knowledge of "what ought to be." Practical knowledge tells "how to do things." Here he does not mean technical knowledge about skills or a means-ends instrumental reasoning. Practical knowledge accrues and matures over time and through practice and apprenticeship or, in his words, "through a history of practical, contingent events."[41] Understanding children and childhood therefore takes the investigator into the difficult-to-chart territory of accrued religious wisdom and presents the challenge of accessing this wisdom's role in today's practices. To study children theologically, in short, demands the study of the conceptual schemes and vocabulary that develop in the religious practices of care for children and in patterned practices, schemes, and vocabulary in history and culture at large.

Making childhood the main focus raises other complex methodological and moral questions: How can adults genuinely understand children? How can the diversity of childhood and its social and political construction across cultures and history be appreciated? Such questions arise directly out of a feminist commitment to respect the voice and experience of the subject. For many years, women have contended with claims about universal human experience that disregarded their views. Children likewise have been disregarded in claims about human experience and must be seen as actors, participants, and contributors in their own right. One final concern arises out of feminist thought: How can adults, especially women and mothers, hear and represent the claims of children without losing progress made by the women's movement beyond rigid roles of motherhood? Can respect for children's subjectivity come without the cost of losing women's relatively new recognition as subjects?

None of these questions can be fully resolved in the space of this essay. They beg for careful exploration as the field of childhood studies and religion continues to grow. One way to proceed for now is to consider children from the perspective of "feminist maternal theology," as I have attempted to define it elsewhere.[42] This is neither the only nor an entirely sufficient pathway to genuine understanding of children or to inclusion of their diversity. It is simply one further step forward.[43] Women may be enabled to hear children precisely because they have stood where children have stood, at the intersection of society's contradictory outward idealization and subtle devaluation of women, children, and childcare. They too have experienced limiting role definitions. Many feminist theologians have not only thought about children; they have acted as primary caregivers. A feminist maternal theology then suggests asking not only how fresh understanding of children might influence motherhood but also how contemporary experience of mothering shapes understandings of children.

As I define it elsewhere, a feminist maternal theology draws upon knowledge located within the practices of mothering as one means to better understand children and other subjects. Philosopher Sara Ruddick, author of the widely recognized book, *Maternal Thinking,* makes the compelling observation that for too long we have remained "ignorant of the perspective, the *thought* that has developed from the practice of mothering."[44] She explores "maternal thinking" from a feminist perspective, well aware of the destructive consequences of restricting women to the home and limiting parenting to mothers. Both the passions of mothering and its cultural devaluation have distracted us, however, from distinctive knowledge gained through close involvement with the care of children. As a result, we have failed to articulate the thinking endemic to maternal practice.

Ruddick claims that maternal thinking arises out of the social practice of mothering, as "practice" has been freshly understood by Ludwig Wittgenstein, Peter Winch, and Jürgen Habermas. In response to the "historical reality of a biological child in a particular social world," the mother "asks certain questions rather than others; she establishes criteria for the truth, adequacy, and relevance of proposed answers; and she cares about the findings she makes and can act on."[45] In this respect, a feminist maternal perspective moves carefully past liberal feminism's critique of motherhood as a source of exploitation and on toward its potential as a site for knowledge necessary to human survival. In essence, to know more about children, we need to know more about the "conceptual scheme" or "vocabulary and logic of connections" that orders and expresses the practices of children and parents.[46]

Maternal thinking has already shaped pivotal insights in feminist theology. In a classic essay, Valerie Saiving put forth the idea, revolutionary for its time, that sin in women does not lie in prideful self-assertion—as many men had defined it—but in self-loss and denigration. This claim rested significantly on her own experience as a single mother raising a young daughter while doing graduate study in the late 1950s.[47] Other equally provocative challenges to Christian conceptions have evolved from the proximity and intimacy between mothers and children, especially in relation to sexual ethics, the sacrificial meaning of atonement, love as self-sacrifice, and Christian vocation.[48]

A feminist maternal theology of childhood extends four core premises of feminist thought in new directions:

- First, the demand to give privileged voice to the marginalized is extended to mothers and children.
- Second, feminist maternal theology challenges the contradictory demonization and idealization of children and women's bodies in the acts of bearing and raising children.

- Third, it enriches debates about theological doctrines of Christian love, sin, and grace by turning to the complex questions of love between the unequal parties of adult and child.
- Finally, a feminist maternal theology stretches claims for justice and liberation across differences to include children and mothers for whom the democratic principle of equality based on formal identity or sameness with the adult male simply does not work.

If the public must rethink its constructions of children and religion, a feminist practical theology is a worthy partner in such reimagining. The study of children calls for a distinctive approach in theology, one that involves both practical and feminist thought. Broadly speaking, a practical feminist theological method promotes two important agendas that would enhance public debates about children: reflection on daily life as central to theology, and respect for the voices of the marginalized as a guiding norm. Reflection on children embodies the theological conviction that the Divine manifests itself in the mundane and that genuine liberation must occur in the most commonplace of places—in the embodied lives of children.

The modern dismissal of children as important subjects and of religion as a public resource is unfortunate. Both leave an entire spectrum of human behavior and history untouched, overlooked, and misunderstood. To effect genuine public change in children's lives requires careful and fair exploration, critique, and revision of religion as a key culture-forming institution. Christianity, as is true for many religions, continues to shape children and to determine how people think about and act toward them more than most people realize. Religious institutions provide family-related moral discourse, communities of social support and control, and frameworks of meaning.[49] Religion shapes shared history and normative visions. Hence, politicians and parents alike would benefit from a richer public understanding of traditions that have formed children and child rearing through specifically religious and moral language and practices. Various religious traditions, including Christianity, have long seen children as part of the common good and a public concern.

Reclaiming religion's importance in the public square therefore naturally entails the reclamation of children's public voice, presence, and participation as a valuable end in themselves. Christians in particular must assert more boldly the claim at the heart of the tradition that declares children a gift and value in and of themselves. Whether in childhood studies or family life, children and their care should never become a challenge undertaken or a subject studied merely as a means to satisfy some other personal or ideological end. Children are neither too difficult nor too silly, but instead profoundly provocative participants in the common life of faith.

3

Princess Dreams

Children's Spiritual Formation in Consumer Culture

KATHERINE TURPIN

I am a feminist and parent to a young daughter. From the beginning days of her life, her father and I provided clothes, playthings, and role models that expressed varied possibilities for how gender can be performed. When a few weeks ago my daughter and I went to see "Disney on Ice: Princess Classics," I engaged in some deep soul-searching. This event represented the end of my illusion that, as a parent, I had primary influence over my daughter's gender formation. Despite my attempts to resist her access to commoditized children's culture with its attendant reinforcement of racial and class hierarchies, we found ourselves participating in one of its classic expressions. How had it come to this?

In addition to personal reflection on this family event, I have approached the experience as an extended case study in this chapter, analyzed in dialogue with research from economists and cultural and educational theorists. Beginning with a description of my own family's relationship to the Disney princesses, I turn to a broader analysis of the role of commoditized characters in the spiritual formation of children, with particular attention to the racial, gender, and class formation inherent in such characters. Finally, I suggest some formational practices that parents and communities of faith can engage, challenging the formation offered to their children by the commercial realm. While my dream of avoiding exposure to commercial formation is impossible, contesting this formation is an important and valuable ministry for adults to perform.

Where Dreams Begin

Our immersion in the princess stories happened slowly. While I tried to sway my daughter by restricting access to these characters and goods, my daughter's classmates shared their dress-up clothes, storybooks, and games featuring the princesses. Through play dates and imaginative free play at her preschool, my daughter became familiar with each of the characters and their basic storylines. Then I made a fatal parenting error. For my daughter's fourth birthday party, I allowed her to choose invitations at our local grocery store. She, of course, went immediately for the Disney princess invitations. This signaled to her guests that princess items were the most appropriate presents. Now we were in the thick of it, including Halloween costumes, books, and movies, and daily anticipation that the princess underwear is clean and available to wear.

By the time the children's mini-paper in our local newspaper featured an advertisement for "Disney on Ice: Princess Classics," we had grown immune to the depth of our daughter's attraction to all things princess. And so, one cold spring day I found myself waiting with my daughter outside the arena for the doors to open. All around us, girls between the ages of eighteen months and six years were streaming in with their parents. Nearly all of them, representing a broad range of racial/ethnic and class diversity in Denver, were dressed in officially licensed Disney princess costumes, mimicking the television commercials for the event. We passed the time counting the number of girls in costumes, but eventually were forced to quit when the number rose higher than my daughter could actually count.

Once we gained admittance to the arena and found a seat, my daughter was so excited that she was almost vibrating. She sat on the edge of her seat, utterly enchanted, occasionally leaning over to give me little hugs and tell me how much she loved being there with me. It was a classic Disney moment. I sat amazed at the production values, the imaginative use of sets, and the skaters' skill. The religious educator in me was fascinated by the way the script drew on the audience's knowledge of the narratives of each of the seven featured princesses, and how the show was constructed to elicit responses from the crowd with just snippets of these stories.

As the show continued, I moved from my initial interest to despair that *these* were the stories dominating the young girls' childhood fantasies. Their much-lamented sexist themes were clear: competition between women for men, with the winners marked by the instant appeal of their beauty; older women resenting rather than nurturing younger women; young women giving up voice and family for romantic love; princesses being imprisoned or placed in a long sleep while princes solve conflicts through violent domination. Character fulfillment, even for the warrior princess Mulan, is marked by dramatic rescue and the resultant romantic involvement.

Throughout the event, I began to daydream about what it would take for my daughter to have the kind of foundational knowledge of Christian narratives that she had of princess narratives. At one point, I began to wonder what "Disciples on Ice" would look like and where the funding for it could be generated. Knowing how incredibly difficult it would be to compete with the Disney production machine and knowing the dearth of stories featuring young women from the biblical tradition, I struggled to imagine such an event that would have equal appeal to my young daughter.

During the intermission, my daughter shared that at the end of the show the princesses would come into the audience and shake hands with all the children. I pointed out the thousands of children in the arena and noted that, with just seven princesses, it would be hard for everyone to get to shake hands. Nevertheless, she was convinced that she was going to meet a princess. At the end of the show, the princesses did step off the rink and began to greet those with rink-side seats. My daughter barreled down the arena steps to get to the rink, dodging other young would-be princesses to no avail. The princesses skated off before Elizabeth could shake a single hand. She was devastated, crying herself to sleep on the way home. Her total report about the show to her father was, "I didn't get to meet the princesses."

Not So Innocent Icons

A few years ago, approximately the same amount of time that my daughter has been alive, Disney discovered that it could repackage characters from its library of hit movies such as *Cinderella* and *Aladdin* into "Disney Princesses" paraphernalia. The princess characters have actually been licensed and marketed since the release of *Snow White and the Seven Dwarfs,* the film that convinced Disney of the potential revenue in pre-licensing.[1] The recent move to package the princesses as a group has been wildly successful even by Disney standards. Indeed, the Disney princesses now compete with other iconic childhood marketing figures such as Elmo, Dora the Explorer, SpongeBob SquarePants, Spiderman, and Barbie for prominence in marketing any merchandise that could conceivably be purchased for children, from personal care items (toothpaste and bandages) to toys and games, food items, clothing, and home décor or utility products. The success of the Disney princess marketing campaign has been so strong that other licensed characters (notably Barbie and Dora the Explorer) have begun princess sub-lines and storybooks. Other book and media products have proliferated the princess theme in more generic forms. Princesses are "in" in every conceivable way, and Disney corners the market with their stable of beloved characters.

The cohort of princesses included in these amalgamated princess products include both the "old school" princesses (Cinderella, Snow White, and Aurora from *Sleeping Beauty*) and the more contemporary princesses (Belle from *Beauty and the Beast,* Ariel from *The Little Mermaid,* and Jasmine from *Aladdin*). In some of the media products in the princess line, Mulan and Pocahontas are also included, though their images are rarely included in the marketing of other daily-use products. Five of the "big six" princesses are distinctly Caucasian. Given the racial heritage of girls in the United States, notably absent from the cohort are princesses of African American or Latina background. One could argue that this lack of focus on the non-Caucasian princesses has to do with the relative success of their movies rather than the racial/ethnic heritage of the princess. However, this merely reinforces the concern that Americans respond better to dominant culture princesses in movie ticket sales and children's products. The princesses with iconic status are almost exclusively marked racially as part of the dominant culture, and young girls who identify and look up to them are idolizing traditional white forms of beauty and female gender performance.

By definition, all of the big six princesses end their stories firmly established as members of the ruling class with seemingly unlimited resources. Indeed, the appeal of the princesses lies in their being rich and having beautiful things. My daughter once wanted to play Cinderella with me. I jokingly told her to do the laundry and the dishes, then she could start in on the bathrooms and floors. She looked at me in horror and replied, "Mama, you know that's not the part of the story I like." To identify with a princess is to be beautiful, wearing beautiful clothes in beautiful surroundings. Other people take care of drudgery and the important work of admiring you from the sidelines. In other words, princesses are exemplars of class privilege.

On the gender front, Walt Disney is reported to have said: "Girls bored me. They still do."[2] The Disney princesses (the "big six," anyway), particularly as presented in their amalgamated form, represent a fairly boring model of womanhood. Communications scholar Janet Wasko notes the similarity in the stories of the princesses:

> The typical Disney heroine is represented by the first one, Snow White, who was innocent, naïve, passive, beautiful, domestic and submissive. While they may display far more intelligence and independence than Snow White, Cinderella or Sleeping Beauty, the more modern Disney heroines (Ariel in Little Mermaid, Jasmine in Aladdin and Belle in Beauty and the Beast) still live in male-dominated worlds, and ultimately find fulfillment through their romantic relationships with Prince Charmings.[3]

The princesses display an amazing lack of relationship with other women in their movies. Despite my own experience with the princesses in a mother/daughter context, six of the eight princesses (Snow White, Cinderella, Ariel, Jasmine, Belle, and Pocahontas) have no mothers. Ariel has several sisters, but she hardly interacts with them in the movie. Additionally, for Snow White, Cinderella, Ariel, and Sleeping Beauty, the primary villains are women, a stepmother in two cases. Wasp-waisted and wide-eyed, the princesses inhabit bodies that defy function as normal vehicles for human life. Despite the use of the term "heroine" for their characters, princesses rarely exhibit their own agency to resolve the conflicts in which they are embroiled in their primary stories.[4] Rather, they are saved by violent conflict or magic performed on their behalf.

Although they are presented as innocent fantasies, these stories have major impact on the identity development and nascent social commitments of young girls. Scholar of critical pedagogy Henry Giroux addresses the pedagogical power of Disney in the lives of young children, noting that its ubiquity and dominance in children's culture constructs children's understandings of self in terms of gender, racial, and class positions. Unfortunately for those who hope to encourage the formation of Christian understandings of justice for the poor and love for the neighbor, these are not the primary ways in which Disney orients its young adherents. Giroux names the persuasive forms of learning that occur in the world of Disney films, the new "teaching machines":

> I soon found that for my children, and I suspect for many others, these films possess at least as much cultural authority and legitimacy for teaching specific roles, values, and ideals as more traditional sites of learning such as the public schools, religious institutions, and the family. Disney films combine an ideology of enchantment and aura of innocence in narrating stories that help children understand who they are, what societies are about, and what it means to construct a world of play and fantasy in an adult environment.[5]

Such influence presents a challenge: how to assess the extent to which these "dominant significations," repeated over time, become a primary referent for children in the process of identity development. Whereas the ancient Israelites were reminded to place their primary, identity-bearing commandment on their doorposts and tie it to their foreheads (Deut. 6:4–9), contemporary children find their identity-bearing stories on their underwear, their sippy cups, their fruit snacks, and their sheets. The endless production of market capitalism means that we can replicate pedagogical persuasion endlessly.

In response to this teaching machine, Giroux calls for transformation in the ways parents and educators assess and address Disney. Rather than an innocent source of pleasure, he calls Disney a "pedagogical and policy-making enterprise actively engaged in the cultural landscaping of national identity and the 'schooling' of the minds of young children."[6] While Giroux does not insinuate that Disney is fulfilling some sinister agenda through its educational activities, the cumulative effect of its institutional and political power, generated through the control of major sectors of the media industry, means that it must be held accountable by parents and educators for what it produces. Addressing Disney's utilization of fantasy, innocence, and desire to shape ideological interests and to legitimatize particular social relations becomes a critical social task.

While Disney's influence on young girls extends well into the "tween" and teen years (evident in the popularity of *Hannah Montana* and the teen idols of *High School Musical*, for example), Disney is not the only children's media and entertainment giant in this pedagogical enterprise. If my young child were a boy, I would undoubtedly be writing this piece about superheroes and Star Wars, and my frustration that the formation offered by these stories emphasizes male domination through strength, power, and exotic weapons and abilities. In all cases, repeated exposure to these stories and artifacts lays a foundation for identity that emphasizes social relations based on particular forms of status and power, which are often inimical to the Gospel. Because they take the form of fantasy and child's play, we often do not respect their power in spiritual formation.

When I have shared my concern about my daughter's interaction with this cultural force, I often get the response: "Every little girl wants to be a princess." However, this "commonsense" assumption is actually a pedagogical achievement with political and spiritual ramifications. Although we recognize that the formation has taken place, we do not often stop to consider the ethical commitments inherent in training children to identify primarily with the wealthy and powerful. While princess stories have been a part of our cultural heritage for many centuries, the depth and penetration of these stories has reached new levels through the commoditizing of their images in consumer culture, extending their pedagogical reach in powerful ways.

Coming to a Store Near You

While lovable licensed characters have been a part of Disney's products for nearly seventy years, the broad commodification of these products into children's lives has dramatically shifted in the last twenty years.[7] Deregulation of advertising in children's television by the Federal Communications Commission (FCC) in the early 1980s has led to program-length commercials and a situation in which even public television shows are bracketed by commercials for sponsoring corporations. Most of today's best-selling toys are linked to media, and many children's television programs, such as *Sesame Street*, are funded through the sales of toys, clothing, and accessories with the images of licensed characters on them.[8] In a parody of the genealogies of the Hebrew Bible, Norma Pecora notes the proliferation of media products that began during the 1980s: "A children's movie begets a children's television program, begets a children's album, begets a children's videocassette series, begets a children's storybook, begets an activity book, and a video game."[9] Disney has capitalized on this pattern; its legendary merchandising activities of characters lead to astronomical sales figures.[10]

The proliferation of products has increased through the idea of "trans-toying," which is the practice of making any product, from toothbrushes to school supplies to oatmeal, into a toy through the addition of licensed characters. Economist Juliet Schor notes that child development experts worry that, as every item in a child's environment becomes a specific toy, children's capacity and scope for imagination are dramatically reduced.[11] Trans-toying creates desire for particular brands of everyday items through the link of licensed characters: "A child of 1, wearing Mickey Mouse diapers, may not be ready to demand a Mickey Mouse storybook—but the time will come—foods, restaurants, diapers, and clothes now build on the exposure offered by the television or motion pictures and the reinforcement of other media."[12] In a recent trip to Target, I found six combined "Disney Princess" videos marketed in addition to their fourteen original individual stories and straight-to-video sequels (which are periodically placed in the "Disney vault" to increase sales through simulated scarcity). As I began to wander the aisles, I also found three CDs, seven activity/coloring books, five kinds of shoes, three kinds of sippy cups, four kinds of underwear, seven kinds of pajamas, and fifty-one distinct toys and games marketed using the "Disney Princess" images. I quit counting before going into the food or personal care aisles. The targeted consumers for these items are girls aged eighteen months to six or seven years.

As children have become increasingly segmented and targeted as a market, companies have realized the economic potential of their desires. Children aged four to twelve made 30 billion dollars in purchases in 2002, a 400 percent increase from 1989. They directly influenced or "evoked" another 600 billion dollars in purchases by their parents through what the advertising industry sometimes calls the "nag factor."[13] Even companies with traditionally adult customers, such as airlines and automobile companies, have begun marketing to children as they realize the impact children have on adult purchases as well as the potential of cultivating lifelong, brand-loyal customers.[14] Susan Linn notes the mounting evidence that indicts this onslaught of direct marketing for harming children: "Childhood obesity, family stress, increased materialistic values, and discontent with body image have all been associated with marketing."[15] She also notes the exploitation of children's and adolescents' insecurities to sell items as a primary strategy of advertisers, quoting numerous marketing texts that fail to explore the ethical and psychosocial impact of advertising campaigns that fill adolescents with images to foster a sense of inadequacy in order to create a felt need for certain products.[16] Children able to engage in regular consumption and those without economic resources to do so are all shaped by the desires and insecurities formed through this marketing.

Studies on the effects of marketing to children have been muddied by the involvement of psychological researchers in the booming business of market research with children. An example of the kind of mixed response of psychological experts on marketing to children is evidenced by Barrie Gunter and Adrian Furnham, professors of journalism and psychology, respectively, and authors of *Children as Consumers: A Psychological Analysis of the Young People's Market.* They note:

> Reaching child and teenage consumers can be a highly skilled exercise… Understanding young consumers' psychology is therefore essential to marketers who wish to reach them… This fact underlines the need for expert help and guidance in researching as well as reaching young consumers… Research evidence should be carefully and thoughtfully utilized to guide campaigns that are designed to expose young consumers to products and encourage direct or indirect purchase behaviour [sic].[17]

Note that the authors do not question the aggressive formation of children as consumers or the use of "expert help" in this formation. Although these authors include a chapter on protecting child consumers, which addresses briefly the concern of exploitation of children for economic gain, they conclude the introduction to this chapter with the following reassurance: "The research literature reviewed in earlier chapters would suggest that while children pass through a stage of vulnerability, they generally emerge from it as informed and knowledgeable consumers able to make their own minds up about what they wish to buy. As they grow older, children develop the abilities needed to challenge the claims of advertisers."[18]

I question how old children have to be to challenge advertisers' claims. Further, do children develop the ability to challenge the system itself, which manufactures desires for nonessential products? Susan Linn, an instructor in psychiatry, bemoans the use of developmental psychology and widespread "expert" research on children to target children as a market. This trend has become such a concern that, in 2000, the American Psychological Association created a task force to investigate the participation of psychological professionals in market research designed to target children.[19] Linn questions the advertising industry's claims about the increasing sophistication of children in reading consumer messages and becoming brand savvy, represented in the conclusion of Gunter and Furnham. Linn notes: "That babies and toddlers request or recognize brands in no way reflects that they are 'savvy' about marketing, which implies a capacity to decode and resist advertising messages. It does suggest that very young children are highly susceptible to marketing, a fact that is borne out by academic research."[20]

Linn further notes that children are unable to distinguish reliably between programming and commercials until about the age of five, and they are about eight before they recognize the intent to persuade in marketing. Even Gunter and Furnham note that, if you use the criterion of whether children can recognize "the total economic relationship between advertising and programming," most sixth-grade children are deficient.[21] Further, they admit that the ability to recognize persuasive intent does not indicate that children, adolescents, or even adults are less persuaded by advertisements to make purchases.[22] Thus, the expert-assisted formation of "savvy" consumers is not in the best interests of children, but rather of the major corporations who market to them.

Many marketers defend the practice of aggressively targeting children by highlighting the benefit to the economy generated by the enormous commodification of children's lives. The desires created by advertising contribute to the common good by sustaining economic growth. Because economic growth is an unquestionable value in U.S. culture, the questions of the spiritual and moral effects of such commercial formation on children rarely receive attention.

Commodification as a Spiritual Issue

Reading secular cultural theorists who assess the influence of media and marketing on children, I am struck by how these authors emphasize the spiritual impact of this system of commodification on young children. For example, Susan Linn notes that relentless marketing undermines children's social and spiritual well-being:

> For instance, the values inculcated by marketing messages, such as impulse buying, unthinking brand loyalty, and a "me first" mentality, are antithetical to values such as critical thinking and cooperation that are essential to democracy. The message central to almost all marketing campaigns—that a particular product can bring us happiness—is contrary to the teaching of all mainstream religions.[23]

Linn recognizes that salvation does not arise from owning the right goods. This is, however, the not-so-subtle subtext of marketing campaigns to which we are exposed in public sectors and increasingly in schools as well. While those of us with traditional religious commitments might reject such a claim in our rhetoric, we are susceptible in daily life to the idea that our happiness depends on owning certain things.

Additionally, one way to demonstrate religious commitment in late capitalism has become purchasing goods from Christian retailers or displaying one's piety through the acquisition of Christian music, clothing, bumper stickers, and bric-a-brac. Rather than addressing the troubling formation offered by consumer culture, such a response allows that culture to structure spiritual practice without conscious critique.

In the sections below I explore the ramifications of commodification for children's spiritual formation.

Creating Commitments Counter to Christian Claims

The claims of consumer culture are countered by basic Christian claims: salvation is enacted by God; God calls people to love of God and neighbor; and God expects people to care especially for the economically vulnerable among us. Feminist practical theologian Joyce Mercer questions the relationship of Christian and consumer values: "How do our daily practices evidence the reign of God amidst the imperial practices of individualism, hyper-consumption, and despair that structure consumerist culture? These are questions of identity."[24] Mercer goes on to challenge the position of North American Christians who are part of dominant cultural groups that benefit from these imperial practices even as they are concerned about educating their children into "alternative meanings and practices of justice, hope, and neighbor-love."[25]

This struggle is one I know intimately as a Christian parent and a religious educator. I was actually much more comfortable when my daughter called out from the backseat of the car, "I wish *I* could be an orphan" (after listening to the Annie soundtrack countless times), than when she declares that she feels like a princess in one of her dresses. My sincere desire for her Christian formation is that she would identify more with orphans and other folks struggling economically than with wealthy, dominant-culture princesses. Unfortunately, her marketing and peer formation often pushes the second kind of formation. This concern is coupled with the ecological and fair-labor issues in the accumulation of products, and the fact that our family's ability to access cheap replicas of the characters on any number of items is often due to the exploitation of the labor of children and their parents in other nations. As Mercer aptly describes, the intersection of children and the complex economic systems involved in media and marketing is not just a personal family struggle but also a global justice issue.

Engendering False Relationships

Given the ubiquitous presence of Disney princesses in my daughter's life and imagination, her deep disappointment in not being able to greet them at the ice show was not surprising. Despite her sense of familiarity and even love for the characters, she has no real relationship with them other than as a purchaser of their icons. One of the concerns of exploiting children's heartfelt connections to licensed characters for economic gain is precisely the false sense of relationship that the practice engenders. Children put enormous amounts of energy and investment in the lives and happenings of nonexistent persons. However, when children are in need of assistance or support, these relationships are only useful tools of escape. They provide neither support (of a material *or* emotional variety) nor, in most cases, an example of agency to inspire young girls.

Among children, their connections to licensed characters provide the social ease of form-mediated relationships through shared knowledge of iconic stories. As a friend noted, you can put any two five-year-old boys who have never met in a room together, and they will immediately break out the imaginary light sabers or Spiderman web and have a form for shared fantasy play. These shared forms may have binding value, but they replicate stereotypical gender roles and hierarchical racial valuing, relying on beauty and violence as means of solving conflict. Thus, while they have the potential to link children across disparate interests and backgrounds, they do so in a way that re-inscribes values that are counter to the theological claims of many religious traditions.

The characters also become a means by which adults connect with children. I have had many relatives ask what my daughter is "into" these days, as they hope to reconnect with her over distances and time apart. While the storylines and characters bridge gaps brought on by lack of day-to-day contact, they gain significance as they serve this relational function. When adults indicate a shared awareness of and interest in the characters and storylines, they reinforce their perceived importance in the eyes of children. While the practice is rooted in an admirable attempt to honor the voices of children and what they value, it fails to provide a counter-narrative to the marketing giants.

The connections forged through shared consumption are not neutral. They are refracted through relations of domination and oppression, through experiences of access to and dearth of resources. As Mercer indicates, "Consumption becomes a way to achieve social solidarity—relational connections with others, even as it also marks identity and status."[26] Anthropologist Elizabeth Chin recently tackled the project of describing how consumption manifests itself in a particular sub-context. She conducted an ethnographic study on the influence of American consumer culture on poor and working-class racial-minority children living in the Newhallville neighborhood of New Haven, Connecticut. She noted that analyses of marketing influences on children often fail to recognize the diversity embedded in consumers' lives across boundaries of ethnicity, gender, race, and class.[27] Chin noted that contemporary commodity consumption influences the Newhallville children as strongly, or even more strongly, than their middle-class, majority-culture peers; however, their participation in this culture is quite different from these more privileged peers. She concluded that contemporary consumption serves as a "medium through which social inequalities—most notably of race, class, and gender—are formed, experienced, imposed, and resisted."[28]

Though shared consumption of iconic stories and products may provide an easy entrance into fantasy play for children from different social locations, it does not erase the real and at times unjust differences in their situations. Educational advocate Alex Kotlowitz explores the meaning of the shared fashions between poor urban and wealthy suburban teens, noting that the connections created by consuming the same fashions are not true connections. In reality, poor children do not have access to the institutional resources of their suburban peers, and suburban young people know nothing about the difficult day-to-day reality of their neighbors. He notes, "And so, in lieu of building real connections—by providing opportunities or rebuilding communities—we have found some common ground as purchasers of each other's trademarks. At best, that link is tenuous; at worst, it's false."[29] Shared commodification, embodied in stories and ownership of status-granting goods, is no substitute for sustained social relationships in which we learn the day-to-day realities of one another's situations.

If It's Not Entertaining, It's Boring

Another spiritual concern generated by uncritical participation in consumer culture lies in its valorization of distraction and amusement. In the church where I served as Director of Christian Education, we often engaged in lively conversations about whether or not worship should be entertaining, both for adults and for children. Many in the congregation felt that if worship was not entertaining it would be boring, a false but convincing dichotomy given our cultural norms. The "-tain-" part of the word *entertainment* has to do with holding, as is evidenced by its presence in words such as *detain* and *retain*. The purpose of entertainment is to capture the attention of an audience for its amusement or pleasure. However, the substitute for superficial entertainment could be a practice of sustained attentiveness generated by an individual or community of faith. Indeed, sustained attention is a fundamental element of almost any form of spiritual practice, and one well worth practicing with children.

The avoidance of boredom has become a fundamental goal for the daily lives of middle-class children in the United States. Suspecting that boredom leads to dangerous or destructive behavior (or incessant whining), modern parents strive to entertain their children throughout the day. This practice has implications for the spiritual development of children. As Schor notes, "If all children's experiences are geared toward excitement, surprise, and thrills, they may not discover that happiness and well-being are mainly gained through an appreciation of the quotidian (that is, daily experience)."[30] A soul tended primarily in the gardens of distraction and amusement may miss the beauty of creation, the subtle movement of the Spirit in the world, the prophetic voice crying in the wilderness.

Additionally, the equation of children's culture with fun and entertainment makes the sharing of stories marked by struggle or suffering seem inappropriate for children, even though children do suffer and might benefit from such stories. I recently taught a preschool Sunday school class using curriculum from a mainline Protestant publishing house that turned the story of Jesus praying in Gethsemane into a mildly farcical story, emphasizing the disciples' repeatedly falling asleep. Making flowers was the central activity of the day. The "compulsory fun" element of childhood culture distorted this story of struggle and vocation into something almost unrecognizable. True, it was only preschool, but the equation of childhood with entertainment and fun can divert us from some of the deepest wisdoms of our religious traditions and stories.

As more and more marketers compete for the attention of our children, "fun" accelerates to more involved forms. Mercer considers the late-capitalist culture practice of intensifying experience through spectacle. Repeated exposure to spectacles such as "Disney on Ice" heightens the possibilities of boredom with everyday experience:

> The constant stimulation of desire shapes children into a state of perpetual dissatisfaction with previously sought-after objects and experiences and into a never-ending quest for that which is novel. Childhood itself comes to be seen as a time defined by constant access to whatever is amusing, fun, and exciting.[31]

This emphasis on excitement and capturing attention through lavish display limits the perceived value of non-entertainment activities with children, many of which are critical for children's spiritual development. For example, extended attention to unjust social situations or to persons requiring extended care (such as children or adults in poor health) requires the ability to put aside the need for constant stimulation and to focus attention on difficult tasks. While the cliché "it builds character" is often used for comedic effect, it embodies a truth: spiritual development requires experiences that move beyond entertainment.

Beyond Princesses and Superheroes: Attending to Children's Spiritual Formation

In the face of intense marketing and other spectacles clamoring for the attention of children, parents and communities of faith must become more intentional about their children's spiritual formation. Many have already begun to develop approaches to limiting the power of consumer formation on their children. The following sections explore some of these approaches and assess their strengths and limitations in reducing the influence of commodification on children's spiritual lives.

A Word on Fighting Fire with Fire

One tactic that many publishing houses and educational programs pursue is the adoption of entertainment genres and production values for the benefit of communicating the Gospel to children. This approach is akin to fighting fire with fire. However, my daydream of "Disciples on Ice" does not adequately address the spiritual formation issues raised by children's entertainment culture. Children's religious education that utilizes familiar licensed characters, such as Bob the Tomato from the VeggieTales series, or an entertainment spectacle format, such as many popular vacation

Bible school curricula, may benefit from the familiarity of their forms and the ability of children to move quickly into them. However, they do not adequately address the issue of false relationships engendered and mediated through these characters, or the speed at which children move on to the next spectacle offered by the culture. Those who take seriously the issue of children's spiritual formation cannot rely on replicating the ubiquitous practices of children's marketing as the most appropriate response to their dominating presence.

"Barbie Is Not Welcome in Our House": The Practice of Abstinence

Another common approach is abstinence from consumer culture. One of my daughter's best friends can repeat the mantra of her parents: "Barbie is not welcome in our house." Concerned about the impact of Barbie on the emerging body image of young girls, her parents have embraced the ancient spiritual practice of abstinence. This was my initial approach in dealing with children's marketing as well: we refused to buy clothing and products with licensed characters on them, and our children do not watch commercial television. The advertising industry itself places the responsibility for protecting children from commercialism solely on parents' shoulders, suggesting that, if they do not like marketing, they should keep their children away from it.[32]

Abstinence is appealing, but it has limits. Linn notes that a social policy of "just say no" is as inadequate for children and commodification as it is for addicts and drugs. She compares the culture of marketing with the toxic street culture in neighborhoods territorially marked by gangs. Despite parents' best efforts, the culture of marketing saturates all communities and "is pervasive and alluring and competes with parental values for children's hearts and minds."[33] As my own attempt to abstain from the princess onslaught indicates, abstinence ultimately does not work, unless you live completely "off the grid" in every conceivable way, or in a well-bounded intentional community with other media-free parents who share noncommercial values. The power of Disney, Nickelodeon, and their cohorts means that they have access to all children in U.S. culture. The question becomes how educators and parents respond to that influence.

"How Could Cinderella Have Made a Better Choice for Her Life?": Contestation

Eventually, parents such as me realize that it is impossible to abstain from commercial influences on our children. What we can do, however, is to contest the values that dominate our culture, and to do this actively with our children. Religious educator Michael Warren argues that religious life itself opens the possibility for contesting the hegemony of media dominance. Media influence on the young is "neither inevitable nor inexplicable." Warren advocates for the development of cultural agency in response:

Understanding how cultural production works and uncovering the human hands at work in it may also show particular persons and groups that they can move beyond being passive consumers of others' significations. They can undertake the production of meaning themselves, first by becoming questioners of the products handed them for their consumption and then by becoming co-creators of their own versions of the world.[34]

Indeed, Warren names this work as part of the human religious vocation, supported by viable religious communities that provide compelling alternative imaginations that help contest media images.[35]

The work of contestation may sound rather sophisticated for young children, but many parents already engage in this work. The same friends who do not welcome Barbie in their house often raise critical questions about the princess narratives with their daughter: "Do you think Cinderella made a wise choice when she decided to marry the prince after only knowing him for a few hours?" "How else could Jasmine have discussed with her father the value of non-princely friends and romantic interests?" Stewart Hoover, Lynn Schofield Clark, and Diane Alters, in their study of families' interacting with mass media, noted that the parents they studied took responsibility for their children's exposure to media quite seriously:

Parents thought and worried about the media and took various overlapping paths to control it—some by imposing time limits or trading off book reading for television watching or video gaming, for example, and others by insisting on (or thinking of insisting on) discussing with their children the media they used. In these ways, parents tried to disembed media, particularly television, from their lives in order to examine and try to control them. At the same time, they listened to, engaged in, and reflected upon the public scripts of the media that they in effect helped fashion.[36]

This parental work is not in vain. Children's interactions with the stories and iconic characters proffered by the media are deeply impacted by the values and responses of those who surround them and by the children's own critical engagement in light of their life experiences.

Elizabeth Chin's study of the Newhallville children supports this conclusion. Despite her claims that the economically disadvantaged young persons she interviewed were deeply impacted by consumer culture, Chin asserts that to assume that consumers are passive recipients swayed by the products and services offered by self-interested corporations is to underestimate their agency and creativity in interacting with the process of consumption. Chin argues that her young informants confronted the market culture and critiqued it from their social location. Faced with limited economic resources, the Newhallville children she interviewed recognized the scarcity of goods to which they have access and the limits that scarcity places on their desires.

Contestation goes even beyond the limits of material goods. Chin points out that the children's critique of consumption includes not only the acquisition of goods, but also the images and ideas that are being sold. Chin relates the story of two young girls and their playful response to the Barbie doll. One of the youngsters, ten-year-old Asia, notes:

> Okay. What I was saying that Barbie…how can I say this? They make her like a stereotype. Barbie is a stereotype. When you think of Barbie you don't think of fat Barbie…you don't think of pregnant Barbie. You never, ever…think of an abused Barbie.[37]

Asia is testing, within the realm of her own experience, the stories that are being sold to her and her friend through the commodity Barbie. Chin pushes her reader to engage in similar contestation. She notes: "It has become increasingly evident that consumption is at once a hegemonic force deserving of condemnation and a realm in which people exercise considerable power and creativity."[38]

I can see such agency and contestation in my daughter's imaginative interaction with the princess characters. When she plays with her princess dolls, she uses them as transparent figures who live through her daily struggles with friends and parents. Despite their high-class representations, in her imaginary world they are not above the concrete particulars of her daily life. They go to work, raise children, and teach preschool. While I still worry about the valuing of class, gender, and racial privilege represented in their stories, this valuing does not run unchecked by the daily experience of my daughter's life. The values and norms that we live in our daily lives exist as a parallel to the fantastic universe of Disney, one that she can draw upon in her construction of selfhood and spirituality.

"At Least Tomorrow Is a Church Day": Forging Authentic, Noncommercial Connections

When we returned home after the "Princesses on Ice" fiasco, my daughter shared her tale of woe with her father about being unable to shake hands with the princesses. Tears streamed down her face as she talked about how we rushed down to say hello, but they skated off without talking to her. Finally, after a long shuddery breath, she announced: "At least I get to go to church tomorrow." She then went off to play in her room.

I was both puzzled and heartened by this announcement. We attend a church that has little formal programming for children, but my daughter has deep connections with the adolescent girl who assists in her Sunday school class, with our ministers, and with other adults and peers in the congregation. These relationships matter to her in powerful ways, despite their seeming insignificance in the face of the multimedia spectacle we had just engaged. She knows the value of these relationships; they are connections with real people who call her by name and love her as she is. These noncommercial connections may be encountered in a variety of contexts: families, schools, neighborhood groups, and so forth. They are vital to the spiritual formation of children, a powerful incarnation of God's love and care mediated through concrete relationships.

Engaging the Powers and Principalities: Changing Social Policy through Collective Action

The deregulation of advertising to children and the encroachment of commodification into public space can be reversed. However, the extended reach and power of corporate interests in children's marketing means that individual parental action is not enough. Many organizations and coalitions have formed to pressure changes in the relentless marketing to children, such as the Center for Commercial Free Public Education, the Center for the New American Dream, and the Campaign for a Commercial Free Childhood. Collective action and social contestation can influence what is marketed to children. For example, Barbie's body type has shifted dramatically in the last few years, as her feet have flattened and her waist- and bust-lines transformed toward more human dimensions. This change was brought about by the relentless critique of feminists, combined with research on the product's influence on children's body image. Similar pressures have influenced Disney. We recently borrowed a Disney-produced Cinderella book from the public library in which she and the prince get together because of their shared interests in veterinary medicine. Shared action can influence the power of marketers, who will sell what people want to buy. Regulation can also protect public media and institutional space for children to develop free of corporate marketing.

Conclusion

While princess dreams may be the most-available version of formation offered to children in a hyper-consumptive culture, they do not have to be the primary and most lasting formation. Effective contestation can have a profound impact on the spiritual formation of our children, and should be considered worthy social ministry by parents and communities of faith. Because the formation offered to children comes through socialization and institutional structures, the counter-formation is also best engaged through communal and social efforts shared by those who hope for different dreams to capture the imagination of children: dreams of justice rather than privilege, of mutuality rather than domination, of care for those who suffer rather than distraction from suffering.

Violence, Boy Code, and Schools

Adolescent Males Making It through Life

RODGER NISHIOKA

Nathan is an easygoing, relatively carefree sixteen-year-old living in suburban Kansas City. He gets into minor hassles with his older sister, but these do not seem to faze him. He does well in school, seemingly with little effort. Tall and lanky, he is a handsome young man with a good number of friends. He is not particularly athletic, but appears comfortable with his body. He relates well with his parents, both of whom are busy with demanding jobs. He regularly attends church with his family and is involved in the youth group. He seems to glide through life. Thus, his response to my question, "What do you think is the toughest thing about being a guy?" was a surprise: "I guess it's just everything, you know? I mean, this may sound lame because I know there's other bad stuff happening in the world, like wars and hunger and stuff, but there really is a lot of pressure to being a guy. Like, it doesn't ever seem to let up."

When I then asked Nathan if this pressure was different from what girls face, he said he really could not say. He added: "I think it probably seems tough to everybody. At least that's the way I see it. I mean, even the other kids who seem to not care feel it. I guess some girls would say that they have it worse, but I think everybody probably thinks that." When asked to give further explanation of the "pressure," Nathan responded, "I think it's a lot of things. Of course there's school and grades and then there's family stuff. I don't have it so bad. I mean, I get along fine with my folks, but a lot of my friends really have serious family stuff going on. I know a lot of adults look at us kids and think we have it so easy, but I just don't see it."

Nathan was one of seventy-seven adolescent males I interviewed across the United States. His explanation of the pressure he feels resonated in all of the interviews.[1] In this chapter, I have chosen to introduce two of the young men, Nathan and Curtis, whose stories represent the larger sample and reveal concerns widely shared among the interviewees.

Curtis is seventeen years old and lives in a small town in South Carolina. He lives with his mom, grandma, and two younger sisters. While his mom is at work, he takes care of his grandmother, who is older and ailing, and his younger sisters. He is an athlete, playing on both the high school football and basketball teams. He also manages to work a few hours each weekend to earn some spending money. Several years ago, Curtis' mother moved the family out of Columbia, S.C., to get away from the city and an emerging gang culture. Curtis loves his family, but says his Mom is "seriously paranoid." He resents that she will not yet let him get his driver's license or a cell phone and that she monitors his computer time closely. Still, he seems to understand it. "Kids can be stupid at times," he says.

While Curtis does not like his mom's strictures, he recognizes that she is doing her best to be a good parent. "She went to college and expects me to go, too," he says. Curtis also appreciates his mom's decision to move from Columbia:

> At first, I was mad about it; but now I understand. Some of the guys I used to hang out with got in trouble. And they were good guys, too. Stuff just happened, and they got involved with the wrong people. I guess it's good that we moved here.

What is the toughest thing about being a guy for Curtis? "I don't know," he says initially. "I mean, I never really thought about it." After reflecting on the question further, he says:

> I think maybe it's different for me, you know, growing up without a Dad and all... I mean, I love my Mom, and she's done a lot for me; but the guy thing, well, I guess it would be nice to have a Dad around, you know, just to relate to. I think the toughest thing for me, though, is that I don't have any time just to hang out. I mean, I'm doing so much stuff–school and practice and work and taking care of my grandma and my sisters. Sometimes I think I just want to go to college for a break, you know what I mean?

Curtis's comments resonate in many ways with Nathan's. Both of these young men, Nathan white and Curtis black, describe lives that are filled with pressure. While their pressures may not appear different from what young women experience, both Nathan and Curtis describe these experiences as *qualitatively* different. Many adolescent males echo the thoughts of Nathan and Curtis. These young men are growing up in a troubling world.

An Epidemic of Violence

October 1997–Pearl, Mississippi. After killing his mother, sixteen-year-old Luke Woodham opens fire at his high school, killing three students and wounding seven others.

December 1997–Paducah, Kentucky. Fourteen-year-old Michael Carneal kills three students at a high school prayer meeting.

March 1998–Jonesboro, Arkansas. Thirteen-year-old Mitchell Johnson and eleven-year-old Andrew Golden open fire on their schoolmates, killing four of them and a teacher.

April 1998–Edinboro, Pennsylvania. Fourteen-year-old Andrew Wurst kills a teacher at a school dance.

May 1998–Springfield, Oregon. After killing his parents, fifteen-year-old Kip Kinkel walks into the school cafeteria and shoots twenty-four classmates, two fatally.

April 1999–Littleton, Colorado. Eighteen-year-old Eric Harris and seventeen-year-old Dylan Klebold shoot and kill twelve students and one teacher, and wound twenty-three other students before taking their own lives at Columbine High School.

November 1999–Deming, New Mexico. Twelve-year-old Victor Cordova Jr. shoots and kills one student at Deming Middle School.

March 2000–Savannah, Georgia. Nineteen-year-old Darrell Ingram shoots and kills two students at a dance at Beach High School.

March 2001–Santee, California. Fifteen-year-old Charles Andrew Williams kills two students and wounds thirteen others at Santana High School.

April 2003–Red Lion, Pennsylvania. Fourteen-year-old James Sheets shoots and kills the school principal before taking his own life at Lion Area Junior High School.

March 2005–Red Lake, Minnesota. Sixteen-year-old Jeff Weise shoots and kills his grandfather and a companion, then goes to school, where he kills a teacher, a security guard, and five students before taking his own life.

January 2007–Tacoma, Washington. Seventeen-year-old Douglas Chanthabouly shoots and kills a student in the hallway of Henry Foss High School.

April 2007–Blacksburg, Virginia. Twenty-three-year-old student Seung-Hui Cho shoots and kills thirty-two and wounds twenty-five others at Virginia Tech University, making this incident the worst school shooting in United States history.

The list is staggering, terrifying, and incomplete. These incidents were reported in the national news. Yet, appearing just off-screen and beyond the headlines were thousands of other acts of violence involving adolescent males, barely mentioned or not mentioned at all. In his book *Lost Boys,* James Garbarino makes a convincing argument that adolescent males are swimming in an epidemic of violence. He cites the FBI reports showing that, of the approximately 23,000 homicides committed annually in the United States, nearly one quarter are perpetrated by a young male under twenty-one years of age. The rate of homicides committed by juveniles rose 168 percent from the mid-1980s to the mid-1990s. Further, the suicide rate among adolescent males has risen 400 percent since 1950. Garbarino goes on to discuss the roles that race and class play in the media's attention to adolescent violence. By and large, says Garbarino, violence that involves poor, inner-city African American and/or Latino adolescent males goes underreported or unreported, while violence that involves middle- and upper-class white adolescent males is given much attention.[2]

What do the news stories and the statistics really tell us? When asked about violence, both Nathan and Curtis acknowledged its reality. Both young men said it is an issue in their schools and in their lives. Nathan portrayed it as more distant, however:

It's not like I feel unsafe. I mean, at school we go through lockdown drills and everything, especially after Columbine, but it's never happened. Sometimes I wonder if there's a kid who's that crazy. There are fights every once in a while. And our school has talked a lot about bullying and not picking on kids, but it still happens.

Curtis attends a large high school that gathers young people from his town as well as the surrounding county. "Yeah, we go through lockdown drills. And once in a while I hear about rumors of stuff like somebody heard once about a kid bringing a gun to school, but it's just talk. It's not serious." Curtis may be more attentive to the issue of violence because of the decision his mother made to move the family away from his old neighborhood. He says:

I hear that some of my old friends are involved in gangs. I don't keep in touch with them much anymore. The teachers at school are all seriously paranoid about gang stuff happening at our school, and they've like banned certain colors and stuff. Last year, they started this strict dress code, but I think they worry about it too much, you know?

What can we know about violence beyond the dramatic incidents and gang activity? Does race and class have something to do with it? Curtis, having grown up with the cautions of the African American community, is sure that it does.

Like, my Mom is always telling me that I have to watch it because, I mean, we're not poor or anything, but she is always telling me that it's safer for a black man to be in the war in Iraq than it is to be living here at home. I'm not sure where she got that, but it may be true. I mean, that's just crazy. Can you believe it? That a black kid like me would be safer in a war than here at home. That's just not right.

Curtis says he feels especially safe now, living in the small town. He is not sure that he has actually experienced racism; however, he is sure that, if his mom had not moved the family, he would be at greater risk for falling into violence.

Nathan believes, too, that class and race have something to do with violence. Drawing upon his experience as a European American in mostly white settings, he says:

> There aren't a lot of black kids at my school. When we lived in Houston, there were more black kids and a lot more Hispanic kids. We do have a lot more Asians at my school now and some black kids and a few Hispanics. Most of the teachers are white so it's kind of weird when we talk about race stuff and I look around and it's a bunch of white kids talking. I know some white kids are scared of black kids; but when we lived in Houston, I had some good friends who were black. We used to talk about race, and I actually miss that. It seems kinda weird to be talking about racism in a school with almost all white kids. I read once that white people think a lot of the violence is black people doing stuff to white people, but actually that's not true; black people are mostly the victims, but we just don't hear about that as much. Yeah, I think race has a lot to do with violence.

One sees in Nathan's comments, as in Curtis's, that their own racial identity and social settings shape their awareness. They are also aware that their perspectives and conversations are shaped by these personal and social contexts. Both Nathan and Curtis think they are living in a more violent time than their parents and grandparents. "I know that's true," says Curtis. "When my grandma is watching TV, like the news, she just keeps talking about how bad everything is now. And she grew up when everything was segregated, and she *still* says things are more messed up today."

Nathan even admits, albeit reluctantly, to the media's influence on today's adolescent males, promoting more violence than found in previous generations.

> Like, I know adults think guys today are more violent because of Xbox and PS2, but I don't know. It may be. I just think that whereas before when kids got mad, they might have called somebody a name or gotten into a fight; now it seems like they get a gun. I don't even know where they get these guns. I think media may be part of it. I guess it has to. I know some kids, all they do is watch these really violent shows.

So what is the attraction to violence? Why do adolescent males act out in more violent ways than adolescent females, who sometimes end up as the victims of this violence? In my reading and research, numerous scholars argue that boys today are struggling with pronounced pressures of how society constructs "masculinity." In her book *Dude, You're a Fag,* C. J. Pascoe argues that masculinity is a configuration of specific practices and discourses primarily conveyed and understood as a form of dominance over and oppression of others, hence the attraction to violence.[3] "Masculinity" is narrowly defined through behavior rather than genitalia. For a young man to be "masculine," he must successfully engage in these practices and discourses or suffer the consequences. Some call it the "boy code."

Deciphering the Boy Code

In his book *Real Boys,* psychologist William Pollack describes a set of rules that boys learn early in sandboxes, on playgrounds, in schoolrooms, at camps, in churches, and wherever else they hang out.[4] These rules are taught and reinforced by parents, peers, coaches, teachers, and the culture in general. The rules are codified through such phrases as "keep a stiff upper lip," "act tough," "be cool," "don't show your feelings," "don't be a wimp," "don't be too nice," and, "just laugh and brush it off when someone punches you." Pollack says that as boys grow up, they learn that these are more than clichés or suggestions; they are strict rules that shape how they must behave to "be a man." To understand the potency of this boy code, we turn now to discover what it is and how it functions among young men today.

Imperatives of the Boy Code

The boy code is taught through many childhood games and through informal interactions among boys, and between boys and significant adults. Drawing upon the work of other researchers, Pollack identifies four metaphors or imperatives at the heart of the boy code.[5]

1. *The Sturdy Oak.* This first metaphor tells boys that they are to be stoic, stable, and independent, like an oak tree. They are never to show weakness, pain, or emotional need. Even to ask for an explanation or for help in a confusing or frightening situation is to break this first imperative in the code. Boys should pretend to be confident in spite of feeling afraid or uncertain, sturdy in spite of feeling shaky, and self-reliant in spite of feeling desperate for camaraderie.

2. *Give 'em Hell.* This second imperative resembles the classic caricatures of extreme athletes and coaches, war heroes, and western gunslingers. The message to boys is that manhood is marked by daring, bravado, and action, popularly conveyed in the "boys will be boys" concept. The concept is then expanded with claims that males are genetically predisposed to be macho, to possess high energy, and to act with

Superman-like courage. Even young boys can be heard "daring" each other to do something, then taunting one another with words like "chicken" if they do not comply with the dare. This element of the boy code tells boys that it is worse to be afraid or to be accused of being scared than to engage in risky behavior that might actually result in injury.

3. *King of the Mountain.* This third imperative in the boy code demands that males achieve status, dominance, and power over others. Understood another way, the "king of the mountain" metaphor teaches boys to avoid shame at all costs, to challenge others, and to prove their worth by putting others down. The world is viewed as a hierarchy, and the code tells boys to climb to the top. Shame comes in failure and losing. This part of the code is summarized by the phrase, "Winning isn't everything, it's the only thing."

4. *Be a Man, Not a Sissy.* This fourth imperative prohibits boys from expressing feelings or urges viewed as "feminine," such as dependence, warmth, and empathy. According to this element in the code, anything that is feminine is taboo. Not only is it wrong to be a sissy, but boys are to ridicule others who show a hint of feminine qualities; their job is to keep others in line. If a boy showing these so-called feminine signs does not change his behavior, others will ostracize him.

Potency of the Boy Code

How real is the boy code for boys today? Neither Curtis nor Nathan had ever heard of the boy code, and both seemed somewhat amused by it. "That's actually pretty funny," said Curtis. "I mean, it's not like anybody ever talks about it that way. I never heard of these phrases." Nathan took a little while to understand it. "So, like, this is unwritten, right? I mean, you're not saying that like this is something all guys are aware of, are you?"

Upon further reflection, both agreed that the code exists at least to some degree. Curtis talked about it first in terms of his athletics:

Oh, man. I'm serious. It's like the worst thing if you show any weakness, you know? You have to be tough. You have to act like a man, or you aren't going to survive. But you know, you don't have to go out for football or basketball or any of the other sports. I know guys who are cool who just don't go for any of the sports, but they're cool guys.

When I asked if these guys were more emotional and more feminine, he admits, "No, I guess not." On the other hand, Curtis does not agree that guys can never show emotions. He explains in this football story:

It may have been that way a while back but not so much now. Like at the start of last season, to get us all pumped up, the coach sat us down and made us watch this movie, *Remember the Titans.* It's about a team that is divided but comes together. At the end, one of the guys gets into a serious car accident, and you can tell these guys really care about each other. You know, when it finished, one of our captains, a white guy, got up; and you could tell he was sorta crying, and it was cool. Like nobody would ever call him a sissy. So I'm not so sure about this code stuff.

Nathan was more certain about the existence and power of the boy code. He remembered when he started high school that one of his friends from middle school was carrying his books "sorta like a girl, you know, like this" (he brings his arms across his chest like he is hugging a notebook), and Nathan and another friend intervened and told him to stop it. "He didn't even know he was doing it, but we told him to stop or he would get picked on," Nathan said. When I asked how he knew it was a rule, Nathan said he just knew. "I mean, it's like there are certain things you just don't do as a guy. You don't sit with your legs crossed a certain way. You don't run a certain way. I mean it all sounds sorta lame, but it's true."

I asked what happens if you do not conform to the code? "Then you better get ready to get picked on," says Nathan. He elaborated with a story. Nathan's school does not allow visible piercings, but girls can have one piercing in each ear. Nathan reflects on how this practice affects boys.

> There are some guys who you can tell have their ears pierced because you can see the hole. It's like they must just take it out when they get to school and put it back in when they leave. But that's really no big deal because it's sorta cool nowadays. But there's another guy who wore like eye makeup and, man, he was always alone. I think he left school because I don't see him anymore. He was older than me anyway, so he might have graduated; but he would get picked on a lot. I used to feel sorry for him, but I never talked to him or anything. I didn't have him in any of my classes.

I pursued the situation further by asking if the boy code is a problem? Curtis frankly responded, "I don't know. I mean, isn't it just being normal to act like a guy? I mean I don't like it when guys act all gay and stuff. Man, in my school, guys joke a lot about being gay and a fag. I think guys should just act like guys and girls should act like girls. Isn't that the way God made us?"

Eager to learn more, I asked if it is really God who decided how guys and girls should act? "I think so," says Curtis. "I mean, isn't that why God made us different?"

Nathan's responses were somewhat different from Curtis's. He can see that, in some ways, the code is a problem.

I guess there are some guys who just don't get into the typical stuff, you know, like you just talked about–the code stuff. I've never really had a problem with it, but like that guy I mentioned, the one who got harassed all the time… I sorta felt sorry for him. I don't know that he actually started out to be different. I think he just was. I don't know if he was gay or anything. At school, guys talk a lot about being gay or a fag, and it's always an insult; but I guess I don't see anything really wrong with it, you know. I don't think that just because you act like a girl you're necessarily gay, just like just because you act like a guy you're necessarily straight. I just think people are different.

But what about the code? "Oh, it definitely is there," says Nathan, "and I guess it's a problem because it forces some people to act like they're not."

The responses of Curtis and Nathan, representing similar ones from other boys interviewed, suggest that the boy code functions differently in different contexts and with different degrees of potency and consciousness. In his discussion of the boy code, Pollack echoes Nathan's comments. The pressure of the boy code forces some adolescent males to devote their greatest energy to being who they are not. After a while, this takes its toll emotionally, spiritually, psychologically, and even physically. Pollack, a clinical psychologist, tells of numerous adolescent males he has encountered who have turned to drugs and alcohol to deal with the pressure of the boy code. Many live with a constant sense of shame, knowing that they are acting out a role that is neither truthful nor generative for themselves. Further, the code forces some young men to separate from their parents before they are emotionally ready. Parents, especially fathers, are fearful of being too nurturing with their sons. They worry that their sons will grow up to be overly dependent and emotional. The code forces many young boys to be pseudo-independent far before they are ready or before it is healthy.

The code also has consequences in peer relationships. When boys act out in ways that go against the code, they are shamed or shunned, leaving some with profound feelings of loneliness, sadness, and disconnection. Pollack says that this shame is similar to what many girls experience in dealing with the pressures about what it means to be "feminine." Ultimately, Pollack says the result for both boys and girls is an intense struggle for emotional, spiritual, social, psychological, and physical health. This struggle is further intensified for boys in their experiences of school, a place of evaluation.

The Troubling World of School

While we may live in a "man's world," at least in relation to power and wealth in adult society, the same is not true for schools, the place where our children spend most of their time and where their success is measured. Pollack and others believe that many boys, due to the violence they experience and the pressure of the boy code, must invest so much energy in keeping up their emotional guard and hiding their deepest and truest feelings that they often have little or no energy left to apply themselves to the tasks of schoolwork. Certainly males still show up at the top of academic lists as valedictorians; but, most often, boys form the majority of the bottom of the class. Overall, says Pollack, boys receive lower grades than girls in school. Drawing upon statistics collected in the 1992 National Assessment of Educational Progress Trend Report published by the U.S. Department of Education, Pollack reports that eighth grade boys were held back 50 percent more often than girls. By high school, boys accounted for two thirds of the students in special education classes. Further, young men made up less than 44 percent of college students. Sixty percent of all master's degree candidates were women, and the percentage of men in graduate level professional education was shrinking each year.[6]

Further evidence of these trends is offered by Michael Gurian and Kathy Stevens. They found that boys are up to ten times more likely to suffer from "hyperactivity" disorder than girls, and they account for 74 percent of all school suspensions. Males in school comprise 70 percent of those students who receive grades of D and F. Of children diagnosed with learning disabilities, 70 percent are boys. Of children diagnosed with behavioral disorders, 80 percent are boys. Gurian and Stevens write that, according to the United States Department of Education, boys are an average of a year to a year and a half behind girls in reading and writing skills. While girls are behind boys in math and science, they have recently made strides to catch up; boys are not doing the same in reading and writing. Of high school dropouts, 80 percent are male. Gurian and Stevens clearly recognize the continuing struggle of girls and women in the society as a whole, but they argue persuasively that the education of girls must not come at the expense of boys. Schools, according to Gurian and Stevens, need to pay attention to the particular needs of all children. Lately, girls seem to be gaining while boys are sadly falling behind.[7]

This cumulative evidence of school pressures needs to be explored and interpreted further, as it reveals pressures with which boys have to deal every day in their school settings.

School Evaluation in the Lives of Boys

As before, we turn to Nathan and Curtis to discover some of the human textures in the statistics offered by Pollack, and Gurian and Stevens. Both Nathan and Curtis are good students and do well in school. When I shared these statistics with them, both raised concerns. "I know some guys really have a tough time in school," says Nathan. He adds:

I know a lot of kids, guys especially, seem to get into trouble a lot and drop out. I guess I didn't realize it happened to guys more than girls; but I can see it, and I think it's true. You know, a lot of time, school is just not real interesting. I have some good teachers, but some of them are pretty boring. I have a friend who is home schooled; and while I'm not sure I'd like it, it seems like he learns more. He's not a freak or anything. I just think his parents thought they could do a better job, and maybe they are. I think I would hate staying at home with my sister though.

Inquiring further, I ask about the idea of girls being more successful than guys at school. Nathan responds:

I definitely think that's true. It just seems that girls get it more than guys do. I'm in several AP (advanced placement) classes; and the girls, whoa, they're always doing better than us guys. There actually aren't as many guys in my AP classes as there are in my regular classes, like my electives.

Curtis describes similar patterns in his school. He talks particularly about how school evaluations and achievement are values in his life, both for him and for his mom. "I know my Mom is always on me about school," says Curtis.

After practice when I come home, I'm usually real tired; but my mom makes sure I eat, and then all I do is homework. I hate my English class most of all. All that writing and reading. I don't even have time to watch TV or get on the computer or play games. I know a bunch of guys on the team who are just barely making it. They think I'm smart. I don't know. I don't think they have a mom who makes them do their work like mine does. If I don't keep my grades up, I don't get to play football or basketball or keep my job so I work pretty hard at school. I try to get most of my homework done in study hall.

When I ask Curtis to respond to the idea of girls being more successful than guys at school, he reflects on gender differences in learning styles and abilities to give attention.

I don't know. I guess it's like this: girls seem to be able to pay attention more than us guys. I'm serious. Some of my teachers are just so boring. I sit there; and then, all of a sudden, I realize I don't know what the teacher is even talking about. Like I just zoned out for, I don't know, 10 minutes. I don't think that ever happens to girls. I don't know how they do it. You know, if I could pay attention—my mom always tells me to "focus,"—I bet I could do just as well as the girls do.

Curtis's responses and his own school achievements transcend the common pattern that Gurian and Stevens and others have found among African-American boys. In fact, Gurian and Stevens write that the troubling world of academic success in schools is even *more* of a challenge for African American males such as Curtis. According to their research, black young men are more likely than other males to be identified as learning-disabled, less likely to participate in advanced placement courses, less likely to perform as well as other boys in math and science classes, and more likely to perform below grade level on standardized tests.[8] In another study cited by Gurian and Stevens, 42 percent of African American males "strongly disagreed that their teachers supported them or cared about their success in school."[9] As with the boy code, we see a great deal of complexity as regards the pressures of school on boys. The big picture shows many different trends related to gender, ethnicity, and other factors. The more particular pictures of Curtis and Nathan show some of the particular ways that these trends affect and do not affect them.

Potency of School Evaluation

In light of the evidence offered here, school, which should be a location of growth and development, is often a place where boys find little success. One cannot generalize about this because the study of individual boys, such as Nathan and Curtis, reveals much nuance. For many young males, however, school is a place where they encounter a "culture of cruelty."[10] In such a culture, boys seek to conform to a group, often any group. At the same time, the group demands conformity and holds the boy up for ridicule for any failure to conform. *Anything* a boy says or does that is different can and will be used against him. Dan Kindlon and Michael Thompson elaborate on this culture of cruelty, explaining that many adolescent males experience ridicule for the television shows they watch, the books they read, the shoes they wear, the color of their socks, the length of their shorts, the cut of their hair, the sound of their laugh, or the length of their stride. In addition, the physical changes (or lack thereof) that adolescent males undergo add to their self-consciousness, whether related to height, weight, musculature, genital development, voice, or hair growth. Given the boy code, adolescent males hide any insecurity or uncertainty to avoid looking weak or vulnerable. Further, many learn quickly that the best way to avoid being a target is to criticize others as a preemptive strike to divert attention from themselves. In this troubling world of tough evaluation imposed by others, say Kindlon and Thompson, no one ends up protected; no one is a winner, there are only greater losers.

Added to the experience of violence and the boy code discussed earlier, young boys often develop a sense of failure within the school system. Pastoral theology professor Robert C. Dykstra writes convincingly about the power of the "loser" image among American males. Predicated upon the notion of failure, Dykstra writes of the totalizing and essentializing power of the term "failure." Dykstra says that the term is often the "epithet of choice" among males today, even more powerful than "nerd," "dork," "geek," "wimp," "freak," "jerk," "slacker," "weirdo," and even "fag."[11] The word is not only prevalent among many adolescent males, but its meaning is expansive—more than simply failing at a particular task. It has come to mark the whole identity of an adolescent male. For many, there is nothing worse to be called. In the interviews that people have conducted after school shootings and suicides, pictures have emerged of the perpetrators. These young men had typically been branded losers many times and had been bullied by their peers and others. Such incidents are common to the culture of cruelty that boys face on a regular basis, whether as participants or observers.

Nathan and Curtis verify the discussion of Dykstra and others. Indeed, they both use the term "loser" as a dreaded label. Nathan says:

> It's tough. I mean, I have good friends at school, and I really get along with most everybody, but there are some kids you just avoid. Either they're mean jerks, and they go after people, or…you don't want to end up getting picked on like they do just because you're around them. I hear the term "loser" a lot. Sometimes kids are just messing around with each other, you know, having fun; but I guess sometimes it could really hurt. Like school is just the way it is, but you know, at church, it's better because there are some kids there that I don't think are liked a lot at their own schools, but we do okay as a youth group. I think it must be tough for some of them at school.

Curtis, like Nathan, recognizes the totalizing nature of the term "loser" that Dykstra and his colleagues describe: "Man, you don't want to be called a loser, you know what I mean? Like, it doesn't have so much to do with losing a game because, when we lose, it's like we all lose together. But if *you're* a loser, then it's about *you*. That's different. That's rough."

I asked Curtis to say more, asking if there were kids whom he would identify as "losers" at his school.

> Well, I mean not really, but everybody treats them that way. There's this one kid that is just a jerk, you know. Like I tried to be nice to him once, and he almost started messing with me. I was like, forget it, man. That's the last time I'm going to be nice to you. I don't know what his problem is. I don't call him a loser, but everybody else does. I guess something's going on with him that just makes him angry all the time. He's a loner, and I guess if I didn't have any friends, I'd be angry, too. I don't know how he makes it through life.

Curtis's last sentence not only verifies the potency of the school culture, with its academic and peer evaluations, but it also sets an agenda for young men caught in the cultural vices we have discussed in this chapter: violence, boy codes, and school cultures. For young men threatened by so many troubling influences, the challenge of "making it through life" can be overwhelming. With Curtis's words, then, we turn to another part of this discussion, seeking hope and envisioning practices that may engender strength in boys' lives.

Making It through Life

After these conversations with Curtis and Nathan and other interviewees, "making it through life" is the lingering question. How do adolescent males do this? Here are two bright, thoughtful, handsome young men with great families. They seem to be relatively popular and are making their way with little trouble. Given the opportunity to reflect in these interviews, however, they both described a troubling world that challenges them every day. Both of them have a vivid sense of the violence in their generation, and both sense that violence is not far from their own lives. This violence is real, even though one of them lives in a gated suburban neighborhood and the other moved to a small town as a result of his mother's deliberate decision to leave a more dangerous urban setting.

Both Nathan and Curtis also deal with the reality of the boy code, though that term and some of its descriptors were not familiar to them until I explained them. They daily navigate through what one psychologist termed the "straitjacket of adolescent male masculinity." Of course, Nathan and Curtis have feelings, as these conversations illustrate; however, they have learned to show their feelings cautiously. Incautious expressions of feelings put them at risk of ridicule. They have learned that they cannot trespass the boundaries of the code, because to do so may make them vulnerable targets.

How does one forge a whole, healthy identity given the weight of the boy code? Young men must also make their way through a schooling system that is as much about educating for life as it is about educating for a future vocation. Everything in their lives, even family and church, revolve around school. Nathan's mother said that when she was growing up, she had the sense that the demands of school were always viewed in a healthy balance with the demands of her family and her church. If anything, she felt like her family carried more weight in the equation. Now, she feels like school has taken over the power position, and she is at a loss to explain why.

Perhaps what is most troubling about the world of adolescent males is that many young men do not have alternative communities and life practices to counteract the epidemic of violence, the weight of the boy code, and the power of school cultures in judging their lives. Many have little support from their families or faith communities. For those who do have supportive, resilient communities, the larger society allows little time and space to support those relationships. It is not surprising that many young men simply drop out of a world that has no apparent place for them and that many others carry their wounds into adulthood. Somehow, we have to do more than help our young men simply "make it through life."

Beyond Just Making It through Life

When I began my research for this chapter, I was more than a little skeptical. I was skeptical that boys were really in trouble. Certainly I was aware that some boys acted out in tragic ways, injuring themselves and others. I was aware that some specific populations of boys, such as African American and Native American males, faced greater challenges in our American society; however, I approached this chapter not at all convinced that boys as a group were in trouble. Now, after much reading and interviews with Curtis, Nathan, and seventy-five other boys, plus interviews with several families and caregivers, I think otherwise. For our boys to do more than just make it through life, we must enable them to embody a new understanding of masculinity. This new vision of masculinity—what it means to be masculine, to be a man—was at the heart of most of my interviews.

Dan Kindlon and Michael Thompson write that boys must be taught that courage and empathy are the sources of real strength in life and that being a man entails such things as emotional strength and vulnerability as well as the development of an internal life that embraces one's feelings.[12] William Pollack calls for revising the boy code. In a similar way that the voices of girls and women have been welcomed in recent years, he yearns for a boy code that allows boys and men to come to "full voice."[13] James Garbarino speaks to parents, pastors and rabbis, school teachers and administrators, and to the juvenile justice system when he says that the most powerful way to dismantle this embedded system of violence among boys is through the power of spiritual, psychological, and social anchors that model nonviolence for boys.[14]

In my research, the most compelling vision came from Michael Gurian. He calls for a vision of manhood that is grounded on four principles: compassion, honor, responsibility, and enterprise. Each of these interact with one another in dynamic ways. Compassion includes an awareness of and caring for one's self, others, and the whole of creation. Honor deals with such values as honesty, character, and decency. Responsibility focuses on one's ability to participate in meaningful ways in the whole of society and, in particular, in playing one's part for the good of the whole. Enterprise deals with the whole self: with one's mind, body, and spirit, as well as the outcome of good work—of contributing in ways so that one grows as a human being.[15] Together, these four principles enable boys to lead lives of integrity—literally lives in which one's life is not compartmentalized, but rather one's relationships are reflected in and related to one's vocation and one's spiritual life and one's recreation.

In a poignant note, Gurian writes that he is hopeful for the future of boys in no small part because of his many conversations with boys and their families and loved ones. At first, given the many struggles boys are facing today, I found this sense of hope incongruent if not disingenuous. I asked Nathan and Curtis if they were hopeful. To my surprise, they both said they were. Curtis was the most sure and the most emphatic:

> Like, in general? Well, yeah. Now, it's not like I think I'm going to end up playing pro football or basketball or anything, but yeah. I got me a lot of hope. I got hope that God watches over me and my mom and grandma and sisters even when times are rough. I got hope that I'm going to college, gonna get a job and a family. I want to take care of my mom the way she takes care of me and my sisters.

Then I asked Curtis what kind of man he would be. His answer was quick and sure: "A good one," he said, looking at me seriously. "I'm going to be a good man." I responded with equal seriousness: he was already that...a good man.

5

"Sometimes I Feel Like a Fatherless Child"

A Feminist Practical Theological Perspective on Adolescent Girls and Father-Loss

JOYCE ANN MERCER

Fatherless children are making news headlines these days. Human-interest stories reporting on the U.S. war in Iraq shine a spotlight on (U.S.) children whose soldier-fathers die in the war or serve overseas in the military. Editorial pages contain columns about children rendered fatherless in the context of "get-tough-on-crime" legislation that has resulted in unprecedented rates of incarceration, primarily among African American men. The purported effects of father absence upon children, youth, and society include everything from heightened financial stress in mother-only families to the flourishing of youth gangs and the increasing levels of disorder in public school classrooms. In this contemporary discourse on fathering, persons who occupy conflicting political and ideological positions on family policy in the United States find themselves oddly joined together in identifying father absence as a significant social issue and problem for children and youth—albeit for very different reasons.

In this essay I explore father-loss in the experience of adolescent girls as seen through portraits of two girls, one drawn from fiction and the other from clinical pastoral practice. These accounts, while not intended to be representative or generalizable to all girls, nevertheless may have parallels in the lives of other adolescent girls we encounter in congregations and pastoral contexts.[1] I use the term father-loss, in distinction from father-absence, to signal the priority and privileging of adolescent girls' *experiences*

78

of a vacuum more than the actual locations of their fathers (i.e., present or absent) in my analysis. As in Rodger Nishioka's chapter before this one, the subtle interplay of gender and culture reveal powerful influences and challenges for young girls faced with father-loss.

A Fictional Account of Father-Loss

Judy Pascoe's fictional account of an adolescent girl grieving the loss of her father underscores many features of the grief experience expressed by girls encountered in pastoral practice. "It was simple for me, the saints were in heaven and guardian angels had extendable wings like Batman and my dad had died and gone to live in the tree in the backyard."[2] The story, *Our Father Who Art in a Tree*, written as Simone's (the fictional girl) first person account of grief lived through her adolescence, narrates the power of father-loss in an adolescent girl's life. Shortly after his funeral, Simone hears her father calling her from the tree in the backyard. When she climbs into its highest branches, she discovers that she can talk to her father, and she begins to visit him regularly in the tree. Soon she invites her mother into the tree as well.

Simone discovers, however, that she risks disapproval and misunderstanding if she shares with too many others this secret experience of connection with her deceased father. Over time, the presence of her father in the tree proves to be a mixed blessing for Simone. While it protects her from the finality of her father's death and a horribly empty sense of loss, it also prevents Simone and her family from getting on with their lives in the present and from reinvesting energy into new relationships with the living. The loss becomes the defining feature of their experience.

Our Father Who Art in a Tree conveys through fiction several key features of the experience of father-loss for adolescent girls. To discover some of those features, I have analyzed dominant themes in the novel.

Imagining a Place Where Loss Is Not

Simone finds a special place to commune with her father in the tree. Father-loss, as with other losses, thrusts grieving persons into liminal space where the boundaries between imaginative thinking and actual experience blur. Is Simone's deceased father actually in the tree? Or is this an imaginal world into which Simone may retreat, treating it as real in order to cope with loss? Grief relocates persons into liminal space, somewhere between what is concrete and "real" on the one hand, and what is imagined, feared, and hoped for on the other hand.

The liminal space of grief is also a space in which theological imagination works to construct meanings that try to make sense of death. This fictional account does not explicitly address theological issues per se; yet, it contains a number of allusions to Simone and her family's religious life. Simone, having learned that she should confess secrets to her priest in the sacrament of confession, does so with a young new priest and discovers that she feels better having told the secret: "Dad's in the tree; we go and talk to him there." This occasions visits from the priest to Simone's mother, who suggests that Simone is engaging in "a form of thought transference...you transfer your thoughts, give them a voice, a persona."[3] Problematically, the priest does not seem to perceive the spiritual elements present in Simone's experience, especially her immediate sense of connection with her father in the tree after his death. Pascoe's prose might be taken as a satire on the priest's reduction of Simone's imaginative act into psychological language, thus diminishing a profound act of theological imagination, which might be likened to biblical visions of a new heaven and a new earth. Simone is able to glimpse this new place where "no more shall the sound of weeping be heard in it, / or the cry of distress. / No more shall there be in it / an infant that lives but a few days, / or an old person who does not live out a lifetime" (Isa. 65:19b–20).

Revising the Self

Another significant feature of grief depicted in Pascoe's novel concerns the power of loss to reconstitute persons' identities. In Simone's case, the death of her father reshapes her identity into that of "the girl whose father died," and, in the case of some busybody neighbors, as "the crazy girl who thinks her father is up in that tree." She discovers that her new loss-determined identity has eclipsed other aspects of her selfhood.

This happened in spite of Simone's desires that secondary school might be a place where she could be someone else:

> [I was] desperate to re-define myself, not to be the girl whose father had died... I longed to be described as something else–the smart girl, the girl who was good at swimming, even the bad girl or the girl who smoked and went off with boys. But I was forever the sad girl whose father had died; that identity was propped up by everyone.[4]

When adolescent girls lose their fathers, as Simone did, they often experience a loss or change in their own sense of self, their identities. This happens at the very time in life when developmentalists assert identity formation as a key issue. Adolescent girls who experience the loss of their fathers must thus construct narratives of identity that account for or make sense of this loss in terms of who they (the girls) are now.

Becoming the Occasion for Others to Confront their Own Losses

Simone's loss seemingly evokes others' experiences of loss, thus adding complexity to many of her relationships. Indeed, father-loss disrupts and alters social relationships with friends, teachers, neighbors, religious leaders, and others, as encounters with a person in grief propel others' own loss issues and experiences to the foreground. As Simone describes her experience of loss, the reactions of other people in her world figure large. Father-loss also brings about a significant change in Simone's relationship with her mother. In effect, Simone "loses" the relationship she formerly had with her mother, as her mother's grief renders her unavailable to Simone.

In grief, Simone must deal not only with her *own* interior experience of loss but also with the actual and perceived reactions of those around her—reactions that, of course, are always mediated through the personal and corporate loss-histories of those others. On the last day of school, Simone bursts into tears as she prepares to leave the classroom and her teacher, the one who had driven her home the day of her father's death. This time, Mrs. O'Grady does not offer to drive her home, and Simone wonders "if it was because it would remind her too much of the day I had driven home with her to my house. My mother half insane at the door, telling me dad was dead."[5] In pastoral practice, girls dealing with father-loss frequently report a sense that others are avoiding them, as if loss were a contagious illness likely to be passed on to others through contact.

A Complex Mixture of Emotions

Since the significance of father-daughter relationships is often under-estimated, so too is the experience of loss in these relationships, with its very complex mixture of emotions, which often go unvalidated. Father-loss engenders a wide range of emotions, some of which conflict with each other and are contradictory, thus difficult to sort out experientially for girls. Pascoe's novel portrays this complexity in the contrast between the emotional experience of Simone at school or in her house, and her feelings when she sat in the tree. From the high branches of the tree, Simone found a way to escape the feelings of loss and longing that so shaped her everyday living with the death of her father.

Of course, Simone could not stay in the tree all the time. And so her movement back and forth becomes a metaphor for the vacillation among diverse feelings in grief: the emotional volatility of girls who find relief and joy in a memory of their father, only moments later to have that same memory dash them into loneliness, resentment, or anger over their loss. Pascoe paints vivid pictures of the emotional complexity of grief, as she takes Simone through moments such as a time of almost forgetting her father only to be dashed into pain with some small and unanticipated reminder of his absence from her life:

> Seeing Katherine Padley's father at my first communion, that set me off. It was the way he took this photograph of her, like she was the most beautiful and the most clever girl in the class. I wanted that, and I howled so much I went red and ugly to the point where even my mother became embarrassed, and she was never one to

worry about causing a scene. She had to drag me out of the church I was howling so loudly, gulping and gasping with despair. I had no idea where the noises were coming from.[6]

Problematically, the pain of loss may be rekindled in unexpected times and places. For children and adolescents, as is true for Simone in the story, this may happen particularly in relation to developmentally situated events (such as confirmation, graduation, etc.), which are rites of passage at which fathers would have been present. Many girls with whom I have worked in pastoral ministry contexts express a similar sense of "being snuck up on" by grief over their fathers in an unexpected moment.

The Incommensurability of Fathers with Other People and Relationships

What Simone learns with time is how specific her relationship with her father is, even in loss. Grieving him, the emptiness she feels cannot easily be filled by other kinds of relationships. She has a sense of uniqueness about the loss of her father. Simone comes to grips with this toward the end of the novel as she at last recognizes that she has been asking the impossible of her mother in the years following her father's death:

> I could be angry with my mother, throw things and yell at her... but it wouldn't change the fundamental problem that she was not my father... I didn't know that all I wanted, all I needed was my father's love... I realized I was asking for something I couldn't have. I couldn't have a father's love from a mother or the other way around. People were separate, and I had to accept that sometimes you don't get the other, or you have it for ten years, or ten days, and you have to make that enough to last for a lifetime... That was a liberation for me, learning this finally, but it came a long, long time later.[7]

Because relationships with fathers occupy a certain unique status among other relationships, simply attempting to replace that relationship with another cannot ameliorate the sense of loss. And yet a common practice for soothing the raw emotions of grief, at least in some North American social contexts, is to seek rapidly to replace the lost one with new relationships.

The portrait of a grieving young adolescent presented by Judy Pascoe's character Simone demonstrates what counselors and scholars of grief and loss increasingly affirm: grief does not go away, and is not finally "resolved." Instead, the experience of loss becomes part of a person's experiential repertoire and character, worn in one's deep interior rather than on the external and easily accessed surfaces of one's persona. Positively, the sense of grief as an ongoing response to loss leads to potentially deepened capacities for empathy with others in situations of loss. Problematically, it may also etch chasms of anxiety, pain, and fear into persons, which deeply alter if not impair capacities for connection and intimacy.

Late in the book's narration, and therefore later in Simone's adolescence, she offers this retrospective look at her own grief process: "I was so angry that he had died, and my only way of dealing with it was to decide he was really gone. I didn't know then—how could I, I was only ten—that you have your parents for life, even if you've never met them. Whether they're dead or alive, they're around for good in you."[8] For Simone, coming to terms with the loss of her father happens over several years as she reconstructs her own identity and a new kind of relationship with him that transcends physical death.

A Portrait of Father-Loss from Pastoral Practice

I turn now to a second portrait of father-loss, drawn from pastoral practice. The two portraits, taken together, reveal the myriad forms and psychological complexity of father-loss. They also shed light on the psychological and therapeutic literature.

Several years ago while serving as a chaplain and clinical social worker in an adolescent treatment facility, I, together with my colleagues, noticed an interesting phenomenon among those teenaged girls who participated in our therapeutic grief groups to address issues related to the loss of their fathers. Many of these girls appeared especially caught in their grief, unable to make therapeutic use of the group with the same relative straightforwardness we observed among peers confronting other types of loss. In several instances, the acute grief of girls dealing with father-loss seemed to be of longer than usual duration in comparison with peers facing other losses. The loss of fathers exerted considerable power over the everyday lives of the girls who came to our group.

Shandra, an African American teen whose father died from complications of chronic asthma when Shandra was sixteen, offered this narrative of her loss experience:

If my mama was the one who left us in a wooden box, everybody'd be supporting me. My church, my neighbors, everybody. They'd be singing gospel songs about motherless children as consolation for my loss! Because, you know, where I come from everybody got to have their mama. Fathers? Who even knows their fathers sometimes? Either they never had one or they in jail, left town, something… "At least you got to know your daddy and he was good to you," they say. "He died in a good way," they say, "not from no gunshot or dope deal." That's right. He died from being sick, not from bad living. He was in jail sometimes, but at least he didn't die there. So I guess he died in a good way like they say. That means, if I start feeling too sad about it, people would ask me what my problem is. Unless I was a boy, needing a father as a role model, I am not supposed to sing that song. It is not supposed to matter as much to me.

Shandra saw her personal sense of loss as being somewhat at odds with perspectives in her community. Many people assumed that fathers are less significant to daughters than to sons. Some in her family and church, such as her pastor and her aunt, later contested the belief that fathers were of lesser importance in their community than mothers. Shandra offered multiple examples to underscore her point, finally saying, "Most people don't know how much my daddy was a part of my life and how much he mattered to me, just 'cause he didn't live with us all the time. I miss him every minute."

Shandra was hardly alone in her experience of other people failing to see her relationship with her father in its full significance. Girls in our groups and throughout the treatment center frequently reported that the importance of their relationships with their fathers was discounted by others. One cultural narrative about fathers and daughters with which Shandra was asked to construct her story, then, holds that, because fathers have a tenuous connection to their daughters anyway, loss of a father should not be particularly significant for Shandra.

How did this cultural narrative affect Shandra?

> I just stopped talking about it to other people, including my mom. If it started getting to me, I'd just get high instead, because I could tell that there was something wrong with me [sarcastic tone] for thinking that my relationship with my dad was any big deal when so many people said it shouldn't be.

Clearly the reigning discourse offered to Shandra and other girls held that mothers were significant to girls, and fathers to boys—but not fathers to daughters.

As Shandra told her story, she also described the impact of her father's death on her faith, set within the context of her family's African Methodist Episcopal Zion congregation:

> They all tell me things like, "I know you are missing your father, but God's your father now." I don't want God to be my father. Let him be Jesus' father. I want my own father. Besides, I am not too happy with God about any of this. Seems like he could have made it different if he wanted to. Why he [God] do this to me? It's very final.

Over the next several weeks that she spent in residential drug treatment, Shandra began to reflect on the extent to which she had tacitly identified God with her father, such that, when her father died, she felt she no longer had a relationship with a living God. God and church used to be "all-important" to Shandra. In rage against God, whom she perceived as taking away her father, she had become increasingly self-destructive in her drug use, as well as harmful to others (through fighting), and stopped going to church altogether.

In treatment, Shandra began to reevaluate her use of drugs and multiple sexual relationships with men, coming to see them less as an internal moral deficit to be judged than as an effort on her part to "medicate away" the emptiness she felt from her father's death and the loss of relationship with God. "It's not like I really think going with these boys can replace my father, but it makes me forget the bad feelings for a little while." The story she constructed in treatment thus accounted for her risky sexual involvements during drug use in two ways, based on her appropriations of some common frameworks used by treatment staff. First, she expressed an understanding of "using sex like a drug" when she needed an emotional escape. Second, she began to tell her own story of promiscuous sexual involvements in terms of her need to fill the void left by the loss of her father.

Countering Dominant Narratives on Fathers and Daughters

Shandra's narrative of father-loss takes shape within a dominant cultural narrative of father-daughter relationships that contains two contradictory strands. First, as explored above, is the idea that fathers are of little significance to their daughters because of gender difference. A further assumption is that fathers who reside elsewhere than in the households with their daughters are particularly insignificant to daughters. Niobe Way and Helena Stauber note that these assumptions are not supported by research with girls, who speak of fathers mattering in their lives regardless of their place of residence.[9]

Shandra maintained a level of resistance to this cultural narrative on father absence in the way she told her own story, insisting that her relationship with her father mattered greatly to her, even though he did not always reside within the household she shared with her mother. Still, the impact of this dominant cultural discourse may be seen in its silencing effects on her. Eventually she stopped talking about grieving her father in the face of strong messages that the relationship should not be very significant for her.

A second strand of meaning in the cultural discourse on fathers and daughters in the United States holds, in contrast to the first, that fathers are *all-important* to their daughters, responsible, in fact, for their psychological well-being, career success, and ability to have a positive sexual relationship with a male partner in adolescence and adulthood. This latter perspective, developed and furthered by the normalizing of psychoanalytic and object-relations perspectives on human development within American culture, has been taking shape through psychological studies on father-daughter relationships since the 1970s. This element of the larger cultural narrative finds expression in the willing assumption by therapists and by Shandra herself that an adolescent girl's sexual behaviors necessarily relate to the presence or absence of a relationship with her father. The fact that this perspective has acquired the status of a taken-for-granted belief about human behavior bears further inquiry.

Eroticizing Father-Adolescent Daughter Relationships

Rachel Devlin situates the notion that a girl's relationship with her father directly relates to her psychological health and her sexual behavior in a discourse on fathers that emerged in the context of a post–World War II American culture. At that time, writes Devlin, the rise of an egalitarian family ideal brought about shifts in fathers' power and authority in families. Stressing the widespread impact of psychoanalysis upon American culture, such that its ideas seeped into the fabric of everyday working understandings of human sexuality, child development, and family relationships, Devlin asserts a post-war cultural shift at work toward preserving paternal power and authority in a new form.

In this shift, the father-daughter relationship was reconstructed as one in which fathers noticed and gave approval of their adolescent daughters' sexuality, and daughters looked to their fathers for such approval. Thus an Oedipalized/eroticized relationship between father and daughter was taken as the norm for father-adolescent daughter relationships. This shift, Devlin asserts, reshaped paternal power for a new time, by

> establishing that girls' psychological health was *inescapably* dependent upon a good…relationship with their fathers; by maintaining that girls' sexual acts were not autonomously undertaken but always reflected prior, Oedipal feelings for their fathers; and, finally, by establishing social conventions that instilled the idea that girls should (and inevitably would) look to their fathers, before anyone else, for sexual approval.[10]

This view of fathers as the first and definitive object of romance by their daughters suggested that the father relationships would shape all subsequent romantic attractions. This idea was depicted as "the preeminent and defining experience of her development" in American psychoanalysis during the 1940s and 1950s.[11] Particularly through the influence of psychoanalyst Helene Deutsch, who wrote extensively on adolescent girls, the idea that happiness in love depended on a girl's attachment to her father became commonplace.

This perspective continued to develop in the psychological literature of the 1970s and 1980s. For example, in 1972, E. Mavis Hetherington pioneered a study of the effects of father-absence on college women.[12] According to her findings, girls whose fathers died displayed high levels of sexual anxiety, shyness, and discomfort around males, avoiding the male interviewer. Daughters of divorced, absent fathers, on the other hand, displayed behaviors that were "seductive" or "inappropriately aggressive in a sexual way." These young women sought out the male interviewer and avoided the female.

Hetherington's study found that these two groups of girls from "father-absent" households had in common their anxiety and difficulty in knowing how to relate appropriately to men. They worked out that anxiety differently depending on the type of loss. The obvious implication of her study was that adolescent girls need fathers in the home in order to be capable of relationships with other men that would not trigger avoidance or aggression. This study's categories of "appropriate" ways of relating to men display a tacit acceptance of (stereotypical) female gender roles in relationships. It also furthered the already strong cultural assumption of how essential fathers were in the production of appropriate female sexual behavior.

Many studies of fathering throughout the 1980s were tied to object relations theory.[13] These focused largely upon the importance of father-presence for the forming of girls' gendered self-understandings and their overall experiences of competency and self-esteem. They (uncritically) theorized a constructive role by fathers as complementing the various relational tasks of development involving mothers. Problematically, then, these theoretical intersections between fatherhood studies and psychological theories built their understandings of distinctive paternal and maternal contributions to children's development upon essentialized role divisions between women and men. Men were assumed to be providers and protectors whose lives naturally open out into the public sphere of the wider world (which they offer in partial ways to their daughters). Women were assumed to be domestic hearth-tenders, nurturers, and caregivers, whose focus is on interior relationships and family.

Even more contemporary versions of Hetherington's earlier research on father-absence carry forward this understanding of fathers as the ones who open the outer world to their daughters. These versions examine the relationships of fathers and their adolescent daughters for effects on academic achievement and, later, career success in young adulthood. The most common conclusion of such research asserts a positive relationship between father absence and low measures of achievement, and between father-presence and high achievement. One study asserts that "the mere presence of the biological father appears to facilitate achievement, regardless of the support he provides."[14]

Much of the psychological research through the 1980s on father-daughter relationships does not question highly gendered, embedded assumptions. Two of these assumptions are that a father: (1) uniquely facilitates a daughter's successful connection with the world beyond the domestic hearth (hence also her success in the work world) by promoting her separation from bonds with her mother that are presumed to be problematic;

and (2) determines her capacities for healthy sexual relationships with men by acting as a kind of "first object" of romantic attachment.

Narrative Interventions as Feminist Critique

The view presented in the previous section was the dominant cultural-theoretical perspective influencing therapeutic models during the time Shandra was in treatment for substance abuse and dependency. In hindsight, it seems readily apparent that the legacy of psychoanalysis and object relations theory leaves adolescent girls in a rather precarious position as "fatherless children." These theories tell stories of girls whose capacities for health and relationship as adult women suffer irrevocable harm from the loss of their fathers. But what if it is not the girls who are broken and damaged, but the theories themselves, trapped in patriarchal perspectives that position women's happiness, career success, and relational well-being at the mercy of their fathers?

The approach known as narrative therapy developed by Michael White and David Epston comprises a valuable lens for a feminist critique of gender-biased psychotherapeutic perspectives. It also holds promise as a means to help girls deal with father-loss. Narrative therapy draws on the work of Michel Foucault and on social constructivist understandings of reality and human experience. These background theories assert that human beings live in and through the narratives they construct in relation to larger cultural narratives or discourses. Often these dominant cultural discourses have problematic or even oppressive effects in people's lives, as they position people to subordinate their preferred stories to a dominant narration in which problems or difficulties become identities. Put differently, "We are subject to power through the normalizing 'truths' that shape our lives and relationships."[15]

Narrative therapy works to excavate a person's story from the dominant discourse shaping it and potentially subjecting that person to repressive forms of power. In narrative therapy, therapists collaborate with help-seekers in an effort to assist them in reauthoring their lives or situations in relation to a "preferred narrative" or preferred identity. The process of narrative therapy invites therapists to assume the posture of a companion-inquirer, who persistently asks questions in an effort to "externalize" the problem, separating it from the identity of the person per se. The search for a new story is grounded in the notion that narrative not only reflects meaning but also creates it. This is not an effort to uncover the "one true story" in a person's experience. Rather, it is a process of reconstituting meanings out of which one lives by "re-storying" a situation to emphasize agency and the productive effects of discursive power rather than the repressive or subordinating effects.

How might a narrative approach to an adolescent girl's experience of father-loss be helpful? I suggested early in the description of Shandra's grief over the loss of her father that Shandra had become "stuck" in an acute mourning for her father that impaired her abilities to engage fully in the treatment process for her substance dependency and also to move on in her life beyond the moment of her father's death. The problem was that Shandra was living a narrative in which she *was* the problem of father-loss. Shandra was embedded in a larger cultural narrative of father-daughter relationships in which fathers were simultaneously of little consequence to girls due to the supposed limits of gender difference, yet also of almost unlimited importance in terms of their assumed ability to shape a daughter's future psychological health. This problem seemed to determine everything about her—from why she used drugs and how much, to how she related to God, and even to her sexual relationships and sexual decision-making. A narrative approach would engage Shandra and her therapist in the joint work of looking for an alternative story in which she could redescribe herself differently in terms of assets and abilities (perhaps latent from early childhood) used in dealing with the loneliness, rage, and sadness she felt over the loss of her father. The rationale is that living into a new narrative can constitute a new reality.

While we were not working out of this framework with her at the time, the pastoral and therapeutic treatment team working with Shandra instinctively encouraged her to develop an imaginative conversation with her deceased father that could support her positive gains in treatment—thus implicitly engaging him as a witness to her new identity and story, that of a girl in recovery who could deal with her feelings by talking to others or through her artistic abilities, rather than through drug use.

In narrative therapy, therapists help clients to notice "sparkling moments," or what White and Epston call "unique outcomes" or experiences not contained within the script of the dominant story.[16] These discrepancies become clues to an alternative, re-storied self-description. In Shandra's case, for instance, times she had enjoyed being with her father and had experienced his joy in her zest for life might become clues to a different way of seeing herself. By identifying small ways in which she was able to resist the deterministic narrative that destined her for unhappy relationships and poor self-esteem, she could find entry points into re-authoring her story.

Instead of framing religious meaning through a dominant narrative in which the Father-God would become a replacement father for her, Shandra might be invited to construct a new narrative about God's nature and being, in which nonparental images could be primary, or in which parentally imaged forms of care might be parallel to (rather than displacing of) human parental relationship. The emphasis upon being a "storied people" constituted in and through narratives is common to both Christian religious tradition and narrative therapy. To integrate this approach in pastoral care would invite Shandra to use her religious tradition and theological imagination to construct alternative religious meanings for this loss. Instead of being destined to live out a dominant cultural narrative on adolescent girls as necessarily and irreparably harmed by the loss of their fathers, Shandra might re-story her experience of loss as one in which losing her father held deep significance for her but nevertheless was a situation with which she coped constructively and ably.

Interestingly, Pascoe's account of Simone offers a window into one such process. Simone's first person narration records the shifts from her initial shock and disbelief at her father's death, to the comfort and pleasure of discovering that she could be with him in the tree outside their house. As the narrative develops and shifts, Simone gradually moves from a story in which she and her sense of loss are the problem, because her father's death seems to end any relationship she can have with him, to a new story in which Simone eventually has a new understanding, a new relationship, with her deceased father. This continues to be true even after the tree where she had reworked the relationship with her deceased father is gone, cut down because of all the problems it was causing the family in getting on with their lives.

Gerald Monk, describing how the process of narrative therapy works, notes the importance of developing an audience or community of witness to the new story. This audience, Monk notes, can include deceased persons, with whom interiorized relationships do not end at the point of death, such that

> therapists using narrative ideas can often encourage clients to contemplate the imagined reactions of a loved one who, though dead, is very much alive in the client's heart or mind. Such relationships can be explored and may become important sources of support and encouragement as the client develops new or more positive self-descriptions.[17]

Clearly, in Simone's experience, her father is a witness to the new and emerging story out of which she constructs her ongoing life after his death. Likewise, Shandra clearly had an ongoing internal relationship with her father though he was deceased. Narrative elements in the practice of pastoral care emphasized her construction of this relationship in terms of her father's positive hopes and desires for her that could support her struggle against drug use.

Implications and Further Questions

From the theoretical heritage of psychoanalysis and object relations psychology, a number of social scientific perspectives tend to address father-loss among girls through a unified lens of fathers' assumed unique and positive contributions to their adolescent daughters' development. These contributions are then deemed missing—and irreparable—when fathers are absent. This cultural narrative on father-daughter relationships finds reinforcement in a companion religious discourse expressing divinity as fatherhood. I suggest that the meanings girls give to their experiences of father-loss take shape in relation to these dominant cultural and religious narratives on fathers, which complicate their grief as they subordinate girls' own narratives of relationship, loss, and selfhood to a cultural discourse mired in patriarchy. In contrast to those psychological approaches to grief and loss, which assume such sexist cultural (and religious) narratives on fathers as normative, a narrative therapeutic approach to father-loss with adolescent girls invites young women to "re-story" their experiences in life-affirming ways.

From the above portraits of two young women, one drawn from fiction and the other from pastoral practice, it is clear that the loss of a father *is* a profoundly significant event in the life of an adolescent girl, reshaping her sense of identity, her relationships with others, her faith, and even the lines between what is perceived to be real or imaginary in life. Within the wider culture, the patriarchal taint of a psychoanalytically informed discourse about whether and how fathers ought to be important to their adolescent daughters skews girls' experiences of father-loss by explaining it within a deterministic generalization.

In contrast to dominant cultural and psychological assumptions, the portraits of adolescent girls offered in this chapter suggest that fathers are, in fact, extremely important to their daughters. The loss of a father has tremendous influence on a girl's life, even when the father has not been living within the home. Further, the meaning of these losses cannot be summarized within the gender-bound categories of paternalism. A narrative approach to such losses emphasizes the possibility of alternative meanings that girls may give to this relationship, as well as the alternative stories of resiliency that can emerge in the face of grief. Further work is needed to explore frameworks for understanding fathers' contributions to their daughters' lives and development that are not mired in problematically gendered assumptions. This will contribute to better understandings of what happens when fathers are absent. Similarly, further work is needed to understand the particularities of grief that adolescent girls experience from father-loss, in its psychological and theological dimensions. Such work can guide stronger pastoral practice with these girls in the future.

6

Healing the Wounds of War

Stories of Faith from the Youth of Bosnia

JOSHUA THOMAS

Brutal inter-ethnic conflicts in places such as Rwanda and Yugoslavia tore societies apart during the 1990s, leaving lasting scars on countless children and youth. This chapter explores the life stories of young people from the city of Mostar in Bosnia-Herzegovina. Their childhoods were marked by violence and social upheaval during the genocidal war following the breakup of Yugoslavia. While revealing diverse ways that traumatic events can trouble young lives, these stories also point to sources of hope, resilience, and faith in the future. This chapter features six such stories, introduced by a brief overview of the conflict in Mostar and followed by an analysis of significant themes along with reflections on possibilities for healing and peace. Because religion was a significant factor in the Bosnian conflict, these stories are particularly valuable for theological reflection about approaches to interreligious understanding and practices of peace-building among young people.

Background and History

My most striking memory of Mostar, in southern Bosnia-Herzegovina, was a sunny afternoon when a group of teenagers was painting a mural outside their high school. In most places, this would have been an unremarkable adolescent scene. But for these teens and this school, survivors of bloody conflict, this was a symbolic act of creation. The young people were covering the scars of war with visions of a brighter future. The school was the Mostar Gymnasium, an ornate building that had housed one of the premier secondary schools of southeastern Europe. Now it stood pockmarked by bullet holes, its façade crumbling and its roof destroyed by shell blasts. The Gymnasium was on the front line of the war in Mostar, and people tell stories about women being raped on its balcony.

As part of post-war reconstruction, the school was being repaired; it would be a place where youth from all three ethnic groups—Serbs, Croats and Bosniacs—could study together as they had before the war. Local teenagers were invited to paint the panels on the metal construction fence in front of the school. Each panel was different. There were brightly colored depictions of TV cartoon characters, peace signs, and yin-yang symbols; but the center panel stood out to me, the one under the infamous balcony. Painted in black and white and gray, it was a modernist interpretation of the crucifixion of Jesus. His life-sized broken body with downcast eyes was hanging from a cross. Some words about peace were written in the local language, but in large letters was one phrase in English: "Jesus, Come back, Please!" In a city where religion was associated with bloodshed, one young person was crying out to this wounded Jesus for help.

The mural embodies the city's ambivalence about religion, portraying it as a source of conflict and a hope for redemption. The Gymnasium stands on the west side of Mostar. That part of the city is dominated by Croat Catholics, visually represented by a huge Franciscan church with massive bell tower nearby. Croats make up about half of the post-war population; others are Bosniac Muslims who live largely on the east side of the Neretva River, which splits this fourth-largest city of Bosnia-Herzegovina literally and symbolically in two. Mostar takes its name from the *stari most*, the "old bridge," which had connected the halves of the city since the sixteenth century, but which was destroyed by artillery shells in 1993.

With the breakup of Yugoslavia, the Republic of Bosnia-Herzegovina was thrust into a brutal inter-ethnic conflict between Croat Catholics (with ties to Croatia), Serb Orthodox (with ties to Serbia), and Bosniac Muslims, who were caught in the middle. This was the bloodiest fighting in Europe since World War II. It pitted neighbor against neighbor in a conflict that included genocide and ethnic cleansing. Ethnic cleansing aimed to drive out minority ethnicities from certain territories to achieve contiguous geographic regions dominated by a single ethnic group. Sometimes, this happened through the outright killing of civilians, as in the massacre at Srebrenica. More often it came by forcibly turning individuals and families into refugees, displaced within Bosnia and abroad. Families were separated, homes were burned, factories blown up, and basic infrastructure, like water and electricity, was destroyed.

The war directly affected nearly half of the population of Bosnia-Herzegovina, with approximately 100,000 people killed, 800,000 driven from the country as refugees, and 1.5 million becoming Internally Displaced Persons, forced to relocate to new homes in a different part of the country. Mostar was subject to two periods of intense fighting. First, the Serbs and the Yugoslav army fought against a united force of Croats and Bosniacs. Then, after nearly all the Serbs of Mostar fled, the two former allies turned on one another, and a second conflict broke out between the Croats and Bosniacs.

Research with Mostar's Youth

I began visiting Bosnia-Herzegovina in 2000 as part of a team of researchers from Dartmouth College led by education professor Andrew Garrod. By then, five years had passed since the Dayton Accords ended the war. The people were in an eerie time of transition. Some hotels, shops, cafes, and restaurants were open again. Schools were back in session, though overcrowded and segregated by ethnic group. Children went to school in two shifts: morning and afternoon. Most of the apartment buildings, especially those near the front lines, were bombed-out shells, with partial walls remaining.

Amid the reconstruction, our work began. Using the framework of cross-cultural developmental psychology, we explored how the experience of war and its aftermath influenced the psychological and emotional wellness of children, adolescents, and young adults over time. Several teams of faculty and students, myself among them, interviewed hundreds of young people in Mostar and surrounding regions over the course of six years, focusing on such themes as moral reasoning, inter-ethnic friendships, and forgiveness.[1]

Our most in-depth interviews were conducted with university students, using a modified form of James Fowler's Faith Development protocol. Over a period of four years, we interviewed sixty young men and women, aged twenty to thirty, about their life stories, important relationships, significant experiences and decisions, and views on issues such as religion and suffering. We conducted a single interview per each student, lasting approximately two hours, either in English or through a translator. Interviews were then transcribed and coded according to Fowler's stages to compare the developmental trajectories of students in Bosnia-Herzegovina with young adults in other contexts.[2] We also looked for common themes and unique trends in the interview content to identify the effects of their war experiences, the sources of meaning and hope in their lives, and areas of continued struggle. Our aim is to draw on this wisdom to suggest ways of working with survivors of traumatic violence, in Bosnia-Herzegovina and beyond.

Stories of Faith

The sixty students interviewed for this project reflect a range of experiences in relation to the war. Some were in Mostar when the war began, while others arrived afterward. Some fled with their families, others were separated from loved ones, and a few stayed in Mostar through the fighting. The students were Croat, Bosniac, and Serb, from Mostar's two ethnically-distinct universities (Croat and Bosniac) and from the neighboring majority-Serb city of Trebinje.

This chapter focuses on the lives of six of these students, whose interviews reflect common sentiments about the effects of war and attitudes toward the future. Their troubles and longings are more about lost friendships and pressures to find jobs than about catastrophic traumas. Some of the youth told more extreme stories of being raped, wounded, or imprisoned in concentration camps. Some children still cannot speak at all. Many teens have become addicted to drugs, and others have committed suicide. There are also inspirational exceptions—highly motivated youth leading peace-building initiatives, starting interfaith musical ensembles, opening business ventures, or running for local government. The six stories that follow represent a more common middle ground and thus can serve as the basis for common responses. These excerpts from the full interviews focus on experiences of pain and struggle, sources of faith and hope, challenges regarding the future, and attitudes toward religion.[3]

Ivana: Energy after the Lost Years

On the eve of her thirtieth birthday, Ivana was heavily engaged in the life of Mostar. An avid yoga practitioner, vegetarian, and volleyball player, Ivana is full of passion and excitement. She aims to be a businesswoman or health professional and serves as president of a new political party for young people, since she considers nationalist parties appalling. "They don't let us breathe," she laments, though she quickly turns from this negativity toward her new project of creating economic opportunities for unemployed young adults. She has also opened an Internet café and works with an international agency as a trainer for youth programs, as well as being involved in her Catholic church. Ivana is optimistic and committed, believing that she "can influence a lot" in her community and country.

Beneath this energetic persona is a life wounded by the deaths of family members during the war. She prefers not to talk about those "lost years," but she is convinced that the war changed her. "It made me stronger in a spiritual way." Ivana has a complex inner life and a strong sense of spirituality. Her faith is individual and personal, "like your name and surname." She respects all religions and believes religion should help people become "real." People don't have to believe in God, but she does, thinking of God as a kind of energy. This energy surges through Ivana's life, helping her transform suffering. She believes that "even in the most tragic and most ugly situation you can find something beautiful." Ivana aims to help other people stop "fighting with themselves" and open up, talk about problems, and move beyond fear. Believing that suffering is mostly a matter of mentality, she keeps busy to stay positive. Ivana attributes her personality to inborn characteristics and to the influence of her family, who taught her a "very wide perspective" and encouraged her to interact with many kinds of people. She is infuriated by individuals, especially religious ones, who don't share her openness. Ivana believes that "the biggest crime is when you use religion for wrong goals which are not human."

Tatjana: "I Shouldn't Have Come Back"

In contrast to Ivana's optimism, Tatjana is convinced that "nothing will be changed for a long time." Most youth, in her eyes, are jobless and hopeless with "no perspective" on life. Tatjana is twenty-one and is studying computer science after being a refugee in Switzerland. During the war, her parents took her away in the middle of the night, and she didn't know what was going on. Tatjana said that the hardest part was leaving her best friends without the chance to say goodbye. The separation from loved ones continued to be agonizing. "Every day we heard that somebody shot somebody," and she worried it was her family or friends. Tatjana talks about life as a refugee, feeling that her self was split: part was in Switzerland, but "part of me stayed in Mostar." Tatjana tries to avoid talking about the war, since it brings up so many bad thoughts. It is "like sores on the mind," she says.

After the war, Tatjana was enthusiastic about returning to Mostar, nostalgic about her childhood. Now she regrets coming back. She understands why so many people her age are leaving the country for opportunities abroad, and she wonders if there will be any future in Mostar. Right now, her university studies, boyfriend, and a few close friends give her life meaning. They help her get on with living, though money is tight and hope for a job is slim. Like many others, she finds joy in "little things," such as close relationships with family and friends, an afternoon of sipping coffee on the street, or word of a cousin's new baby. Unlike Ivana, who sees herself as having energy and power to make change, Tatjana reflects a more common sentiment of powerlessness, believing that "we can't do anything, we're just ordinary people." She focuses on her private life and hopes to find some measure of happiness there.

Tatjana turns to God for guidance in this private life; this helps her to be truthful and to take care of others. Like Ivana, her religion is private, and she shares few details of her faith. The child of a mixed Serb-Muslim marriage, Tatjana never identifies herself as belonging to a particular religious group, although she attends the majority-Muslim university. She insists on respecting all religions and thinks most people have good intentions, no matter what their religion. "They are just trying to do good things, to have a world without hate."

Jakov: Blaming the War

"When something is wrong around here, we say, 'Ah, the war.' The war causes everything. But that's not true." Jakov, a twenty-three-year-old student of education, takes a cynical view about his life, peers, religion, and the country as a whole. He thinks people use the war as an "excuse." He realizes that he does this too, preferring to spend days playing video games rather than getting involved in the community. Jakov was a refugee in Croatia during the war, living in "a huge hotel that used to be a nudist resort." He laughed, "but we weren't a nudist refugee camp!" Like Tatjana, Jakov was awakened one morning by his mother, who gave him a bag and said, "You're leaving." His aunt and uncle took him across the border to Croatia, while his parents and older brother stayed behind. He thought he would be gone for seven days, but it was four years. "Suddenly you don't have anything but one bag. For months these are the only things you have left of life." Jakov, a Croat, had to leave behind his best friend, a Serb. Now in university, Jakov continues to have a "complicated social life" with friends from all ethnic groups. People look at him strangely when he goes to restaurants or clubs on the Bosniac side of town, but he says, "If I'm hungry, I'm going to eat."

Behind Jakov's wit is profound confusion: "I'm not sure I really know who I am now." Dislocated in many ways, Jakov spends a lot of time alone, though he is close to family and friends. In those alone times, he wonders about his future. "Sometimes I have this feeling that every man on earth knows what's happening to him except me." Jakov tries to be optimistic, but worries about getting a job and finding a woman to marry: "Will I have a car I like? Will I be satisfied?" Like Tatjana, Jakov focuses on small pleasures, such as joking and drinking and smoking, and his plan to get a dog.

Sometimes he wonders what God would say about the things he does, but he thinks the church is corrupt and is not a good teacher of morality. Jakov is angry that the Catholic Church in Mostar is spending money on cathedrals and bell towers when so many people are poor. The church interferes too much in politics, he thinks, and religion should be about helping people lead a "decent life." But Jakov is not sure what this means for him. He wants to go to the United States or Africa to travel, maybe get a good job. But he usually leaves big questions unanswered, hoping things will work out over time. "I think one of my biggest problems is that I don't know what to do."

Andrej: Rebuilding a Life

"I am twenty-one years old, but I feel like I've lived fifty years!" Describing himself as a hyperactive child and hardworking student, Andrej lives a life full of possibility and pain. Andrej spent the beginning of the war worrying about his father, who was in the army, never sure if or when he would come home. Then the fighting came to Andrej himself; the Yugoslav army surrounded his hometown. "It was all around us. You can hear bullets hitting the ground around you. My mother said, 'Lay down!'" He remembers the sounds of gunfire and grenades, as they scrambled to get away. In the confusion, he was separated from his parents, fleeing instead with his aunt and uncle. For two weeks he heard nothing from his family, then received wrong information that soldiers came to his house and killed them, and finally learned the truth that they were alive. Andrej's home *was* destroyed, and he said: "I lost everything except my family. I fled with only what I was wearing." Some people told him that kids do not understand what is happening during war, but he did. "We realized that this was no joke. Some people go insane because of war. But for me, I grew up quickly."

Andrej felt as if someone had taken part of his life, his childhood, and "threw it away." The war forced him to worry about whether he would make it another day, whether a bomb would come in the night. Now uncertainty continues with the economic situation of his country. Most of his friends "don't have a prospect for the future, won't have a better life." He sees himself as an exception, however. He has a sense of adventure, as a survivor both of war and of serious injuries. During childhood, he broke several bones in accidents. In college, he collided with another player in a soccer match and broke his leg and hip and nearly lost his life. Recuperating in the hospital and learning to walk again, he remembers seeing the children of his hospital roommate coming to visit him; in that moment, he "realized that there is meaning, there is something to live for."

Now, Andrej wants to live for his children, to give them a future and teach them how to live a good life, as his father did for him. He sees Mostar as his town, and Bosnia as his country. He wants to make both into places that would be good for his children. "I don't hate any people. I love all people." He knows that rebuilding the country will take a long time and a lot of effort from many people, and Andrej is ready to do his part. "One individual is nothing, but society works when a group of people are doing something good together." For Andrej, this togetherness includes people from all ethnic groups. He longs for the day he could unite with Serb, Croat, and Muslim youth, to "sit with them and talk with them about our past and maybe about some future together." God is a part of that future, too, One who helps him in the struggles of everyday life. He believes God has protected him from danger, but wonders why God seemed not to protect everyone. As do others, Andrej hates when religious leaders talk about politics. He nurtures a private spiritual life through conversations with God each night, and he believes that the biggest difference is not between religions, but between people who live their lives by "spiritual things" and those who live by "material" ones.

Emira: Losing Everything

Emira thinks materialism is a problem with young people, too. "I'm not a materialist, except for these boots!" Laughing, as she acknowledges her expensive shoes and fashionable tastes, she says that she wants to fit in with her friends. She would rather not be materialistic, but feels the need to "be part of this world." Money is a huge issue in Bosnia: few people have any, and most want more. Emira thinks materialism is a way for people to try to be happy, move on with life and not think about the war.

Like many others, Emira lost all her material possessions in the war, and her house was burned. "We had just one blanket and the clothes on my body." Emira's family fled from their home on the Muslim side to one vacated by a Serb family on the Croat side of the front line. Her family was later forced out of that home when the Croat army took it over. A neighbor took them in and made Emira's family false Croat identity papers. Emira had another set of false documents when she went to the Muslim school during the war. A journalist made her an ID saying she was Austrian, then drove her to school every day. Besides dodging bullets to go to school, Emira had to carry buckets of water to her family's apartment from the one working spigot on her block. "I started to live independently when I was fifteen because I had to." Emira loves and mourns her independence, for it makes relationships hard. "Sometimes I feel like I'm alone and so empty, but the worst thing about independence is sometimes I just need someone to hug."

Like Jakov, Emira is confused about the future, finding herself "in the middle of nowhere" in terms of values, religion, and career. She wants a life beyond material things, a chance to "go farther," but she is unclear how to get there. She is spiritual, but suspicious of miraculous intervention. God is about feeling "complete and satisfied."

Dragoslav: An Artist's View

While most young people pursue careers such as marketing, computer science, or education, Dragoslav is an artist. He attends the art academy in Trebinje, a majority Serb city a modest drive from Mostar. A poet and actor, Dragoslav focuses on painting now. He left home at fifteen to study art in a special high school. "There was nobody to control me, and I could decide what to do." He thinks artists are a unique type of people, and he identifies with the "world of art more and more." Besides family, a close group of artist-friends are his support. He talks to them about everything, but avoids people who are not "complex persons" like his friends. Dragoslav gives few details of his time during the war, but talks of how hard it is now, when young people are becoming addicted to drugs and alcohol to deal with past pain and dim prospects for the future.

Dragoslav tries not to plan too much, taking a spontaneous approach to life. "They all say artists are a little bit crazy!" He finds that art, as with religion, gives him purpose. He considers his artistic talent a gift from God and tries to nurture it. Though "not an especially religious person," Dragoslav is well-read in the history and religious traditions of Asia and Africa. Pointing to other inter-ethnic conflicts, Dragoslav thinks they were all caused by "one sort of people, with the same mentality of being divided by religion. It's not God's punishment. They are the ones to be blamed." He voices a widespread fear that the war in Bosnia-Herzegovina might start again, as he worries about his country's reputation, "marked as if we were a wild people." He wonders if the war destroyed everyone's future, isolating the country from the rest of the world.

Still, Dragoslav is not fatalistic, and he resists any notion of God controlling people "like pawns." He also rejects the way some religions blame other ones for their problems. Dragoslav believes there is "one God for all of us" and that people can understand different religions. He compares religion to language: although Bosnia-Herzegovina has three official languages (Serbian, Croatian, and Bosnian), everyone can understand the others. "It's just that there is a different way of looking at it."

Wounds, Wisdom, and Hopes

While they reflect a diversity of life experiences, these six stories also point to common themes regarding the nature of the wounds felt, wisdom gained, and hopes shared by the youth we interviewed. First, their physical, emotional, and spiritual wounds came primarily from *prolonged disruption of the fabric of ordinary existence* more than from acute traumas.[4] Most youth were told that the fighting would last only a few days; instead, it was years. Whether that time was spent huddled in the basement of apartment buildings, or moving house-to-house ahead of advancing armies, or stranded in refugee camps with only a blanket and the clothes they wore, these youth experienced profound uncertainty about the most basic aspects of life. Often isolated from important relationships and surrounded by physical destruction, they expressed anxiety about not knowing where their next meal would come from, when the next artillery shell would fall, who would be the next to die, when they would return home, or if they would even have a home on their return.

Uncertainty and anxiety have continued since the war, mostly due to rampant unemployment and political instability. Many young people question whether a united, multiethnic Bosnia-Herzegovina is possible or desirable. Some are optimistic, and international organizations hope this generation will lead efforts toward a prosperous and peaceful future. Other youth are more cautious about getting involved in politics, preferring to focus on the already daunting tasks of building what they call a "normal life"–spouse, home, job, and children.[5] Such "normalities," and the pleasures of family, friends, and a good cup of coffee, seem to be the only reliable sources of joy.

Amid this uncertainty about daily practicalities, these young adults exhibited a deep wisdom forged during the conflict, manifested most clearly in *nuanced inner lives.* They value spirituality but question religion, acknowledge their heritage but reject rigid ethnic identities, and refuse to accept or reject individuals solely because of religious or ethnic background. Many youth attribute these sophisticated attitudes to growing up "too quickly" because of the war. Some have lived independently since their early teens and were responsible for younger siblings. Others were left with nothing to do during the war but stay inside and ponder big questions, such as the surrounding death and suffering. Though most students we interviewed identified themselves as religious people and spoke about their experiences in religious terms, they rejected the perceived corruption of formal religion in favor of an intimate connection with God. This God, like their faith, transcends any religious tradition. In a significant finding, *not one of the sixty youth interviewed believed their religion was the only true way,* despite teachings to that effect by their religious leaders. Exclusivist rhetoric only increased suspicion and confirmed their belief that using religion to motivate hate is one of the worst sins.

Likewise, *few students saw ethnicity as their primary identity,* despite politicians touting that rhetoric. Not many identified with the "Bosnian" national label either, reflecting in part a weak central government and the country's division into two semi-autonomous entities. Instead, hometowns, families, friends, or occupations offered a sense of wider connection to most youth, while others preferred to see themselves simply as human persons. *Although the war may have increased nationalistic loyalties for some sectors of the population, for a significant portion of young people, it had the opposite effect.* The war discredited exclusive ideologies and the leaders who espouse them.

Not only do these young adults reject rigid ethnic labels for themselves, they bring that same, nuanced perspective to their views of others. They refuse to believe that members of a particular ethnic group are all good or all bad, largely because of childhood experiences ironically reinforced by the war. Many of the interviewees told stories of close childhood friends from opposite ethnicities. Some are children of mixed marriages themselves. Even more remember people from the "other side" saving their lives during the war, by hiding them in their homes, helping them escape, creating false identity papers, or providing food and supplies. These acts of resistance were not isolated incidents, but common features of their stories. *The dichotomous notion that some groups of people are all good and others are all bad simply does not fit their experience.*

Even now, however, the social pressures to conform to ethnic separation are strong, for fear of renewed violence. Eating at the wrong restaurants, going to the wrong school, and especially marrying someone from the wrong ethnicity exact a great social cost. People say they want their life, city, and nation to be more integrated, but they believe it is not yet possible. The wounds of the war are too fresh. With the exception of highly motivated persons like Ivana, the active hopes of these young adults center on creating a "normal life" for themselves and their families, rather than on working toward peace and reconciliation on a wider scale.

Possibilities for Peace-building

Despite their reluctance, young people remain important partners in building a peaceful, united future for Bosnia-Herzegovina. Formed by complex experiences with people on all sides of the conflict, the young adults we interviewed exhibit the very attitudes that scholars of peace-building identify as crucial to post-conflict recovery. Chiefly, *they are unwilling to accept rigid boundaries between religions or ethnicities, and they refuse to give exclusive loyalty to a particular group.* They reject nationalistic mythologies that inter-ethnic conflict is historically inevitable, although they are realistic about the fragility of peace. They embody an alternative perspective, committed to undoing patterns of hatred and including people of all ethnicities in their individual and collective future.

Reflecting on Bosnia and Rwanda, Jodi Halpern and Harvey Weinstein suggest that *empathy* and *rehumanization* are key steps toward reconstructing society after massive inter-ethnic conflicts.[6] The young adults from Mostar possess these in abundance. The supposed enemy never stopped being human to them, because each young adult had a close relationship with at least one person from another group. These relationships proved strong enough to outlast any violence done on behalf of that religion or ethnicity.

> What young adults require now are mechanisms to support greater interaction with peers from other ethnic and religious groups, and the political and economic promise that would motivate them to make an investment in Bosnia-Herzegovina's future. Instead, estimates are that over ninety thousand young people left Bosnia-Herzegovina between 1996 and 2001, and many now see leaving as their only hope. Critics of internationally-driven youth programs designed to get the "best and brightest" to stay in Bosnia-Herzegovina note the short-term approach of these efforts. This has left young people disillusioned and youth peacebuilding initiatives sporadic and haphazard.[7]

In contrast, the Mennonite scholar and practitioner John Paul Lederach argues that transformation of conflict in deeply divided societies requires a "comprehensive, integrative, strategic approach." It requires a long-term commitment and cross-group encounters for people to "articulate their past pain and to envision an interdependent future."[8] In this respect, Lederach echoes insights from narrative therapy, developed by Michael White and David Epston.[9] This psychological approach aims to help people recognize and name the problematic narratives shaping their lives and to construct more preferable alternatives. By examining the way people link certain experiences into a plot line that perpetuates suffering, the therapist creates space for clients to form alternative ways of understanding their experiences, drawing on their own resources for healing.

While many young people in Bosnia could benefit from such individual re-authoring, the task of upsetting a narrative of inevitable division and hopelessness requires Bosnia-Herzegovina as a whole to re-author its future. However anxious the young adults may be about their economic futures, their complex understanding of ethnic and religious identity is a gift to the wider process of reconciliation. *They already represent an alternative story to the default narratives of separation and inevitable conflict.* Were these young adults able to include more peers from other ethnicities in their social networks, their witness to an alternative way of life for Bosnia-Herzegovina could be even stronger.

Religion and Peace-building Approaches

In narrative therapy, support structures are required if a new story is to last, amid pressures from the old narrative. Providing this support is one area in which religious communities have a vital role to play. Because religion has been a marker of divisive identities in Bosnia-Herzegovina, it must take part in healing the wounds it helped create. *Despite a personal belief in God, however, no university student among the sixty interviewees named local or international religious leaders or communities as positive actors in pursuit of peace.* Instead, they saw the leaders as corrupt, hate-inducing, or irrelevant. This section identifies some ways in which religion might be a constructive partner in peace-building, supporting the young people who are already poised for peace. These conclusions are necessarily suggestive and tentative, since the most fruitful approaches would be generated in collaboration with young people and religious leaders themselves, in light of local contexts and the particular viewpoints of the Orthodox, Roman Catholic, and Muslim communities.

My initial reflections point to four peace-building approaches: (1) rebuilding public trust in religion through a reorientation toward peace, (2) establishing religious communities as sites for inner and social healing, (3) engaging in theological reflection about wartime experiences, and (4) prioritizing interreligious learning as a strategy to prevent violent conflict.

Rebuilding Public Trust through Reorientation toward Peace

Rabbi and scholar Marc Gopin argues that within every religious tradition lies a "reservoir of prosocial values" that can be mobilized for peace-building efforts.[10] Attending to "prosocial" aspects of religion rather than violent ones is a commitment that religious leaders and grassroots communities must make. It requires a choice to reorient the energies of religious communities toward peace-building and reconciliation, rather than violence and division. Accomplishing this reorientation requires both interior and public actions.

Gopin speaks of the inner orientation this way: "To have a clear sense of one's uniqueness and to combine that with a willingness to explore and visit other worlds of meaning, without destroying them, are central ingredients in religiosity that is oriented to peacemaking and conflict resolution."[11] Again, the young adults of Mostar embody this identity of *uniqueness and openness,* with inner lives ready to engage others. The public actions of reorientation require high-profile religious leaders to distance themselves from nationalist politics and to speak and preach about their religion's prosocial values in terms that are *intelligible and authoritative within their religious communities.* Likewise, when they visibly endorse concrete acts of multi-religious cooperation, such as joint efforts to address poverty or healthcare, or participate in interfaith dialogue programs, they are authorizing others to follow in their footsteps and catalyzing a reorientation toward peace.

Establishing Religious Communities as Sites for Inner and Social Healing

Religious communities bring particular gifts to the process of peace-building, including the ability to serve as *supportive shelters for mourning and anger,* in which people acknowledge the wounds of war in their lives. Rather than suppressing or avenging hurts, religion can help people name, release, and transform feelings. Contemplative prayer, testimony, rituals, and song are practices that might channel these powerful emotions. Such proposals echo the conclusions of Evelyn Parker's chapter regarding ritual and testimony in relation to the anger of African American youth.

Additionally, religious communities represent *venues for rebuilding the social fabric* that unraveled during the war. Generations of citizens might hear each other's stories and begin to empathize with persons from other ethnic and religious backgrounds. Beyond this work of rehumanization, religious communities could act from their own commitments to care for the poor and marginalized to develop cooperative, multi-faith responses to common social realities, such as poverty or substance abuse. This process might also fire the imaginations of young people to embrace hopes for the future that extend beyond their individual lives and into the work of societal healing.

Engaging in Theological Reflection about Wartime Experiences

Religious communities can also be *venues to grapple with theological dimensions* of the stories of Mostar's young adults. This process could begin with the young adults themselves, who are at a time in life well-suited for struggling with complex issues, argues Sharon Parks:

> Never before in the human life cycle (and never again) is there the same developmental readiness for asking big questions and forming worthy dreams. In every generation, the renewal of human life is dependent in significant measure upon the questions that are posed to us during this era in our meaning-making. The dreams those questions seed yield the promise of our shared future."[12]

By and large, the young adults we interviewed lack the sophisticated theological language to interpret their complex life experiences and nuanced inner journeys. In this light, conversations between young people and religious leaders could begin with students sharing their rich experiences, and then move into a critical engagement with the intellectual and spiritual resources of Bosnia-Herzegovina's religious traditions. Not only would this process help young people better conceptualize the significance of their experiences for societal renewal, it would also bring the insights of their life stories to bear on the religious traditions themselves.

For example, these conversations might focus on the pluralistic commitments these young adults exhibit. Most of the people we interviewed consider themselves both religious and open to other traditions, an attitude justified by personal experiences of God outside their own community and by ethical concerns for the harm done in the name of religion. These perspectives resonate in mystical and moral theology that could bolster or modify their intuitive viewpoints.[13] In this sense, theology can strengthen the religious identity of individual young adults and thus contribute to the creation of a critical mass of people who *reject exclusivist and nationalist rhetoric precisely on religious grounds.*

On the other hand, their experiences might *bring new perspectives to traditional religious concepts.* Inter-ethnic wars and genocide represent massive dilemmas for understanding the causes and cures of suffering. Most young adults from Mostar take a pragmatic approach, believing that bad things simply "happen" and that, with a positive attitude, one can grow stronger through the tragedies. The underlying questions are seldom far away, however, like how and why the war happened in the first place, or why some people who pray to God for protection are kept safe and others are killed. Intentional theological reflection would invite the kind of serious grappling with these questions that is currently absent in the young adults' stories. From these conversations, new insights might emerge about the nature of the human person, the means of redemption, the function of prayer, and the role of God in individual and collective futures. Not only can young adults learn from their religious tradition and others, but they also have a lifetime of insights to share. These may well reshape theological understandings in their home country and beyond.

Prioritizing Interreligious Learning to Prevent Violent Conflict

Most of all, religious leaders need to listen deeply to the stories of these young adults, with their wounds, wisdom, and hopes. *Wherever we are in the world, all of us have a religious responsibility to make the lives of the millions of children and youth who live in violence part of our sacred consciousness.* Inter-ethnic conflicts and religion-related violence remain part of our contemporary context for ministry. These narratives of suffering and hope must be allowed to transform our practice, making *interreligious learning and peace-building ongoing priorities of practical theologians and religious educators.* Gopin argues that religious communities are better at preventing conflicts than solving them. Our response to inter-ethnic conflict and genocide must include a sustained commitment to interfaith solidarity and attitudes of empathy, humanization, and openness.

Conclusion

The stories of young adults from Mostar show that youth may be leading the way in these efforts to heal the wounds of war. The conflict during their childhood has made them suspicious of exclusive divisions, and they are ready to move "beyond hate." Already in their inner lives, they show that it is possible to hold together deep faith in one's own religion and openness to other traditions, even after living through violent conflict. Their lives bear witness to the devastating consequences of war and social upheaval on children, but they point as well to vital sources of hope and faith that can be nurtured by religious communities into transformative practices of peace-building.

PART TWO

Choosing Life in a Troubling World

7

Yearnings, Hopes, and Visions

Youth Dreams and Ministry Futures

MARY ELIZABETH MULLINO MOORE

"What are your dreams for the future?" I asked two young men. Both responded: "I want to make a lot of money." Curious, I asked why this was important to them. One said honestly, "I don't know." The older one replied, "I want to be free to do anything I want to do and to give my family whatever they want and need." These responses reveal something of the materialistic captivity of youth, but what of the idealistic visions? Are they dead? I suggest not. In addition to materialistic visions, youth are filled with hope. The largest problem that youth face is the shattering (sometimes battering) of their hopes. Shattering can be caused by privations of poverty and other forms of marginalization, by lack of accepting and loving communities, by lack of encouragement or active discouragement, and by lack of a worldview into which youth can fit their hopes. In fact, the two youth whom I have quoted both face more than one of these difficulties. What yearnings are submerged under their desire to make a lot of money?

The purpose of this chapter is not to deny the realities of materialism, but to dive beneath these realities to more fundamental inner realities of youth. What were the two boys really saying to me underneath their materialistic camouflage? I cannot answer that question on the basis of the two interviews, but some realities do present themselves. Both of these young men have struggled with school, and both long for success. One has struggled all of his life with poverty, and one with parental judgment and abuse. Neither has grown up in a religious community, and their responses to my questions about their spiritual lives were, "I believe in God." The older one added, "I want to live a good life, and that is about it." These young men have had little experience of encouragement, accomplishment, religious communion, or theological framework to nourish their lives.

The purpose of this chapter is to explore the yearnings and hopes of young people, alongside disruptive impediments and promising visions. The chapter begins with a focus on hope and impediments, then turns to yearnings and visions of youth. It concludes with visions for youth ministry. Resources for the study come from narratives, ethnographic studies, and interviews with young people, as well as from reports of youth ministry in diverse parts of the world and religious traditions.

Hope and Impediments

Youth do yearn for much, but many have abandoned hope; impediments seem insurmountable. For this reason, I pause at the outset to acknowledge the role of hope in the lives of young people. Psychologists and educators have long studied the power of hope to strengthen people in the face of life struggles and to guide their daily life choices.[1] In ministry settings, hope guides the processes of goal-setting, planning, and evaluation. More fundamentally, hope raises questions of spiritual and social ideals. John Dewey defined ideals as "possibilities that someone has judged *ought* to exist."[2] His definition suggests that, ideals are not yet actualized, but they are within the range of imagination. Someone, or some community, considers them to be possibilities of high value.

If hope is an important force in young lives, the present world situation is sobering. To glimpse a few fragments of that situation, we turn to snapshots of youth in the United States. Some statistical figures are actually encouraging, having improved in the past fifteen years, though improvements are fragile. Poverty for children under age eighteen declined from 22 percent in 1993 to 16 percent in 2000, but rose back to 18 percent in 2005.[3] Improvements are also evident for young people in female-householder families. The percentage living in poverty was 54 percent in 1993, and 43 percent in 2005. Between 1980 and 1993, two thirds of black children in households headed by women were below the poverty line. In 2005, the numbers had dropped to 50 percent (compared to 50 percent of Hispanic children and 33 percent of white, non-Hispanic children). Similarly, child hunger is lower, and birth rates among adolescents have declined, reaching a record low in 2005 of 21 births per 1000 young women ages 15–17 (compared to 39 births per 1000 in 1991). Violent crime has also declined, both with youth as victims and as perpetrators. Youth aged 12–17 who are victims of violent crimes have declined from 44 violent crimes per 1000 youth in 1993 to 14 per 1000 youth in 2005. Youth perpetrators, aged 12 to 17, have declined about the percentage from 52 violent crimes per 1000 youth in 1993 to 17 per 1000 youth in 2005. Further, 88 percent of young people aged 18–24 had completed high school credentials in 2005, compared to 84 percent in 1980, with more marked percentage increases for Hispanic (57 percent to 70 percent) and black, non-white Hispanic youth (75 percent to 86 percent).

These figures seem promising, but they are still challenging. They reveal that youth cannot be approached simply by grim statistics, nor by tales of youth who have committed or been victimized by heinous crimes. At the same time, for 18 percent of America's children to live in poverty, and for 43 percent of youth in female-householder families to live below the poverty line is unacceptable. For youth to be victims in 14 violent crimes for every 1000 youth and to be perpetrators in 17 per 1000 youth is tragic. Further, while the poverty figures have been rising or holding steady in the years since 2002, the percentage of children living in affluent families has also risen, revealing an increasing gap between rich children and poor children.

This exploration of statistics is revealing, but the numbers reveal nothing about the inner lives of youth—the challenges they face and the hopes they cherish. For this, we turn to recent studies of young people's hopes and dreams. These are also sobering. In a study of higher education, Chitra Golestani asked classes at the University of California at Los Angeles, "Do you believe a better world is possible? Do you believe that peace is possible?"[4] Only 5 percent of the students respond positively to these questions. This is particularly revealing, given the high academic achievement of UCLA students. In a 2001 study of university students across the country, 200,000 students responded to a survey asking which of twenty goals motivated their decision to go to college. Sixty percent of the students chose the option "being well off financially."[5] These studies reinforce the consumerist realities described in this book by Katherine Turpin, David White, and others. Yet, what yearnings and hopes underlie the statistics and mark the inner landscapes of young people?

Yearnings of Youth

What yearnings and hopes, if any, supersede the materialistic dreams arising in youth and youth-serving institutions? To this question, we now turn, exploring five yearnings that youth carry with them, if only adults will notice.

Yearning for the Holy

The first yearning is for the Holy and is exemplified in an historical story. In 1820, fourteen-year-old Joseph Smith was disturbed by the religious experiences of his Presbyterian home and of the revivals that swept upstate New York where he lived. The Baptists had established churches with farmer-preachers, and the Methodists had done the same with circuit riders; thus, he had opportunity to observe multiple forms of church. He also observed the tensions that emerged among people adhering to different denominations. People often sought a church after being converted at camp meetings, and the churches competed for the seekers. In such a context, Joseph was haunted by the question of which church was right and true, especially since he believed these decisions would affect his immortal soul. He wrote later, "I knew not who was right or who was wrong, but considered it of the first importance to me that I should be right, in matters...involving eternal consequences."[6]

The young Joseph Smith, in his eagerness to sort right from wrong, turned to the avid reading of scripture and to prayer.[7] In the book of James, he found a guiding insight, namely to ask God for guidance in prayer. One text particularly spoke to him: "If any of you is lacking in wisdom, ask God,...and it will be given you" (1:5). Joseph Smith began to pray with increasing fervor. Then, on a bright spring day, Joseph Smith went to the woods to pray, where he experienced a dark and foreboding visitation from Satan. He cried to God for help, and then saw a pillar of light descending upon him, filling him with God's Spirit. He saw two images of God as Father and Son, whereupon Joseph asked God which of the Christian sects was right. According to Smith, God then declared that all of the sects were wrong. Further, God forgave Joseph his sins and promised that he would receive a full disclosure of the Gospel at a later time. That vision lived with Joseph for days, during which he felt his soul filled with love. Indeed, the vision lived with Joseph for the rest of his life.

Fourteen-year-old Joseph gradually told his story to family members. They believed him, but clergy did not. He expected the Methodist minister, who was a religious enthusiast himself, to take him seriously, but was sorely disappointed. Later, he wrote, "I was greatly surprised at his behavior; he treated my communication not only lightly, but with great contempt, saying it was all of the devil, that there were no such things as visions or revelations in these days."[8] The ridicule against young Joseph began to fall out on his family as well. Life became more difficult, leading Joseph to rely more heavily on the vision to validate his experience and anchor his life.

Reflecting on this narrative of almost two hundred years ago, I am struck by several insights. First, Joseph Smith was *actively seeking and pondering questions that were of eternal importance to him,* as they were to adults in his day. The effects of revival movements, religious fervor, competition among churches, and the yearning for salvation played a role in his journey. His yearnings and his search were not qualitatively different from those of adults in his community, but his seriousness was intense. Second, Smith was *preparing himself with Bible study and prayer* as he awaited answers. Third, Smith *experienced a theophany* that was deep and real to Joseph. Fourth, *the church did not accept him or his experience.*

Though Joseph Smith could be analyzed psychologically, the question here is not whether his particular visions represent a healthy life or norms to be emulated; neither is the question whether the Church of the Latter Day Saints, which he founded, is a credible Christian church. The question is whether the churches near the young Smith might have offered space for him to reflect on his early visions and to seek God's direction, and might have mentored him on the journey. What might have been the effect on

Joseph Smith's community and church history if his vision had been taken seriously from the beginning? How often do youth have such experiences, only to be ignored, rejected, or humored by their elders, including elders of the church?

Yearning for Community

A second story points to a second yearning of youth, namely the yearning for community. A Native Canadian high school in Saskatoon, Saskatchewan, has responded to the lonely cries of Native youth with the following mission statement:

> The Joe Duquette High School (The Saskatoon Native Survival School) is a healing place which nurtures the mind, body and soul of its students. The school offers a program of studies which affirms the contemporary world of Indian people. The school supports the uniqueness and creativity of the individual and fosters self-actualization in a cooperative environment. Our focus is on healing all members of the school family. Consequently, our philosophy expects: a caring, a forgiving, and a believing environment.[9]

The communal values of Joe Duquette accentuate the "healing place" of the school itself, the values of Indian culture and people, a cooperative environment, the "school family," and intentionality in creating a caring, forgiving, and believing environment.

In such a school, community is a proclaimed value, and it is also the resource from which the school program is designed. The primary practices thus include:

- Daily sweet grass ceremonies in classrooms, followed by the "talking circle" (passing a "talking rock" from speaker to speaker around the circle)
- Involvement of elders, who lead ceremonies, tell stories, and teach skills and traditions
- Cultural camp for one week every summer, with traditional ceremonies, setting up of tepees, interacting with elders, and participating in cultural workshops
- Open admission and expected attendance (awards for good attendance and a requirement for re-admission if a person misses five days consecutively—all in the spirit of valuing each person's presence in the community)
- Courses in regular academic subjects, plus Cree language, drumming, dancing, singing, sewing, and beadwork
- Support circles for those with special needs, plus gender circles
- Infant care program for children of unwed moms (and others), emphasizing similar values and activities as found in the high school

- Emphasis on staff collaboration and on communal decision-making
- Administration through Parent Council, Department of Education, and Catholic School Board, working through a liaison committee and management committee

This partial list of regular activities reveals the emphasis on interconnected communities, including elders, students, staff, children, and administrative bodies. Further, the communal emphasis is grounded in spirituality. In their first report, the ethnographers did not include spirituality and spiritual practices in describing the school. The students and faculty objected, insisting that the ethnographers could not understand Joe Duquette without understanding Native spirituality, which is foundational. In short, the community of Joe Duquette includes the present students, faculty, staff, and administrative bodies, as well as the larger Native community and the spiritual community of Cree people.

As one present teacher explains, the school responds to the profound longing of Cree young people for community with one another and with their people. Few such schools exist, and the effort to establish and maintain them is enormous; yet, Joe Duquette meets needs of young people that are not met elsewhere. Rarely are institutions so intentional in educating their young people in and for community. What might be the effect of creating more intentional communities for young people within their schools or religious communities; drawing upon the resources of elders; receiving young people as they are; caring for their distinctive needs (spiritual, intellectual, recreational, creative, ethical, psychological); expecting attendance as a part of covenantal relationship; and providing smaller communities to meet diverse interests and special needs?

Such communal life is important to most young people. Echoing the words of the Joe Duquette teacher, Evelyn Parker sees a similar yearning among young people affiliated with gangs, and she asks similar questions of faith communities.[10] Youth are hungry for vital community in most of this fractured world.

Yearning to Understand the World

A third story introduces a third yearning–the yearning to understand the world. James Fowler, author of faith development theory, describes a fateful moment when he was fourteen years old. Someone gave him a book about the providence of God, thinking that he would be interested.[11] At that young age, Fowler read the book avidly and became convinced that "religion could not have meaning without some conviction of God's presence and God's activity in the world."[12] This passion grew in him through high school, college, and graduate school, where he encountered the writings of H. Richard Niebuhr and Erik Erikson. These early influences fed Fowler's curiosity, and helped shape the research and theory that marked his life contributions.[13] Further, he has continued to build upon his early trust in God's providence and his growing realization that human life has meaning, which is constructed and reconstructed over a lifetime.

With a closer look, one can discern Fowler's long-lasting commitments to his discovery at fourteen years of age, namely that "religion could not have meaning without some conviction of God's presence and God's activity in the world." At the same age as Joseph Smith, James Fowler was buffeted by the questions of his day, as Smith had been by questions of his time. Rather than leaving him to his own devices in searching, someone gave him a book. Rather than ignoring or chiding him for his discoveries, people listened. Adult guarantors rewarded his yearning to understand the world by planting a few seeds and watching them grow. What might be the effect for young people today if people took their questions seriously, or took their own questions seriously and expected youth to be partners in the process of dialogue and discovery?

Such encouragement could have far-reaching effects. The yearning to understand the world is, in fact, interlocked with the other yearnings we have considered. Consider, for example, Viktor Frankl's psychological discoveries about meaning-making—the connection between a person's yearning for transcendence (broadly understood) and yearning to understand and function in the world. Frankl witnessed in Auschwitz that the people who were able to search for (or reach toward) meaning beyond the death camp were the ones most able to survive.[14] Frankl did not posit a simple cause and effect relationship. He certainly recognized the forces that were beyond the control of death camp prisoners. He did posit, however, that a searching spirit could be life-giving—whether the searching was grounded in intellectual reflection, human relationships, or other sources of meaning that transcended the duress of devastating situations.

One sees this searching spirit in many young people, expressed in explicitly religious, implicitly religious, and nonreligious frames. Sometimes it is expressed as the simple love of learning. Alice, a fifteen-year-old girl, told me, "There is so much we don't know in history, and I would love to figure it out."[15] Alice is in awe of ancient civilizations, such as ancient Egypt, and she hungrily reads everything she can find. Jonathan Tompkins, in Patricia Hersch's *A Tribe Apart*, sought to understand the world and explore mystery in a more unusual way.[16] Jonathan, a serious young man who laughed at his mother's interest in attending a circus, embarked on a four-day vision quest in the wilderness, hoping to mark his last year of high school and seek vision for the future. After his third night in the wilderness, Jonathan realized a dramatic shift: a new self-knowledge, awareness, empathy, and "belief in his capacity to change."[17] He felt joy as well as remorse regarding his relationships of recent months, and his life was genuinely changed when he returned. Hersch concludes Jonathan's story:

When he got home, he never shared the details of his journey into the wilderness and into himself with his friends or his family... He left the next morning with his mom to look at colleges. School started a few days after he returned. One thing changed for certain: when the Big Apple Circus came to Reston that October, Jonathan Tompkins took his mom.[18]

Jonathan's vision quest, similar to James Fowler's reading and Alice's Egyptology, led him to a new understanding of the world and his place in it, even in the whirl of adolescent life.

Yearning for Ethical Guidance

Already implicit in the other yearnings of youth is the yearning for ethical guidance, which takes many forms. The African Methodist Episcopal Church and some other churches in the United States have begun a movement among young people regarding sexuality and ethical decisions. Young people are encouraged to pledge sexual abstinence before marriage.[19] The motivation for this pledge comes from the dreams of young people for education, vocational options, and fullness of life without premature commitments to long-term relationships. The movement is also intended to help youth avoid the social traumas and personal losses that attend early pregnancies. Whatever the motivations, many young people are making this ethical commitment with enthusiasm.

In another vein, ethnographic studies of youth in congregations reveal high interest in social issues, high commitment to ethical values, and eagerness to dialogue with one another and trusted adults regarding the ethical issues that they face.[20] In one suburban white congregation, for example, youth express a desire to reflect on war and peace and to develop political negotiation skills. In that congregation, training in conflict mediation and discussions of just peace have led at least one youth to attend an international just peace conference, and a large group of youth to negotiate with administrators in their high school for more just treatment of students.[21] In an intertribal congregation, youth express their admiration of Native American elders and their own desire to learn from them about how to live well.[22] In an inner-city Roman Catholic parish, youth participate actively in local political campaigns and also make efforts to welcome new people who do not find a welcoming place in other communities.[23] In a Midwestern congregation, youth learn the values of their families as they work closely with them in their small church and rural community. They often praise adults in their congregation as worthy examples of value-shaped daily lives.[24] In a Roman Catholic parish on the Navajo Reservation, youth express their desire to hear more from their elders so that Navajo values will not be lost when the elders die.[25] In a small Korean congregation, youth want to talk with other youth about their ethical values so as not to be formed only by their parents' values.[26]

The differences in youth of these congregations are obvious, but the deep commitment of these young people is similar. They share an eagerness to seek ethical guidance, discuss ethical values with peers and adults, and make good decisions. What might be the effect for young people today if people assumed that youth really cared about ethical living and were actively seeking ethical guidance? What might be the effect if adults and congregations were more concerned with the ethical yearnings and deep ethical commitments of youth (sometimes embryonic and sometimes well-developed) than with their *own* dreams for the young people?

Yearning to Make a Difference

Another yearning naturally follows, the yearning to make a difference. I recently participated in a conversation with three Mormon mothers. All three have teenage boys. One has a son who is presently on his mission; one has a son who is preparing for a mission next year; the third has a son who is mentally challenged and wants to go on a mission when he finishes high school (even if he is well into his twenties when he completes his schooling). The conversation initially focused on the first two mothers; then they asked the third if her son wanted to do a mission. She responded that her son wants this badly and that she and her husband have been thinking of ways he can do it.

One of the other moms said, "That is great; I can imagine a hundred things he might do!" They all agreed, and the conversation continued to surface ideas. The desire of this boy to make a difference in the world by serving on a mission was intense. His parents recognized it, as did members of his ward. This boy was not to be excluded from significant work simply because he had special learning needs and challenges.

This young man's dreams to make a difference are echoed by twenty years of interviews by members of my youth ministry classes. I have asked students to interview youth (female and male, young and old) about their relations with God, with other people in their families and friendship circles, with their churches, and with the world. One common response has appeared in more than 85 percent of the interviews (more than 200 interviews to date). These youth expect to make a difference in the world. Some say that they will make a difference by living good lives and relating with their own families and friends with love. Others say that they can and *do* make a difference by being critical of hypocrisy, injustice, and lovelessness, and by making efforts to reshape the worlds in which they live. Still others have already taken risks in their lives to make a difference for others, as fifteen-year-old Alice did when she intervened with a friend suffering with anorexia. Almost all the youth interviewed have articulate visions of how the world could be, as well as commitments to contribute positively. Some of these commitments are being enacted in the present; others are directed to the future.

When these visions to make a difference in the world are supplemented with recent research, one discovers ways in which youths' yearnings to make a difference are connected with the other yearnings we have discussed. For example, the qualities of altruistic behavior–giving of self for others–correlate with the ability to function in social relationships (bonding, empathizing, participating in caring behavior, and so forth); the ability to solve problems; and the ability to form global connections.[27] Further, researchers have discovered correlations between empathy and school achievement, and between social skills and academic performance, suggesting relationships among capacities of self-giving, living in community, and seeking to understand the world.[28]

What might be the effect on youth if the adults in their lives listened to their dreams? What might be the effect if their communities gave them opportunities to make a difference in the present, both as individuals and as communities of youth? What might be the effect if adults encouraged their dreams and supported their preparations for further contributions in the future? Combining anecdotal narratives with psychological and ethnographic research suggests that the possibilities for young people are far-reaching.

Visions of Youth

The yearnings described thus far have parallel visions. Theologically, I am saying that God is present in the world, and is present in the yearnings of youth. Indeed, the yearnings of young people often point toward God's New Creation. What is needed is for youth to be heard, accompanied, and guided on their journeys so their nascent yearnings may grow into visions.

- *Relationship with the Holy: Youth yearn for the Holy because they are already awake to the presence of God*–the prevenient grace of God that has been working in and around them from the beginning of life. Because youth are awake to God, however grandly or embryonically, they often envision more.
- *Community: Youth yearn for community because God is Holy Community (expressed by Christians in the Trinity) and because God calls people into covenantal community with one another.* Because youth can glimpse this community of God, they envision more.
- *Meaning-making: Youth yearn to understand the world because God is Wisdom, and Wisdom-Sophia was present with God in the creation of the world.*[29] Because youth glimpse the wisdom of God, they hunger to know more.
- *Faithfulness: Youth yearn for ethical guidance because God provides a cloud to guide people by day and a pillar of fire by night.* Because youth glimpse the possibility of walking with God, they envision more.

- *Vocation: Youth yearn to make a difference in the world because God has been creating from the beginning of time and promises to create the future—as God of creation and new creation—and God calls human beings into the vocation of enjoying and participating in God's work.* Youth glimpse the nascent presence of God's new creation and the call of God to participate in God's work; therefore, they envision more.

If youth are filled with overwhelming yearning, then we owe them respect, response, and companionship on the journey with God. We need to see the visions toward which youth yearnings point. If we do not, we will be thwarting youth, as the Methodist minister did to Joseph Smith and as the dominant culture did to the Cree youth of Saskatoon.

I recall how I, as a young person with visions, was likewise thwarted, never finding safe places to share my visions. When I proposed that the youth be given opportunities to share their faith in one of the informal evening services of our local church, I was told that youth could not be trusted to prepare a service that would be meaningful for others. When I assured the adult leader that the pastors could still preach and we would simply prepare and lead the liturgy, the idea was still rejected. The next year, when one of my classmates was asked to preach on the Sunday morning after Christmas, I concluded that the real opposition had been to me—a mere girl—who might be president of the Methodist Youth Fellowship (MYF) and the subdistrict MYF, but should be silent in church. That early experience awakened a determination in me. In the intervening years, I have worked hard to create opportunities in worship, teaching, and service for youth to share their faith. The thwarting I experienced has borne good fruit for others. *Youth yearnings represent the eschatological presence of God, and their visions point to God's eschatological future.* We cannot ignore these without ignoring God.

Visions of Youth Ministry

Youths' visions, however human, are gifts from God. When youth share their visions, they are fulfilling *God's* promise that our sons and daughters shall prophesy and our young men shall see visions (Acts 2:17–18; Joel 2:28–29). This does not mean that their visions are fully true, fully false, or in between; it *does* mean that their visions are gifts of God to be taken seriously as signs and symbols of what God is doing in the world. With this awareness, we turn to visions for youth ministry. These visions are already emerging among youth in churches, synagogues, temples, and public schools around the world. At the same time, they have not yet come to full fruition. They do suggest accents upon which we can build as we envision the future of youth ministry.

Transcendence

The youthful yearning for the Holy stirs a *vision for youth ministry that engages young people with the transcendent.* Youth's search for transcendence is not always expressed in conventional ways, as might be gathered from the nineteenth-century story of Joseph Smith. Smith's vision was apparently threatening to the Methodist pastor in whom he confided, perhaps reminding the pastor of the dramatic spiritualities of the revivalist period that he found problematic and certainly challenging the pastor's beliefs. Similarly, we see a lack of conventionality in contemporary spiritual expressions of many youth and young adults, reflected in young people who wear religious symbols on jewelry and sing songs of death and life and holy mystery, but deny any sacred value or relevance in their religious communities.[30]

Many people around the world are paying attention to youth and their yearnings. Hans-Günter Heimbrock, of Frankfurt, Germany, says that the holy is reappearing in youth culture across Europe, beginning to replace Max Weber's "demystification of the world" with "the return of the holy." He concludes that, in European multicultural societies, religious education is increasingly important in the schools to help youth develop competence to participate in religion with their intellects, senses, and feelings.[31] This is important for the well-being of the larger society. Fred Smith draws a similar conclusion from the United States urban context, particularly from African American boys. He says that youth need a sense of transcendence, which can help counteract pathogenic factors of racism and materialism.[32] At the same time, he recognizes that youth often encounter "deviated transcendence" and then place transcendent confidence in that which is not itself transcendent, such as material things, or success in school, or one's gang or community of friends. These themes are echoed in many other studies of youth and youth ministry. Transcendent vision is urgent for young people.[33]

Communion

The yearning for community stirs a *vision of communion in youth ministry.* This takes many different forms. David Mitchell looks to the community of the Million Man March and other communal ministries to find models for empowering youth ministry, especially as they face what he calls the "Destructive Capitalistic Personality Complex."[34] Gregory Cajete echoes the Joe Duquette High School as he seeks to recover Native ecologies of education—engaging youth in the rituals, traditions, Native communities, and earth practices of their people.[35] At the same time, Yaacov Katz is working with an Israeli government commission to develop a core curriculum that will solidify a democratic society in Israel.[36] He recognizes that Israel is at a turning point that requires building up a democratic way of life—politically, economically, and religiously. He sees Israeli youth as the people who will have an opportunity to give leadership in that direction; hence, a core curriculum lays groundwork for developing a democratic communal ideal within the larger society.

Thus far, I have described the work of creating communion as if it takes different forms from community to community, but what of diversity *within* communities? Of course, the communities referred to above are themselves diverse. That is one reason that Katz emphasizes democratic ideals. Others are doing important work on building community within pluralized societies. Sissel Ostberg of Norway has coined the term "integrated plural identity" to describe the experience of young people who live in multicultural contexts and have plural identities within themselves, calling for integration.[37] She emphasizes the role of dialogue in such societies. Heid Leganger-Krogstad, also of Norway, advocates dialogical education as well, but she supplements this with "diapractice." Diapractice is cooperation that "takes place among pupils across difference in lifestyle, beliefs, and values to solve practical (and simple theoretical) tasks in the school context or in the local community."[38] Diapractice includes singing, playing, dancing, cooking, eating, playing sports, dramatizing, and working in student councils. The idea emanates from efforts between Christians and Muslims in Africa, who have learned that relationships move in more positive directions when people work together at a practical level rather than limit their interaction to verbal discourse about beliefs and values.[39] We see in these studies a recurring emphasis on community life with the rich textures of collaborative talk, action, and problem-solving. Communion, while important for all communities, holds particular value in communities of diversity, which youth communities often are.

Whereas a vision of communion sounds joyful, it is very complex. Young people expend much energy negotiating their identities in relation to gender, culture, and social boundaries.[40] This lays a burden on youth ministry and youth educators in schools. The first challenge is to help youth encounter the cultures of their people, especially if they are living in multiple cultures or as immigrants in a new homeland.[41] The challenge then is to provide opportunities for young people to live in community with other youth and, at the same time, to negotiate and renegotiate their identities within those communities. This leads naturally to the next vision.

Wisdom

The yearning to understand the world has its parallels in *visions of wisdom and meaning-making in youth ministry*. This has been an emphasis in youth ministry for generations. In Turkey, Mualla Selcuk and others who work with her in the Cabinet of Education are developing an approach to peace education that draws from the Koran, encouraging young people to discern meanings in the Koran that help them make sense of life and help them envision and work toward a better future. In the Koran, Allah is portrayed as the One who guides the human, so youth are encouraged to "develop a sympathetic awareness of the dialogue between God and humankind taking place in the Koran" and to see how that dialogue actually relies on the efforts of young people today.[42] Youth are taught the wisdom of the tradition and they are encouraged to engage in religious practices that turn them toward God for guidance. The tradition forms the roots of the educational tree, the reflection process and search for meaning form the trunk, and the fruit of the tree is the youth's ability to make choices.

Similarly, Graham Rossiter, professor for the Australian Catholic University, sees the search for meaning to be the primary task of young people, which needs to be encouraged, supported, and resourced through religious education. He wants youth educators to encourage youth to wrestle with contemporary music and film in dialogue with religious traditions, all the time searching and forming their unique identities as children of God.[43]

Faithfulness

The yearning for ethical guidance is easily misunderstood, and people often offer forms of ethical guidance that youth reject, resent, or ignore. The vision stirred by this yearning can be called a *vision of youth ministry that inspires faithfulness.* Even the older youth quoted in the opening words of this essay connected his desire for money with the ability to care for his family. This young man does not have religious frameworks with which to ponder a vision of faithfulness, but he has vague yearnings and hopes that could be enhanced.

Around the world, we see youth ministers and educators responding to the youthful desire to be faithful. Kasonga wa Kasonga, at the Christian and Family Life Desk in the All Africa Conference of Churches, describes how African churches work to provide ethical guidance to youth regarding sexual behavior.[44] Mualla Selcuk in Turkey describes how her country works on peace education grounded in religion, focusing on a common saying from Muhammad, "Be moral by the morality of God."[45] Heid Leganger-Krogstad and other Europeans describe how they are developing religious education for citizenship.[46] Michael Warren describes youth ministry that supports youth in resisting destructive forces in materialistic culture.[47] These are all efforts that take youth's vision for faithfulness seriously, and attempt to journey with youth toward that vision.

Vocation

Finally, the yearning to make a difference stirs a *vision of youth ministry that calls and equips young people in their vocation.* This is a well-established theme in youth ministry, but one that has never had enduring and full-faceted attention.[48] It is also a well-established practice in Christian churches, which frequently send youth mission teams to build houses and churches, or to lead children's events and classes, or to visit retirement homes. Despite the common practice, the full nature of youth yearnings to make a difference and to find meaningful vocation is often overlooked. The mission trips and service projects are often seen as one event among many, as an occasional foray into another world, without full engagement and reflection on that engagement. This, of course, can be valuable in itself, but is rarely sufficient for inspiring, guiding, or satisfying the pull toward vocation.

One exception to this is reflected in the ethnographic study of James Youniss and Miranda Yates in a Roman Catholic school. What is described in their book is far more than an annual mission trip; it is a framing of the whole curriculum and life of the school around service.[49] Another exception is told in David Halberstam's *The Children,* in which a small group of young adults, well-schooled in nonviolent protest, led a movement of youth and young adults to protest the discriminatory practices in Nashville, Tennessee, in the 1950s.[50] Young people, aged from seventeen to twenty-three, were the principle leaders of the lunch counter sit-ins and other protests that eventually fed into the larger civil rights movement, which eventually turned many laws and practices in the U.S. on their heads. Young people with a strong sense of vocation awakened a nation to their vocation. Young women and men were prophesying and seeing visions, and that made all the difference.

Conclusion

I am saddened by the opening stories of this chapter, the stories of two youth who expressed their future dreams in terms of making money. The sadness of individual lives oriented around money is extended when we look into a world that cries out with a multitude of physical, spiritual, and relational needs. The visions expressed in this chapter suggest a place to begin again—a place where youth are encouraged to express their yearnings and develop their visions into embodied realities. Such stirring of vision is urgent for young peope and their communities. In a world crying out for peace and justice, in a world that longs to know and respond to the compassionate, challenging presence of God, we need the prophecies and visions of the young. We need their yearnings and their action. Let us listen, encourage, and respond!

(Non)Cosmetic Ministry

Reclaiming Hope Among Abused Adolescents

KAREN MARIE YUST

Kendra and Jesse read aloud ancient words from Ezekiel, translated for today.[1] Kendra begins, "Dry bones, listen to what the Lord is saying to you," and Jessica continues: "I, the LORD God, will put breath in you, and once again you will live. I will wrap you with muscles and skin and breathe life into you. Then you will know that I am the LORD" (37:4b–6, CEV). They continue this scripture dialogue through verse 14, which Jesse recites: "I will bring you home, and you will know that I have kept my promise. I, the LORD, have spoken" (CEV). Then they return to their seats alongside their peers at the Germaine Lawrence School in Arlington, Massachusetts.

I distribute sheets of paper on which I have photocopied a drawing of a bone. I ask the fifteen girls, two staff members, and a local church volunteer, "Where are the dry bones in your lives? What are the things you worry are dead or dying in you or in your friends that you want God to bring back to life?" Several minutes of scribbling ensue, as all heads bend over paper bones. "Do you have any more bones?" ask a few girls. I hand them a couple more sheets, and they continue to write. I put words on my own paper and wait for them to finish.

When all writing ceases, I invite three girls to gather up the bones and bring them to the altar. There they lead us in the "prayers of the people" by reading the anonymous petitions one by one, each followed by the girl reading saying "Spirit of God," and our shared response, "Hear our prayer." Thirty-six dry bones are laid on the altar awaiting God's enlivening breath. They are only a fraction of the bones in the valleys of death and despair known by the approximately two hundred girls at Germaine Lawrence, but identifying them in our weekly worship service is a sign that hope blooms even in such valleys.

For over two years I ministered with adolescent girls ages ten to eighteen in this residential school and treatment center for young women with histories of severe abuse and behavior disorders. Seventy percent of the students had attempted suicide at least once prior to their admission, and many had bounced around among several foster homes or spent time in hospitals for eating disorders, substance abuse, or other self-destructive behaviors. Quite a few had lived on the streets at some point in their lives when they attempted to run away from neglect, abuse, or yet another unfamiliar stop in an inadequate foster care system. A few others broke deviant behavior stereotypes: they were female sexual abusers and fire setters. All had been referred to Germaine Lawrence because they needed the Center's highly structured behavioral modification therapy to help them "reduce their maladaptive behaviors, to develop age-appropriate social skills, and to make enough progress to enable them to live in the community safely again."[2]

From the moment I became their chaplain, these girls couldn't wait to haul me into a corner and ask me really hard questions, such as: "Where was God when my dad would get drunk and hurt me?" "Why did God let my grandmother die when she was the only person around to take care of me?" "Will God forgive me for the things I did while I was a runaway?" These conversations frequently occurred while we were painting our nails the most amazing array of colors I have ever seen. Greens, black, and electric yellow predominated, topped off with a coat of glitter. Together, sprawled on dorm living room floors, tucked away in borrowed counselor offices, and hanging out around kitchen tables, we talked and learned about the depth of God's love and the breadth of God's acceptance, as God's mercy flowed over us like polish on a nail.

Over time, three of these young women requested baptism as a sign of their acceptance of God's grace and proclamation that they are indeed God's beloved children. Others responded in other ways. By exploring the life stories of four of these young women, I will identify theological and psychological themes, and then illumine, critique, or extend these themes in light of their lives. I will also explore religious practices that touched their hard realities. To that end, I have analyzed my journals, sermons, and materials collected from the girls during the two years that I spent with them.

Anna and the Power of Lament

One of the young women who chose baptism as a beloved child was named Anna. Anna had been physically and sexually abused before she was adopted at the age of ten. I met Anna on an Ash Wednesday. She didn't know it then, but her adoptive parents had decided to rescind the adoption; they could no longer imagine a way to love her through the turmoil of her anger and rebellion. I was her pastor as she learned to cope with this awful revelation. I also became the model of a stable and reliable adult in Anna's life, visiting her weekly in addition to seeing her in chapel each Sunday afternoon.

Anna's major spiritual concern was a familiar one: she wanted to know why bad things happen to "good" people. She brought a copy of *Chicken Soup for the Teenage Soul* with her to one of our private pastoral care sessions and slung it across the room, demanding, "Who writes this shit?!" The book was a gift from her adoptive grandmother, who wanted Anna to believe that, despite her adoptive parents' unwillingness to ever see or talk with her again, everything would work out if Anna would only trust in God. Not surprisingly, Anna wanted nothing to do with such a trite spirituality. Instead, she found greater solace in biblical laments and stories about the people of Israel on the shores of Babylon. Exiled from the home she had known for five years, with no realistic hope of return, she knew her story would have no *Chicken Soup* happy ending, just as the Israelites' fortunes had no short-term reversal. She began to learn that a longer view of justice is sometimes required and that she could cry out to God for justice without being accused of lacking faith.

Prayers of lament are powerful meaning-making tools for adolescents caught in situations that make no cognitive or emotional sense to them. Walter Brueggemann, in describing biblical lamentations, says that they "are powerful expressions of the experience of disorientation. They express the pain, grief, dismay, and anger that life is not good."[3] When a teenager names what is wrong in her world, she is evoking divine and social recognition of her experience in its disorienting form and also moving toward the assertion of a modicum of hope that her experience can be transformed. True laments possess both "candor and anticipation."[4] In this section, I will engage with the young women's experiences in dialogue with biblical texts and Brueggemann's commentary on lament, seeking to illumine the power and qualities of lament that speak to young people on their sometimes ravaging journeys of faith.

The personal laments found in the psalms model a specific shape for prayers of lament that adolescents can emulate. They typically begin with *an invocation of God's presence or an address to God.* Psalm 12 begins simply, "Help, O LORD..." (v. 1a). Psalm 28 employs a longer invocation:

> To you, O LORD, I call;
> > my rock, do not refuse to hear me,
> for if you are silent to me,
> > I shall be like those who go down to the Pit.
> Hear the voice of my supplication,
> > as I cry to you for help,

as I lift up my hands
   toward your most holy sanctuary. (vv. 1–2).

Many teens prefer a short invocation, as that more closely resembles their daily speech, but they appreciate knowing that ancient religious peoples were not afraid to demand God's attention.

The second element of biblical laments is the *complaint*. The psalmists state emphatically (and often with metaphorical hyperbole) that they face a problem requiring God's immediate attention. The author of Psalm 12 complains that he has no models of godliness because human beings "utter lies to each other; / with flattering lips and a double heart they speak" (v. 2). Psalm 28, attributed to King David, complains about "wicked" persons who claim to want peace in the community but have "mischief…in their hearts" (v. 3). Adolescents can relate to these concerns. They have little difficulty understanding what a complaint is; the challenge they face is overcoming their hesitancy to complain to God when the little knowledge they have about religious practices suggests that complaining is disrespectful of God. A guided walk through the book of Psalms provides numerous examples of religious forebears who dared to complain and whom God heard. If they could do it, says an anxious teen, perhaps I could try as well.

The biblical lament's third element is *an expression of confidence or trust in God*. Psalm 12 recalls, "The promises of the LORD are promises that are pure" (v. 6a). David proclaims in Psalm 28, "The LORD is my strength and my shield; / in him my heart trusts" (v. 7a). For adolescents who have little, if any, experience of divine trustworthiness or knowledge of God's acts in history as described in biblical narratives, this aspect can be difficult to frame on their own. My task at Germaine Lawrence was, in part, to introduce the students to the stories of scripture in ways that might help them trust God to care and stand up for them. Each week in chapel, I would proclaim the good news. One week, I likened the Israelites' desire for a king (1 Sam. 8:4–22) to my then two-year-old son's refusal to hold my hand in parking lots because he wanted to imitate his nine-year-old brother. I suggested that Israel was misguidedly trying to prove to the countries around it that it, too, was a strong and capable nation. Then I compared my reaction to my son's behavior with God's response to Israel.

> When Michael [my son] runs away from me, I'm often tempted to get mad at him, especially since I've explained to him over and over how dangerous parking lots are. But God didn't get mad at the Israelites, although God certainly had good reason to be angry. Instead, God told Samuel to warn the people about the corruption and discrimination a human king would bring to Israel.[5]

We reflected on this story in light of how the desire to be like everyone else can get us into significant trouble. We also noted that the people were right to complain to God about previous leaders who had abused their authority and to insist that God provide more suitable leadership. Our discussion thus provided a story of God's responsive care, which was useful in their laments.

Other sermons explored the Israelites' longings during exile to go home, linking those desires to the wish every Germaine Lawrence girl had for a loving place to call home for herself. Preaching from Zephaniah 3:14–20, I shared how God responded to the Israelites when they were discouraged about returning home:

> God had not abandoned the Israelites. Instead, God sent a prophet into their troubled lives and messed-up homes. And this prophet, named Zephaniah, came bringing good news: God has promised to lead you home! God has promised to gather up all of you who feel like outcasts, and to take care of you. Instead of being despised by other people, you're going to be praised. So stop worrying! God is by your side, and God will always be with you.[6]

A sermon interpreting Jeremiah 29:1–7 and Luke 17:11–19 also picked up on this exile theme. The Jeremiah text tells the story of the people of Jerusalem and Judea after an invading Babylonian army took them prisoner. The Luke text focuses on a group of lepers forced to live outside a village in a mini-refugee camp. In the latter case, God acts quickly to heal the lepers so that they are able to go home again almost immediately. But in the former case, God works at a much slower pace and through different means.

> The people of Jerusalem wondered if God had abandoned them when the Babylonians took them away from their homes. They felt all alone and scared. And so God sent them a message. The message said: "Make a new home in the place where you find yourselves. Work together and grow strong. Learn to live peacefully. Take care of yourselves and each other. Treat the place you are as a home away from home. And, someday, when you are stronger and wiser, healthier and better prepared to face the ups and downs of life, you will have your own home again.[7]

All three of these stories became examples of God's trustworthiness that girls might invoke as expressions of trust in God as they prayed their prayers of lament.

The fourth element of a personal biblical lament is *a petition specifically requesting action on God's part*. Teenagers are often surprised to discover just how explicit and graphic the petitions of the psalmists are. Psalm 12 bluntly requests, "May the LORD cut off all flattering lips, / the tongue that makes great boasts" (v. 3). Psalm 28 employs a retributive justice theme: "Repay them according to their work, / and according to the evil of their deeds; / repay them according to the work of their hands" (v. 4). Brueggemann suggests that these kinds of petitions articulate the human "yearning for vengeance" and "legitimate and affirm [the] intense elements of rage" that we feel when oppressed.[8] However, these petitions also affirm that "vengeance belongs to God." They speak to God's sovereign role in fostering "moral coherence and moral order" in the world.[9] Psalms of lament do not provide humanity with a "license to kill" in James Bond fashion, but they do encourage imaginative, gut-wrenching, cathartic expressions of our deepest longings for God's justice in an unjust society.

Adolescents agree with the retributive justice sentiments of the psalmists; but, as with the complaint aspect of lament, they are nervous about speaking their mind to God. Biblical testimony regarding this practice, as well as habits of truthful speaking cultivated in the therapeutic realm, helped the young women at Germaine Lawrence learn to voice explicit petitions. Among their requests during one week were:

- "I want to pray for my dad so he can stop his drinking."
- "I believe that if I try really hard I can make level. I pray that I can make level in my heart."
- "I pray for my mom and hope she gets her wish to have a baby of her own."
- "[I pray] that I get to leave Germaine Lawrence School soon so I can go back home with my family or get my own place."[10]

An expression of praise or vow to praise is the fifth element of biblical lament. Psalm 12 phrases this aspect as a simple statement claiming God's protection (v. 7), whereas Psalm 28 offers a joyous song:

Blessed be the LORD,
　　for he has heard the sound of my pleadings.
The LORD is my strength and my shield;
　　in him my heart trusts;
so I am helped, and my heart exults,
　　and with my song I give thanks to him. (vv. 6–7)

Brueggemann suggests that we need to read the praise and thanksgiving psalms in concert with the lament psalms to appreciate fully the language of celebration and joy essential to our movement in lament from disorientation amidst the chaos of crisis to reorientation toward God's wholeness.[11] The young women at Germaine Lawrence also found the means to praise God in hymns, songs, and weekly celebrations of the eucharist.

For the young women, however, integrating their complaints and petitions with their praise took time and consistent modeling. We regularly used a "prayers of the people" format that included an invocation of God by the prayer leader and the response, "Hear our prayer," from the assembly after every petition. I scripted the invocations so that the girls heard different praiseworthy attributes of God affirmed over a period of weeks and months.

This practice built a larger faith vocabulary for the girls to use in praise of God, both in their laments and in their other prayers.

Keisha and the Appeal of a Mythic-Literal God

Keisha was another beloved child of God struggling to make sense of her life. In her struggles, she reveals something of the developmental power of mythic-literal understandings of God. In so doing, she reveals how developmental stages may inform our interpretations of the spiritual formation of adolescent girls who are journeying through abuse and violence. Keisha's story also stretches developmental discourse, revealing that supposedly immature developmental imaging of God may play a useful formational role in the lives of young women caught in abusive life situations.

Referred for treatment after she sexually abused a younger sibling, she was beginning to understand how chronic abuse at the hands of a male relative helped to explain but did not excuse her own behavior. Oscillating between the burdens of residual denial and overwhelming guilt, she needed to learn how to forgive herself and rebuild her relationship with her family as they all began to implement measures and practices designed to keep everyone safe and foster respect and self-esteem. Forbidden to wear jewelry (because sharp edges might tempt her to mutilate herself through "cutting"), she used eyeliner applicators to draw bracelets and rings on her arms and mine as we talked about how to make sense of being both victim and victimizer in a broken world.[12]

Keisha's spiritual questions stemmed from her ambivalent view of herself and her previous exposure to conservative religious teachings. She imagined a God of retribution, quick to anger and eager to punish. While she wanted to avoid punishment, she also believed that she deserved to suffer because of what she had done. One week during chapel, I told the girls the story of Thomas (Jn. 20:24–29). I identified him as a disciple who wasn't afraid to ask questions about God and challenge what he heard from others. I then invited each of them to become like Thomas by writing down their own questions about God and Christian faith. Keisha asked, "I heard Jesus would come back and pick out all the Christians and leave the rest to burn on Earth—is that true?"[13] In the ensuing discussion about their questions, Keisha admitted that she was afraid of being "left behind" because of the bad things she had done.[14] She could not reconcile the merciful God she was meeting in chapel with the wrathful God she'd heard talked about on television. Over time, however, she began to make sense of the idea that God could be a lot like her counselors at Germaine Lawrence: setting appropriate expectations, reinforcing those expectations with positive and negative consequences, and always offering another chance to succeed even if someone had really screwed up.

While Keisha's concept of God as behavior modification counselor emphasized responsibility more strongly than grace, it was a developmentally useful interpretation for a young person feeling out of control in a fearful and dangerous world. Abuse may deprive an adolescent of typical childhood experiences. The teenager will not see the reliability in the relationship between causes and effects in interpersonal relationships. Such a youth can benefit from opportunities to explore again the developmental tasks of middle childhood. She needs a chance to consider God as a model of "simple fairness and moral reciprocity."[15] She needs to see God as a force that can organize her world into something less chaotic and more predictably just. Such a God can reinforce treatment structures that highly value consistency, caring, and a rewards-based system for encouraging behavioral goals. This God-view will not ultimately sustain a teenage girl who has already learned through experience that not every bad act is punished. This God-view does permit her to see the possibilities and limitations of dependence on "simple cosmic moral retribution" while she experiments with new ways of defining herself and her relationships. In particular, this mythic-literal interpretation of God described by James Fowler[16] can assist young people in reconfiguring their engagement in some of the developmental tasks Melvin Levine has described:

> (1) to sustain self-esteem; (2) to find social acceptance, primarily with peers; (3) to "reconcile individuality with conformity"; (4) to identify and emulate role models; (5) to examine values; (6) to feel successful in the family; (7) to explore the freedom and limits of autonomy; (8) to grow in knowledge and skill; (9) to become reconciled to his or her own body; (10) to handle fears; (11) to limit and control appetites and drives, including food, sexual drives, material wants, the seeking of attention; and (12) to "know thyself," or to develop self-awareness.[17]

Tasks seven, ten, and eleven especially benefit from a transitional attachment to a divine being who values and models reciprocal fairness for humanity.

Other research reinforces this perspective. Emily Crawford, Margaret O'Dougherty Wright, and Ann Masten, in a review of studies exploring the relationship of spirituality to resilience, note: "The belief that a loving God is in control, even though we may not always understand God's will, may allow some youth to reframe trauma."[18] This reframing breaks down presumed cause and effect correlations in a teen's life, permitting a young person to draw new relationships between actions and reactions.

As in any dynamic process, the conceptual connections with which a traumatized young woman is experimenting are marked in pencil, subject to erasure as their effectiveness is evaluated and alternative approaches are tried. Since faithfulness is a lifelong transformational practice, it is not appropriate to expect adolescents to do their spiritual work in indelible ink. The use of a Mythic-Literal God-image by Keisha and her peers is a means of resiliently reframing their suffering so that it no longer overcomes their hope for a better future. As Fowler and Mary Lynn Dell observe, "Where earlier deficits in the self and in one's patterns of object relations have not been worked through and healed, they become factors that can inhibit the use of cognitive abilities in the tasks of identity and ideology construction in adolescence."[19] Keisha's God, imaged as behavior modification therapist, was her means of working through the deficits in her previous object relations.

Natalie and the Necessity of Radical Hospitality

A third beloved child of God at Germaine Lawrence–although not one who chose baptism during my ministry there–was Natalie. Partial to the Goth look, her cosmetic ministrations to my face during our conversations in the dorm living room gave new meaning to "clergy black."[20] Natalie's question during our discussion of the Thomas story echoed Keisha's concern. Natalie wrote, "I personally don't go to church anymore because my mom does vudu [*sic*], and I have been studying for about 1.5 years and haven't been to church in 8 years. Is it true when I die I can't go to heaven?"[21] After the service, she walked over to me to say goodbye, as she assumed she would no longer be welcome in chapel. I assured her that she remained a welcome member of the congregation and suggested that we get together to talk when I came to her dorm for dinner later that week. We left the conversation option open, with Natalie in charge of deciding whether we would find a corner to ourselves or simply keep our interaction general as part of the group.

I arrived half an hour before dinner, and it was clear Natalie had been watching the door for me. I barely had time to greet the other girls in the house before she pointed to her cosmetic kit and asked if she could do my face. Agreeing, I let myself be led to a quiet spot near an end table and sat down. Natalie proceeded to make me up and tell me about her study of magical religions (Vodou, Wicca, Santeria) and her fascination with the ability to manipulate spiritual powers. In response, I told her about the undergraduate world religions course I had taught the previous year, and I offered to loan her some articles and books about these topics.

She put down the eyeliner, gave me a piercing look, and said, "Isn't that against the rules?" I asked her what rules she meant, and she replied, "the rules of being a minister." In her limited church experience, clergy never talked about anything but Christian beliefs and moral standards. She had heard churchgoing neighbors condemn her mother for her "Satanic" practices. She had expected to shock me, even as she was trying to connect with me through her story. That I was willing to explore these other religions with her and discuss how they were similar to and different from Christianity both delighted and amazed her. I had validated her quest for a spiritual path that she could embrace by choice rather than by society's expectations. Furthermore, I had offered to shelter her within the Christian community and explore those options alongside her. Together, we were discovering something about radical hospitality.

Goth culture and magical religions can have strong appeal among abused adolescents. Voltaire, a present-day namesake of the eighteenth-century Enlightenment writer, is an author and participant in the Goth scene. He writes:

> Things that appeal to Goths tend to pertain to the dark aspects of human existence—such as death, romance, and feelings of loneliness and isolation. Not so surprisingly, many Goths are drawn to the scene due to experiences of abuse, discrimination, or systematic ridicule at the hands of "normal" people (or "mundanes" as they are called in the scene).[22]

At any given time, three or four Germaine Lawrence students would be participating in Goth culture to the extent permitted in their particular program.[23] When Natalie chose to share her Goth and Vodou interests with me, several other girls migrated to the fringes of our conversation. They would occasionally interject comments and questions based on their own encounters with Goth culture in their home schools or during their times on the street. Many were sympathetic to Goth preoccupations. They saw a connection between a Goth fascination with death symbols and a Christian focus on Jesus' crucifixion. They were also well acquainted with the overlap in Goth and Christian symbols on gravestones in the old cemeteries that dot almost every churchyard in New England. Thus, our discussions of Goth culture became an entry point into discussions of soteriology and eschatology.

A ministry of radical hospitality begins with the questions adolescents are asking from within the cultures and contexts in which they reside. It permits teens to explore the characteristics, beliefs, and practices of other cultures in conversation with and in the safety of a Christian community. However, it is not a relativistic practice in which "anything goes" and all interpretations of the truth are valued without question. It is an intentionally safe and welcoming context in which to describe, discuss, encounter, listen, wonder, and discern what God is doing and saying in the world and how God is revealing Godself among God's people. To borrow Parker Palmer's words, it is "a space in which the community of truth is practiced."[24] As such, it eschews both an objectivist religious approach that declares what is true for all without regard for differences in human experience and, also, a subjectivist acceptance of personal experience as the entirety of truth. It embraces instead a process of meaning-making that "requires listening in obedience to each other, responding to what we hear, acknowledging and recreating the bonds of the community of troth."[25]

Germaine Lawrence students already have some experience with such a community as part of their treatment program. When a girl engages in behavior that negatively affects school or dorm life, one aspect of taking responsibility for her actions is "doing restitution." This practice involves writing out one's reflections on the inappropriate behavior and sharing those reflections with other girls in the dorm during a daily group discussion time. The other girls respond in turn with comments about how the behavior affected them as well as with affirmations of the offender's new insights and commitments as a result of her reflection. When Sasha did restitution for giving herself a tattoo, she named her behavior as "dangerous and wrong," spoke of her "regret" that her behavior upset her peers, and indicated that she would have acted more responsibly if she had "chosen to get a tattoo professionally done, or not get one at all."[26] Her peers responded with admonishments that reinforced Sasha's conclusions about the inappropriateness of her previous thinking and actions, alongside statements of forgiveness and support as Sasha moves on. This almost daily group work facilitates personal and communal discoveries about the true meanings of grace (characterized by affirmations) and accountability (embodied by admonishments).

The girls' habituation into a practice of radical hospitality through regular experiences of "doing restitution" suggests that good ministry with adolescents need not be primarily about protecting them from poor decisions by reinforcing certain moral standards. Ronnie and Charles Blakeney contend that religious leaders and social scientists concerned with the power of religion to deter serious juvenile misbehavior are not considering the most constructive connection between the two. They write, "The question isn't, 'How does spirituality protect youth from delinquency?', but rather, 'How does spirituality help young people learn from their mistakes and not get stuck on a delinquent trajectory?'"[27] Intentional Christian spaces (such as the chapel services at Germaine Lawrence and informal group and personal pastoral visits) that welcome adolescents' struggling to relinquish unhealthy behaviors and reorient their lives create opportunities for youth to reflect on their mistakes alongside others in the community. Such spaces may reveal Christian perspectives and spiritual practices capable of sowing and nurturing hope in the fertile soil of battered and bruised souls.

Gillian and the Gift of Service

Gillian's status as a beloved child of God was vehemently contested by Gillian herself. The first time I met her, I knew immediately that she was a "runner," for she wore no shoes.[28] I also guessed that she was a "cutter" (from the scars on her arms) and that she likely struggled with an eating disorder because of the close watch the staff kept on her eating habits. However, the most obvious thing about Gillian was that she was a knitter. Multiple skeins of yarn tumbled from a plastic bin at her feet as her knitting needles flashed. She had no time for nail polish, eyeliner bracelets, or black lips. Her mission was to knit as many hats for babies in the neonatal intensive care unit at Boston Children's Hospital as she could produce in her free time. A counselor had told her of the hospital's desire to put homemade hats on their littlest patients so their care wouldn't seem quite as institutional and impersonal. Gillian knew about being institutionalized; she understood the sometimes-impersonal nature of group care. So she began to knit, enlisting her dorm mates in rolling yarn balls and tying off ends. She eventually taught several other girls how to knit as well, until the entire dorm spent parts of most evenings making hats for hospitalized newborns.

A residential treatment center like Germaine Lawrence is populated with adolescents who perceive themselves as persons unworthy of living. They embody this belief directly through suicidal talk and attempts, and indirectly through self-destructive behavior, such as "school failure, cutting, sexually acting out, drug or alcohol abuse, running away, eating disorders, aggression, or firesetting."[29] It is tempting to cast them as victims primarily in need of compassionate care, or as out-of-control delinquents crying out for a firm hand. While both characterizations tell something of their stories, they miss another important aspect of these young women's lives. They are teens looking for a purpose in life that binds them to other people rather than leaving them isolated and alone.

No matter how much suffering these young women had endured or how much anger they were learning to control, they exhibited an amazing desire to help those less fortunate than themselves. In August 1998, I shared with them stories and photos from my travels earlier that summer to Honduras. They enjoyed participating vicariously in my mountain hikes to distribute medicine in remote villages and my adventures exploring the Mayan ruins in Copan. I assumed their interest stemmed primarily from their own desires to travel to exotic places and engage in their own exploits. What I did not realize is that they had formed a tentative bond with the villagers whose likenesses and crayon drawings I had brought back with me. The truth of that bond became apparent when news of hurricane-induced mudslides in Honduras made international news the next year.

When the girls arrived for chapel the weekend following the media reports, they immediately asked if I had news about the villages I had visited during my trip. They wanted to know if they could write notes and draw pictures for the families in Honduras to show that people in America were praying for them. Stunned by their outpouring of compassion and overwhelmed by the urgency of their need to do something, I quickly assembled paper and markers for their use. I left the school that day with a large manila envelope stuffed full of inspirational cards for people in Honduras who had lost so much. The bulging envelope was from girls whom most people think have nothing at all to give.

Gillian's knitting and the Germaine Lawrence congregation's response to a natural disaster both point to an important way in which victims of trauma become survivors with hope for a better future. The ability to help others suggests that one is not worthless and not without power. Gillian and her band of knitters were able to affect the experiences of tiny babies and their parents. The students who made cards in chapel had the power to comfort distraught families thousands of miles away. Their assertions of worthlessness and powerlessness were, if only briefly, overcome by the conviction that they were capable individuals who could make a difference. This conviction, "that others and the self are good and worthy people," is an essential aspect of resiliency and meaning-making.[30] Opportunities for those who are being served to offer service become a transformational gift for traumatized youth.

An Unconventionally Conventional Youth Ministry

Carol Lytch claims that conventional congregations attract teens by offering three things: "a sense of belonging, a sense of meaning, and opportunities to develop competence."[31] While the Germaine Lawrence congregation is not conventional, the four significant aspects of its ministry revealed by the stories of Anna, Keisha, Natalie, and Gillian correspond to Lytch's findings. Because of the congregation's practice of radical hospitality, each participant felt that she belonged. Even young women who never attended chapel services identified themselves as members of the spiritual community because of regular dorm dinners and informal conversations with the chaplain. Girls in crisis knew they could ask a counselor to call the chaplain, and many did. The rules of reporting were relaxed in pastoral care—the chaplain was only mandated to share threats to the student, her peers, or her counselors—so girls could talk about past illegal activities or struggles related to their treatment without legal or programmatic consequences. Counselors reinforced the radical nature of the spiritual community's hospitality by calling in the chaplain when they thought a girl's overall treatment would benefit from a more confidential space to work through issues.

The adoption of a regular practice of lament and the encouragement of the teens' attraction to a Mythic-Literal God reinforced a broader sense of belonging and also generated a sense of meaning. The students at Germaine Lawrence discovered that they are part of a long and diverse line of people beloved by God as they learned about God's promises and God's active presence in the world. They also acquired practical theological frameworks within which to identify and interpret their experiences as connected to God and the Christian community. They were no longer restricted by the debilitating interpretations of their experience that had driven them into treatment. Participation in communal practices of lament and experimentation with a view of God that emphasizes reciprocal justice provided spiritual means to reorient themselves alongside the cognitive behavioral means offered in the general treatment program.

The gift of service opportunities helped girls develop competencies as caregivers rather than care-receivers. While outreach ministries such as the hat and card projects did not originate with the chaplain, they emerged because of the teens' desire to live out their faith in tangible and competent ways. As empowered members of a spiritual community, they offered one another specific ways to transfer the downtrodden-victim identities of their old-wineskin pasts into the new identity wineskins of compassionate survivorship. Such offerings carried a greater transformative power precisely because they originated with the young women themselves and thus represented their own recognition that competency as a caregiver is an important personal and spiritual skill.

In light of this analysis, my ministry with the students at Germaine Lawrence might be characterized as unconventionally conventional. The unconventional stories of the girls who comprised the spiritual community radically shaped the way in which I interpreted the lectionary texts I preached and the communal practices I emphasized. On the other hand, these abused and seemingly hopeless adolescents were attracted by the same "hooks" of belonging, meaning, and competency-building that draw well-nurtured teens into the life of the Christian community.[32] There was, however, one notable difference: a rather unusual dependence on cosmetics. These young women seemed much more comfortable working on life issues while making up themselves and their religious leader. Painting nails a glittery neon yellow, drawing the links of a bracelet around a wrist in dark brown, applying black lipstick, even knitting caps to outfit newborns, are all cosmetic activities. Such activities created spaces for a non-cosmetic ministry that helped the girls at Germaine Lawrence to reclaim hope. And so they discovered the courage to pray, "Let peace, joy, harmony, trust and kindness return to our daily lives."[33]

9

Living Out Loud in a World That Demands Silence

Preaching with Adolescents

VERONICE MILES

Today was her birthday, and the telephone conversation extended well past an hour. When I asked Rashida how she felt being thirteen, she explained that thirteen meant she was a teenager and she should begin to think about serious things, such as God and family, politics and war, the environment, college, and the future. Delighted and amazed, I listened as she signaled in no uncertain terms that she wanted to become one of my dialogue partners. She had opinions that mattered and were worth hearing. I felt as though a dam had broken; a flood of insights, unarticulated until then, came rushing out–thoughts that she had been saving for that moment when she finally turned thirteen.

Thirteen was Rashida's entrée into adolescence, years during which young people take up important tasks of making meaning for their lives and discovering their place in the larger scheme of things. What does it mean to live a good and successful life? What does the future hold for me? Where do I fit, and what does my life have to do with those with whom I share this planet? Such important questions confront adolescents as they begin to imagine how they might live meaningfully into the future.

Determining how to live meaningfully necessitates sifting through numerous perspectives, listening for those that resonate with one's own sense of the world, and discarding those that appear inadequate. This is an arduous task, especially for adolescents who live in the United States. As citizens of one of the wealthiest nations in the world, U.S. youth inherit the prosperous and influential images the represent the national persona.

These images of wealth and material prosperity remain the prevailing symbol of success, albeit many youth find it inconsistent with their lived experience. U.S. youth are also coming of age in a world in which global stability is tenuous. War is no longer a rumor, impoverishment persists, and genocidal cries echo throughout the globe, hoping to awaken someone to the injustices that force people's *backs against the wall.*

These cries are difficult to ascertain amid the cacophony of competing sounds and images that saturate our visual and acoustical horizons, transmitted incessantly from the media. The media moderates our exposure to other persons while selling us an image of the *good life* defined by individual achievement, money, and power.[1] It fashions and sustains public image and perception, creating a unique cultural milieu with the media as its primary purveyor of meaning. *Meaning* becomes a lucrative commodity, packaged in the accoutrements of prosperity and sold to the viewing public. Adolescents who assent to the media's portrayal of life find it difficult to imagine alternative possibilities for their lives. Thus one of the most demanding tasks of young people is unmasking the media's distorted representations and discovering an authentic way to live in relationship with other persons. I call this learning to *live out loud.*

In this chapter I explore several alternatives for Christian communities desiring to nourish adolescents' ability to *live out loud.* That is, communities that are willing to become their co-journeyers and dialogue partners. I focus primarily upon preaching as one conduit through which adolescents learn to live out loud and discern meaning for their lives. *Meaning-full preaching* releases persons to perceive and engage reality in light of the Gospel's vision of a world in which sustenance is available to those who hunger and thirst for the necessities of life.[2] The trajectory of the Gospel is indicative of the Hebrew expression *shalom,* which signifies God's commitment to health, wholeness, and prosperity for all persons. Meaning-full preaching thus invites adolescents to live the Gospel as members of a community committed to creating a world in which God's *shalom* can become a reality. This chapter is concerned with the power of proclamation within a shared communal ethos to enhance adolescents' ability to live out loud.

Living Out Loud and the Power of Community

History is replete with stories about persons and communities who chose to *live out loud* when faced with seemingly insurmountable suffering. Not the least among them are twentieth-century youth organizations such as the African National Congress Youth League (ANCYL) organized under the leadership of Nelson Mandela in 1944, and the Student Non-Violent Coordinating Committee (SNCC) that grew out of a sit-in against racism at North Carolina A&T University in 1961. These youth organizations aggressively resisted the oppressive structures that ordered their existence and refused to relinquish their vision of a new reality. Yet, the vision was not theirs alone. It mirrored their communities' passionate determination for a just and liberating reality.

In ancient Israel, young people supported their community's ongoing struggle for freedom. In some instances this meant resisting oppression from without, as in Daniel and his comrades' refusal to eat the Babylonian king's food.[3] Others, such as Zelophedad's five daughters in the book of Numbers, transgressed social and religious boundaries by resisting oppression from within their community. These five young women discovered new meaning within the contradiction of their community's deeply rooted systemic patriarchy and its history of liberating praxis. I begin our conversation about meaning-making and community with retelling their story.

In Numbers 26 and 27, we meet Mahlah, Noah, Hoglah, Milcah, and Tirzah, young Israelite women and daughters of a Mannasite named Zelophehad. They were gathered with all Israel in the plains of Moab near the Jordan River as Moses and Eleazar the priest conducted a national census. The census assessed Israel's military readiness and determined how the property in the trans-Jordan would be divided. But for Zelophehad's family and for the Mannasites, the census presented a dilemma. Zelophehad was dead and had no sons to receive his inheritance.

This was problematic because his daughters were born at a time in Israelite history when property and inheritance rights passed through the male bloodline. They, like all other women, were not entitled to own property. Without an inheritance in the land, Zelophehad's name would be lost among the Mannasites. More distressingly, with no brother to receive their inheritance, the five sisters and their mother would become dependent upon other male family members, their father's brothers, for their survival.[4]

As participants in a patriarchal society, these young women had learned kinesthetically—in doing women's things and not doing men's things—that women were prohibited from certain places, such as being counted in the census. On the other hand, they were members of a proclaiming community with a strong legacy of liberating praxis, which likely emboldened them to transgress the patriarchal boundaries of their society. Consequently, in Numbers 27, they approached Moses and Eleazar at the tent of meeting and demanded an inheritance among their father's brothers.[5]

Their petition created a dilemma for Moses and Eleazar. No precedence had been set for granting their request. Nonetheless, "Moses brought their case before the Lord" (27:5), and YHWH agreed that Zelophehad's daughters should receive their father's inheritance.[6] YHWH's "yes" extended justice to a set of circumstances that had presumably gone unchallenged, creating a generative ethos in which *shalom* could become the normative expression of community. The ordinance was imperfect; it did not completely abolish disparate inheritance laws. Nonetheless, its imperfection should not negate the reality that these five young women initiated a change in their community that may never have happened if they had not spoken. They chose to *live out loud.*

To *live out loud* is to resist distorted representations of reality and embrace alternatives that create wholeness and well-being for oneself and for other human persons. Though the evidence might imply improbability, persons who *live out loud* know intuitively that possibility has not been exhausted. They respond to the pulsating rhythm of a world "sighing, crying and whispering wholeness, wholeness, wholeness," inviting those who will to synchronize their hearts to this universal pulse.[7]

To say that the world demands silence is to disclose metaphorically the processes by which the present order and its benefactors distort and inhibit our ability to respond to universal cries for wholeness. This does not negate silence in its actuality, for restraint from speaking can be a powerful form of resistance, evinced in acts of civil disobedience and silent protests. Speaking is also not limited to vocal expression, as nonvocal communities can attest. Thus, I explore "silence" here as that which results when structures and powers rob persons of the ability to sense their deep desire for wholeness and live accordingly. *Living out loud* is not primarily about sound or speaking; it is a way of being, perceiving, and behaving that reflects our commitment to the hope of *shalom* as tangible reality.

Expanding the Meaning-making Paradigm

The five women in Numbers chose to *live out loud* by embracing possibility rather than surrender their agency to delimiting aspects of their community. The dilemma in which they found themselves necessitated a definitive shift from the social norms that defined their existence as women in ancient Israel to that which secured their well-being.[8] Their decision to transgress the socioreligious boundaries not only secured their well-being; it also cast new dye into the fabric of their culture. Similar to these five women, I, too, am concerned with the power and possibility of discerning meaning when the socioreligious context in which we live warrants transformation rather than preservation.

Charles Foster describes meaning-making as the dynamic interaction between cognition and affect, thought and feeling, which ultimately shapes "our knowing and doing."[9] He argues that the "*cognitive* actions of discerning, comprehending, thinking and understanding" and the *affective* experience of "coherence, discovery and possibility" contribute to one's sense of purpose.[10] Persons thus make meaning for their lives by discerning patterns of thought, feeling, action, and interaction that are significant for living in the present and into the future.[11] This ongoing process of meaning-making shapes our commitments and choices; they, in turn, provide "impetus to our actions."[12]

Similarly, Robert Kegan refers to human persons as "meaning-making organisms" and contends that human existence is itself the "meaning-making context."[13] Adolescence denotes a transitional phase within this recurring process. During adolescence, adults anticipate that youth will begin to "think reflectively, inferentially, connotatively and thematically," as they reconsider their world in light of their expanding relationships.[14] They are to become good citizens, "sharer[s] in the idea and activity of preserving the societal bonds of the commonwealth."[15] But what are youth to do when systemic oppression inhibits their ability to participate equitably in the commonwealth?

The systemic violence and oppression that confronted Zelophehad's daughters, as well as the members of the ANCYL and SNCC, were severe. The relational paradigms that constituted their communities were grossly inadequate, and alternatives appeared improbable. Nonetheless, each chose subversive action rather than assent to the givens. Their responses reveal two additional processes, *intuition* and *conation.* I will thus explore *intuition*–pre-reflective impressions, experiences, and convictions–and *conation*–intentional, purposeful yet often unconventional actions–as essential aspects of meaning-making, particularly in the lives of youth facing systemic oppression.[16]

Henry Mitchell explains that human persons store information, impressions, and experiential encounters gathered through a lifetime in the intuitive consciousness. He contends, "This input is not examined, adopted or organized in a *consciously* rational manner. It includes a wide variety of insights from culture, family, church, school and community, and individual experience."[17] People gain intuitive knowledge from experiences that often appear routine, inadvertent, or insignificant, but are actually powerful in shaping perceptions. One might say, then, that the experience of Mahlah, Noah, Hoglah, Milcah, and Tirzah as girl-children in a community for which overcoming adversity was commonplace enriched their perception of what might be possible for their lives. Even though systemic patriarchy demanded silence, the liberating praxis that constituted their community energized them to resist and contest. Intuition, therefore, reflects a way of knowing grounded in experience rather than reason or rationality.[18]

Conation, intentionally choosing an efficacious course of action even though or especially when the evidence does not support the choice, is also essential. Conation is purposeful, willful, and intentional action that resists annihilation and compels persons to act upon what they believe to be possible and necessary for life. Participants in the ANCYL and SNCC engaged in conative action as they contested systemic oppression. They acted without guarantee, but with purpose and conviction to secure new life for themselves and their communities. Conative actions are un-reasonable, when reasonableness is understood as nonresistance or acquiescence. Persons who discern meaning conatively subvert existing patterns of relationships, not randomly or emotionally but decisively, drawing upon cognition, affect, and intuition to determine risks and accomplish their purpose. Conation and intuition work cooperatively with cognition and affect, creating a synergy by which adolescents can resist oppression and discover meaning and purpose for living.

The Power and Danger of Media Representations

The meaning-making paradigm that I have described does not occur in isolation. It requires an experiential context in which adolescents and adult co-journeyers can *mind* their world. To *mind* the world is to view it as objective reality, unmask the mechanisms that sustain oppression, and "open the way to surpassing and repair."[19] In the contemporary U.S., the media's contentions regarding the good life are incessant. Hard work yields success, it claims, as the systemic inequities that relegate many people to the margins of society remain hidden.[20] Proffered by advertisers and big businesses that stand to amass great wealth should they convince us that their view of the world is preferable, the media thwarts our ability to notice limits and to envision communal well-being as a viable social commitment. Herein resides the power and danger of media representation. Not only do these representations appear reliable, but their iconic quality also elicits mimetic behavior. Thus, when persons *mindlessly* appropriate media versions of reality, the world appears closed and static, leading persons inadvertently to surrender their agency and live as silent reflections of a media-contrived world.

Michael Warren explores the iconic quality of media images and contends that they are not simply visual depictions or portrayals of some aspect of reality, but representations that persons accept as reliable characterizations of the real world.[21] Because humans are imitators by nature, we incorporate these representations into our understanding of reality and emulate their qualities without pausing to "think about them, understand how they work, [or] make judgments about their value."[22] These representations appear harmless but they are by no means inert. Their mimetic power intensifies as the noticeable similarities between the viewer and the mimetic subject increase.[23] Thus, Warren contends that icons possess latent power that can "trigger a way of imagining ourselves...of inviting the viewer to imitate the qualities of the person or reality represented by the icon."[24] Consequently, they give meaning to what we see; they shape patterns of thought and feeling that undergird human behavior.[25]

Warren's investigation of media images encourages me to consider again the sheer magnitude of media representations. They appear inescapable, persistently and repetitively instructing, selling and re-presenting with hopes that they might form us in the media's own image. We repetitively view a television commercial, for example. Before we realize it, we are purchasing the prescribed item. Repetition and constancy of exposure amplify this mimetic power by legitimizing the item's necessity and co-opting our imagination.

This process may seem harmless; however, when one's thoughts and feelings are shaped by images that repetitively and consistently devalue persons and communities, the implications are enormous. Persons and communities already exist within wider culture contexts that influence their ability to live as subjects of their existence. While one might welcome repetitive exposure to life-affirming representations, negative images can reify oppressive systems that objectify rather than promote subjectivity. In other words, private patterns of thought and feeling can alter our existence, especially if one agrees that humans construct the societies in which they live.

Patricia Williams argues, for example, that we create our world through narratives and myths: "I do think that to a very great extent we dream our world into being. For better or worse, our customs and laws, our culture and society are sustained by the myths we embrace, the stories we recirculate to explain what we beheld."[26] Similarly, Patricia Hill Collins defines repetitive images or myths as "controlling images" and contends that they are "designed to make racism, sexism, poverty, and other forms of social injustice appear to be natural, normal, and inevitable parts of everyday life."[27] Warren also agrees that "what we see tends to construct a way of seeing and can…become institutionalized in patterns of interaction between persons."[28] The media's potential for influencing our perceptions and consequently how we fashion our world is undeniable.

Perception frames what we are likely to accept as reliable and normative for living, as well as what we deem just, necessary, and politically efficacious. Distorted representation can diminish our perceptual acuity and lead to unwitting consensus with the current order. Consenting to the current order seems grossly inadequate in a world in which numerous youths continue to suffer under social structures that refuse to count them in. Therefore, a liberating word that releases adolescents to anticipate and create new possibilities for living is imperative.

Formulaic Living and Social Devaluation

One of the media's most powerful narratives is that life is simple and formulaic, neatly packaged and predictable. The narrative repetitively promises happiness, fun, exhilaration, power, contentment, love, popularity, and success if one would simply purchase the right paraphernalia. M. Shawn Copeland argues, "This society promotes the confusion of comfort, convenience, (hyper) masculinity, (hyper) femininity, and sex with the 'good life'–that is, with authentic happiness, self-realization, and personal fulfillment in community."[29] Without regard for systemic barriers, the narrative insists that the accumulation of material goods *is* the formula for a successful and meaningful life.

Imbedded within this formula is an evaluative mechanism that assigns value to persons and things based upon their ability to acquire and maintain the material goods, social standing, or physical characteristics indicative of the good life. For example, most characters portraying the *good life* are white-skinned, male, affluent, and powerful. They wear the latest fashions, drive expensive cars, and use the latest technology—with product logos prominently displayed. The *good people* typically win. Few die without some type of retributive justice or vindication. Blacks, Hispanics, Asians, or other *racialized* groups seldom portray *good people* and are often excluded altogether.[30] Tragically, numerous adolescents see persons with whom they share ethnic, racial, or gender similarities depicted as unremarkable or *bad people,* perpetuating devaluation and negation.[31]

Devaluation circumvents the meaning-making process and can lead to unreflective imitative behavior (silence) when negating representations are appropriated without critique. This is powerfully portrayed in Evelyn Parker's investigation of "emancipatory hope" in the lives of African American adolescents. She maintains, "Within the polyphonic environs of black adolescents, life, religious culture, media culture, school culture, and family are all struggling for power to shape the consciousness of adolescents."[32] The youth in her study demonstrated what Parker defines as "fragmented spirituality," the inconsistency between their belief in a powerful and transforming God and their hopelessness regarding God's power to dismantle racism.[33] She discovered that the primary source of fragmented spirituality was *ventriloquation of media culture:*

> Ventriloquation of media culture regarding racism fragments the spirituality of adolescents who are in the throes of ideological becoming. The assimilation of words from characters and personalities on television who present a defeatist attitude for confronting racism prohibits youth from weaving together language, religious meaning, and moral practice that are indicative of expectation and agency for dismantling racism.[34]

Imitation of negating media images thwarts agency and leads to hopelessness and defeatism, particularly as it relates to injustice, oppression, and dehumanization. Hopelessness and defeatism inhibit creative action and domesticate human imagination. When persons are not able to conceive alternatives, they inadvertently perpetuate the same unjust and oppressive systems that initially distorted their understanding. In other words, formulaic conceptions of reality create and sustain silence.

Formulaic Living and Youth Culture

Hip-hop has become the signature expression of what it means to be young, popular, powerful, and successful in the twenty-first century. Hip-hop professes to be more than a musical genre—it claims to be a way of life for its artists and for the youth who define themselves as members of hip-hop culture. From the perspective of its proponents, hip-hop dismantles class and racial boundaries, evinced by its far-reaching acceptance and influence among youth.[35] Yet, as we will discuss, hip-hop has also become one of the media's primary vehicles for perpetuating formulaic conceptions of reality.

Developed in the late 1970s and early 1980s, hip-hop was created by young people such as Grandmaster Flash, DJ Kool Herc, Sugar Hill Gang, and popularized in the 1980s by many, including Queen Latifah and MC Lyte. These artists spoke truth *to* power *for* the powerless and *from* their own contexts of struggle. They *lived out loud* by representing reality from their perspective and engaging the world on their own terms. As hip-hop's popularity grew, the potential for living the *good life* became a reality for many of its artists. But it also involved accepting recording contracts with the very powers that they had critiqued so vigorously.

While recording contracts with large recording companies provided the exposure necessary to distinguish hip-hop as a genre and secure its credibility among youth, contracts with companies that were less passionate about the message and more concerned with making money meant that hip-hop was no longer the property of its creators alone. Participation in mainstream media also exposed their messages and images to commodification by recording companies, clothing lines, and advertisers who continue to profit from hip-hop's popularity and widespread appeal. Eventually, artists within the genre learned that living the good life required them to make important decisions regarding the monetary value of their product and the integrity of their message. During a recent appearance on Russell Simmons' *Def Poetry Jam,* artist DMX lamented and critiqued hip-hop's loss of control over its message and urged artists and adherents to reclaim their voice and unique identity.

Hip-hop's insistence upon voice and uniqueness resists homogeneity; thus, its messages are varied. For some artists, hip-hop means articulating socially conscious messages, naming oppression, and speaking truth to power. Others, however, perpetuate the individualistic message of hedonistic material consumption that permeates much of U.S. culture. Numerous adolescents, especially African American males, have told me that they plan to *make it big* or *blow up* in hip-hop so they can purchase the much-desired trappings of success. Few have thought critically about the content of their message, but almost all hope to *get rich* in the music industry. They invoke the catch phrase "bling-bling," which has come to mean material accumulation, money, and recognition and which, for many, speaks to their value as human persons.

While *bling-bling* does mirror the mainstream media's characterization of the good life, the evaluative mechanism that I have identified is most notable in the misogynistic, dehumanizing, and denigrating images evident in some of hip-hop's rap lyrics. For example, in her critique of 2 Live Crew's song "Hoochie Mama," Patricia Hill Collins challenges the acceptance of disaffirming images of black women:

> Despite the offensive nature of much of 2 Live Crew's music, some Blacks argued that such views, while unfortunate, had long been expressed in Black culture (Crenshaw 1993). Not only does such acceptance mask how such images provide financial benefits to both 2 Live Crew and White-controlled media, such tacit acceptance validates this image. The more it circulates among U.S. Blacks, the more credence it is given.[36]

Further, if hip-hop's claim to cross-cultural appeal is accurate, then the *hoochie* image is not only given credence in the minds of Blacks, but in the minds of people throughout the U.S. and the world. Perpetuation of such images legitimizes the victimization of women and other vulnerable persons and places hip-hop at risk for committing what comedian Vince Morris describes as "lyrical genocide." Far from the transformative and imaginative possibilities that are born when young people *mind* the world in which they live, genocidal lyrics recirculate negative sexualized and racialized images that consent to the annihilation and dehumanization of Black people, in general, and Black women in particular.

Whenever we negatively represent a person or group of persons without noticing how our representations perpetuate oppression, we reinforce historical patterns of relationship that prevent persons from living as human subjects. Also, by exercising "freedom of speech" without thoughtful consideration of the capacity of words to create images and the power of images to elicit mimetic behavior, genocidal lyricists co-opt imagination and create patterns of interaction that reflect their assertions. The artists and those who *mindlessly* appropriate their messages forfeit the opportunity to create meaningful relationships, resist distorted representations, and imagine alternatives to the lack that exists in the present. Instead, they propagate, intentionally or unwittingly, the meaning that is handed to them by those who benefit most from the current order. They relinquish the possibility of *living out loud* for the certainty of living in silence.

Countering the negative effects of artists such as 2 Live Crew, progressive hip-hop artists such as Jill Scott, India Aire, Mos Def, Mary J. Blige, Dave Chappelle, and numerous poets in the largely underground, spoken-word movement grapple with life, love, loss, hardship, and injustice from a decidedly transformative and liberative perspective. Evelyn Parker suggests that "progressive rap" reflects the prophetic voices of young people as they express a form of *holy indignation* and "seeks to transform systems of injustice by transforming the perspective of their [the systems'] victims."[37] Therefore, as modern-day prophets, progressive hip-hop artists appear committed to unmasking oppression and publicly articulating the painful realities that these systems create.

While not representing a utopian or romanticized view of reality, their artistry reflects intentionality about deconstructing the present and proposing alternatives for the future. For example, in her recording, "I'm Not My Hair," India Aire resists prevailing images of beauty by speaking of her struggle with breast cancer and her revelation that her hair was not indicative of her worth as a human being. In one of the choruses she asserts, "I am not this skin. / I am a soul that lives within."[38] Aire discovered meaning for her life that transcended formulaic notions about beauty, being, and acceptability. In so doing, she encourages others to discover the *soul that lives within.* Similarly, spoken-word artists articulate messages of survival, resistance, and liberation as they continue the tradition of speaking truth to power and evoking the imagination of the powerless, which began with artists such as David Nelson, Umar Bin Hassan, and Abiodun Oyewole, members of the 1960s group The Last Poets.

Given its liberative focus and insistence upon speaking truth to power, progressive hip-hop offers an alternative to the silencing effect of formulaic media representations. If hip-hop is as pervasive in youth culture as many suggest, then its artists share in the task, whether they choose to or not, of helping adolescents grapple with their questions and decisions at this crucial moment in their development. I say this, not unaware that many hip-hop artists are also trying to make meaning—discerning risks, considering possibilities, and negotiating relationships. While progressive hip-hop may assume the role of dialogue partner, I caution against hip-hop becoming the sole or predominant perspective to which adolescents are exposed. Churches and other trusting adult co-journeyers must remain faithful dialogue partners, which includes engaging the world of hip-hop and listening attentively for young people's prophesies, complaints, hopes, and dreams as they traverse the waters of adolescence.

Meaning-full Preaching

The determination that frames this discussion is that churches and other worshiping communities can become life-affirming "holding environments" in which adolescents discern meaning and learn to *live out loud.*[39] Communities of faith can become cross-generational, dialogical contexts that provide space for inquiry and reinterpretation, confession and contestation, laughter and lament as adolescents explore meaning. My emphasis upon dialogue suggests that churches are not required to shield adolescents from the various perspectives to which they are exposed. Rather, their task is to envisage a world in which *shalom* can become a tangible reality for all persons, hopeful that adolescents might also find this image a compelling and inspirational alternative to the media's formulaic representations of reality. Churches must remain committed to proclaiming the Gospel in word and deed, testifying to the reality it represents.

For preachers concerned with helping adolescents learn to *live out loud*, this Gospel testimony involves engaging youth in sermonic encounters through which they can discover meaningful connections between their lives and the biblical witness.[40] It also involves welcoming adolescents as active participants in the life and ministry of the church. I call this approach to preaching *meaning-full preaching: preaching that invites adolescents, along with all persons, to live the Gospel as participants in a shared communal ethos that is committed to creating a world in which God's shalom can become a reality.*

Meaning-full preaching is concerned with helping adolescents mind the present—unmask representations of reality that inhibit well-being—while imagining a new reality. Thus, meaning-full preaching is intentional about exploring adolescents' questions, hearing what they have to say, and inviting young people to engage the biblical text imaginatively and reflectively. My hope is that meaning-full preaching might embolden adolescents to recognize the contradictory nature of their existence, speak truth, and stand against injustice. Therefore, I appeal to those who are willing to preach the good news of the Gospel and to make that news real in the lives of adolescent and adults alike.

Grounded in Good News

The Gospel is not simply an idea, but rather the imaginative construct that constitutes the church. It is the church's ongoing practice of loving God and neighbor and the church's commitment to a just and liberating existence for all persons. The church perceives the Gospel among biblical prophets such as Isaiah, Micah, and Amos, who declare that suffering and oppression are not the final shape of our world, admonishing us to "let justice roll down like waters, / and righteousness like an ever-flowing stream" (Am. 5:24). We sing of it in Psalm 82 as the psalmist portrays the God of Israel urging the Divine council: "Give justice to the weak and the orphan; / maintain the right of the lowly and the destitute. / Rescue the weak and the needy; / deliver them from the hand of the wicked" (vv. 3–4). These images powerfully shaped Jesus' life and ministry and continue to speak today.

Many modern Christians engage most potently with the Gospel through the life of Jesus and his announcement of a new reality. In Luke 4:18–21, Jesus envisages the cessation of poverty, captivity, and suffering, and the advent of a new social order. He reads from the prophet Isaiah:

> "The Spirit of the Lord is upon me,
>   because he has anointed me
>   to bring good news to the poor.
> He has sent me to proclaim release to the captives
>   and recovery of sight to the blind,

to let the oppressed go free,
to proclaim the year of the Lord's favor." (4:18–19)

He then proclaims, "Today this scripture has been *fulfilled* in your hearing" (4:21, emphasis added). The word *fulfilled* meant that a divine promise was about to be realized; it signaled a fundamental change in the order of things. [41] It further revealed God's commitment to justice and condemnation of disparities between the poor and privileged. Jesus' suggestion that *this scripture has been fulfilled* exerted a claim upon those who heard it. It demanded an active human response to divine intent. The proclamation still summons us to participate in bringing the reality that Jesus announced to fruition.

Each sermon is an opportunity for the news of the Gospel to be fulfilled as *promise* and *call.* Meaning-full preaching communicates the promise of the Gospel and invites adolescents to participate in making that promise a reality. This is no easy task, given the mimetic and representational power of media constructs of reality. Consequently, meaning-full preaching requires a commitment to disrupt the stability and force of media images, while also helping young people discern possibilities for living the Gospel in their everyday lives. Those who are serious about being co-journeyers with adolescents enjoy the remarkable challenge of *making the Gospel real* in their imaginations.

Making the Gospel Real

Making the Gospel real involves creating sermons that adolescents can understand: sermons that honor their experience, respond to their questions, and welcome their participation in the shared communal ethos that we call church. Meaning-full preaching, therefore, necessitates sermons that are intelligible, accessible, and invitational for adolescent hearers.

Intelligible preaching is preaching that one can understand. It makes the message clear and comprehensible, lucid but not condescending. Intelligibility includes the use of language that is familiar to the hearers and that awakens the imagination. Thus intelligibility is not only concerned with intellectual coherence but with helping adolescents envision imaginative possibilities for living the Gospel, possibilities that may not have been readily apparent given the prevailing cultural milieu. Intelligibility also includes choosing evocative words, phrases, stories, and analogies that can bridge the gap between the ancient world of the Bible and our contemporary world. [42] These choices might include language that elicits sensorial engagement with the text—e.g., sounds, images, smells, taste, and sensations, as well as descriptive language that illumines theological and sociopolitical aspects of the text. Intelligible preaching invites adolescents to engage the Gospel cognitively, affectively, and intuitively, with hopes that it might aid them in choosing that which gives meaning to life.

Meaning-full preaching is also accessible preaching, intentional about engaging the world of adolescents. Caution! I am not advocating preaching that is full of youth cultural jargon, which can become as stale and cliché as any formulaic expression. Rather, I am suggesting that preachers remain cognizant of the world in which adolescents live–their joys and struggles, questions and concerns, future aspirations and fears. What concerns youth about war or the ferocity of racism, sexism, classism, and heterosexism in U.S. culture? What do their music, poetry, and protest literature say about how they view God, the church, or its proclamation? Accessibility requires that preachers listen attentively to young people, with hopes of integrating their understandings into our sermons. This might include preaching the lives of biblical youth, such as the five young women in Numbers, or of historical youth who have made significant contributions to the world, exemplifying their Gospel commitments to well-being.

Accessible preaching is also preaching that explores perspectives, expands alternatives, and invites adolescents to engage fully in the process of discerning the promised shape of our world. It announces the good news of the Gospel over against the media's repetitive formulaic assertion regarding happiness and success. However, good news is not always pleasant news, especially when it challenges practices and commitments. What are similarities between the plight of the rich young man whom Jesus instructed to "sell your possessions, and give the money to the poor" (Mt. 19:21) and the plight of those saturated with media's message that material wealth gives meaning to life? How might Peter's epiphany that "God shows no partiality" (Acts 10:34) collide with the disparity in value that alienates persons and communities from each other based upon life circumstances or the ways they were created? There are no simple answers to these questions. In fact, accessible preaching resists the lure of simple answers. It struggles with the complex questions that confront youth and adults alike. It sustains a creative tension between celebrating shalom when it is expressed and deconstructing practices and attitudes that inhibit new creation.

The invitational character of meaning-full preaching grows out of this ambiguity between situational expressions of shalom and the ongoing necessity for shalom in this world. Meaning-full preaching proclaims, with thanksgiving, that many oppressive structures, such as apartheid in South Africa and Jim Crow laws in America, have crumbled. However, it does not ignore the suffering that persists among those whose deliverance is yet to come, and among those whose emancipation has revealed ever-deepening levels of systemic oppression.

There is much work to be done! Meaning-full preaching acknowledges that no historical period or liberating movement reflects the complete actualization of shalom, while it also affirms that all who are created in the image of a Creating God are called to participate significantly in shaping and sustaining a world that reflects God's intent for creation. The Gospel as shalom calls forth a reality in which the hungry are fed, those who thirst are refreshed, strangers are welcomed, the naked are clothed, the infirmed are healed, and those who are incarcerated are no longer abandoned.[43] Ultimately, those of us who preach with adolescents hope that together we might experience the Gospel as promise and call. We pray that, by the aid of the Holy Spirit, our sermons will offer nourishment for the journey and embolden young people to stand as living testimonies to the power of the Gospel.

Some Last Words

Creating a shared communal ethos that can nurture adolescents to *live out loud* can be a difficult and sometimes lonely journey. It demands courage to proclaim, "Today the scripture is fulfilled in your hearing" among the privileged and oppressed. Similarly, it requires us to listen for the voices of those who have been silenced and marginalized in a world that is increasingly intolerant of those voices, and encourage them to speak. That is, encourage them to press the social and religious boundaries of their world and dare to *live out loud.* Therefore, I offer three last words to preachers who seek to create a communal ethos in which adolescents might experience the joy of living *out loud.*

The first word is to *establish dynamic and generative relationships with adolescents.* Engage them as dialogue partners who, as Rashida reminded me, have opinions that matter and are worth hearing. As adult co-journeyers, preachers need to abandon dominating and repressive relationships, and accompany adolescents on their journey of discovery. Preachers can listen for the prophetic voices of youth in their music, poetry, and complaints, seeking to understand the deep yearnings of their souls. Adult co-journeyers are not required to abdicate their identities and become caricature adolescents, but rather to approach youth with genuine regard.

Second is to *engage adolescents as dialogue partners and to remain in conversation, even when conflicts emerge and resolution seems improbable.* Adults are bequeathed the responsibility of seeking common ground and maintaining a dialogical exchange from which creative insights and actions can emerge. Conflicting points of view are inevitable. Rather than allowing them to foreclose conversation, adults and youth alike might best view them as opportunities to acknowledge frustration and carefully peel the socioreligious layers that keep them apart. Whether because of a generation gap or simply different experiences, beliefs, and ways of being, conflicts arise from human uniqueness. Dialogue can foster a dynamic exchange of ideas through which adults and youth might learn together and gain an appreciation for an expanded range of possibilities. Also, both develop oppositional abilities that can strengthen their critique and resistance of the thematic story of media.

The last word is to *proclaim a meaning-full reality; foster well-being, unmask distortion, and release young people to imagine their world through the lens of the*

Gospel. The concept of meaning-full preaching grew from my encounter with Mahlah, Noah, Hoglah, Milcah, and Tirzah and with members of the ANCYL and SNCC. These were proclaiming communities that valued and practiced communal well-being. In each case, young people articulated a vision of reality that departed from the oppressive ordering of existence. They chose resistance and contestation despite the resounding "no" of their social and religious contexts. Inspired by them, I encourage preachers and worship communities to retain their proclaiming quality and to utilize preaching as one means by which persons might tell the story. To that end, I stand with other proclaimers of the Gospel, hoping and praying that adolescents might embrace the practice of *living out loud.*

Subversive Spirituality in Youth Ministry at the Margins

SUSANNE JOHNSON

In light of the exclusion and pain disadvantaged adolescents experience in a class-ridden society, how do impoverished inner-city black youth in Wichita, Kansas, marginalized Chicano youth in Albuquerque, New Mexico, and innumerable other at-risk youth across the United States defy the odds and engage in transformational ministry at the margins? This chapter explores how certain groups of so-called "at risk" youth live their Christian spirituality in ways that uplift, transform, and sustain them personally and also give public expression to faith for the good of their respective communities and neighborhoods. Spirituality lived at the margins and on the underside of society may hold important corrective insights for spirituality lived in the mainstream. As the apostle Paul suggests: "God chose what is foolish in the world to shame the wise; God chose what is weak in the world to shame the strong; God chose what is low and despised in the world, things that are not, to reduce to nothing things that are" (1 Cor. 1:27–28).

Specifically, this chapter focuses on the dynamics of faith-based youth community organizing (YCO), a strategy through which marginalized and excluded teenagers, along with their adult mentors and community partners, utilize their collective power to hold local public leaders, groups, and institutions accountable for securing greater equity and justice for underrepresented, underserved youth in the community and to address their well-being. Across the nation, but little noticed by mainline churches, YCO groups are retrieving youth from the clutches of gangs and other forms of self-destruction, then initiating them into a life that kindles their spirituality, captivates their imagination, quickens their hope, and capitalizes on their passion. In settings shaped by the perspectives and practices of faith-based organizing, youth ministry stands in stark contrast to conventional youth ministry in the mainstream. By attending to the remarkable narratives of resistance, transformation, and hope among poor and working-class young people, who are often invisible to the dominant church and who experience much of the brunt of this "troubling world," we can potentially rethink and revitalize the ways that congregations practice youth ministry in the mainline. At the very least, we will gain reverence and respect for God, who works in and through Jesus Christ, and in and through all things, to redeem and renew creation "from below."

What Is Youth Organizing and How Does It Work?

Through faith-based youth community organizing (YCO), young people are equipped with a complex set of skills, strategies, and perspectives that enable them to resist, address, and transform personal and social evil and to effect change in their neighborhoods, schools, and community institutions.[1] In the tradition of organizing, young people learn to connect traditional resources of Christian spirituality to the social, economic, and political realities that shape their daily existence and that of their families. In the U.S., members of faith-based YCO groups belong to welfare and working-poor families. Most are youth of color, many are bicultural immigrants, and they tend to live in blighted inner-city neighborhoods, though YCO groups can also be found in suburban and rural areas. Several qualities of faith-based organizing are important to identify if we are to learn from them.

First, faith-based YCO trains youth and their adult mentors in the art of public life and public theology. Further, it rehearses them in realities of the pluralistic, globalized society that the U.S. now reflects. Believing that leaders are made, not born, YCO groups are known both as "universities of hope" and as "universities of public engagement," which provide on-the-job mentoring of young people in skills and knowledge that they need to participate in public life and to contribute to the common good. While adult mentors bring spirituality, maturity, commitment, leadership strengths, and relational gifts to the young people, they do not always have expertise in grassroots organizing. Many are co-learners with youth in this regard. Rather than being a sage-on-a-stage, adult leaders are often a "guide-by-my-side."

Second, the theological framework of faith-based organizing is a socially engaged spirituality shaped by "a biblical foundation, an eschatological orientation, [and] a political responsibility."[2] In contrast to Christian education and youth ministry that exhorts youth to go out and witness to God's reign in the world, leaving them to figure it out on their own, faith-based YCO groups concretely and corporately practice the presence of God's reign in their communities. Through instruction and immersion, young people practice the presence of God, particularly in disinvested, impoverished, and crime-ridden inner cities and in blighted rural areas. Youth appropriate a biblical spirituality with feet rather than a disembodied spirituality with wings.

Third, *YCO uses participatory action research, critical pedagogy, and popular education methods to equip youth in their ministries.* These approaches prepare teenagers with affective, cognitive, and enactive skills needed to effect personal, social, and structural transformation in their neighborhoods, institutions, and communities. Echoing approaches described by David White in this volume, YCO involves youth in a cycle of participatory action, informed by the educational work of such luminaries as Paulo Freire, Henry Giroux, Ira Shor, and bell hooks.[3] We will return to this cycle later in the chapter.

Fourth, YCO engages with youth in relation to the several overlapping institutions that form their lives. The premise is that young people form Christian self-identity as they practice their faith in the context of multiple, overlapping communities, institutions, and settings, not strictly within church youth ministry programs (or Christian families); therefore, the focus of youth ministry is the overall context in which youth form their sense of self over time. While participation in institution-based formal settings—such as Sunday school and other forms of church-located youth ministry—is decisively important for young people, formation of self-identity and exploration of vocation actually occur over a span of time within multiple, overlapping contexts.

These interrelated, interdependent community settings are what sociologists refer to as "mediating institutions." Included among them are families, churches, schools, libraries, youth clubs, sports organizations, youth-serving nonprofits (such as Campfire, Scouts, YMCA), along with *local* government, judicial, health, and business entities. Such settings provide a buffer zone between life as more privately lived in bonds of interpersonal and familial relationships, and life as more publicly lived in larger systems of government and corporate business. The mediating role is particularly significant in relation to larger systems, which, however remote, play a decisive role in shaping daily realities, functioning, and malfunctioning of young people and their families.

Fifth, YCO creates community partnerships. A major YCO strategy is to draw local mediating institutions together into collaborative, multi-sector partnerships that ideally include representatives from civic, government, and business sectors of society. Through the power generated by collective action, marginalized young people around the country (and globe) are transforming the public culture of conversation in their local communities and regions. The collective power, participation, and input of adolescents from the underside can help ensure that the agenda of their cities and various youth-serving institutions are imbued with greater justice for teenagers who live outside the dominant circles of power.

The Power of Deep Listening

The agenda for faith-based organizing groups comes directly from grassroots young people themselves, not from adult sponsors or teachers, youth ministers, youth steering councils, denominational youth manuals, or prepackaged curriculum resources. The agenda is generated from deep listening in scores of conversations, considered to be the mainstay of youth organizing. Youth organizers invite their peers into intentional, focused dialogue, the nature and content of which is carefully elicited and guided by the organizers. They hold conversations with diverse persons, not simply young people in the organizing group. The conversations require artful, balanced guidance, for they are neither formalized interviews nor casual conversations over a Coke.

In one-on-one dialogues with peers, normally thirty to forty-five minutes, the youth leader invites another young person to articulate and reflect on concerns in their workaday world that provoke a sense of urgency or intense passion. The youth try to get beneath surface conversation and evoke that which is most fully alive in their fellow human beings. They want to know something about the hurts, hungers, and hopes pulsing within their friends and peers, and the extent to which these peers feel compelled, energized, angry, or motivated to do something about their life situations and that of others. Far from being mere tools for information gathering, the dialogues are intended as genuine efforts to connect with and care for others and to build enduring relationships.

In one-on-one dialogues with adults, youth organizers engage with teachers, school principals, school board members, pastors, mentors, mayors, elected city officials, parents (theirs and others'), and a broad range of business and civic leaders. While these conversations may elicit new issues, they are conducted especially to further reflection on youth-identified agendas from the peer conversations. Dialogue with various adult stakeholders is a way to illumine issues from other points of view and to build enduring, collaborative, public relationships.

The one-on-one dialogues are considered so important that youth receive training in how to conduct them. In role-plays carried out in front of other group members, youth practice skills associated with "deep listening." Role-playing is followed by debriefing, evaluation, and critique, through which group members aim to help one another improve listening skills. In reflecting on the art of deep listening, youth meditate on their own previous experience, utilizing questions such as: When have I personally felt most deeply listened to and cared for? What was the impact? When and where have I offered to listen deeply and attentively with another? What obstacles to listening do I face, and what can I do to overcome them and to deepen my capacity for listening? What happens during, and as a result of, encounters when deep listening occurs?

From Deep Listening to Participatory Action Research

Deep listening is the mainstay of YCO, but it leads into participatory action research. Young people engage in studying a situation, identifying the cutting issues, and developing and implementing responses. The basic flow follows a common pattern, though the movements are intertwined.

Sharing Personal and Social Narratives

The heart of participatory action research is the sharing of life stories, and the typical locus is "house meetings." Groups of young people gather in church basements, living rooms, local clubhouses, and other youth hangouts to share their personal and social narratives. Here teenagers assure one another of a mutually respectful, confidential environment where they can freely share concerns, worries, hurts, and hopes for themselves and for their families, neighborhoods, schools, and workplaces. They give one another space to talk about the experiences and ongoing realities that exert pressure on their lives and on the lives of their families. They talk about their passions and dreams, what they envision, and what it will take to get there. This includes naming obstacles that must be removed or reduced to secure the full flourishing that God intends.

When young people open up and share their life stories in respectful, safe settings, they begin to realize that, in their perplexity, pain, and passion, they are not alone. As they attend to their multiple narratives, they also begin to detect underlying patterns that connect their experiences–previously thought to be unique or idiosyncratic–to the stories and experiences of their peers in similar situations.

Engaging in Critical Social Analysis

When youth probe into their stories, they engage in critical social analysis. They begin to grasp the connection and dialectic between individual and collective reality, between personal and social transformation. The personal becomes the political, and the political is seen to have intensely personal bearings. Stimulated by reflective inquiry and group discussion, young people see how their own lives are played on a larger stage, and how their individual stories intertwine with larger ones. The stories are mutually embedded, influencing the plotlines and outcomes of one another. Even the globalized world insinuates itself into their workaday world, and that of their family and neighborhood, as when the company that employs their parents shuts down and relocates overseas, sending the local economy and their families into a downward economic spiral. Pervasive economic, social, and political forces play a hidden and not-so-hidden hand in the story of where they have been and where they are going: many to jail, a few to Yale.

Engaging with Hurt and Hope

Often intertwined with critical analysis is the act of exploring hurt and hope. Helping adolescents tap into authentic and real Christian hope requires their tapping into the real hurt in their lives. When their pain and passion remain inward and unvoiced, their lives are mired in hurt, helplessness, and hopelessness. If their personal and socioeconomic worlds are to undergo radical transformation, they must grasp the surface symptoms and also the underlying roots of their hurts and hungers. This is the real meaning of "radical," a term from botany that means tracing or following the stem down to the actual root. Follow the pain; trace it down to its underlying roots. By attending to the greatest pressure points of pain in their individual and social lives, youth are enabled to trace it to its roots and to discern where the Spirit opens new potential for radical change. Personal insight and collective awareness often deepen in this step, opening toward transformation and redemption, healing and wholeness, as promised by the Gospel in which the spirituality of these young people is rooted.

Cutting Issues

After young people listen to the hurts and hopes of their peers through numerous one-on-one dialogues, along with a more limited series of house meetings, they cluster the themes and then prioritize, focus, and fashion the identified pain and problems into a realistic agenda. Groups devote considerable time and attention to narrowing amorphous problems, then framing them into specific, "winnable" issues. This is referred to as the skill of "cutting issues." This process pares youth concerns into realistic bite-size portions. If this is not done, the tendency is for youth to become overwhelmed with the enormity of social problems and to sink into a sea of despair and hopelessness.

The distinction made between *problems* and *issues* is that socioeconomic and political problems are so large-scale, amorphous, persistent, and slippery that groups do not know where to dig in, while issues are looming problems that have been scaled down to manageable size, brought into sharp focus, and made "actionable." Skyrocketing high school dropout rates, for example, is a large-scale social problem that forecloses the future of many students, especially youth of color, and burdens the economy. No matter how full of faith and passion they are, one group of teenagers cannot solve a problem of such magnitude. However, a youth group *can* collaborate with their local high school principal, school board members, and teachers to get college preparation courses included in their school's curriculum, along with intensive help for students through small learning communities. A faith-based youth group in Philadelphia did precisely that, and nearly tripled their high school's graduation rate!

Addressing Issues with Research and Action

After manageable issues have been identified, they are then further broken down into specific, sequential steps. Next, various *ad hoc* action research teams are formed to carry out background research, conduct interviews (with relevant power brokers and stakeholders), collect relevant data (including demographic statistics), brainstorm possible strategies, and choose the best option for addressing a given step. The teams bring recommendations to the collective group, and the group finalizes and carries out action plans calculated to guarantee winnable results. At every step along the way, and at the end of every meeting, the group conducts a reflective evaluation. By means of critical evaluation, members gain insight into themselves, the group functioning, the consequences of their actions (intended and unintended), and the possibility for more effective future meetings and more faithful actions approximating God's reign. The entire process of *participatory action research* is an ongoing, continuous cycle.

Young people whose families have been pushed to the underside of society often are so accustomed to being on the losing side of life that, to build self-confidence and hope, they need to begin with small victories achieved through small steps. For this reason, groups generally address initial issues that are amenable to direct action and are deemed to be easily *winnable.* After boosting their self-confidence and building their collective power, groups then proceed toward larger issues that have ever-widening spheres of complexity and influence.

The Personal Meets the Political in Albuquerque

From this general description of YCO, we move now to a case study of one example of YCO in Albuquerque, New Mexico. While the agenda for faith-based grassroots groups routinely emerges in the ongoing one-on-one conversations and house meetings, it is sometimes set in motion by a public crisis seen as salient to youth and their ongoing concerns. Such crises have their own antecedents and prehistory, but the crises themselves open opportunities to crack open *cultures of silence.* By way of their ongoing training, young people are ready to seize such moments when potential is heightened for untruths to be unmasked, false assumptions to be questioned, prejudicial policies and programs to be exposed, and the light of God's love and justice to be shined on the situation. Faith-based organizing operates on the premise that public crises must be embraced, heightened, focused, and sometimes even provoked as one step toward the redemption and transformation of socioeconomic, political (and hence personal and spiritual) realities.[4] Only by passing through disequilibrium and disorder can life be reordered in ways that more fully reflect the vision of God's reign in human history.[5]

YCO in Action

A public crisis presented itself to Chicano young people in Albuquerque, N.M., when security guards at a local shopping mall arrested a group of them and then banned them from stepping foot on the premises thereafter. In a thinly masked attempt to hide their prejudice, store proprietors at the mall underhandedly and unjustly used a local ordinance as the pretext for filing a legal complaint, which then led to the arrest. The ordinance prevents young people from congregating in public assembly without the presence of parents or guardians. While this is reasonable, store proprietors abused its intent. In response to the unjust arrest, Chicano youth in Albuquerque convened themselves, shared and reflected on their stories of pain and struggle, then strategized and organized a public outcry and action against specific racist actions and attitudes aimed at Chicanos, especially teenagers. Along with their parents and other supportive adults, the youth marched up and down the hallways of the shopping mall throwing brown dollars through the air to symbolize the revenue generated by youth of color in Albuquerque. They also held public rallies and undertook successful legal action against mall owners.

YCO in Context

Reflecting on this brief case, one sees quickly that *attention to context* is an important feature of faith-based youth organizing. In contrast to many youth ministry models that are, to varying degrees, decontextualized, disembodied, dehistoricized, individualistic, and generic, the ministry of faith-based organizing is place-based, situated, communal, and contextualized, while also being contemplative, interpersonal, and relational. Grassroots organizing affirms that "reality" differs for various people and groups, depending on their *social location,* which includes ethnicity, gender, and socioeconomic and geo-political circumstances. For example, the act of discerning vocational direction by middle-class and upper-middle-class young people involves questions and options that arise from the assumptive world of their social location. This is vastly different for young people living on the underside of society.

Consider the life of a teenager who lives in a home that has no food in the cabinets on some days, where heat and electricity are occasionally cut off in the winter, where siblings die from inadequate medical care, where filthy rats scurry across the floor at night, where gunshots whiz by or through the windows, where streetlights are shot out and never replaced, where abandoned structures are used as meth labs and crack houses, where unidentified dead bodies are occasionally found in back allies, where loved ones die in drive-by shootings, where less than one-fourth of teenagers graduate from high school, where adults hang out on porches and street corners because no jobs are available. For such young people, vocational questions are quite different from those of their middle- and upper-class counterparts. Their questions about "how I stay alive" are not simply existential and spiritual. They are literal.

Chicano young people in Albuquerque today cannot adequately understand their own personal stories of pain, deprivation, and struggle—nor the ongoing redemption and transformation of them—unless they see how their lives are conditioned by a larger story and animated by socioeconomic, political, and cultural forces *played out in specific, localized ways.* Historical and global forces are embedded in local events and conditions in Albuquerque and its environs. The history of Albuquerque and all of New Mexico is a story of outside forces seeking to colonize, dominate, and exploit native peoples and natural resources. Though people of color—the majority of the population—have paid the greatest price for this history, they have also developed traditions of resistance. As one of the most culturally diverse states, New Mexico's majority population includes Chicanos (indigenous Mexicans), Native Americans (especially Pueblo Indians whose ancestors have been in the region for many millennia), Mexican immigrants, and smaller African American and Asian/Pacific Islander populations. Albuquerque is a region of extremes that includes a host of wealthy high-tech headquarters and transnational corporations, alongside *colonias,*[6] such as Pajarito Mesa, which is a counterpart to the poorest neighborhoods in the two-thirds world. Youth of color are brought up in the crossfire of these cultural and economic forces.

Diversity in Faith-Based Youth Organizing

Before moving to conclusions and proposals, one more mark of YCO needs attention, namely its embrace of diversity. While high school cafeterias, congregations, and clubs are generally places where teenagers segregate by ethnicity, class, culture, and grade level, faith-based youth organizing groups are one of the few places in U.S. society in which adolescents seek out and celebrate diversity. Grassroots community organizations underscore equity across lines of gender, age, race, class, culture, denomination, theology, and sometimes faith traditions (with a few including Jewish youth).

Much of the social and political activism among young people in the U.S., especially on college campuses during the 1960s, was inspired by the philosophy of Saul Alinsky, considered to be the grandfather of faith-based grassroots organizing. The groups discussed in this chapter descend from the Alinsky tradition.[7] Trained in sociology and criminology at the University of Chicago, Alinsky began his work in the 1930s in squalid slum areas, which came to be known as "Back of the Yards," spawned by the meat-packing industries in Chicago (the focus of Upton Sinclair's *The Jungle*). In his studies of gang members, he concluded that much criminal activity owes at least part of its development to a sense of powerlessness and hopelessness that poverty breeds in young people.

Though Alinsky was politically left, it would be a mistake to over-identify the grassroots organizing tradition with liberal theology, for it is practiced by a broad spectrum of denominational and theological traditions. At the beginning of the twentieth century, evangelicals were among the Christians most active in multiethnic organizing efforts to unionize workers; end abuses of child labor; achieve women's suffrage; and end abusive treatment and squalid living conditions of poor, disenfranchised immigrants. In certain arenas today, this dimension of evangelical tradition is being recovered. Christians Supporting Community Organizing (CSCO) was founded in 1997 for the express purpose of enlisting Evangelical, Holiness, and Pentecostal congregations in the faith-based organizing movement growing across the U.S. and around the globe.

Faith-based youth organizing is also geographically diverse, taking place in urban, suburban, and rural settings across the U.S. For example, Voices of Youth organizes youth in grades nine through twelve who live within an impoverished two-county rural region in central North Carolina. Youth United for Change draws together Latino, African American, Asian, and Caucasian youth from four high schools in the predominantly minority, low-income North Philadelphia area. Hope Street Youth Development (HSYD) is a grassroots youth group located in a predominantly African American neighborhood in the northeast part of the large Midwestern city of Wichita. The diversity among and within YCO efforts is part of what they have to contribute to reconceptualizing youth ministry. We turn now to that question.

Subversive Spirituality in Ministry at the Margins

The ministry and spirituality of young people involved in faith-based grassroots organizing is counterintuitive to the notion that ski trips and pizza parties are the best way to attract teenagers. Faith-based YCO efforts resist the temptation to "McDonaldize" ministry into fun, quick, and easy weekend "McEvents." Moreover, they expose and dispel the myth that vital youth ministry requires a dynamic young "pied piper" whose job is to magnetize adolescents into the church, where they are seen and treated as *recipients of* rather than as *participants in* ministry. In comparison to YCO forms of ministry, many mainline churches trivialize the interests and capacities of adolescents, especially for theologically reflective social praxis. What is needed is a form of ministry with young people that supports subversive spirituality at the margins. Such ministry will have several prominent qualities, which I develop here.

Holistic

An overriding feature of faith-based youth organizing is its holistic spirituality. It generally relates three key dimensions of Christian spiritual formation: *orthodoxis* ("right beliefs"), *orthopraxis* ("right actions"), and *orthokardia* ("right affections"). Much mainline youth ministry, by contrast, latches onto one or another of these dimensions as primary. Indeed, the history of Christian formation is full of fierce debate as to whether the affective (*orthokardia,* or "heart"), cognitive (*orthodoxis,* or "head"), or enactive (*orthopraxis,* or "hands") dimension of faith is of primary importance.[8]

The "great divide" is often expressed in debates between those who emphasize Christian formation as promoting right believing *(orthodoxis)* and those who emphasize right living in the world *(orthopraxis).* The former stresses Christian beliefs and doctrinal content, often emphasizing biblical knowledge and salvation through Jesus Christ. The latter stresses emancipatory praxis, often in solidarity with excluded and marginalized peoples. Many practical theologians and religious educators do, however, hold these together. Thomas Groome's "shared praxis" approach to ministry is seen as a way to witness to and participate in the reign of God, which is breaking into human history through the person and work of Jesus.[9] This approach is theologically informed activity that involves mutuality with peoples on the underside of society.

Another major emphasis in Christian spiritual formation is *orthokardia,* promoting a heartfelt, experiential sense of God's personal presence and activity in one's life. Typically, one Person or another of the Trinity is emphasized. In this approach, Christians engage in historic devotional practices aimed to cultivate mystical, spiritual, experiential dimensions of faith. This is the *major* (but not exclusive) thrust of the contemplative approach to youth ministry currently growing in popularity.

Biblical portraits of spirituality and faith assume all three dimensions to be equally important, with *no one of them elevated above or viewed as logically prior to the others.* Nevertheless, false wedges are driven between the dimensions, as well as false wedges between *divine agency* and *human agency.* If Christian formation involves learning how, over the course of a lifetime, to participate more fully and faithfully in *what God is doing through Jesus Christ* in and for the world, these debates are false in their dichotomizing. Even when these three dimensions of Christian spirituality *are* acknowledged to be equally important, however, one usually predominates, supported by either *linear* logic or *pie-slice* logic.

In linear logic, the "journey inward" is declared to precede the "journey outward." This is not supported biblically; nevertheless, some youth ministry models are structured on this very premise. The epithet misleadingly assumes that engagement in acts of justice, service, and mercy is the *consequence* of having cultivated attentiveness to God through contemplative prayer and related devotional practices. The biblical witness reverses this logic, however, and claims that time spent in the presence of the least and last in society is a *precondition* for entering into authentic worship and relationship with God.[10] As Jürgen Moltmann writes: "the kind of thinking that makes distinctions...between inner life and external reality...reflects the sickness of division" that Jesus came to heal.[11]

In pie-slice logic, the various dimensions of spirituality are compartmentalized, as though the aims and purposes of engaging in each are distinct rather than directed toward the selfsame ends: deeper attentiveness to and participation in the life of the triune God, or involvement *in who God is* and *what God does.* Bible study is the usual fare, with service or mission projects as occasional events. Contemplative prayer practices and retreats are altogether different occasions, with fellowship activities peppered along the way.[12] These diverse activities are lined up side by side, like individual books on a shelf or, to use another image, like slices of a pie (which can only be dished out one slice at a time). No wonder there is so much compartmentalization between "Sunday" and "Monday" living, and disconnection between faith and life. Christians have difficulty seeing how the pieces are integrated in their workaday world.

Centered on the Presence of Jesus

Another contribution of YCO to the practice of subversive spirituality with youth is its focus on Jesus. The church would do well to emphasize its unique spiritual emphasis on *the presence of Jesus.* In his book, *The Church in the Power of the Spirit,* Moltmann names settings—known in some church traditions as *means of grace*—in which believers are assured and promised the *efficacious, experiential presence of Jesus.*[13] These include settings where the community: (a) shares bread at the Lord's table (1 Cor. 11:24–25); (b) proclaims the good news and opens scripture together; (c) encounters the poor, excluded, discarded, and marginalized (Mt. 25:31–46); and (d) experiences the final consummation and renewal of all things, now being actively inserted into the present (Mt. 28:20; Jn. 6:39–40; Rev. 21:1–4; 2 Pet. 3:13).[14] The last setting refers to the concrete practice of eschatological hope.[15] Moltmann contends, "Hope finds in Christ not only a consolation *in* suffering, but also the protest of the divine promise *against* suffering."[16] Christian spirituality is thus inherently subversive; it involves "living in the light not of the way things *are,* but of the way things *will be* in God's future."[17]

Disruptive

A third mark of subversive spirituality in youth ministry is disruption, a theme familiar to theology, in which religious experience often disrupts the status quo. James Loder contends that faith arises in, and depends on, relational encounters with witnesses of faith, preeminently encounters with Jesus.[18] In contrast to a developmental focus on continuity, Loder underscores the *event* quality of faith as it is practiced in historical situations in which people seek to participate faithfully in God's own faithfulness. This is disruptive. Walter Brueggemann advances a similar notion. Biblical narratives are interested in believers choosing a particular *faith stance* within a given historical situation.[19] These often run counter to status quo socioeconomic or political arrangements; thus, they cause upheaval, wrenching transitions, and painful transformations (such as the civil rights movement). Brueggemann says, "The struggle to embrace covenantal modes of life is the story of faith development in Israel. That struggle is acute because covenantal practice is inevitably *subversive* of other modes of life. Maturation then is characteristically *subversive.*"[20] From Brueggemann's perspective, biblical narratives portray *mature spirituality as subversive spirituality.* From this perspective, spiritual formation will nurture in adolescents the courage to critique and live outside dominant systems of *empire.* Spiritual formation empowers them to construct alternative systems to those that give advantage the few to the disadvantage of the many. Faith *disrupts* business as usual.

Standing in contrast to this biblical view of faith is the popular conception that, in light of the magnitude of perils posed by contemporary culture, coupled with predictable developmental stressors, adolescents need to be equipped to offset the *risk factors* in their lives by accumulating *protective factors,* faith being one of these. Attendant to this idea is subtle classism. Middle- and upper-middle-class youth are told that faith is the protective *human capital* and *social capital* that helps them navigate successfully through adolescence. "You've got the whole world at your feet" is the mantra they hear. Low-income, "at-risk" youth are encouraged in faith for its *inhibitive* function; it is a mechanism of social control. Thus, research is done to correlate faith with reduced rates of juvenile recidivism, criminal and gang-related behavior, and risky behaviors, such as alcohol and drug use, sexual activity, and truancy. Such perspectives reveal no trace of faith as lived, for example, by Dr. Martin Luther King Jr.—a Spirit-led faith so radical and countercultural that the Good News manifests itself as disruptive and subversive. This disruptive vision animates grassroots young people in their ministries at the margins.

The formation of a full and integrated Christian self-identity requires young people to be immersed in *holistic* practices of spirituality. This is not merely a matter of engaging the affective, enactive, and cognitive dimensions of teaching-learning. Rather, young people are initiated into the plenitude of meeting places with Jesus—through worship, breaking bread, encountering the underside of society, prayer and meditation, and acts of sociopolitical resistance against forces that thwart God's promised future. The congregation assumes responsibility to engage growing young people in practices *recalibrated* to ever-widening spheres of complexity and influence, depth and breadth. These practices are then integrated into larger strategies, such as those found in faith-based youth community organizing.

Open to Encountering Jesus on the Underside

Another mark of subversive spirituality is that it opens people to encounter Jesus on the underside of social hierarchies. One group of middle-class young people met on the first Saturday of each month in poverty-stricken West Dallas, building relationships with poor residents and working with them on projects, such as making kitchen tables for recent immigrants and building extra rooms on tiny, wood-frame houses. After a brown-bag lunch, usually outdoors, the group read scripture, engaged in biblical-theological reflection on their engagements, asked critical questions about what it means to encounter Jesus on the underside of society, probed why infrastructures are allowed to crumble in one part of the city but not in others, and reflected on future action. Then, they worshiped, prayed, and shared the eucharist.

What images of God are embedded in the hidden curriculum when prayer, meditation, and other devotional practices are introduced at retreat centers, amidst shady pine trees, with the sound of silence broken only by whippoorwills and the hum of cicadas? Lacking funds for such weekend retreats, low-income teenagers find solace in God portrayed as *the habitation of justice.* What does Sabbath rest mean to teenagers who are major breadwinners in their families, struggling to graduate from high school while holding a patchwork of low-wage jobs after school, evenings, and weekends? In middle-class mainline churches, such cases are isolated exceptions; in poorer neighborhoods, they are the norm. Given that scripture writers equally emphasize *labor* and *rest,* biblical spirituality is aborted when we help advantaged, well-employed people find rest, but neglect to help disadvantaged, unemployed people find labor.[21] Just as rest needs to be adequate, so does labor; minimum wages are not living wages.

Young people can gain a profound sense of the purpose, power, and presence of Jesus when they contemplate or pray the "Jesus Prayer"[22] while sounds of police sirens, barking guard dogs, boom boxes and hip-hop, shouts and wails of children, and pimped-out cars with loud exhausts sound in the background. Where the "blooming buzz" insinuates itself into prayer may be where Jesus wants attention drawn anyway. For middle-class youth, the eucharist is more deeply saturated in meaning when celebrated arm in arm with marginalized poor persons within the context of their neighborhood! Authentic witness to the Gospel, holistic experience of spirituality, formation of mature Christian self-identity, faithful participation in *missio Dei,* and revitalized youth ministry depend on spending more time where pathways to Jesus come together and form a crossroads. At these intersections, youth find the abundance of life promised and secured through the life and ministry, death and resurrection of Jesus Christ.

Conclusion

Churches have been investing much energy, time, and money to revitalize youth ministry in the United States. One implication of this chapter is that, in this "troubling world," renewal efforts will inevitably be shortsighted and theologically thin if they do not include meaningful encounters between youth in the mainstream and youth at the margins. A major task of Christian theology—especially Christian eschatology—is to help believers see human history from the perspective of those on the underside (Mt. 25: 31–46). Joerg Rieger expresses this well:

> Aware of the blind spots of the dominant perspective, the view "from below" introduces a critical element: Nobody experiences more severely what's wrong with the way things are than those who are crushed by these things. We need this point of view in order to evaluate where things have gone wrong and where *we* need to change.[23]

If ministry is animated by a spirituality that disrupts the status quo, and if we in mainline churches *are* the status quo, then the spirituality of those who dare journey from center to margin will be subversive. The gospels say that we cannot see the realm of God unless we look from the undersides and margins. This perspective reverses *colonialist* and *neocolonialist* approaches to mission and ministry. All authentic spirituality, all authentic practical theology, all authentic Christian witness, begins in such *reversal.*

In recent years, works attending to interracial, inter-ethnic, and intercultural issues have increased in youth ministry. However, many publications still fail to take adequate account of the radically diverse population of adolescents in the U.S., especially neglecting issues of *class difference.* Differences in people require different approaches to youth ministry and spiritual formation. Further, every approach to youth ministry and spirituality is laden with assumptions about race, class, culture, and theological perspective. Remembering this is itself subversive. What is offered in this chapter is an invitation into subversive ministry in which diverse approaches are welcomed, but always with an accent on holistic, Jesus-centered, disruptive, and margin-walking spirituality.

11

With New Eyes to See

Helping Youth Develop Religious
Imagination to Encounter Holy Ground

CLAIRE BISCHOFF

My interest in identity was piqued my inaugural year of teaching middle school religious studies, the same year that I first saw *Merchants of Cool*, a Frontline documentary. In it, journalist Douglas Rushkoff hypothesizes that, in media and advertising, the representations of youth have been collapsed into a prevalent stereotype for each gender. Young women are portrayed as "midriffs"–perfect bodies valued solely as sexual objects. Young men are depicted as "mooks"–jokers who are only interested in bodily functions and sex.[1] Since the complexity of my students' lives contrasted sharply with these one-dimensional caricatures, I wondered how the students' engagement with media culture affected their understanding of themselves, their relationships with others, and their places in the world.

While identity has garnered much attention in relation to education, Mary Elizabeth Moore bemoans the preoccupation with identity to the neglect of imagination.[2] This neglect is surprising to her, since she understands imagination as crucial for both education and identity. Imagination enables people to see the world and to envisage alternative worlds, to know ourselves as we have been and are now, and to dream of who we might be in the future.[3] Also heralding the importance of imagination, Maxine Greene writes, "Of all our cognitive capacities, imagination is the one that permits us to give credence to alternative realties. It allows us to break with the taken for granted, to set aside familiar distinctions and definitions."[4] Imagination helps us reinterpret past experiences in light of the present and envisioned future, make new connections between seemingly divergent realities, ground our hope, and empathize with others' realities. Without imagination, we might always be who we have been, and change would be slower in coming in the world.

Imagination is not a singular perspective, for many imaginative lenses are available to us to view our lives and world. As consumers in a capitalist democracy, we learn to see with economic and political imagination. As inheritors of the legacy of Freud in a largely technocratic society, our vision is shaped by psychological and scientific lenses. Those of us who work with youth in faith communities have another crucial perspective to offer: that of religious imagination. Maria Harris describes religious consciousness as "one that sees the holiness in things, the sacred in things, and the teaching capacity in things of the earth."[5] Cultivating religious imagination with youth reaps a benefit that is common to all forms of imagination in that we are enabled "to see more in our experience, to hear on normally unheard frequencies, to become conscious of what daily routines have obscured, what habit and convention have suppressed."[6] Religious imagination can foster the sort of wide-awake and creative vision that is crucial for the identity work of youth. More importantly, from a Christian perspective, religious imagination invites young people to recognize the holy ground of their lives, to see God working through, in, and with themselves, others, and the world. Inviting youth to envision transcendence in the everyday, to contemplate the more of their experience, and to believe in God's promises for the future summons them to imagine the world in radical, transformative ways.

In this chapter I consider questions of identity that adolescents face, as well as visions of education that promote imagination, recognizing that these topics have rarely been reflected on together, even though imagination is a critical component of identity work. I begin by identifying some of the difficulties youth face in their identity work, particularly in naming an identity that is enduring yet adaptable, drawing on media culture in thoughtful and responsible ways, and making identity decisions when adults are largely absent from their worlds. In response to these challenges and based on work I have done with young people in diverse Christian settings, I propose three responses that address the identity challenges and assist young people to develop religious imagination: story sharing and theological reflection on life stories, media viewing and theological reflection on popular culture, and meditative practices.

Identity Challenges for Youth

Adults who study and work with youth have relied for decades on Erik Erikson's assertion that the process of discerning one's identity is the normative psychosocial crisis of adolescence.[7] Despite challenges to Erikson's normative claims and increased attention to how identity changes and develops throughout life, what does seem to hold true, at least for most

adolescents in the United States, is that questions of identity are vital.[8]
Youth may question who they are and how this present identity relates
to who they have been in the past and to who they will be in the future.
Becoming more aware of others' perspectives, they may be concerned
about how to present themselves in different settings and how to reconcile
their own self-image with how others understand them. While youth face
a multitude of difficulties today, I highlight in this section three challenges
to forming identity.

Promise of Narrative for Naming an Enduring yet Adaptable Identity

One identity challenge confronting youth is developing a sense of
themselves that is coherent over time but is also flexible enough to adapt
to maturation and change. According to Erikson, meaningful cultural
ideologies to which youth can commit themselves are an essential ingredient
for developing an enduring identity. However, Erikson wrote in a modern
world in which ideologies still were invested with power. Youth in this new
millennium live in an increasingly postmodern world, a world in which
"no schemes, let alone systems, seem to be available that could hold the
increasing varieties of human experiences together."[9] Due to a lack of
meaningful cultural ideologies, youth may struggle to make the sort of
long-lasting ideological commitments that undergird a durable identity.

Youth striving to name enduring aspects of their identities also
experience an increasingly global and diverse world, a world in which
they are likely to interact with people of different religions, ethnicities,
political persuasions, and sexual orientations. Further, modern technology
enables young people to be immersed more fully in communications and
relations, resulting in what Kenneth Gergen terms "social saturation,"
or the self being infused and shaped by multiple others.[10] In contexts of
diversity and social saturation, youth may be overwhelmed by the plethora
of identity options and prematurely settle on an identity, thus foreclosing
future identity development. Conversely, adolescents may be attracted to
the idea that they can be different people in each new surrounding. The
danger here is that identity becomes totally diffuse, a danger that may be
particularly acute for young women.[11]

For naming an enduring yet adaptable identity, "'narrative' may prove
a helpful metaphor for understanding the nature of identities," since a
narrative sense of self allows for continuity and integration at the same time
as plurality and malleability.[12] Narrative identity is generated by reading
and interpreting one's life history and telling one's story. Here integrity is
not the result of sameness across different environments, but of integrating
aspects of identity within the framework of one's life story. As religious
educator Heinz Streib explains, "Narrative identity, in a single thesis, invites
selfhood and subjectivity, it invites particularity and pluralism, it invites
subversiveness and difference."[13] Narrative identity preserves particularity

and pluralism because it arises from the multiple and unique experiences of the individual, and it is open to difference and subversion since it can always be reinterpreted and retold. The narrative self retains continuity in the form of one's life story, but it is never a once-and-for-all identity, since it is open to revision in light of new experiences or reinterpretation of past experiences.

While narrative may be promising for youth striving to name an enduring yet adaptable identity, many youth are not encouraged to tell the stories of themselves. This is particularly true for young women. Studying the connection between women's ways of knowing and self-concepts, Mary Belenky, Blythe Clinchy, Nancy Goldberger, and Jill Tarule found that many women had difficulty naming themselves, a problem compounded by the reality that "all women grow up having to deal with historically and culturally engrained definitions of femininity and womanhood—one common theme being that women, like children, should be seen and not heard."[14] Much attention has been paid to the phenomenon of lost voices among young—usually white, heterosexual, middle-class—girls in adolescence; but the voices of youth who do not fit the normative ideal are also lost through marginalization and criminalization.[15] Further, we need to heed how *all* adolescents are silenced by dominant cultural narratives that celebrate the ideal of youth without taking into account the particularity of young people's lives.

Promise of Media Engagement for Relating Identity to Culture

A second challenge to identity work is engaging with media. It is no secret that adolescents watch a lot of television, many from the comfort and privacy of their own bedrooms.[16] Entire networks, such as the WB and MTV, target youth. A simple search on Google reveals that television watching is associated with obesity, violence, intimate sexual behavior, substance abuse, poor grades at school, and a short attention span, to name the most prevalent negative correlations. Whatever the actual effects of media culture, young people need ways to engage media thoughtfully and responsibly.

Those who work with youth are concerned about the impact of media culture on identity development, although no consensus has been reached about the nature of that influence.[17] Two opposing opinions exist: one worried that youth have too many identity choices, the other alarmed that identity options are overly limited by media culture. As a representative of the former group, Kenneth Gergen is troubled by the "experience of the vertigo of unlimited multiplicity," what he names "multiphrenia," and how this experience is amplified in a media culture.[18] For Gergen, both increased communication with real people and engagement with media culture contribute to a socially saturated self, since "media figures do enter significantly into people's personal lives."[19] To make his case, Gergen argues that if religious adherents are influenced by their meaningful relationships with figures such as Jesus and Buddha, who are no longer palpably present in these relationships, then consumers may also have relationships with media figures that shape them. As the self becomes inundated with real and fictional others, the number of "oughts" multiplies—that is, demands on what one should be doing and who one is in relation to these other selves. As young people plug into television, the Internet, and iPods, they may experience a dizzying array of relationships and have difficulty finding themselves in the mix.

At the other end of the spectrum are a number of religious educators who argue that media culture leaves adolescents with less subjectivity to form their identities. Young people are forced to accept an identity from an increasingly narrow range of options presented by the media. Even more problematic, the identities from which they can choose often do not speak to their lived reality, as mass media culture champions dramatic aspects of youth culture and idolizes adolescents as highly sexualized beings.[20] As argued in *Merchants of Cool,* adolescents see a lowest common denominator image of themselves reflected through media culture, thus limiting the imaginative possibilities for their identities.

Religious educator and media scholar Mary Hess is less pessimistic about how media affects identity development. According to Hess, many people have an instrumental view of how media influences people. This view assumes that producers create media with a particular message, which is then transported in various forms to consumers, who receive the exact message that producers intended. Finding this instrumental view outdated, Hess draws on postmodern media scholarship to provide a more nuanced vision of how people consume media:

> Postmodern media scholarship suggests that mass media are best described as naturalized aspects of our cultural environment, raw materials we use in shaping our identities, our relationships, and our communities. Rather than being reliably produced and predictably consumed, mass media "texts" provide space for creative negotiation and even resistance between the author of a given media "text," the receiver of that text, and the context in which the text is produced and consumed.[21]

In this understanding, media culture provides material from which adolescents can choose to narrate their identity, but it does not dictate identity. In her study of young women's use of media culture, Bettina Fritzsche found that adolescents utilize media culture as a toolbox from which to take what they need for crafting their own identities.[22] Instead of demonizing media culture, it may be better to conceptualize it in this way. Thus, the adult mentors' roles are to help youth gain the critical thinking skills to choose salutary and appropriate tools from the box. For those in

Christian faith communities, this may be similar to helping youth develop hermeneutical skills to read biblical texts with a critical eye.

The promise of a cultural toolbox becomes even more important if identity is understood from a narrative perspective. Stories provide orientation for our lives, and much of our self-understanding is embedded in the narratives of our cultural, social, political, ethnic, and religious groups.[23] As Alasdair MacIntyre writes, what we are "able to do and say intelligibly as an actor is deeply affected by the fact that we are never more (and sometimes less) than the co-authors of our own narratives... We enter upon a stage which we did not design and we find ourselves part of an action that was not of our making."[24] While the stories that orient human lives traditionally have been the meta-narratives of religion and culture, in a postmodern age when the validity of these meta-narratives is challenged, people may need to draw upon other narrative resources, such as media culture. Thus an alternative and potentially more useful way of framing the question of how media influences adolescents is to ask how the narratives presented through media culture inform young people's life narratives and how we can assist youth in drawing on media narratives in salutary ways.

Promise of Willing Listeners for Doing Identity Work

A third challenge for youth is to tell their stories in a fast-paced, individualistic culture while caring and committed adults are largely absent. Many have written about the dominant individualism in Western cultures and particularly in the United States; less has been written to address the influence on youth. Although they specifically interrogate cultural discourses of girlhood and female identity, Sinikka Aapola, Marnina Gonick, and Anita Harris discuss this prevalent Western identity discourse of the twenty-first century. This neoliberal discourse of individualization "promotes a social world where the individual is fully self-responsible."[25] In this discourse, youth are what they make of themselves, which becomes problematic for those young men and women who cannot simply be whoever they want to be because of structural factors that affect and limit their life choices. Aapola and her colleagues explain:

> Embedded in the concept [of individualization] is a sense that a life of success and happiness is within reach of girls [and boys] who learn the skills and/or have the characteristics necessary for continued self-invention. The constraints of gender, race, class, sexuality, disability, and ethnicity on this bright future is covered over by the suggestion that an individual can overcome all with the right attitude and drive.[26]

Young people are held responsible for making the correct choice about higher education, taking advantage of job growth by utilizing technological skills, and reinventing themselves to fit new labor markets.

When the individual alone is accountable, failure is understood solely as the individual's fault without regard for meaningful cultural constraints. While many youth "enjoy greater flexibility in imagining their life trajectories," they have to balance choice and risk with minimal structural supports.[27]

Compounding the limitations of the neoliberal choice biography is the fact that many adolescents do not have adult conversation partners to support them in their identity work. According to journalist Patricia Hersch, ours is an era when adolescents "are more isolated and more unsupervised than other generations," making them, in effect, "a tribe apart" without much guidance from adults.[28] Based on three years of observing eight adolescents in one United States town, Hersch concludes that many adults are not willing to meet teenagers where they are. However, she did find that youth were eager to talk when an adult made time to listen.

While we might expect faith communities to be places in which adults and youth actively listen to each other, this is often not the case. As David White notes, youth are frequently marginalized in faith communities, both spatially, as youth rooms are relegated to basements or eliminated to address space shortages, and ministerially, as youth are freed to have dances while adults do the serious work of the church.[29] Unfortunately, when adults do attempt to interact with youth, it is often to talk *at* them rather than to attend to their stories. We decide what we think youth need to know about the faith tradition and pass on this requisite knowledge in an instrumental fashion. Further, as White articulates, youth ministry "has undergone a seduction or abstraction from its own sense of place," that is, it has shifted attention from specific youth in living communities to a cohort approach to youth utilizing impersonal, nationally developed curriculum.[30] Utilizing generic curriculum may implicitly inform youth that we are not attending to their particular needs and experiences.

Beyond being marginalized in faith communities, youth often do not receive any assistance in linking their life experiences and choices with their religious tradition and identity. Church becomes an obligatory Sunday activity, divorced from school, family, friendships, romantic relationships, and media culture. Based on expansive survey and interview data, Christian Smith found that, while many teens *said* that religion was important in their lives, little evidence in their interviews supported this claim.[31] Some interviewees even affirmed outright that religion had nothing to do with the rest of their lives. If youth struggle to connect religion and the rest of their lives, that is probably because we are not inviting youth to discuss the rest of their lives in the context of the faith community.

Facing the reality of adults' absence from their lives, youth are probably doing the best they can, relying on peer groups to aid them in discovering what it means to be young women and men in our society. For instance, in their ethnographic study of gender identity performance in female friendship groups, Pamela Bettis, Debra Jordan, and Diana Montgomery found that the girls' emphasis on loyalty and relationships created a safe base from which to play with a variety of female identities.[32] Similarly, in her research on gender identity narratives with junior high students, Marnina Gonick found that research space provided the young women "with an opportunity to ask each other questions about their experiences, to explore sameness and differences, as well as to check, compare, share, and make meaning together of this experience."[33] The power of peer groups both to challenge and to affirm our self-narratives is avowed by feminist theologians and pastoral caregivers, who recognize that women's groups help women resist and reshape destructive personal and cultural messages about female identity.[34]

With New Eyes to See:
Developing Religious Imagination with Youth

The three identity challenges I named above—narrating an enduring identity that is adaptable to difference, drawing on media culture thoughtfully and responsibly, and doing identity work with listening peers and adults—are all thwarted by limited vision or a lack of imagination. In this section, I introduce three responses to these identity challenges that cultivate the religious imagination of young people—story sharing and theological reflection on life narratives, engaging with and reflecting theologically on media culture, and meditative practices. Not only do these responses invite youth to see beyond the givens of their world, thus invoking the ability to imagine the world as it is not yet, but they also induce youth to grasp the world through theological, sacramental eyes. In other words, youth are encouraged to practice seeing how God is working in and through their lives and the world. By inviting youth to employ religious imagination in faith communities and in concert with their daily experiences, we support youth in encountering the holy ground of our world and their lives.

Sharing and Reflecting Theologically on Life Narratives

The first response is to provide youth with what Carol Lakey Hess calls "safe houses" within which they can share their life stories.[35] Dori Baker has done this with girlfriend theology, and I have done it in the Stories of Gender project.[36] Both of these projects involve meeting with small groups of young women to share and reflect on their stories. While my project aims specifically to discover how girls construct female identity, what the young women told me in their exit interviews reveals the importance of story sharing for youth ministry.

The participants spoke of the story sharing groups as a novel opportunity to reflect on their stories in a formal setting. Alexa felt the experience was special "because I never had a chance to talk to anybody about my experience, and it was exciting to hear feedback on what people thought about it." Lauren expressed the young women's appreciation for having an adult take interest in their life stories. She said, "People actually care [about young people] that are old, kind of like you…it's nice to know that you actually care what teenage girls think." Lauren also valued knowing that other young women shared her experiences: "It's not just you going through this and you're not the only one who's ever gone through the same thing. There are other girls as well, and you can come together and talk about it without just having people look down upon you."

In addition to appreciating good listening, the young women found the story sharing groups to be opportunities for healing. Being able to disclose the story of a broken friendship helped Idana become "calmer about the situation." When I asked her if the story sharing model would be good for churches to adopt for working with youth, she suggested doing it once a month to "kind of help us get over some things that may be going on. Even if we're not over it, we'll be able to, maybe, start a process of getting over it." Thus, story sharing provides a space in which adolescents receive affirmation from both peers and adults and in which they may work toward healing by appropriating painful past events as part of their life story.

Beyond the opportunity to share and reflect on their stories, the young women welcomed the chance to think about where they saw God in each other's stories and their own lives. For many it was the first time they had been asked to think of God as present in their lived experience. Shantell remarked, "And with the whole relating it to God, like I said, I hadn't really thought in that type of perspective or what not, and it, you know, it kind of opened my mind to something different." This new perspective is something Emmy planned to continue to cultivate, saying, "It'll make me look for God more in things now than what I used to."

These reflections on God were not only mind-opening, but they also empowered the women to resist damaging cultural values, such as the stringent ideal for feminine beauty and identity. In one group, the participants worked together to articulate their belief in a God who knows the "true you" and loves you no matter what. Their exchange is worth quoting at length:

Claire: "Where did you hear or see God in Lauren's story?"
Bethany: "The whole part about being who you want to be and not what other people think you should be."
Emmy: "Yeah, and how you're his [God's] child, too."[37]
Bethany: "How you're his child no matter what. No matter what you do, no matter what you say, he will always love you."
Lauren: "And he sees you for who you really are and not–"
Bethany: "Not what people want you to be and what you think you should be. He sees you, who you really are, no matter what happens. And no matter what you do to yourself either or do to your body, with tattoos and piercing, he still sees who you really are."

Lauren: "He sees through all the bad things that you do. He sees deep down inside of you."

These young women drew on their religious tradition to counter destructive cultural scripts of femininity. In so doing, they echo the vision of cultural-defying, theologically grounded vocational identities described by Don Richter, Doug Magnuson, and Michael Baizerman.[38] The young women described a link between their experience of struggling to be accepted and their belief that God is the one person who always accepts them. Their reflections suggest that story sharing opens space for youth to imagine their life stories through a religious perspective; it encourages them to make connections between their theological beliefs and personal narratives. Further, it creates opportunities for people who work with youth to suggest other theological insights that might be useful to young people struggling to articulate a constructive identity.

In addition to using theological reflection to contest common cultural narratives, story sharing can also challenge a neoliberal, individualized notion of identity in which youth are told that they can choose to be whomever they want to be, spurning critical consciousness about how sexism, racism, classism, heterosexism, and ableism (among others) influence their identities.[39] In short, the sharing of life stories may be an important way to stimulate transformation. First, youth may come to recognize how structural and cultural factors influence identity as they hear commonalities among their stories. The discovery by Bethany, Emmy, and Lauren that they all felt pressure to measure up to an unattainable standard of beauty led them to discuss the possible origins of this standard and to brainstorm how they could support each other in resisting this pressure. Second, imagination may be stirred as young people encounter contradiction through the stories of others, contradictions that open new horizons for their own narratives. For instance, Shantell explained how her participation in the group led to a broader vision of gender identity:

I guess with everyone's input and their stories and...and their perception of what it means to be a girl, [this] has actually, I guess, broadened...broadened my idea of perceptions of what I thought it was to be a girl. So now instead of just having my ideas of what's a girl, I have, like, each and every one of their ideas, too.

Listening to others' stories can help us "cultivate multiple ways of seeing and multiple dialogues in a world where nothing stays the same."[40] Beyond the benefits story sharing has for promoting a more nuanced way of seeing the world, it also promotes empathetic relationships as we come to understand others, not through generalities, but through the specificity of their experiences. As Mary Elizabeth Moore stresses, respectful human relationships—ones that can be built through story sharing—undergird justice and peace in our world.[41]

Engaging with and Reflecting Theologically on Media Culture

A second response for ministry with youth is to discuss and reflect theologically on products from media culture, such as television shows, music videos, Web sites, and movies. In spring 2005, I studied the practice of television watching and how youth make meaning through this practice. I gathered weekly with a group of five young women at a local Methodist congregation to watch and discuss *The OC,* a popular Fox drama at the time.[42] The focus group discussions I conducted after the show each week attended to the portrayal of romantic relationships, sexuality, and sexual behavior. I learned two important lessons through the lively process. First, simply by talking with the young women about how sexuality and romance were portrayed on the show, I came to understand their sexual worldviews better. The conversations helped me imagine their social and romantic worlds through their eyes and logic. Second, I discovered a nearly complete disconnection between the young women's religious lives and their television watching practices. For the most part, they did not believe that television influenced their beliefs, and they struggled to answer my question of whether television might have anything to teach us religiously.

Based on this participatory action research, I propose that engagement with media products become a regular practice of ministry with youth. Let me point to five reasons for this proposal. First, good education meets students where they are because we cannot walk with students on their educational and spiritual journeys if we do not know from where they begin. As educator Robert Kegan writes:

> Since what is most important for us to know in understanding one another is not the other's experience but what the experience means to him or her, our first goal is to grasp the essence of how the other composes his or her private reality. The first truth we may need to know about a person, in other words, is how the person constructs the truth.[43]

With adolescents, as with most people, simply to ask, "How do you understand the world?" does not work well. Instead, as I did with the young women and *The OC,* engaging and discussing media products with youth enables one to gain a better understanding of how youth understand a variety of topics. From this basis of understanding, we can engage youth in discussions about alternative ways of seeing the world, offering religious imagination as one resource.

Second, the practice of engaging with and discussing media products can aid in developing media literacy skills, a crucial skill in a mass-mediated culture. In our focus group discussions, the young women offered targeted critiques of *The OC,* but they could have been pushed to consider more systemic issues, such as how ethnicity and socioeconomic status are represented on the show. Our discussions would have been a great opportunity for me to ask questions that could lead to deepened critique.[44] Further, by inviting youth to problematize media products in the context of faith communities and with theological commitments in mind, we can shape the imaginative lenses through which young people engage media culture. The young women I worked with approached television with interpretative frames that were largely divorced from their faith lives. As a religious educator, I would like to see their interpretative frames influenced by their religious imaginations of faith communities, but this will only happen when faith communities share the burden of media education with schools and families.

Third, pragmatically, engaging media enables groups to deal with sensitive topics without forcing adolescents to discuss them based on their own experiences. Television shows, for instance, keep issues such as premarital sex distant enough that youth can discuss them, while also evoking empathy with the issue. Discussing media culture may help youth develop enough trust that they will eventually feel safe discussing issues in their lives. Additionally, narratives in media products have the power to extend the range of people with whom we might empathize by exposing people to the lives of others, whom they may never personally encounter.[45] As philosopher Richard Kearney claims, "Stories 'alter' us by transporting us to other times and places where we can experience things *otherwise*."[46] In conclusion, encountering a variety of stories through media products (as through story sharing) may be important for the development of empathy and ethical sensibilities, particularly if this encounter happens with some framing by the youth minister. This does not replace engagement with real people, but it may be a good starting point.

Fourth, when we engage with and discuss media products in faith communities, we can discover how God is working in and through popular culture.[47] Even if people are uncertain about whether God works in this way, discussing media products in a church setting sends the implicit message that apparently a-religious products *do* have something to do with our faith lives, and may encourage young people to consider how their faith relates to the rest of their lives. In any case, it seems fruitful to wonder, along with Mary Hess, "What would we do if we would ask, not what is our community of faith's perspective of this piece of media (translated into: do we approve or disapprove of its apparent content, or do we know how we can 'use' it), but how is God speaking to us and through us in the midst of this conversation?"[48] This sort of work gives young people permission to expand the appropriate boundaries of religious imagination to include media culture.

Finally, studying the worldviews of adolescents and the popular media of their cultural worlds reveals something about God and the world. As such, this study contributes to the accumulating wisdom of practical theology.

Friedrich Schweitzer writes, "Traditionally, theology has devoted its utmost care to the study of its sources in the Bible, tradition, and history; today, theology must learn how to study the world of contemporary adolescents with similar effort and care."[49] This is what Don Browning would call descriptive theology, a form of theology that "is interested, of course, in *all* situations–occupational, familial, educational, governmental, legal, military–that are part of life and that engender practical questions to be addressed by Christian action."[50] Adolescents spend a sizable portion of their time engaged with media culture. Those of us who care about adolescents would do well to attend to the studies done by scholars in other fields about how youth are influenced by media culture, then to consider how we can do theology with young people in a way that contributes to theological wisdom. We also need to consider how we might help young people bridge their engagement with media culture and their engagement in faith communities, thus contributing their theological wisdom directly to communities of faith.

Meditating

A third response for ministry with youth is to invite youth to engage their religious imaginations through meditative practices, through which they may better come to know themselves and God's presence and guidance in their lives. Silence and guided meditation are two such practices grounded in Christian tradition that may be useful to Christian young people in their identity work. In our plugged in, technological world, silence is a rare experience. Our Christian ancestors appreciated the importance of silence as a way to quiet self and make space for listening to God. When teaching middle school religious studies, I offered the students a Lenten challenge: to open class every day with silence, starting with one minute the first day and adding a minute each day. By the end of Lent these young people were spending the first twenty minutes of class in meditative silence. While I am not naïve enough to believe that every student took full advantage of the silence (a few nodded into sleep), a number of students commented positively. They appreciated a time to settle themselves, to think about their lives, and to converse with God in their unique ways.

The other favorite practice of the students was guided meditation, which we did both in the church sanctuary and our classroom. I would encourage them to get comfortable, close their eyes, and then follow my instructions. Usually, I would begin by having them relax their bodies and focus on their breathing, followed by guiding them through a scene, biblical or otherwise, and concluding with having them silently ponder questions in conversation with God. Again, I know that some students took this as an opportunity to catch up on sleep, but many found this to be an exciting new form of prayer. One of my favorite meditations centered on having a conversation with Jesus about personal gifts and vocational callings. Other meditative practices could also be used, such as *lectio divina* or Ignatian meditation, to offer young people options from their faith tradition for prayer and discernment.

All of these meditative practices offer youth much-needed time for silence, reflection, and prayer. They offer tools for discernment that young people can utilize throughout life, tools that may be particularly useful to youth facing the pressures of the neoliberal individualized choice biography. Instead of making decisions alone about who they will be and bearing full responsibility for these choices, through meditative practices young people may develop what E. Byron Anderson calls a theonomous identity, "a processual identity emerging from, in, and toward a relatedness to a relational God."[51] Youth may come to understand that their primary identity comes from God's call to be in relationship with God and be more attuned to God's work in their lives. In a world in which adults are often absent, prayer and meditation enable youth to encounter the caring presence of God and the Christian communion of saints, living and dead, who can walk with them on their journey. Meditative practices offer a time apart, a time for visioning the self and the world in new ways, a time for experiencing the God who is the ground of our religious imagination.

Conclusion

A major task of adolescence is to begin forming an enduring yet adaptable identity through a narrative understanding of the self. This task can be challenging in a pluralistic, mass-mediated society in which adults and young people often do not have much time for meaningful contact and conversation. In our faith communities, we can assist youth with this task by creating spaces in which they can share their life stories, reflect on media culture, and practice silence and meditation. What unites these three responses for youth ministry is that they dare youth to take a leap–to discern the identity to which God is calling them and to reflect on God's work in and through their lives, media culture, and the larger world. These responses all cultivate theological reflection and religious imagination, a way to encounter the sacred ground of our lives and see ourselves in a hoped for future. Through practices that foster religious imagination, we invite youth to see the world through new eyes, to cultivate their own theological understandings, and to develop religious identity as an important aspect of their life stories.

12

The Power of Testimonies

Spiritual Formation and Ministering with Youth

ALMEDA M. WRIGHT

The second Sunday of the month was special because the young people knew that it was their Sunday. They could go to the "small church" and have their very own worship service, where they sang their music, led and created the order of worship, and heard a sermon specifically related to their experiences.

While I have attended my share of "youth church," I was surprised when the youth minister opened the floor for testimony sharing. I was admittedly anxious as I waited to hear what would come from the mouths of the young people. I did not know what to expect, but I was impressed that the youth minister seemed nonanxious about the youth's wreaking havoc on the liturgy. As I sat on the edge of my seat, waiting for the first testimony, a young woman approached the pulpit. When she stood behind the "sacred desk," her peers applauded. They gave verbal and nonverbal affirmation as she told of what God was doing in her life.

This seventeen-year-old young woman explained that, when she first came to the church, she was a mess. She described herself as being "wild, very wild" and as being really mean, having a "real hot attitude." She testified that the youth minister really helped her, by being one of the few people to take time with her and to put up with her "resistance." She thanked him. Then, she transitioned from her past to the good things in her life now—training for track and being voted "most humorous" and "best legs" in senior superlatives at school. She then asked the group to pray for her father, because she did not know where he was. She was open and vulnerable as she shared this, but she did not dwell on the negative. She again switched to more hopeful news—her recent SAT scores and her college choices. She ended by asking the community to keep her in prayer.[1]

As I left that youth service, the testimony period stood out in my mind. I was struck by my initial anxiety about the practice and perplexed by the persistent feeling that this service was truly a rare occurrence. I reflected on the fact that in many churches Sunday worship, including youth church, is an orchestrated affair; therefore, the idea of devoting time in the middle of worship to extemporaneous sharing and receiving of adolescents' testimonies *was* truly novel. This novel privileging of the concerns and testimonies of youth also raises questions about the ongoing, customary church practices with youth.

In this chapter I look particularly at the practices of African American churches with youth. I seek to respond to practices that silence adolescents, particularly marginalized adolescents, as African American youth often are. In naming the problem of "silencing" or "voicelessness," I recognize that, among African American youth, the predominant issue is not that they have lost their ability to speak for themselves or that they feel they have nothing worthwhile to say. More often, the things that they say are not deemed significant or credible by others; therefore, when they choose to speak, the youth sense that "no one" is really listening or caring about what they say.[2] In this chapter, I explore the practice of sharing testimonies as a corrective to this silencing and as a part of adolescent spiritual formation. I draw on examples from two African American churches that have incorporated youth testimonies into their regular youth church services, annual Easter worship, and Youth/Young adult services. By examining these two examples, I highlight the power of sharing testimonies in youth identity formation, community building, and "speaking truth to power." I further point to parallels between the practice of sharing testimonies and the "re-narrating step" in feminist narrative therapy.

The Black Church and Ministry with African American Adolescents

Working with Black Youth traces the trends of youth education and ministry in the Black church through history. The volume notes how the church changed in response to social, economic, and political factors, as did its educational ministry with youth.[3] Of particular interest for our discussion is the description of Black church youth education in the Civil Rights and post–Civil Rights era. Grant Shockley argues that, even though Black churches were "squarely behind the struggle for civil rights...during this period," the educational ministries of Black churches declined in vitality: "Their combined programs never reached more than a major fraction of black youth."[4] Essentially, Shockley points to a "widening gap between the Black church and its youth" by the mid-1960s, which paralleled a similar trend toward decentralizing the Black church's function in the Black community. Shockley's historical overview also points to some contemporary issues confronting the Black church and African American adolescents.

In spite of Shockley's hope that creative practices with youth would prevail, church historian Albert G. Miller, in his 1997 "Princeton Lectures on Youth, Church and Culture," describes a "chasm" between the Black church and Black youth.[5] Miller observes the "scarcity of youth" in the Black church, recounting the difficulty Black pastors name in recruiting and keeping teenagers and young adults.[6] He goes beyond describing this gap, however, and argues that the Black church is "irrelevant" to the concerns of Black youth. Miller supports his conclusion by citing a study by C. Eric Lincoln and Lawrence Mamiya, who asked why youth and young adults were missing in Black churches. Surveying more than 2,100 Black ministers, they found that 21.5 percent thought "youth were not given a chance by adults to participate in a meaningful way in church programs." In addition, 25 percent thought youth were "bored" and did not find "a relevant program for them" in the church. Based on his own experience with African American youth, Miller is also convinced that "many [youth] leave the church, in part, because they feel the church preaches, exhibits, and lives a Gospel that is not relevant to their concerns in the world. They are looking for a Gospel that is willing to speak the truth to those in power, to challenge the racist and exploitative situations in which many young people find themselves, and to affirm their cultural values."[7]

Echoing themes similar to Shockley, Miller, Lincoln, and Mamiya, Anne Wimberly urges Black churches and communities to take seriously the concerns and narratives of Black youth.[8] She, with the others, calls us to think seriously about the concerns of adolescents and the practices of Black churches in responding to these concerns. Her concern is not only to attract and keep youth involved, but also to address the underlying needs that African American youth name, especially their yearning for a sense of purpose and a place of belonging.[9]

Sharing Testimonies

Recognizing the dilemmas of declining relevance, a growing chasm between young people and the church, and the lack of meaningful opportunities for youth to participate in church life, I propose that all is not lost. The youth testimony service recounted above, though a rare occurrence, offers hope that churches can still be a conduit of transformation in the lives of African American youth. As Miller and others suggest, African American adolescents are issuing a clarion call to the church. They ask how we plan to minister with youth, to respond to their concerns, and to validate their witness.

The youth testimony service suggests ways to critique the Black church and ways to reclaim some of its historical practices. The tradition of testifying within the African American church community suggests ways that the church can respond to the crisis of irrelevance in youth ministry and the consequent experiences of voicelessness, invalidation, and hopelessness among a generation of African American youth.[10] In this section, I look at the tradition of testimony sharing in Black churches and at the new manifestations of this practice with African American adolescents.

Testimony as Vital Practice of African American Christian Worship

Although W. E. B. Du Bois[11] characterized his first southern Negro revival by "the preacher, the music and the frenzy," my experience, generations later, of southern rural revivals demands the addition of another element—the testimony.[12] From my childhood in rural Virginia, I cannot remember attending a revival that did not begin with a praise and testimony service—characterized by an elder standing to tell what the "Lawd" had done for him or her. These accounts of how God was still speaking and moving in the lives of ordinary people had the power to "set the church on fire."

This time of praise and testimony prepared the congregants for the remainder of the service. More than preparation, these services provided a forum for sharing struggles and transforming individual concerns into communal concerns. As sociologist of religion, Cheryl Townsend Gilkes, notes in her discussion of pillars of Afro-Christian worship:

> Testimony transforms the collection of worshipers into a community. Oppression and suffering make testimony important for psychological survival. Testimony does not resolve black problems but does transform them from private troubles of distressed individuals into public issues of a covenant community... Testimony can be a form of protest.[13]

Gilkes discusses the ways that testimony is essential to forming community and creating the "shared experience" that Black religion addresses. She also argues that testimony served as "antecedents to movements for social change." Thomas Hoyt, in his discussion of testimony as a practice of Christian faith alongside other practices, notes the community-building and change-producing functions of testimony sharing:

> Although only one person may be speaking at a time, that person's speech takes place within the context of other people's listening, expecting, and encouraging. In testimony a believer describes what God has done in her life, in words both biblical and personal, and the hands of her friends clap in affirmation. Her individual speech thus becomes part of an affirmation that is shared.[14]

Here, Hoyt points to the two dimensions of testimonies: (1) to testify to the church and world about the action of God and (2) to testify to God, telling God the truth about themselves and others. The dual dimension of Christian testimony illustrates the many functions testimony has in African American churches.[15]

Both Hoyt and Gilkes combine their reflections on testimony services with an analysis of the social-historical conditions that have led African Americans to need to testify and the myriad ways testimony connects the Christian faith with their lived experiences. For example, testimonies have been vital in the life of African American communities because the practice of testimony gives primacy to the voices of ordinary, and often marginalized and oppressed, people. Within an oppressed community, it was and is significant to have a safe space in which one's concerns and experiences of hostility and dehumanization can be voiced and heard, and in which strategies for redressing those experiences can be shared. Gilkes also points to the fact that, even within the Black church, the voices of women were historically oppressed–for, often times, women were restricted from preaching in Black churches. Testimony services, however, gave women a place of primacy. Their experiences were illumined and affirmed (becoming the content of much of the male-dominated preaching).[16]

In noting the interconnection of testimony and other pillars of African American worship, Hoyt illustrates the transformative power and call to action of the testimony. Hoyt asserts that, in the preaching moment, "testimony requires a response from those who receive it. Preaching is a witness intended to evoke other forms of witness... The testimony of preaching is a prophetic testimony, one that makes compelling claims on both preacher and hearers."[17] In other words, testimony-preaching makes claims on both preacher and hearer, calling communities to respond to God's blessings and mandates for justice.

Gilkes and Hoyt together outline the foundation of the practice of testimony in the African American Christian community. The power and vitality of testimony in a community is manifest in the ability of testimony to build that community, call for and catalyze social change, give primacy to marginalized voices, and move beyond the community to speak to others and to God.

Old Tradition–New Manifestations

While the extemporaneous praise and testimony services of my youth are a rarity in most contemporary African American churches, the power of testimony and the practice of sharing from daily experiences lives on, manifest in new ways.[18] After attending and reflecting on the youth testimony service recounted at the beginning of the chapter, I became more attuned to, and began to search for, ways that public testimony sharing is now being reappropriated in African American churches. I discovered the significance of the spiritual practice in the lives of youth and young adults. In this section I reflect on two African American churches that have incorporated the practice of testimony sharing as part of worship services for special events, such as Easter programs, youth and young adult worship services, and women's conferences and retreats.[19]

In the first congregation, located in Boston, Massachusettes, youth testimonies have been integrated into the life and worship of the church in a variety of ways. One year, the Sunday school superintendent revamped the

Easter program by including formal public testimonies. Moving from their typical program of toddlers reciting poems and elementary-aged students reenacting the crucifixion, the Sunday school superintendent recruited adolescents and young adults to share their "testimonies of life"–giving the youth a vital role in the worship service as well as an opportunity to be transformed in the process. During the service, an adolescent female shared a very emotional testimony. I vividly remember Christy standing in front of the congregation in her white dress, sharing and crying because she felt really blessed and honored. She discussed her struggles in high school as she worked to resist peer pressure and violent confrontations with other girls. Christy also shared her family struggles–living with her mom only, and how they had endured despite her mom's job changes. The sharing of her testimony was a truly transformative moment for her. She had been a very involved, but critical (even cynical) youth, but she shifted. Instead of only critiquing the program that year, she became integrally connected and interwoven with the success of the program and the renewal of her church community.

On another occasion, this church incorporated testimonies into the annual young adult worship celebration. During the service, a young woman shared the testimony of her journey to graduate school. Although she was very hesitant at first, Michelle agreed to share her experiences as an African American female, getting her Ph.D. from MIT. Like Christy, Michelle recounted how sharing her testimony was transformative for her own life. Michelle writes that after testifying she became connected to more people in the community. People reached out to her, encouraged her, and in turn she was reminded of the fact that the entire church community was interconnected. Michelle writes:

> The entire experience strengthened me and encouraged me... Reflecting on my testimony and the responses drove home for me how interconnected we really are; we really do have a responsibility to share with and support one another as we walk with the Lord. I also felt a personal triumph in having been obedient in sharing what God had put on my heart to say. The experience helped me to realize how much God had been changing me and growing me.[20]

In sharing her story and struggles, Michelle followed the traditional testimony ritual of telling how God is still moving and acting in the lives of God's people, but she also went far beyond that. While Gilkes and Hoyt refer to testimonies as a means of sharing strategies for coping with problems, Michelle's testimony also emphasizes the power of testimonies to inspire and encourage others. For example, Michelle recounted, "One person said she decided to go to nursing school after hearing my testimony." In Michelle's experience, the act of sharing a testimony both spoke of God's tremendous blessings and exemplified for other young African American females possible career paths. Michelle's testimony served to plant seeds of hope and possibility—possibly transforming the perspectives of other youth and congregation members.

In addition to the occasional inclusion of public testimony sharing, another congregation—in Atlanta, Georgia—incorporated testimonies into the bi-weekly youth worship services and held special forums for "sister sharing" during their women's conference. During the bi-weekly youth services, youth engage in leading all aspects of worship and engage in the practice of sharing from their life experiences, connecting those experiences with the goodness of Jesus. In the youth worship service, the experiences of youth, in their own words and on their own terms, are given primary attention and respect. The young people have an opportunity to discuss any situation from their lives. No problem is deemed inappropriate or too trivial.

For example, one session I observed occurred right after progress reports were given out. Many youth testified about their grades, both in thanks to God for blessing them to do well and asking for prayers to do better. On that morning, a young woman, Dana, testified about her struggles in school. She testified that the previous year she had been "up to her tricks, skipping class and all that crap." She also noted that she was failing and still needed prayer for science, because she had an "F," but it was "a high F, a 68.8." Expanding upon the traditional structure of testimony sharing, Dana layered her testimony with references to triumphs and struggles, laced it with some humor (about her high F), as well as acknowledged the many ways that she saw God blessing her in spite of her current struggles. In the Atlanta church, both the youth and the youth minister named the practice of sharing testimonies as essential and vital to the youth worship service—noting that youth church would not be the same without having the opportunity to share and hear the testimonies of others.

The Atlanta church also exemplifies not only the ways that testimony sharing is being reintroduced into the life of African American churches, but also exemplifies, in the contexts I observed, several ways that testimony sharing is being reformatted (breaking with the traditional form and structure of the practice). For example, during their Women's Conference the conveners set aside a special session for the adolescent women of the church. In this setting the young women were invited to share their testimonies and experiences as they related to the conference theme of healing and transformation. The young women, using improvisational techniques, dramatized particular experiences from their lives; in a sense, they shared their testimonies in drama. The more powerful aspect of this session, however, involved the responses to the skits. After each skit the young women had to name the struggles of each youth and then to name strategies for coping with and overcoming the situation.

In this forum, the practice of testimony looked very different from the experiences of my youth, but the content and function were the same: in the context of community, young women came together to share of their struggles and to reflect on ways that God was moving and capable of moving in their situations. The young women also participated in the transformative dimensions of testimony sharing by communally responding to one sister's struggles. This particular youth thus transformed her struggle from an individual to a communal one, where she received advice for coping and overcoming. In reflecting on the tradition of testimony sharing in the African American church and the new manifestations of this practice with adolescents, I see many implications of the practice for the lives of African American youth. A reiteration of these spiritual practices within the African American church promises to be relevant to the needs of adolescents.

Implications for Ministering with Youth:
Content and Function of Youth Testimony

While appreciating the lament of Black pastors and scholars about the inability of churches to retain, or even attract, African American youth and young adults, my concern about the relevancy of the church's ministry with youth goes beyond making sure that there are more Christians or church members. I draw upon womanist and feminist scholars such as bell hooks, who asserts that the goal of education is transgression and freedom; N. Lynne Westfield, who asserts that her bottom line in womanist religious education is justice; and Mary Belenky and her colleagues in feminist epistemology, who assert that the aim of education is the development of women's authentic self.[21] I understand ministry with youth as journeying with youth in such a way that youth are able to move beyond struggling for survival to construct, hear, and affirm their authentic selves or voices and to be empowered for the work of individual and communal freedom and justice.[22]

Additionally, Kenda Creasy Dean and Ron Foster in *The Godbearing Life* inform my understanding of ministry with youth. They outline a relational and practice-based approach to ministry with youth. One of their underlying assertions is that the last thing youth need is another activity or program, not because programs are inherently bad, but because, at this point in their development, adolescents are in need of relationships.[23] For Dean and Foster, a "practices" approach to youth ministry is not about having a list of things or skills that each youth must perfect; instead, youth should allow "practices to master them." Dean and Foster define practices as "constitutive acts of a community that identify us as, and form us into, people who belong to that community." They further outline practices as constituting "the daily rhythm of our life together."[24] Building on these ideas, they characterize practices in a fivefold manner: (1) practice requires doing—that youth actually take part in doing something and not simply talk about it; (2) practice "does" things—noting that the practice has the power to teach, heal, celebrate, etc.; (3) practice involves others–emphasizing the communal nature of our ministry; (4) practice is ongoing–it's not just a single event that we plan enjoy and move on; and (5) practices have standards of excellence.[25]

Reflecting on my understanding of ministry with youth, the characterization of practice as active, transformative, communal, and ongoing is helpful, as are the manifestations of testimony in the African American Christian context that I have described. In light of these insights, I outline some functions and implications of this practice as part of the larger African American community, and potentially part of other communities of faith as well.

Youth Testimony as Expression of Adolescent Struggles

First, the ongoing and effective practice of testimony sharing gives youth workers an entry into the lives and experiences of African American youth. Many times adolescents are regarded as reticent and reluctant to express what is truly on their minds with adults. Developmental psychologists also point toward the fact that many youth are not yet capable of verbalizing their feelings fully; however, the practice of testimony models a way of sharing one's concerns and struggles beyond peer group or even family. As observed at the youth testimony service, the practice of testimony created a forum to voice the unique concerns of adolescents. The young people were able to talk about their struggles in school, at work, with friends, and even with their parents. They were also able to share stories of progress–to articulate how they viewed success for themselves and to enumerate their future goals. In light of congregational observations, one can conclude that a vital element of testimony is the witness to what is happening in the lives of youth. The practice offers insights for youth pastors and workers about the lived experiences of youth and how best to empower the youth to meet their needs.

As Gilkes notes in reference to the testimonies of women, "In any pre-revival devotional session, one can hear a litany of the social problems affecting black women;"[26] similarly, the testimonies of youth give us a better understanding of the world in which youth are living and struggling. Instead of assuming that we know what youth are dealing with or even trivializing their concerns as only transitory, youth testimony sharing affirms their concerns as valid. It also transforms their concerns into communal concerns with communal resources and strategies for addressing them.

The role of testimony as a descriptor of adolescent struggles and the need to pay attention to the testimony of youth is further emphasized in Albert Miller's lecture, cited above. Miller reflects on the "Boston Miracle" and the youth violence crisis in Boston during the 1980s and 1990s. He concludes that youth have much wisdom to share both with their peers and with the broader community.[27] The "Boston Miracle" refers to the miraculous decline in youth homicide rates during the 1990s as a result of African American Christian ministers becoming concerned about and connected to the youth in the streets and gangs of Boston. Many African Americans living in Boston at the time had a sense of hopelessness, thinking of the youth as a "lost" generation. However, the Boston Miracle reminds us that developing relationships and listening to the stories and concerns of youth–those committing violent crimes and those afraid to go outside because of them–can effect change for the entire community.

Youth Testimony as Formative of Community

Many of the examples shared throughout this essay, from the role of testimony in traditional Afro-Christian worship to the "new manifestations" of testimony, point to the importance of testimony for community building and formation. The examples illumine how in testimony sharing youth connect with each other and receive peer advice for how to cope with particular issues. Also, youth and adults connect with each other and recognize that, regardless of age, wisdom can be gained from their shared stories. In actively listening and being concerned, one can no longer diminish the concerns of the other. Instead, we take responsibility for bearing one another's burdens.

The practice of testimony builds explicitly Christian community as well, for we share of our ordinary experiences and lace them with reflections on how God is working in us. In testimony, we pull from and connect with the biblical community and "cloud of witnesses" contained in scripture. In turn, we form an understanding of what it means to be part of a wider community connected with the Divine.

Finally, the practice of testimony builds an African American communal identity in that we share from our experiences and history as an oppressed people and a people of great heritage. Therefore, in the practice of giving and hearing testimony, African American adolescents can become more connected with their history and legacy–and better equipped to counter stereotypes about what it means to be African American.

Youth Testimony as Formative of Identity

Beyond providing connections in the adolescents' ever-increasing social sphere and community, the practice of testimony sharing has the power to aid adolescents in their process of identity formation.[28] Dr. James Fowler, in his discussion of *Faith Development and Pastoral Care,* notes that one of the developmental hallmarks of adolescence is a newfound ability for "mutual perspective taking." During adolescence, youth become able to imagine the perspectives of others. This, in turn, affects how youth come to see themselves. For example, Fowler describes this phenomenon in the couplet, "I see you seeing me: I see the me I think you see... / I construct the me I think you see."[29] Fowler writes that typical adolescent views of the world and of themselves are influenced by the opinions of others; therefore, having their perspectives validated and received in a community of faith is crucial for an adolescent's self image. The community, significant adults, and youth ministers have the capacity during this stage to reflect back to youth the positive attributes that they observe and, in effect, contribute to the youth's sense of self.

African American adolescents, as well as other marginalized groups, have a particular need for adults to reflect back positive images. Often African American adolescents, specifically those from lower working class and working poor communities, struggle to understand who they are as individuals as well as how they are perceived as part of a historically oppressed group. In dealing with issues of race (and ethnicity and class), the adolescent has to make sense of "I see you seeing me and I see the *me* I think you see," by reworking and countering the historical legacy and stereotypes inherent in being part of a collective, under-represented and stigmatized "me."[30] Therefore the practice of sharing and affirming testimonies serves to reflect back to young people that they are not stereotypes from popular culture, but are distinct and precious individuals.

Youth Testimony as Transformative Care–Re-narrating Life Stories

Another consistent theme from the congregations described in this chapter and from discussions of testimony in the literature is the idea that testimony is transformative care. As noted earlier, testimony has the ability to transform individuals into community members, to transform their individual struggles into communal struggles, to transform a youth's self image, and much more.

During a follow-up discussion about the practice of testimony sharing in one church, one youth minister noted that many of the youth come from homes and situations that are abusive or where they are struggling with absentee parents–situations compounded by race, gender, and economic concerns. He added that he never wants the youth to remain in the place of only seeing the negative dimensions of their situations. Instead, the youth minister saw the testimony time as a way of transforming or re-narrating their life stories to include elements of success and triumph and as a way of "encouraging themselves." As the youth minister shared his perspectives, he noted that this process of being honest with one's self and confronting both the triumphs and struggles is essential to both youth and adult development. He observed that the experience of speaking honestly empowers youth to deal with "their stuff"–and not blame others for particular life events. The pastor went on to describe the importance of helping youth learn to not use bad experiences or their parents as "crutches," but to grow beyond focusing on the negative aspects to a place of rethinking and reframing their situations in terms of their power to transform and/or withstand particular situations.[31]

This youth minister's reflections parallel the main concepts of narrative pastoral care, as presented by Christie Neuger in her work *Counseling Women*. Her narrative pastoral approach asserts the need for people to come to voice in their situations (e.g., to testify about what is going on in their lives), but to also come to a place of clarifying their stories. Neuger outlines the "5 Rs" of clarifying one's story in transformative pastoral care: *remembering, reframing, reversing, re-imagining, and restorying.*[32] If we are mindful of the many dimensions of the practice of testimony, we see that each of these "5 Rs" is included. The initial act of testifying helps young people and community remember the situations with which they have been struggling. In testifying, youth also begin to reframe these situations, placing them into the context of their larger life stories. With the help of their peers and ministers, they can begin to take new perspectives on the situation. For example, in the Atlanta church's youth testimony period, a young man shared a complex story of a "shady week" and the struggles and triumphs in his life. In the act of sharing and receiving applause and verbal encouragement, his struggles were reframed within the context of his triumphs. He left the pulpit encouraged that, although his situation had not changed, he had a different way of looking at it.

In the process of getting new perspectives, Neuger points to the fact that people need not simply look from a different angle, but can also reverse truth claims and elements of their lives that are incompatible with their goals toward wholeness. In the context of community, youth can thus begin to reverse negative claims about their lives and re-narrate their life stories (imagining a new situation and reclaiming their power to move toward it).

Youth Testimony as Speaking Truth to Power

In addition to the community building, identity forming, and re-narrating roles of sharing testimony, youth testimony has the ability to "speak truth to power in love." While it is true that youth workers and churches gain valuable insights into the lives of youth by listening to youth, youth also offer correctives and alternative visions of how the world *should be* in their testimonies. In discussing the particular ills and problems they are confronting, youth often cause a breach in the status quo (and a break from the norm). They articulate the wrongs they encounter and, within a community of faith, seek to address these ills. As many educational theorists note, the power of naming and speaking into existence a reality different from the norm, or different from the reality named by oppressors, is transformative. For example, Brazilian educator Paulo Freire wrote, "To speak a true word is to transform the world."[33] Freire's discussion of "naming the world" parallels the practice of testifying among an oppressed group of people, for he points to the fact that naming is not the power or privilege of some elite group, nor can any one person say a "true word" alone or for another person or group. Instead, Freire points to the ways that naming is done in dialogue, in community.

In other words, the practice of testifying empowers youth to reflect critically on their lived experiences. Within an affirming community, they can begin to speak a word of correction—reflecting on the dysfunctional aspects of their current situation and proposing collective ways to challenge or respond to this dysfunction. Similarly, religious educator, Evelyn Parker, in her chapter on "sanctified rage" in this volume, discusses the ways that youth testify in the new manifestations of "rap music." This is a way to speak truth and express rage about their current situations.[34]

Youth are also called into the practice of thinking about and even questioning how God is working in their lives and communities and, further, to question how God wants them to respond. Whereas in more traditional practices of testimony sharing, only a particular vision of God is espoused, youth testimony sharing has the potential to name questions and struggles with how God is operating (or not operating)—and to bring those individual questions into a place of sharing about how others also have questioned God and wondered about where God is/was in a particular situation. In other words, new manifestations of testimony empower youth to share new understandings of how the Divine works and to name places where it seems that God is not working *yet*.

Conclusion

"The power of testimony is to give voice to the faith that lets people run on to see what the end's gonna be. Stories like these, told in the context of oppression, are... 'testimonies charged with hope.'"[35]

In making space for adolescent voices, communities of faith also need to respond to and be accountable for the testimonies shared by young people. When young people shared in the youth worship service, another dimension was added to the community, modeling "testimony" and calling the youth to think about what was happening in their lives in light of how they understood God and the community of faith. The time of sharing testimonies was never seen merely as an opportunity to gripe and complain, but it served as a forum for describing a situation, often a situation of struggle, that held out a hope or gave witness to the power of God and the community to "turn the bad situation around." Even if the situation was ongoing, the youth testifier would often end by requesting the community to pray for her or lift her up. Typically, before the young person left, several of his peers would reach out to him. Many times the youth minister or other adults present would also let the youth know that they were available to listen and strategize with the young person on how to deal with his or her situation.

Testimony, or testifying, is an essentially hopeful spiritual discipline. While the skeptical scholar in me wonders about the ability of testimony sharing to hold the hard situations and theological conundrums, the practitioner recognizes that, even in the face of unresolved circumstances and problems, people long for, even need, hope and faith so they can "run on to see what the end's gonna be." The practice of testimony empowers youth to "tell it like it is," not to be ashamed of their experiences, but to share their experiences in the hope and knowledge that their stories will be received by an encouraging community, and will also serve as encouragement for others. The practice of testimony aids in the process of helping youth find their authentic voice, a voice constructed and reconstructed in light of communal witnessing and listening.

13

Sanctified Rage

Practicing Holy Indignation with
Teenagers in the Black Church

EVELYN L. PARKER

Allie, a seventeen-year-old African-American girl from Chicago, was enraged as the policeman pushed her boyfriend's body against his new black Volvo.[1] Although they were speeding, the harsh verbal and physical actions of the police officer were not needed, thought Allie. As the policeman roughed up her boyfriend and hurled racial insults at both of them, Allie felt every muscle in her body tighten. She was furious! After pulling her boyfriend's pockets inside-out, his coins falling on the pavement, and punching and probing every part of his body, the policeman received a call on his lapel walkie-talkie. His responses to the person calling suggested that her boyfriend was not the suspect they were searching for. The officer indicated to the person on the other end that he would not search "the female companion." In a rude and sarcastic tone, void of an apology, the policeman told them they could go.

This was not the first time Allie had experienced the dehumanization of racial profiling from the Chicago Police. Although she was tempted to return verbal insults to the policeman, she channeled her rage into gathering information, writing the officer's badge number and other information from his police car so she could report the incident to the proper authorities. This experience launched her crusade against racial profiling by police officers and her commitment to transform society from this form of injustice. But who would join her in this campaign? Although Allie is admired as a positive leader by her peers from the Southside of Chicago, their relationship has never demanded commitment to social causes. Also, finding supporters among her peers at school, located in a north shore suburb, was highly unlikely. Perhaps her history teacher would be interested. She knew her parents would be supportive, but what about her youth group, her pastor, and her congregation? Would they welcome her outrage at this racist imposition of "driving while black"? How can the African American church be a sanctuary for Allie's rage? How will the congregation nurture her indignation for the purpose of transforming unjust systems and social policies?

This chapter examines rage in the lives of African American adolescents, as well as the root causes of black youths' rage, the effects of rage on their spirituality, and how the church can be a setting where anger can be transformative for youth, the church, and society. I explore questions about the nature of anger in black teenagers, the consequences of anger that is not appropriately channeled, and the opportunities for ministry with black teenagers who are a tinderbox for explosive anger due to the systemic problems of race, class, and gender oppression. I reflect on potential practices of the church in light of "holy indignation." I first introduced this idea in *Trouble Don't Last Always: Emancipatory Hope among African American Adolescents,* in a chapter entitled, "I Snapped, Man: Teenage Rage." In that chapter I analyzed the life stories of Allie, Andre, and eighteen other high school teens from the Chicago area. I found that these black teens were angry as a result of the pain they carried inside. My constructive response was holy indignation.

Rage can be characterized as human passion felt in the depth of one's heart, mind, and soul in response to an undeserved attack, betrayal, humiliation, or any other dehumanizing act. Rage is volatile human fury or unstable human anger. It can result in violent behavior in some situations, or cause psychological impairment, such as depression. As with many emotions, rage can be destructive, but it can also be constructive. The life of Malcolm X is an example of constructive rage that sought to transform injustice.[2] Holy indignation is a form of constructive rage. It is "the freedom to express anger against injustice in the sacred space of the Christian church and also the public square of North American society."[3] This essay offers holy indignation and invites possibilities of constructively addressing anger in black youth. Rage and anger are used interchangeably in this essay. This human passion can have a unique form in the lives of some African American teenagers.

The Nature of Black Teenage Rage

A number of psychologists, pediatricians, and sociologists highlight the problems of angry African American teenagers in North America through empirical studies. One study particularly revealing of psychosocial issues is Michael R. McCart's 2006 study in which he interviewed thirty-six African American youth between the ages of ten and eighteen years.[4] These youth were among those who had received treatment for violent interpersonal injuries in a Wisconsin pediatric emergency room. The project sought to determine the psychosocial concerns of these youth in relation to their injuries. The youth reported 178 different concerns, which were content-analyzed and placed into ten thematic categories. The category labeled *anger/aggressive behavior* had the highest percentage of respondents, 78 percent. The other categories included *general internalizing symptoms* (61 percent), *peer difficulties* (53 percent), *parent/family conflict* (50 percent), *posttraumatic stress symptoms* (47 percent), *academic concerns* (42 percent), and *physical health concerns* (39 percent). The study concluded:

> African American assault victims are experiencing a broad range of psychosocial needs. To bolster youth recovery and reduce the risk of future injury, researchers and practitioners need to identify effective methods of assessing these needs in the emergency department so that youth victims of interpersonal violence can be referred for appropriate follow-up services.

Even though the root causes of anger are not specified, this research draws our attention to the connection between black teenage anger and the resulting violence. One might thus ask what options youth might be offered for channeling their rage?

Other studies have pointed to racial discrimination as a cause for black teens' anger. One such study by Carol Wong, et al., examined the face-to-face experiences of African American adolescents with racial discrimination in school. In the sample of economically diverse black seventh and eighth grade youth, experiences of racial discrimination by teachers and peers at school were predictive of "declines in grades, academic ability, self-concepts, academic task values, increases in depression and anger, decreases in self-esteem and psychological resiliency, and increases in problem behavior." The study also discovered that a clear and positive ethnic identity buffers the black teen who suffers such discrimination.[5]

Wong's research points to the problem of racial discrimination, the systemic problem of racism in North American educational institutions, and its effects on black youth. Racial discrimination and racial prejudice practiced by schoolteachers and peers correlates with anger and other potentially destructive behavioral responses in black teens. Such research cannot give definitive evidence of causation, but it does pose questions for further research regarding the causative power of discrimination. Further, this research does not resolve value questions regarding the positive and destructive values of anger, but it does reveal anger to be a powerful force in young lives.

Although Wong's empirical research does not explicitly study social class, the work of William Julius Wilson in his classic *The Truly Disadvantaged* helps us understand the connection between current and historical racism in North America and the struggles of poor inner-city blacks. Discrimination in education and employment practices has perpetuated the cycle of poverty and despair among black youth growing up in the inner city. Poverty disproportionately influences the African American community. One need only recall the televised images of poor blacks during the aftermath of Hurricane Katrina in New Orleans to understand this point.

Likewise, bell hooks and other black feminist and womanist theorists have consistently argued the troubling effects of the triple travesty of race, class, and gender inequity levied against African American women and girls. Poor black girls living in the inner city may not imagine choices beyond pregnancy, drugs, and gangs, all of which are expressions of internalized anger. These issues have been documented by anecdotal, biographical, and empirical evidence. Certainly, they were recurrent themes for the girls I interviewed for *Trouble Don't Last Always*.[6]

The research findings of McCart and Wong, et al., illustrate the relationship of black teenage anger and the physical and psychological toll it has on them. The research also points to the fact that the lives of angry black teens are complicated by economic deprivation, political powerlessness, and social instability. However, this research has not helped the church and community to understand these systemic social, political, and economic problems in North American context and how they are related, historically, to black rage. The combined pressures of abject poverty, an underemployed/unemployed father, substandard housing, and an incarcerated mother may cause either an internal emotional and spiritual meltdown or an external eruption. By no fault of their own, angry black teens do not understand injustices on this level. They rarely have opportunities for critical reflection and discourse that help them name the sources of their anger. If this leads to an *internal* meltdown, it may manifest itself in drug addition, sexual promiscuity, depression, bulimia, anorexia, or other internalized self-destructive behavior. An example of an *external* eruption is dealt with in detail below.

Expressions of Destructive Rage

It might be helpful to consider an example of an *external* expression of rage among black and white teens that is destructive. Consider fight/fighting clubs, which are clandestine groups that use violence, intentionally or unintentionally, as a radical form of psychotherapy. These groups surfaced among all age groups after the novel titled *Fight Club*, written by Church Palahniuk, was popularized in a movie of the same name.[7] Fight clubs are a recent phenomena in the Dallas-Fort Worth area, where black and white teens, both girls and boys, engage in bare-knuckle fighting while someone videotapes the event with the intent to make a profit from selling the visual image. For fifteen dollars, a person can purchase black-on-black and black-on-white brutal bloody brawls, a total of fifty fights, for their visual pleasure. The juvenile authorities discovered this phenomenon after police responded to a fight that resulted in life threatening injuries for several Arlington teenagers. At first glace, the Arlington fight club, known by the DVD titles of *Agg Townz Fights* and *Agg Townz 2*, appears to be uncontrolled testosterone. Upon closer examination, one finds a blending of adolescent delinquent behavior, media influence, and misappropriated entrepreneur creativity, fueled by deep-rooted anger.

Authorities in New Jersey, Washington, and Alaska have discovered more than a half-dozen teen fight clubs operating for fun or profit in their states. Fight club participants are suburban high school kids, not just gang members or juvenile criminals. One example was documented in a newspaper article, revealing the far reach of the phenomenon and the media interest: "Chase Leavitt, son of U. S. Health and Human Services Secretary Mike Leavitt, was arrested for participating in a fight club at a Mormon Church gym in Salt Lake City in December 2001, when his father was Utah's governor."[8]

While empirical data is inconclusive, I posit that this form of violence is practiced among black teens because it allows them to express deep-seated anger that is otherwise difficult to articulate. Black teens involved in fight clubs are expressing intense rage. Black rage resides in the depths of the African American psyche as a result of enslavement and the atrocities committed to enslaved black people.[9] This rage has been passed on from generation to generation and manifests in this generation of black youth that experience injustice through the various systemic forms of racism, sexism, classism, and heterosexism. Black rage expressed through the participation of youth in fight clubs is one example of destructive rage.

Other forms of destructive rage evidenced externally include black teenage gang culture. Black teenage rage is often misdirected at other black teens as they engage in the predatory practices of violent gang culture.[10] "Life without meaning, hope, and love breeds a coldhearted, mean-spirited outlook that destroys both the individual and others."[11] Fight clubs, violent gangs, and other forms of destructive rage merit theological analysis.

Theological Reflection on Destructive Rage

Many black theologians, such as Michael Dyson and Cheryl Kirk-Duggan have written about the problem of black anger from a theological perspective, focusing on effects seen in black women, men, and children. A succinct and publicly influential account of the rage that surfaces in African Americans from systemic social ills is offered by Cornel West in his seminal work *Race Matters*. Among the factors that West identifies are white supremacy, market-driven values, economic inequities, and gender oppression:

> The accumulated effect of the black wounds and scars suffered in a white-dominated society is a deep-seated anger, a boiling sense of rage, and a passionate pessimism regarding America's will to justice.

Under conditions of slavery and Jim Crow segregation, this anger, rage, and pessimism remained relatively muted because of a well-justified fear of brutal white retaliation. The major break-throughs of the sixties—more psychically than politically—swept this fear away. Sadly, the combination of the market way of life, poverty-ridden conditions, black existential *angst*, and the lessening of fear of white authorities has directed most of the anger, rage and despair toward fellow black citizens, especially toward black women who are the most vulnerable in our society and in black communities.[12]

West points to domestic violence in the black community as a manifestation of black rage. It destroys relationships between partners, children and parents, and webs of other relationships, as well as between perpetrators of domestic violence and God. Destructive rage of this nature is external to the person committing the act.

Angry black youth internalize some forms of destructive rage. An example is misogynist practices among black adolescent females seeking gang or club membership. Potentially lethal games or initiation rites among black girls such as sexual activity with known HIV/AIDS partners is an example of an internalized misogynist practice. For a black girl to go through an initiation rite that is high risk and potentially life threatening suggests that relationships within that gang matter to her. What do girls engaged in such practices think about themselves and their relationship to God or any other divine source? How would they respond to the words, "Present your bodies as a living sacrifice, holy and acceptable to God," from Romans 12:1? These questions are among many others that help us think about the theological implications of a black girl's need to be in relationship with others and her internalized rage.

One such implication is ecclesiological in nature. This is, What role must the black church play in the problem of rage among black youth? I contend that an African American church that seeks to be relevant to the black community must take seriously the problems its youth and their families face. These problems include the rage that results when institutions, systems of power, and practices of culture are oppressive. Black adolescent rage is a problem for the black community and the African American church. The church is invited to conceive imaginative ways to help angry black teens gain a clear sense of who they are to shore up their sense of self against attacks by racist individuals and systems. Later in this essay I will offer ways to address the problem of rage among black teens and the role of the African American church.

First, I want to point to a roadblock that can hinder the ecclesial mission and ministry to black youth. Unfortunately, black rage and the black church have not been associated in popular imagination or church practice. Expressing anger or rage in the black church has been traditionally perceived as a cultural taboo. In light of the resistance, we turn in the next section to examine this phenomenon in the black church.

Respect the Lord's House

Since enslaved Africans in North America established black religious institutions, they have been cultural centers of meaning, value, and authority that have sustained the black community.[13] Members of the black community revered black religious institutions, including black Christian churches, so much that a set of codes and rituals were developed to maintain a high level of respect for the black church. This emphasis on respect has complexified the church's relationship with anger and its expressions, which we will explore after a brief investigation of respectability.

Dress Codes

Dress codes, specifically for women, have traditionally included dresses with hemlines at or below the knee, dresses with sleeves (preferably three-quarter length), and a prohibition of "erotic" colored dresses (red dresses). Women should always wear a hat, doily, or other appropriate head covering during worship. Dress codes and relevant practices for women are illustrated in the Official Manual of the Church of God in Christ (COGIC). This denomination is representative of dress codes among African American congregations, particularly during the first half of the twentieth century, when many of these congregations were formulating policy and rules for communal life.[14] The section on "Practices Disapproved: A. Immodest Dress" offers guidelines for modest dress in all settings. Members are cautioned against "dressing in a sensually provocative manner" because such dress "produces inclinations to evil desires."[15] "Social occasions call for attractive and dignified attire; one attiring oneself on such occasions should always be mindful of Scripture that admonishes to dress in modest apparel. II Tim. 2:9."[16] The Official Manual of the Church of God in Christ also offers dress codes for clergymen and clergywomen. The extensive section for women outlines appropriate dress for women who hold offices on national, state, and local levels. The guidelines for "The Laywoman" amplify on scripture to make the case for modest dress among women and girls. This section is quoted below.

> It is hoped that this dress code will encourage the laywoman to return to the old fashioned standard of dressing as becometh holiness… We feel that this code amplifies the expression of the writer, St. Luke, who said in the book of Acts, "and they had all things common." It is hoped that all of our women will refrain from wearing unnecessary gaudy attire but will join with our leading women in reminding the world that there is a "difference."
>
> We close by admonishing our young women and girls to let your manner and your clothing reflect the Jesus that you sing and

testify about. The world is looking for an example, a model, why not be that one.[17]

As you can see from this passage, the burden of maintaining "respect" for the COGIC is demarcated along gender lines. The dress code evolved out of the need to address a concern for black women travelers, their respect, and their safety against ardent racists. COGIC and other Sanctified Church women were encouraged to practice this dress code to "counter the stereotypes used as rationales for abuse of black women."[18] What was initially intended to support and protect black women has evolved, more or less, into a practice to promote respect for the church.

Other dress codes have emerged in the black church that prohibit contemporary styles among teenagers such as sagging, oversized pants, which are worn in a way that allows the pants to fall below the hips and expose undergarments. Sagging is practiced among both males and females, although males more frequently. Another contemporary style involves low-rise jeans worn among young women that show midriff and undergarments. Dress codes point to the politics of ecclesial respectability.

Rituals

Rituals in African American congregations have also emphasized respect and respectability. The codes of behavior have included never allowing children to play in the pulpit and never leaning or standing on the altar railing. Some denominations require choir members to kneel at the altar for prayer before entering the choir loft; this is a way of respecting the sacred place and the ministry of music. Preachers and other members of the pulpit are required to kneel in front of their chairs for prayer before sitting as a means of giving reverence to the hallowed place of the pulpit.

Rituals of respect vary depending on the identity and culture of the African American congregation. In my small southeastern congregation when I was a teen, we knew the time for worship had come when the traditional call to worship rang out: "The Lord is in his [sic] holy temple. Let all the earth keep silent before him [sic]." The time had come to be still and silent in respect to God. Such rituals signify being in the midst of the Holy One.

Respectability and Anger

These dress codes and sanctuary rituals have been traditional evidence of respect for the Lord's house among African Americans. Although strict practices of reverence are not as common in contemporary congregations, many people, especially among the older age-level cohorts, still hold beliefs in these conventions as they give honor to God and God's church.

Herein lies the problem of anger and its relationship to the black church. Respect for the black church through practices and rituals prohibit any practices related to the expression of rage in the church. At best, anger felt by teenagers is acknowledged in youth groups and in the Sunday morning sermon. Many adults in the black church feel it inappropriate to express anger in the Lord's house. Also, for some, it is downright blasphemous to express anger against God. Many believe that God's wrath will strike you down if you express anger toward God. Generation after generation of parents have taught their children that God will not be pleased with them if they disobey the conventions of respect in the sanctuary. For these reasons, black youth have carved out other venues for expressing their rage. Popular culture is such a setting.

Rage in Popular Culture

While the expression of black rage in the African American church is a cultural taboo, black rage is liberally expressed in popular culture, especially in hip-hop culture. Hip-hop is a cultural meaning system embraced by many African American youth as well as youth from other racial/ethnic groups.[19] It includes practices and processes of making meanings from things encountered in everyday life. Various genres of hip-hop culture might be considered as expressions of rage.[20] Rap music and graffiti, discussed below, are included, along with movies, cartoons, and video games as expression of rage identified with hip-hop.

Anthony Pinn writes, "Hip-Hop first emerged as a cultural and creative response to the matrix of industrial decline, social isolation, and political decay endemic to New York City's Bronx section."[21] Teenage Puerto Rican and African American rap artists of the Bronx, who faced fewer and fewer socioeconomic opportunities and accompanying marginality, considered their creative abilities as a form of political response. Hip-hop culture emerged as an ontological and epistemological alternative for New York youth. It includes its own language, dress code, movies, videos, video games, television shows, visual artistic expression, dance styles, and musical forms.[22]

Graffiti art or Tagging (writing names, symbols, and images on public facades) emerged as early as 1971 as Hip-Hop's visual artistic expression. Interestingly, tagging did not originate in the inner-city [sic], but in New York's Manhattan. It was initiated by a Greek teenager named Demetrius in the late 1960s, who took on the moniker of Taki 183. While working as a messenger, traveling by subway to all five boroughs of the city, Taki wrote his name all over the subway cars and stations. Inner-city youth were fascinated by tagging and adopted this art form as a rite of initiation for gangs as well as revealing their existence in a society that renders them invisible.

Hip-hop culture packages rage for consumption, in positive and negative forms, especially among teenagers. Gangsta rap music and videos with lethal litanies directed at women and girls, as well as any opposing persons or groups, are an example of negative rage. In other words, the rage destructively attacks individuals. The rap artist 50 Cent, for example, has performed such songs as *I'll Whip Ya Head, Boy*, expressing destructive rage with lyrics that, if acted out, would maim and kill. Most, if not all, of 50 Cent's music can be categorized as negative. Arrested Development, a popular rap group during the 1980s, has been categorized as progressive rap music.[23] Kanye West, a contemporary of 50 Cent, is perhaps also a progressive rap artist. West and Arrested Development often give expression to positive rage against systems that oppress communities. West has performed such songs as *The Glory*, rapping lyrics about his fury against war. This song of positive rage contrasts to an earlier song, *Gold Digger*, which gives the illusion of positive rap; however, upon closer examination, it implies misogyny.

Various forms of hip-hop culture provide a meaning system for positive expressions of rage. This meaning system, however, must be practiced within a community. The black church is one possibility for the positive expressions of rage through rap music, break dancing, graffiti art, and other genres of hip-hop culture. Some churches do allow such expressions of positive rage. Since the advent of hip-hop gospel music, such as Kirk Franklin's *Stomp* in the mid-1990s, some black churches have invited the religious music of hip-hop artists, including rap music.

While listening to and creating hip-hop gospel music as a channel for African American adolescents to express anger is important, their rage also needs to be a transformative force in the church and society. Given the authoritative role of the Bible in Christian congregations, a good source for examining rage is scripture.

From Anger to Boldness[24]

Anger and rage, as stated earlier, are volatile human fury that results from an undeserved attack, betrayal, humiliation, or other dehumanizing act. Anger is common in biblical narratives, even occurring in Jesus, who turned over the tables of money changers in the temple (Mt. 21:12–13; Mk. 11:15–17; Lk. 19:45–46; Jn. 2:13–22). In these texts, Jesus demonstrated a transformative form of anger that raised the consciousness of onlookers regarding the sanctity of the temple. Another example of the transformative power of anger can be found in Acts 2. The followers of Jesus Christ used their anger through the power of the Holy Spirit to act boldly when confronted by unjust powers. Jesus had promised his disciples that the Holy Spirit would come to them when he left. It is the Holy Spirit that transforms anger into acts of boldness for justice. On the day of Pentecost:

> And suddenly from heaven there came a sound like the rush of a violent wind, and it filled the entire house where they were sitting. Divided tongues, as of fire, appeared among them, and a tongue

rested on each of them. All of them were filled with the Holy Spirit and began to speak in other languages, as the Spirit gave them ability. (Acts 2:2–4)

As the apostles and the believers were speaking in the languages of devout Jews and other peoples from far and near, many onlookers were amazed and perplexed; they asked the meaning of this miracle. Others sneered and accused the believers of being drunk. Galileans are thought lacking in linguistic talent,[25] and that accusation probably made Peter indignant. Perhaps he said, "How dare they say such a thing of Christ's disciples. We have been waiting and praying patiently for the coming of the Holy Spirit as Jesus promised. How dare they mock us!" Then, in the power of the Spirit, Peter stood, eloquently clarified what was happening, and proclaimed the risen Christ.

Now let us fast forward from the day of Pentecost to the early days of the Church and the work of Peter. In Acts 4, Peter and John were witnessing in the temple, teaching the people, and proclaiming resurrection from the dead. They had just healed a crippled beggar, much to the chagrin of the Sadducees, who had Peter and John arrested. These Jewish leaders had a problem with the apostles' healing and teaching, as well as the fact that about 5,000 people who heard what they had to say had become followers of the way. The two apostles were probably angered for being arrested on a trumped-up charge. The next day the rulers, elders, and scribes assembled in Jerusalem with the high priest and other members of the high priest's family. In their presence, Peter, filled with the Holy Spirit, explained the series of events again, giving testimony to the risen Jesus Christ. They were amazed at the boldness of Peter and John, two uneducated and ordinary men. After the religious leaders deliberated, they decided to release Peter and John with a warning not to speak anymore in the name of Jesus. Peter and John responded:

> "Whether it is right in God's sight to listen to you rather than to God, you must judge; for we cannot keep from speaking about what we have seen and heard." After threatening them again, they let them go, finding no way to punish them because of the people, for all of them praised God for what had happened. (Acts 4:19–21)

After Peter and John were released, they went to their friends and reported what they had experienced. When their angry and dismayed friends heard what had happened, they raised their voices and fervently prayed. According to the text, "When they had prayed, the place in which they were gathered together was shaken; and they were all filled with the Holy Spirit and spoke the word of God with boldness" (Acts 4:31). The Spirit of God empowers followers of Jesus Christ to have courage, to act audaciously.

The disciples of Jesus Christ, as revealed in these texts from Acts, embodied a spirituality that predisposed them to transform their anger into a positive force to promote the reign of God. The followers of Jesus were willing to allow the Holy Spirit to possess their minds, bodies, and souls in every way, including anger. Their anger was channeled into a positive force of courage to confront unjust religious and political powers of authority.

I am not suggesting that angry black adolescents are predisposed in the same manner as the early disciples. However, the experience of the early followers of Jesus has implications for black youth. Positive anger generated and transformed by the Holy Spirit within black youth can transform social, political, and economic injustice in the church and society. As described earlier, anger, especially from racial and economic stressors, takes a psychological toll on black youth. In like manner, racial and economic injustice fractures the spirit and breaks the soul of a black teenager whether churched or unchurched. Youth who allow the Spirit of God to direct their thinking and actions have potential to turn the world upside down, just as did Peter, John, and other followers of Jesus Christ.

Violence to the spirituality of black teenagers is rampant–that is to say, violence to their "ways of knowing and being in the world that inform and shape their beliefs in God, the values they hold, and the practices they manifest" is rampant.[26] Rage caused by the demons of racism, classism, sexism, and also heterosexism shreds the spirit of an African American adolescent. These are demons that black youth, especially those in the inner city, may be incapable of naming. How then can the black church suture the fractured spirituality of black teens? If their rage has any redeeming qualities, how might the black church utilize their redemptive rage?

Holy Indignation as Redemptive Rage

I contend that black adolescent rage, when the Holy Spirit works through that rage, has power to save humankind from sin, which includes race, class, and gender injustice. When black adolescent rage is placed in God's redeeming embrace, known in Jesus Christ, it has power to transform those sins that denigrate and dehumanize all our sisters and brothers, regardless of age, race and ethnicity, socioeconomic status, or sexuality. This redemptive rage is *holy indignation.*

When the Holy Spirit works through teens' holy indignation, this is God's saving work. Holy indignation means righteous anger and its positive expression in the context of the African American church and the larger society. It is the freedom to express anger against injustice in the sacred space of the church.[27] Holy indignation in the church includes the positive expression of rage through music, dance, visual art, and the spoken word, as well as in the public arena through social activism and protest as nonviolent direct action. I advocate that the black church become a sanctuary, literally and metaphorically, for African American adolescent rage. This requires the church to welcome adolescent rage so that rage may be shaped, through the power of the Holy Spirit, into a positive force, a transformative emotion for the good of humankind.

An important starting point for holy indignation is the public expression of anger and rage in the church. The church needs to be a context that holds youth rage and encourages its expressions and its transposition into holy indignation. Such a movement requires change in contemporary church practice. One important change would be to create spaces for youth to express themselves through ritual performance, especially to express their rage. Rap music and liturgical dance are helpful examples of art forms that could become part of these rituals, creating opportunities for youth to express rage publicly and within a safe (sanctuary) community.

To be clear, I am advocating for black youth to be allowed and encouraged to talk about the anger they feel at an appointed place and time in the church. Whether they share their rage in weekly worship or youth ministry programs all depends on the local congregation. Such expression of adolescent rage is the spiritual discipline of testimony, in which youth speak "truthfully about what they have experienced and seen, offering it to the community for the edification of all."[28] According to Thomas Hoyt, testimony is "telling the truth to God about our lives and bearing witness to others about God's redemptive activity in the world."[29] When black teens are allowed to tell the truth about their anger before the congregation, they are participating in the communal practice of testimony. One can rightly argue that this form of testimony does not follow the common prescription of testimony in the African American church, in which words of thanksgiving and celebration of conversion experiences are shared.

Nevertheless, when teens and adults tell the truth about their pain, laying it naked before the gathered community, they are testifying. This form of testimony, expressing holy indignation in the sanctuary, requires educating the congregation about new ways of testifying before God in the community of faith. In some ways, testimony as holy indignation is a pouring out of pain and struggle already practiced in black congregations. In many congregations it is common to see tears streaming down a person's face as he or she shares troubles before God and the congregation. The agony and sometimes anger is a precursor for the type of holy indignation I have described.

Subsequent to the ritualizing of black adolescent rage, and in conjunction with this form of testimony, black teens should be engaged in consciousness-raising educational ministry that will help them understand the systems of injustice that cause their anger. Consciousness-raising ministry helps young people become aware of political, social, economic, and sexual forms of power that are often clandestine in nature, yet manifest in destructive and dehumanizing ways. The goal is to help black youth become aware of powerful entities that set policy on state, national, and global levels, affecting their lives and the lives of those they love. Consciousness-raising ministry helps youth become exegetes of the many contexts and cultures that intersect their lives. Such skills of reading and interpreting their social realities will keep them alert to inconsistency, incongruity, immorality, and illogical activity in church and society. The youth ministry approach in David White's *Practicing Discernment with Youth,* as well as that in *Trouble Don't Last Always,* seeks to engage teens in consciousness-raising and transformative ministry.[30]

Through ritualized opportunities to testify and express adolescent rage and through consciousness-raising educational ministry, congregations can experience the redemptive activity of Jesus Christ anew. At the same time they will also experience the sanctification of the church. Holy indignation is sanctifying rage and brings new life, new possibilities, and new hopes through the power of the Holy Spirit.

14

Welcoming the Vernal Season of the Heart

Discoveries in the Youth Discipleship Project

DAVID F. WHITE

This golden stage [of adolescence] when life glistens and crepitates...has wrought a great work in the world and infected it with love of beauty everywhere. It is the vernal season of the heart and the greatest stimuli for the imagination... Their bud is curiosity... Staring, experimenting with sensation, surprise, active observation, the passion to touch, handle, taste everything, often apparent cruelty due to the lust to know.[1]

Muted chuckles emerge from the corner where sixteen-year-olds, Raymond and James, are huddled over a computer screen creating a Web site to warn youth of the dangers of being exploited by the media. Chairs scrape loudly across the wooden floor as Sarah and a group of six girls rearrange the furniture to make space for a skit illustrating healthy ways of dating and relating to the opposite sex. Jeremy and Jennie create a mild distraction to the thespians, dragging garden tools across the room from the community garden. Salim engages in heated debate with Pastor Melissa about the church's role in the Middle East. Still other young people spill onto the front steps of the gothic urban church, eating watermelon and chatting casually with some adults. These are the sights and sounds of the Youth Discipleship Project, sights and sounds of the Spirit alive in youth.

This chapter is a reflection on the curiosity, creativity, and energy of youth, what G. Stanley Hall calls "a vernal season of the heart." Sometimes in our projections about youth as the *future* of the church or society, we

210

obscure a truth expressed by G. Stanley Hall that young people bear certain kinds of beauty that involve curiosity, creativity, and energy. Speaking theologically, this suggests that teenagers represent spiritual gifts for the church and the broken world, gifts bearing witness to the beauty of God. Yet, especially in a culture that inhibits such vitality by plopping the young before TVs or teaching that happiness consists of consuming goods, flourishing must be cultivated by alternative activities and relationships. What activities and relationships will enhance the creative capacities that Hall observed and for which Christian faith hopes? These were core questions that guided the Youth Discipleship Project. Taking such questions seriously might constitute distinctive approaches to the church's ministry with youth. To guide the investigation, I offer an extensive case study of the development of the Youth Discipleship Project, its findings and its failures.

Beginning in 1993, a few seminaries, with encouragement from the Lilly Endowment, recognized that they might claim a role alongside congregations and denominations in exploring alternate approaches to youth ministry.[2] In 1997, the Youth Discipleship Project (YDP) at Claremont School of Theology inaugurated an experiment to enhance the church's capacities to empower youth as agents of faith in their congregations, communities, and world. In this chapter, I will describe this experiment in practical theological pedagogy, especially as it evolved in the critical third year of the YDP. To this end, I will first present the basic form of YDP, much of which continued through the life of the Project. In a later section, I will describe the discoveries that sparked a significant shift in the program's focus. The value of such a retrospective account is that it sheds light on contextual learning and on the dynamics of leadership required to follow the leading of the Spirit and to enhance the vitality of ministry with youth. Such a project might be replicated, of course, but it is more likely to inspire other projects and approaches to youth ministry. That is our hope. Below is a brief description of the activities and relationships that formed the pedagogical heart of YDP.

Core Pedagogy

The above picture of young people engaging in creative actions that nurture their spiritual gifts—creating a Web site, a skit about dating, and a communal garden; arguing politics and theology; and relating with adults—did not emerge spontaneously. It involved creating pedagogical spaces "in which obedience to truth is practiced."[3] Recent research focuses on the *creation* of adolescence as a time bridging childhood and adulthood. The research reveals that contemporary adolescence has rendered youth relatively alienated from their families, local communities, and the earth—from their own hearts, minds, souls, and bodies, thus inhibiting the vitality and curiosity that Hall observed in 1904.[4] Further, some argue that such distraction inhibits youth's capacities to sense the Holy in their lives.[5]

If young people are to reconnect to their minds, hearts, souls, and bodies, to God and others, they must first learn alternative practices. The question of how to empower young people to live into their giftedness was central in the YDP. Thus, YDP adopted a practical theological pedagogy. Specifically, we invited young people to:

1. *listen*–attend to situations that evoke their passions, such as anger, sadness, frustration, joy, or feelings of connection;
2. *understand*–analyze the systemic forces in which these situations are constituted;
3. *dream*–imagine their life situations as illumined and reshaped through biblical and theological reflection and prayer; and
4. *act*–discern, strategize, and respond to God's call in the world.

This pedagogical process involved young people with adults in learning communities, exploring questions and strategizing faithful responses.[6] The communities participated in a range of pedagogical activities including: drama and art groups to express their life stories, study groups to explore the social conditions and theological possibilities for their lives, and covenant groups and daily worship to pray and attend to God's call upon their lives. In addition, youth participated in plenary groups to share their findings, and in action projects to address emergent issues and contribute to their local communities. These activities will be elaborated subsequently.

The YDP hoped to engage young people in navigating the diversity of Southern California, helping them to reach across ethnic, regional, and class boundaries to establish lasting partnerships with each other in God's work. Tolerance, understanding, and solidarity–witnessed through the youthful actors, Web designers, theologians, or farmers–are signs of God's reign. They are also practical necessities in an interdependent world in which people are increasingly aware of the enormous price of intolerance. Underlying these commitments to empowerment and solidarity, we placed hope in a God who seeks to heal the world by lifting us into a dance toward God's reign. We sought to empower youth as agents of faith, capable of resisting domestication and engaging in joyful partnership with God within this blessed and broken world. To fulfill these purposes, we invited approximately sixty diverse young people to join twenty adult leaders at local colleges or nearby mountain retreat centers in Southern California to form four-week residential learning communities.

Programmatic Elements

What would make sixteen-year-old Amanda, with little interest in school, grasp the complex needs of a community and the environment and develop a sense of urgency to till and plant a vacant lot for a vegetable garden? What activities and relationships would spark her passion for learning, compassion, and action? A good pedagogical theory is not enough;

theory must be embodied in concrete structures. The core structures of the YDP program included study groups, plenary groups, covenant groups, and worship. Though many aspects of the program were to change from year to year, these remained constant through the three summers of YDP.[7] Of course, some learning happened in other spaces, but the relationships, activities, and conversations begun in these groups spilled into informal reflections and helped form a learning community. In a sense, living in community created favorable conditions for this pedagogy; and the pedagogy created a more favorable community. The programmatic structures made space for both.

Selection Process

In the first two YDP summers, young people from across the United States were invited to apply for the summer community.[8] We sent application materials to churches, Christian schools, youth organizations, denominational youth departments, and ministers across the United States. Of the five thousand sets of application materials sent out each year and the hundreds of applicants, only sixty youth were chosen to participate. These sixty were chosen according to a range of criteria, including: regional, ethnic, gender, and class diversity; community involvement; self-awareness; commitment to the church; intellectual curiosity; and their church's readiness to support them upon return home. Instead of identifying and recruiting only academically successful youth, we viewed our role as cultivating curiosity among diverse youth, equipping them to explore questions and respond to God's call into partnership. We assumed that, whatever their academic achievement (as typically measured), many youth hold deep curiosity about their world, their faith, and their place in God's world. These capacities are important for partnership in God's redemptive work.

In creating the application materials, we recognized that God sometimes speaks in and through diverse modes of intelligence, not just linear rational expression. In addition to written essays, we allowed young people to submit art projects to express their commitments. In and through these alternatives, some were much more articulate than they might have been if limited to written essays. In using these alternate forms of expression, young people were already engaging in one of the rhythms of our core pedagogy—telling their stories through poetry, drawings, drama, songs, and creative writing. By recognizing artistic expression as a way of knowing, we affirmed our understanding of God's incarnation—that in Christ God lived in human flesh, and God continues to move in and through the bodies, souls, and hearts of youth.

We also recognized that living and working in contexts such as the YDP community demanded readiness in youth—including emotional and relational readiness to work collaboratively. We discovered that a caring community of adults and youth could help build relational capacities in youth, provided we had a critical mass of youth and adults with relational abilities and plans to hold young people in care while inviting them to work with and care for others. Selection was thus done with great care–discerning which youth were prepared to work in this unique context.

Study Groups

"I can't believe this is so much fun!" said Roberto. "I've never had fun using my mind before!" The excited speaker was a sixteen-year-old African American young man, who discovered the joy of connecting his heart and mind with the world around him. In the summer program, young people worked daily in groups of twelve to explore their lives–what made them angry, sad, frustrated, joyful, loved, appreciated, or connected. Roberto was in a group of young men who seemed to ache for answers to a single question: "Why were young men of color in their community continually harassed by police?" According to Roberto and his friends, the police in their neighborhood rousted them daily, stopped their cars for no reason, and surveyed them suspiciously at they shopped at local malls. They told stories about friends who were serving sentences in prison or juvenile detention centers. Many other youth were visibly moved by their stories; they decided to study the situation and find ways to respond.

Roberto and his friends, like other youth and adults, participated in one of the five study groups, each composed of twelve young men and women from diverse communities. Roberto's story is only one example of those told by young people in these groups–some evoking sadness or anger, while others evoked joy or delight. Each study group was facilitated by an adult whose aim was to find different ways to facilitate young people in telling their stories of life in their communities, including their hopes and dreams for their futures. A variety of means were utilized, including simple discussion, guided meditations, videos, music, art, storytelling, poetry, and drama. In the telling of these stories, young people were teaching each other and the adults about their worlds and God's work in their midst.

Ultimately, the curriculum for these groups–the subject of their listening, understanding, dreaming, and acting–emerged from the young people and their life situations. Each group selected one or two themes that articulated their common concerns. These themes were explored critically, theologically, and strategically, as young people considered potential responses. Themes identified by young people included: police harassment, media manipulation of youth, inane forms of schooling, problems with parents, environmental racism, sexual harassment of women, and pressures on boys toward violence and productivity.

Plenary Groups

In addition to daily study groups, YDP held daily plenary sessions that served as opportunities for groups to share findings about their chosen themes. In these plenary sessions, study groups took turns teaching the entire community about their topic and reflecting with the groups how their respective themes were related. Our hope was that, by the end of summer, the young people would gain deeper insight into their themes and situations, and see how these were interwoven. One benefit of exploring the relationships among themes was the opportunity to discover root causes. Seeing situations as discrete is more likely to suggest responses than perpetuate problems. For example, one group presented a plenary about the entertainment and fashion industries, focusing on how they form youth's ideas about how they should speak and dress. They pointed out that creating ever-evolving youth niche markets of music and fashion often alienate young people from their parents and local communities (creating a rift in norms and values, a phenomenon that Quentin Schultze and his colleagues call "the big chill").[9] These young people gained a more comprehensive view of the market culture when they discovered how much the entertainment media influenced boys' attitudes toward violence and women's attitudes toward sexuality and dating. Studying these issues side by side revealed their common relationship to consumerism and media exploitation and intensified the youth's concern to resist consumerist patterns. Such overlap sparked endless dorm conversations and provided a sense of solidarity.

In addition to group reports, the plenary sessions became venues to highlight research that represented underlying themes common to several of the groups. For example, we invited guest speakers or reviewed video resources to help us reflect on racism, gender inequities, or consumer economics. At still other times, plenary sessions became opportunities to rehearse, via dramatic skits or discussions, ways to address injustices or to participate in ongoing works of justice, beauty, or study.

Covenant Groups

In addition to critical and theological study, YDP recognized the importance of inner spiritual life and small groups to support youth. If, as theologians insist, God works best through love and not fear, then our challenge is to "fear not."[10] Yet, fears are not always conscious. They require prayer and reflection to become evident as inhibitions to faith and then to be resisted.[11] Identifying and resisting our inhibitions to faith are best done alongside trusted others who can challenge and hold us accountable.

The significance of youth struggling with their inhibitions can be seen more clearly in a particular instance. Over a period of several days, certain study groups explored the dynamics of advertising—how advertising intentionally exploits the emotional voids of adolescents, such as desires for intimacy, identity, meaning, community, or even a connection to the Holy. The purpose is to create affinities with advertisers' products. The youth explored the role of fashion in adolescent peer culture—how peer status is to some degree determined by what fashions teens consume. They also learned how important it is for marketers to create discontent with "outdated" products to create desires for new ones. Young people accepted these ideas as long as they remained abstractions. However, when a guest speaker made these ideas personal by explaining how Nike athletic shoes are made and sold, he struck a defensive chord in our teens. "Nike is not so bad, I love Nike!" some argued with conviction–even in the face of the speaker's evidence, such as Nike's exploitation of sweatshop labor, and the problem of urban teens who have killed each other for shoes. Many young people defended their Nike products. The speaker noted, "You would have thought I was speaking ill of their mothers!" A simple awareness of Nike's practices of exploitation was insufficient to challenge young peoples' entrenched habits of consumption. A change began to take place as covenant groups examined, through prayer and journaling, the hopes and fears that were represented in their defense of Nike. Some realized that Nike products had become a source of identity for them. Others feared rejection by peers or being "out of step" with fashion trends. Only through prayer, journaling, art, and dramatizations of their inner struggles were they able to begin to diffuse their inordinate attachments to these products.

To provide space for young people to attend to these attachments and inhibitions, young people met daily with small groups of six to eight other youth and two adults for spiritual reflection and practice. These small covenant groups engaged youth in a wide array of contemplative practices. At their best, these covenant groups served as an opportunity for group spiritual direction–functioning in response to the findings of their study groups and attending to how God is lovingly calling them to address the broken world, including their gifts and inhibitions for such work.

Worship

Worship was a near constant reality in the YDP community, occurring on Sunday mornings and every evening. Each Sunday the study groups "made pilgrimage" to various churches in the area, introducing youth to the ethnic and religious diversity in the Southern California area. We visited mainline Protestant churches, evangelical churches, Pentecostal churches, Unitarian churches, African American churches, Quaker and Mennonite churches, and Catholic churches of every ethnic variety. Sometimes, the churches were chosen according to themes studied in the study groups. For example, one group studying race made pilgrimage to a local congregation known for its theological and political response to racism.

Young people often responded to these pilgrimages with emotions ranging from delight to suspicion, especially in going to those churches with unfamiliar styles. These pilgrimages always prompted lengthy conversations about God, the church, and history, as well as much inner reflection about their resistance to certain styles. While few ended up adopting a different worship tradition, many left with a greater confidence that God works in many ways across traditions. These pilgrimages also fostered understanding of individuals for each other. We frequently overheard conversations in which young people confided sentiments such as, "I feel like I know you much better since I've been to a church like yours."

In addition to these Sunday pilgrimages, young people took turns each evening creating worship experiences for the YDP community. In these worship contexts, the influence of their various religious and ethnic traditions was evident. These were not simply opportunities for youth to reproduce the worship of their home communities. These worship creations became exercises in "playfully" reinventing worship to include experiences from other worship settings. We saw, for example, Presbyterian youth learning to sing gospel music, African Americans experimenting with contemplative prayer, and Hispanic Baptists crafting formal liturgy.

Rethinking YDP as a Contextual Project

"This is hard!" exclaimed Jeremy, "It doesn't seem right."

"What?" I asked, wanting to respect Jeremy's complaint, since he had gone to the trouble of speaking to me in private under cover of darkness, out of earshot of other youth.

"I mean, I'm not so sure I want to tell them about my neighborhood. I sort of came here to forget about that for a while." In his gentle manner, Jeremy was telling me that he and others were resisting the core pedagogy that engaged them in reflecting on their culture, local and popular.

"Say more," I encouraged.

"O.K., for example, you know when you are meeting someone for the first time, you don't say, 'Tell me about your family or community, or something like that'; you say, 'Hey man that's a cool shirt... Have you heard that new Snoop CD?'"

"O.K., right." I nodded. I began to realize that I had not been a sufficient student of youth culture to anticipate this concern.

This conversation with Jeremy took place in the second year of YDP in a mountain retreat in Idyllwild, California. It continued over many days and included many staff and youth. It helped to confirm a suspicion about the youth's inhibitions and revealed the etiquette of young people to engage in small talk, especially talk of popular culture, when getting to know others.[12] In essence, Jeremy's question and the many conversations that it prompted helped to verify our observations that, despite our hope that youth would eagerly explore their home contexts, their foremost concern was to negotiate the exigencies of life in the YDP community. For Jeremy, the demands of meeting new people and establishing common ground with them took priority over reflecting on his home context.

Youth also evidenced other priorities, such as resolving conflict and finding their place in the community. Ironically, as young people made their chief priority the emergent task of negotiating the YDP community, they avoided encounters with diversity and reflections on the wounds and blessings of their home communities. Rather than reflecting about the social locations that made their lives dissimilar, youth preferred discussions of popular culture—music and rap artists, television and movie actors, and fashion—to create a basis for friendship. While we appreciated young peoples' desire for unity, we nevertheless suspected that such unity represented something like pseudo-community, not mindful of the particularities of their lives or the possibilities of mobilizing with each other for change. This insight was one of several that prompted a new model for contextualizing YDP within familiar communities.

In light of these difficulties and other practical and theological considerations, we suspected that our original decision to move youth from their local contexts into college or retreat settings may have contributed to their hesitance to explore their social locations. After scrutinizing our experiences over two summers, we implemented changes to ground youth more deeply in their communities so as to reflect our theological commitment to enlarge the capacities of congregations to empower youth.

The most significant and determinative change in our third year was to work directly with and within local congregations in a single community in Pomona, California, instead of with individual youth gathered from across the country. We also decided to organize the YDP community rather like a day school, allowing youth to remain in their homes and neighborhoods at night (except for a few evenings when we hosted coffeehouses or dances) and to join together during the day. Our intent was to keep them geographically and emotionally close to their community, family, and congregation, while creating opportunities for them to reflect critically, theologically, and appreciatively on these contexts. The reasons for this shift were manifold. Below are the most significant.

- *Contextual reflection.* We hoped that engaging youth within their home contexts might *maximize their ability to reflect on their lives and communities.* Grounding YDP within their communities kept their experiences of these communities immediate enough to compel study and response. For example, a young man might be better able to recall the fear of being rousted by police when living in and reflecting on his familiar home environment. Also, grounding the project amid friends, family, and congregations removed some anxieties of navigating a new environment.
- *Community engagement.* We hoped that a localized model would allow us to *engage youth in more direct and immediate action in their home communities.* While in previous distant retreat settings, we succeeded in leading young people in general reflections on adolescent life, the distance precluded the opportunity for youth to engage in concrete action within their communities. We hoped that living and reflecting

within a community might enable us to move more quickly from reflection to action and back to reflection, thus enhancing our learning.

- *Support through family and congregational relationships.* Perhaps our most important hope was that *home communities, families, and congregations could reinforce growth of youth over time,* thus enhancing the sustainability of the project. The young people could be supported by people whose love for and knowledge of them extends years backward and forward. Moreover, if young people were going to become agents of change in their communities, they could work more effectively with their congregations, families, and youth groups than alone. We hoped to enhance the capacities of congregations to be more attentive with youth, helping them to create pedagogical spaces and discover their resources for supporting youth.

All of these hopes and more were grounded in our theological perspective: that the church is a context for nurturing relationships, in which lives can be formed in interdependent partnership with others and with God. As we reflected on our work in the first two years and on our new questions, we discovered several theological commitments about which we wanted to be more intentional. In sum, we accented the church as a tangible witness of Jesus Christ in history—a sacramental glimpse into God's nature and purposes. If the church is to embody God's nature and purposes, Christians must continually assess God's call on the church as a body. The work of Christian formation is never an individual endeavor. It involves our being held by a committed and intentional community, seeking to respond to God's call in a particular time and place.

In conclusion, our rethinking led us to believe that our hopes for young people could best be fulfilled within the communal context of churches living in the creative tension of their daily ministries, and within the theological context of witnessing to Jesus Christ and practicing sacramental presence in a particular time and place. These practical and theological insights became guiding principles as we reshaped the summer program.

Restructuring YDP: Relocating and Redirecting

In light of these guiding principles, we set out to help young people forge connections with their churches and communities, which meant relocating and redirecting the YDP. This one decision generated an array of other changes, generating the "whirling, buzzing confusion" of YDP's new pedagogical context, which I now introduce. In dialogue with staff and participants, we made five key changes: grounding the project in five partner congregations, integrating church staff, drawing on the resources of each congregation, educating congregations, and making worship pilgrimages to each congregation.

Grounding YDP in Partner Congregations

Having selected Pomona, California, as our "ground," the YDP administrative staff met with local pastors in Pomona to build relationships and recruit churches that shared our perspectives and purposes. In conversation with these pastors and congregations, we framed the invitation to join YDP as an opportunity to join with other congregations, their youth, and God as partners in their community. We found no lack of pastors and churches that were eager to engage such a partnership. Five congregations were selected on the basis of their diversity, the congruity of their ministries with our aims, and their need for such work with youth. Another criterion was the churches' creativity in witnessing to Christ in their communities, for we wanted young people to observe diverse ways of serving God.

We determined that the YDP summer community would spend one full week in each church,[13] conducting our daily worship, study, plenary, and covenant groups. These five churches were spread geographically around the city. They were ethnically, denominationally, and economically diverse: (1) an ethnically diverse urban Lutheran (ELCA) congregation; (2) an Anglo-American suburban Presbyterian (USA) congregation; (3) a rural Hispanic American Baptist congregation; (4) a United Methodist congregation in a transitional neighborhood; and (5) a Pentecostal African American congregation.

Each congregation had unique wounds, blessings, and ministries with the larger community. For example, the rural Hispanic congregation had established a large community vegetable garden. The urban Lutheran congregation had a long record of fighting on behalf of civil rights in their community. The black Pentecostal congregation had founded a school for teaching black heritage, dignity, and responsible citizenship. Once these congregations were selected, each church set up a small steering committee of four to ten participants to select twelve youth for this project and to remind the congregation to pray for their youth, our program, and their church's growth in forming and embracing the gifts of youth. Partnership with these congregations was key to relocating YDP in this local context.

Integrating Church Staff

Whereas in previous summers the YDP staff was largely constituted of seminarians and doctoral students, we sought, in this new incarnation of YDP, to integrate local church pastors, youth leaders, and Christian education directors into our work. Staff training involved four weekend retreats spread over the nine months prior to the summer. In these training weekends, adult staff formed themselves as a Christian community of practice—which would later draw youth alongside them in community. A key priority of these training events involved orienting and training staff in the pedagogical approach of the program. Our hope was that the church staff people might find value in this approach to youth ministry and attempt to sustain some version of it in their congregations following the summer program. More important, however, the church staff folks made important contributions. They became our guides to understanding the young people and their communities, and they contributed important insight about practical approaches.

Exploring and Enlisting the Resources of the Congregations

Once the summer began, each week became an opportunity for young people from host congregations to express pride in their church and religious and ethnic traditions, while also exploring the forces within their community that limit fullness of life and faith. They did this in diverse ways. For example, each congregation insisted on preparing food for our roving community of youth and adults, often providing food that bore some relationship to their ethnic or church identity. Also, pastors and laypeople from each congregation provided an introduction to the history, theology, and practices of their particular congregation, as well as their understanding of the social context of their community.

As various study groups struggled to understand issues such as poverty, racism, ageism, sexism, or environmental degradation in their communities, pastors provided insight from the standpoint of their particular biblical and theological traditions. It was heartening to see groups of twelve youth filing into the pastors' offices to glean their theological perspectives. It was also fascinating to observe how the questions raised by curious young people challenged pastors to consider new theological questions and possibilities.

Educating Congregations

We knew that one failure of our original vision of empowering youth was our inability to change the assumptions and patterns of congregations who considered youth incapable of assuming important roles. We addressed this problem by engaging church leaders in evaluating the assumptions and patterns that support or suppress youth empowerment. On one night each week, we engaged congregational leaders in discussions about youth in the life of their congregations and communities. Leaders selected from the host church of that week gathered for the purpose of reflecting on ways to create space for youth empowerment in their congregation's life and to share with each other their own successes and struggles.

These conversations yielded a number of potential and actual experiments: involving youth more significantly on church committees and worship, mentoring youth as leaders, offering more intergenerational mission opportunities, providing resources for families to empower their youth, engaging youth in the church's traditional rhythms of worship, and pastors' listening to youth's ideas for more lively worship styles.

Making Worship Pilgrimages to Partner Congregations

In an effort to engage youth in appreciating the diversity of ethnic and religious expressions represented in the community, the entire YDP summer community made worship "pilgrimages" to one of the five congregations each Sunday morning prior to the summer community's relocating in that church for the coming week. These worship pilgrimages provided opportunities for young people to gain more complete understanding of the religious communities of other youth and, by comparison, to know their own traditions better. The rituals, languages, stories, and practices of each congregation, while holding enough common ground to be familiar, also involved distinctively different expressions of Christian faith.

Each congregation contributed distinctive perspectives for interpreting God's work amidst the charisms and limits of its distinctive community. For example, the African American Pentecostal worship emphasized celebrating God's benevolence and responding in gratitude, while the Mexican American Baptist worship emphasized humility, community, and hard work for the common good. The urban Lutheran congregation embodied their faith commitments by showing generosity and hospitality to our group of young people. The suburban Presbyterian congregation revealed creativity in the music and artistry of their worship, embodying their commitments to God's freedom and continual renewal. We realized, in every case, that these were not random acts. They represented characteristic ways of understanding God's work and call.

In addition to revealing something about their theological commitments, the worship and practices of these congregations also revealed something about their social contexts and their struggles in being faithful. For example, the Mexican American Baptist congregation was set in a working-class community that rarely received a fair share of public funding for streets, schools, or law enforcement. They saw their neighborhood garden of flowers and vegetables as an attempt to bring beauty and bounty to this community—an act of faith in a God of beauty and providence. Similarly, the urban Lutheran congregation's hospitality with the youth mirrored their ministry with the homeless in their community. These idiosyncratic perspectives on the world and on God's call were condensed in the worship of these congregations—through sermons, scripture choices, songs and hymns, testimonies, and prayers. Not surprisingly, many themes emphasized by the YDP youth mirrored the theologies and ministries of their respective congregations.

The value of the worship pilgrimages cannot be overstated. While the congregations had already invested in the work of our summer community by contributing participants and staff, and by praying, the pilgrimage Sundays gave congregations an opportunity to meet the entire YDP community of youth and adults and to celebrate and commission the youth for ministry.

Fruits of Contextual Ministry

The YDP case study offers insight about meeting youth in the "vernal season of their hearts" and empowering them for faithful action. The YDP youth expressed their vernal season in many ways: crafting dynamic worship, creating poems and songs to express their feelings about the broken world, creating plays to express their hopes and fears, creating Web sites about violence and consumerism, creating T-shirts that warn teens about media exploitation, creating murals for their churches, and protesting legislation that criminalized minority youth. The case study reveals internal goods as well.

Increasing Contextual Awareness

The case study highlights values and practices of contextual awareness. Young people gained greater appreciation of the wounds and blessings of their own and other neighborhoods and churches. They regularly expressed surprise at how different life was for young people living only a few blocks away. The practice of moving through different neighborhoods and studying diverse contexts in relation to their generative themes increased their awareness of their own and other contexts. Young people from host churches came to see their churches and neighborhoods through the eyes of visiting young people. They saw disparities in material and social conditions, in ethnic and religious cultures. I recall the day we first traveled to the working-class Hispanic Baptist church. Two upper-middle-class Anglo girls confided to me their fear as our rented van jogged down a street with giant potholes and "tagged" signs. By midweek, these same girls delighted when the neighborhood children ran from their houses to greet them each morning. YDP youth came to celebrate how various congregations embraced their partnership with God in their particular contexts. Further, they developed more complex understandings of context, and began to imagine how to extend their own visions of partnership with God, both within and beyond their local neighborhoods.

Deepening Practical Theological Discussions

A second contribution of the case study is to reveal the significance of practical theological reflection for young people. For many young people, Christian faith exists in certain—usually marginal—practices and spaces. By developing habits of thinking about their lives from God's perspective, and about God from the perspective of their lives, young people grew into habits of thinking about God as an integral part of all of life. They also grew in considering themselves—their values, actions, commitments—in partnership with God's work in the world. By the end of the month, these youth had learned to consider topics such as politics, economics, race, gender, beauty, art, work, and play through the lens of Christian theology.

Enhancing Solidarity across Boundaries

Another fruit for youth ministry is the possibility and practice of solidarity. Cultivating friendships and moving temporarily into the neighborhoods of new friends helped YDP young people gain fuller understanding of the practices, values, and beliefs of others. It is easier for young people to appreciate the goodness of another ethnic, class, or religious community when they have eaten at their tables, prayed their prayers, sung their songs, and played with their children. Further, young people develop stronger bonds of loyalty, respect, and concern for others when their hearts have been broken by their stories. One significant learning moment occurred when youth from the upper-middle-class, European American Presbyterian church recognized the disparities in public resources afforded them in comparison to others. They raised questions about the diminishing tax base, loss of jobs, high crime rates, and deteriorating schools in other parts of the Pomona community. The young people, in that moment, recognized their common bond as humans and Christians. They encountered the concerns of others and committed to a common struggle for a more just world and a more humane city.

Increasing Community Involvement

Joining each other in a month of living and studying moved many young people to respond by forming small action groups to address their concerns. Some youth created a Web site to warn about local businesses that exploit young workers by underpaying or overworking them. Others created a theater production that illuminated problems in dating relationships and gender roles. Still others went to a city council meeting to protest a recent spate of police violence against youth in that community. These acts did not, by themselves, transform the community of Pomona, but they represented patterns of empowered Christian discipleship that may grow into more transformative dimensions as these young people influence friends and relatives and continue to engage issues.

Involving Youth More Fully in Their Congregations

Several congregations that participated in this community experiment had been struggling to discern how to engage their young people in meaningful ministry. Some of the congregations admittedly had fallen into patterns of treating youth as incapable, dangerous, or irresponsible, relegating them to minor roles and trivial programs. This project revealed the capabilities of youth and sparked the imaginations of congregations concerning possibilities for youth ministry. Following the summer program, several congregations actively sought to create a different quality of space for young people.

Conclusions

These few results do not exhaust the ways that the localized version of YDP bore fruit for youth and youth ministry. Certainly they reveal enhanced friendships and religious practices among young people and their congregations. We also know that several of the youth groups continued to meet in partnerships of recreation, study, worship, and/or community action. A longitudinal study would have been illuminating, but insights from the one summer and ensuing months are sufficient to point in promising directions.

The Youth Discipleship Project, and its engagement with five congregations, represents a glimpse of hope for the future of youth ministry. Specifically, a hope was born that ministry with youth might cross boundaries of difference in forming opportunities for friendship and solidarity, might empower youth to partner with God in God's work of healing, and might integrate youth more fully into their congregations' work of knowing and responding to God. The experience and testimonies and actions of participants keep that hope alive for me. Thus, I close with an invitation to local congregations to consider the visions, rhythms, and practices described here as possibilities for engaging with youth as partners with God in healing their communities.

15

Transformative Listening

JENNIE S. KNIGHT

On a hot, smoggy July morning, twelve high-school youth and two adults sat in a circle in a college classroom, talking about gender and sexuality. As part of the inaugural year of the Youth Discipleship Project at the Claremont School of Theology, sixty youth from across the country and twenty adults had come to live as community for one month on the campus of Scripps College in Claremont, California. Our intention was to engage with youth in ways that addressed their central concerns, focusing on "generative themes"—issues around which they had the most emotion and worry. When we unwitting adults facilitated initial exercises with the youth to identify their generative themes, two-thirds of the youth wanted to explore issues of sexuality and gender. A lucky twelve were chosen from this majority to be in a month-long exploration group about the topic. Ironically, but not surprisingly, when the adult group leaders gathered to decide which groups they would lead, no one wanted the topic of sexuality and gender. Finally, one brave man agreed to lead the group. As co-director of the project, I agreed to join him as a female presence in leadership.

On our first day of discussion, in a group of ethnically and economically diverse youth, equally divided between males and females, the discussion turned toward sexual harassment and sexual violence. The room was alive with laughter as the students told stories of almost constant verbal and physical sexual aggression, both in and out of school. We, the adult leaders, were horrified. When girls told stories about being grabbed repeatedly in school, with no intervention by adults, they laughed as if it were simply a funny inconvenience.

I asked, "Doesn't it bother you when that happens? Don't you get angry?" One girl responded, "You do the first time." I asked, "Then what

226

happens?" Several girls responded, saying, "You get used to it. You just become numb to it."

The girls also admitted (and several boys confirmed) that, at some schools, girls initiated sexually harassing behavior toward boys as well. They did not see girls as innocent victims. The discussion revealed a highly sexualized, aggressive culture that boys and girls alike negotiate on a daily basis.

The discussion later turned to the story of a girl who was gang-raped by an entire sports team at the high school of one of the youth present. The entire group of youth laughed raucously at the story. I felt physically ill. As they described the details, I felt overwhelmed and asked them to stop for a moment.

One of the girls exclaimed, "But you said you wanted to hear us!" I had to admit that she was right. I encouraged them to continue the discussion, hoping that our questions and leadership might enable them to move beyond laughter to critical, faithful reflection about these extraordinarily painful issues in their communities. In the following weeks, two of the girls in the group revealed that they had been sexually abused by an adult male in their lives.

Listening to youth, to the sometimes shocking, often distressing details of their experiences and to their sometimes incongruous emotional responses can be painful for adults. Many of us would rather avoid such discomfort. In the experience just described, we invited the students to share their truths about issues of sexuality and gender, and we were flooded with a torrent of disturbing stories and emotional responses by the youth. However, once we had promised to listen, the youth held us to that commitment. The result was a powerful revelation of deeper truths as the community unfolded.

In this chapter, I draw upon the extensive research of the Youth Discipleship Project (YDP), conducted during two month-long summer programs, as well as over the course of a two-year partnership project with twelve economically and ethnically diverse congregations. This is the same YDP that David White describes in the previous chapter. The focus of this chapter is to demonstrate the importance of listening to youth about their lives and their passions. As the story above reveals, our engagement in listening to youth was transformative for adults and youth alike. I place our findings in conversation with other significant studies of listening with adolescents. Through this conversation, I argue for youth ministry in which listening to youth is of central importance.

Previous research reveals that listening is equally important for girls and boys, yet their experiences and approaches to relationship are often quite different. Similarly, we discovered in the Youth Discipleship Project that, while youth of diverse backgrounds often share similar concerns (including alienation from adults, racial/ethnic stereotyping, violence, and gender/ sexuality issues), these concerns look quite different in diverse contexts. Thus, listening to youth requires paying attention to their particularities. Adults who aim to strengthen the selfhood and faith of youth need to listen to them in ways that not only affirm their feelings, but that also help them think critically about the sociocultural dynamics at work in their communities and empower them to act for positive change in light of their faith. To do this effectively, adults must take risks: acknowledging their own feelings, thinking critically about social issues, and taking action for social change. An approach to youth ministry that engages people in serious listening to youth thus leads to transformation in youth and adults alike.

Listening as the Foundation for Ministries with Youth

Listening to the voices, feelings, and experiences of youth is central in many approaches to youth ministry. However, a close exploration of the Youth Discipleship Project, in which a particular form of listening was foundational, can reveal significant new directions for future ministries with young people. In both the summer residential Youth Discipleship Communities and the two-year Church Partnership Program, we guided youth and adults through a process of discernment about the concerns and passions that were closest to the hearts of youth.[1] The process culminated in youth and adults taking creative public action together to address their concerns in positive ways.

The discernment process is based on the educational philosophy of Paulo Freire. In Freire's pedagogy, listening to a community and its concerns must always come first. Listening can take many forms—not simply through direct conversations, but also through drama, observation, and spiritual practices.[2] After listening, the community's concerns are re-presented to the community through "codes" (pictures, stories, skits, film clips, and so forth), so people may view them with critical distance and reflect about their causes and possible solutions. Based in this approach, the discernment process moves from practices of *listening* to practices of:

- *understanding* (thinking critically about particular themes and discovering their root causes);
- *dreaming* (reflecting on the resources of one's faith tradition and discovering a word of hope and guidance about how to address the theme from a faith perspective); and
- *acting* (planning and implementing an action project to address the theme).[3]

The process is a spiral in which people continually return to previous movements, and in which adults accompany youth as they move back and forth in the understanding, dreaming, and acting phases of the process. Listening remains the core throughout.

The exploration group described above reflected critically about their concerns related to sexuality and gender. They asked questions about why their churches had remained silent about these issues and how sexually aggressive realities influence the daily lives of youth. They dreamed about how churches could be safe spaces, sanctuaries of honest, loving communication and guidance. As their action project, they wrote and sent letters to approximately seven hundred congregations, outlining their feelings and concerns and advocating that churches need to provide a space for youth to talk about sexuality and gender issues without judgment, but with loving adult guidance.

The Power of Listening Adults

The presence of unflinching adult listeners is a key factor in youth's development into adults who are able to claim their voices; to create and maintain relationships with others in which their feelings are valued and respected; and to resist cultural forces such as sexism, racism, or classism that can cause them to devalue themselves and their abilities.[4] Boys and girls alike struggle to assert an authentic self-identity and to stay connected in genuine relationships in a culture that demands that they conform to stereotypes.[5]

Recent research reveals the alarming extent to which many boys and girls lose access to significant aspects of their emotional lives (and thus to significant parts of themselves) because of their struggles either to conform or to resist. The presence of empathic, nonjudgmental adults to listen to their feelings and experiences can help them gain critical awareness about themselves, their relationships, and their culture, including the cultural stereotypes that influence their formation. Such listening allows both girls and boys to affirm their whole selves in relationship with others and to strengthen their resistance to destructive influences in their lives without sacrificing their capacity for vulnerability. This research on female and male selfhood has profound implications for ministries with youth; thus we turn to representatives of that research to further our understanding of the needs and possibilities for listening to young people.

Listening to Girls

> *To listen to girls whose voices are ordinarily met with silence in the larger world is to invite disruption, disturbance, or dissolution of the status quo. To support the strengths, intelligence, resilience, and knowledge of girls whose culture or class are marginalized by society is to support political, social, educational, and economic change. It may be easier to sacrifice girls than to support their development, and when girls sense this, it may be hard for them, with the best of intentions, not to give up on themselves and sacrifice their own hopes.*[6]

Foundational studies of listening with girls have been conducted by a team whose research emanated from Carol Gilligan's early work on women's development. The result has been a series of research projects focused on young women in diverse cultural and religious settings. One of these projects is a helpful anchor for exploring the value of listening with girls. Jill McLean Taylor, Carol Gilligan, Amy Sullivan, and a larger group of women researchers from diverse ethnic and class backgrounds tracked the development of a group of twenty-two teenaged girls of different ethnicities, all poor and working class, from the eighth through eleventh grades. Through a series of interviews over these years, they found that one of the most important factors in girls' development, emerging with the ability to claim their voice and to stay in relationship, was for them to have a woman other than their mother who listened to them without judgment.

The authors focused on the girls' ability to maintain connection and relationships, without sacrificing themselves—their voices, feelings, opinions. This ability depended not only on their particular family situations, but also on their class, cultural, and racial backgrounds. The authors explain that, prior to adolescence, "many girls demonstrate a strong sense of self, an ability to know and voice their feelings and thoughts, and to give authority to their experience."[7] However, during adolescence, a shift takes place for many girls: they find their relationships threatened when they express their complex feelings and experiences with assertive voices.

For middle-class girls, this shift appears when they face pressure to shape themselves into a dominant cultural image of femininity *and* into ideals of maturity and adulthood that have previously been held for men but are now expected of women as well. One pressure is toward the cultural feminine ideal of the "perfect girl," who is selfless, "always nice and good, never hurts other people's feelings, who either lacks or can control hunger and sexual desire, and who contains her feelings, especially anger."[8] The other pressure is toward ideals of separation and independence associated with adulthood. Caught between these two ideals, girls often fear they will lose important relationships either way: either by giving up their feelings and voices to others or by giving up their relationships with others and learning to be self-sufficient. They find no easy in-between. Girls often dissociate from their bodies and feelings during this time, for the sake of maintaining inauthentic relationships and an image of perfection.

The authors of this study discovered that the girls they interviewed from low-income backgrounds, regardless of ethnicity (including girls of Portugese American, Irish American, African American, and Hispanic descent), did not feel the same pressure to conform to the "perfect girl" image that middle-class girls of diverse ethnicities do. Rather, they often claim the right to their voices and feelings, only to find themselves rejected and in danger of retaliation by adults and peers. Adults often do not want to hear what they have to say because it threatens the political, economic, educational, gendered, and raced status quo of society. Over the course of the study, these girls often became increasingly isolated from authentic relationships–choosing to be independent and seemingly strong to avoid risking further rejection and retaliation.

Faced with these pressures, girls choose several strategies of resistance. Some choose "covert resistance" to avoid the negative consequences of speaking out. While they appear outwardly to comply with conventions, they "go underground" with their feelings and knowledge. The danger of this conscious strategy of self-protection is that, when a girl has no confiding relationships, some kinds of knowledge can be lost to her, such that she becomes dissociated from her feelings and from herself. Girls who choose to speak out and act against relationships that feel false; against conventions that require silence or self-sacrifice; and against stereotypes based on race, ethnicity, class, or sex face the potential reactions of other people and of social systems that are threatened by their protest. Thus their "overt resistance" has its share of dangers for girls growing up in a society that demands that they conform.[9]

The girls who most successfully navigated this treacherous terrain of adult and youth pressures to conform–who were able to maintain access to their own thoughts and feelings and to healthy, authentic relationships, while also resisting social stereotypes–were better able to talk through their feelings and thoughts about all topics with a trusted adult. Unfortunately, for many youth, experiences of such listening are rare. One girl in the study, Ana, describes an aunt who listens to her and shares from her own experiences, saying, "She's crazy." The authors explain:

> Taking girls seriously, especially girls who might be labeled at risk, often means validating what girls know and feel to be true, and so it is perhaps no accident that Ana also says of her aunt "she's crazy." The label "crazy" that Ana affectionately ascribes to her aunt also reflects the cultural marginalization of unconventional women.[10]

Women (and men) who risk listening to youth and sharing honestly with them from their own experiences are often willing to challenge social norms and resist conformity themselves. They are willing to risk marginalization to maintain their integrity. These are the types of adults who can guide youth toward a similar form of selfhood through listening and through example. The challenge is for adults to do this critical work themselves so they might be present for youth in the ways they most need.

Listening to Boys

As with girls, boys also need adults to listen empathically to them, to affirm the full range of their emotions, and to challenge societal stereotypes. William Pollack and his research team have documented countless hours of interviews with hundreds of boys and their families from diverse ethnic and economic backgrounds across the United States. Based upon their findings, they argue that one of the primary reasons why, statistically, boys are falling behind girls in most areas of education is that boys are shamed at an early age to present to the world a "mask of masculinity" that conveys an image of "toughness, stoicism, and strength," when in fact "they feel desperately lonely and afraid." In 1998, boys were twice as likely as girls to be labeled learning disabled, made up 67 percent of high school special education classes, and constituted 71 percent of school suspensions. Only 58 percent of male high school graduates attended college, compared to 67 percent of females, and they were developing emotional problems at alarming rates. Boys were up to ten times as likely as girls to be diagnosed with a serious emotional disorder, and four to six times more likely than girls to commit suicide.[11] Rodger Nishioka discusses these concerns in his chapter as well.

While adolescent girls often experience a crisis of identity at adolescence, boys are forced to separate emotionally from their caregivers at the traumatically early age of about six years old. They are socialized through shame from a young age to regulate and deny emotions and characteristics that are not considered masculine, such as sadness, fear, and vulnerability. The result is that boys can mask and then lose awareness of major aspects of themselves at a young age. By the time they reach adolescence, boys are deeply invested in "saving face," in maintaining their image of masculinity at all costs to avoid the unthinkable shame of having their true vulnerability exposed.[12]

At the same time that boys become "hardened" into men through this process of solidifying their "mask of masculinity," society now presents them with conflicting messages that they are also expected to be sensitive and respectful in relationships with girls, able to share their feelings, and able to shed sexist "assumptions about male power, responsibility, and sexuality." Pollack argues that this confusing complex of often contradictory messages functions in society as a "Boy Code," an impossible ideal that boys experience with frustration, anger, depression, and plummeting self-esteem.[13]

As with girls, empathic adults who listen carefully to the verbal and nonverbal messages of boys can make an extraordinary difference in helping boys reclaim their whole selves and experience authentic relationships. However, because of painful experiences and shaming messages about sharing their feelings, boys need particular kinds of listening by adults. To access the inner lives of boys, adults need to:

1. create a safe, shame-free environment for conversation, in which the boy recognizes true empathy on the part of the listener
2. let boys know that the adults are available to listen, but allow boys to come to them on the boys' own timelines
3. connect with boys through "action-talk"–creating a space for conversation during a shared activity

4. listen with their complete attention, without interruption, and convey empathy through facial expressions, tone of voice, and the sharing of similar experiences

5. provide boys with affirmation and affection for who they are and for their genuine sharing[14]

These approaches to listening to boys require that adults be willing to shed their assumptions and fears about how boys and men are *supposed* to feel and behave. For men, this may involve healing from their own "mask of masculinity" so they can avoid perpetuating the cycle of shame for the next generations of boys. For women, it may involve recognizing the ways they place unrealistic shaming expectations on men and boys in their lives and then distance themselves emotionally from boys because of those expectations. For adults to be genuinely empathic with boys, they must be comfortable with their own emotions and be willing to share those with the young men. As is the case when listening to girls, they must also be willing to challenge social stereotypes and the ways they are enforced. They must be willing to seek wholeness within themselves and in society as they affirm and nurture the wholeness of boys. All of this requires change on the part of adults; therefore, many adults avoid listening carefully to youth.

Challenges to Listening between Adults and Youth

The discussion thus far reveals the crucial role of adults as listeners and the potential for the transformation of adults in the process. To listen to young people without judgment or condemnation is to invite them into critical thinking about their situations and to help them develop healthy strategies of resistance that do not involve sacrificing themselves or their relationships. Listening also encourages youth to express their complex feelings about topics that evoke discomfort in the larger society (taboo topics such as sexuality—as the above discussion of the YDP summer program demonstrates). Such listening requires adults to do the same work in their own lives. Unfortunately, adults often have not developed critical strategies of self-reflection and resistance or healthy patterns of relationship for themselves. They have not been willing to risk marginalization: to challenge social conventions and claim wholeness for themselves, their relationships, and society in general. Therefore, too often, they are not willing and/or able to be the listening presence that youth so desperately need for healthy development. Those adults who are willing to engage in the process of thinking critically and reflecting honestly with youth often find themselves challenged in ways that can disturb their equilibrium. Even those who consider themselves self-aware and critical about social issues can be pushed to new awareness by listening to the experiences of contemporary youth.

When I have asked seminary students and adult youth leaders in churches if adults avoid listening to youth, they have responded with an unequivocal "yes," and have offered several common reasons. First, these conversations confirm that many adults avoid listening to youth because they resist remembering their own adolescence. They are glad to be safely (more or less) on the other side of a difficult time in their own lives. Being in relationship with youth, even superficially, often brings to the surface insecurities and emotional pain from adolescence that many adults long to avoid. Inviting youth into genuine relationship, in which both the youth and adult share honestly about their experiences and emotions, increases the risk for adults of facing painful memories and feelings they would prefer to forget.

Second, some adults would rather not know about the realities of youth's lives. In spite of negative feelings about their own adolescence, they would rather imagine nostalgically that life for teenagers is the same as it was for them. Even with all of the difficulties of adolescence for previous generations, adolescents today face an overwhelming set of cultural pressures that few adults can even imagine. To listen to youth is to be forced to recognize distortions in our culture and the ways they shape the lives of our young people. This recognition challenges adults to work for significant social change. As the earlier discussion indicates, many adults are afraid of this risk; to listen to youth is to risk change. Hearing the stories can force adults out of their self- and generation-absorbed denial into a conviction for action that invites "disruption, disturbance, or dissolution of the status quo" and supports "political, social, educational, and economic change."

In addition to these inhibitions to listening to youth, particular cultural dynamics also impede communication between youth and adults in diverse contexts. Most of our partner congregations in the Church Partnership Program of the Youth Discipleship Project identified particular cultural dynamics at work in their congregations and communities that impede communication between youth and adults. The combination of these complex factors contributes to a cross-cultural phenomenon of alienation between youth and adults. In a part of YDP not described in the previous chapter, leadership teams of adults and youth in twelve ethnically, economically, and denominationally diverse congregations from Arizona, California, and Hawaii worked together to discern generative themes of youth in their communities. A dominant theme that emerged in most of the congregations was alienation between youth and adults. This alienation took different forms in different cultural contexts, however.

In a suburban United Church of Christ congregation east of Los Angeles, the youth felt very lonely at home because their parents work long hours. They felt alienated by the pressures that their parents placed upon them to succeed academically and financially. The youth were not convinced that they wanted to repeat the so-called "American Dream" that they saw, often unhappily, in their parents. In another middle-class, mostly European American Disciples of Christ congregation, many adults feared and mistrusted youth because of general cultural prejudices and fears, such as the assumption that youth are disrespectful, irreverent, and uninterested in spirituality.

In a Hawaiian United Methodist church where many members were Tongan, the Tongan youth felt great pressure to "save face" so their families would not be ostracized by the Tongan community. In particular, the Tongan girls had many responsibilities within their families, preventing them from participating in most youth-related activities. While many Tongan families move to the United States with the hope of educational and career success for their children, the intense pressure for girls to devote much of their time in helping their families prevents them from studying and preparing for college. The girls were frustrated by contradictions in their parents' words and behavior.

In a Unitarian Universalist congregation in Southern California, the research team discovered that a well-intentioned denominational history of promoting "Youth Autonomy" since the 1960s had left their youth feeling alone. They found difficulties in communication between youth and adults and a lack of inclusion of youth within the congregation because of these communication problems. A significant number of adults in this congregation felt that they had nothing to offer youth and expressed that they did not know how to reach out to them.

In a small South Los Angeles congregation, largely African American in membership, only a few adults were involved with youth in the congregation. Many adults were single parents struggling for the survival of their families. Some resented the attention given to the youth group because they were in desperate need of help themselves. The youth felt that the adults did not understand the pressures of "street culture" on them. Also, adults judged youth unfairly, and some disrespected them.

In a Korean/Korean American congregation, the language barrier between the Korean-speaking adults and English-speaking youth was the greatest source of alienation. In addition, youth felt confused by parents telling them that church is their most important priority, yet pressuring them to study and succeed academically rather than attend church events. Youth also felt resentment when adults stereotyped and gossiped about certain youth who did not live up to their standards of academic and social success.

As these examples demonstrate, cultural location shapes the contexts for youth's relationships with adults. Alienation caused by a variety of economic and cultural factors results in a breakdown in communication between youth and adults at a time when youth greatly need the compassionate, challenging, listening presence of both parental and nonparental adults. Through listening to youth (and adults) in each congregation, the pain of alienation and the root causes of that alienation for each community were uncovered. Only after careful listening were congregations able to gain critical understanding, to dream about how their faith traditions could guide adults and youth to live together differently, and to act together to make changes in their congregations, communities, and society at large. As a result, adults and youth alike were transformed.

Listening for Personal and Social Transformation

The conversation between the findings of the Youth Discipleship Project and research about the listening needs of adolescent girls and boys reveals the transformative potential of listening to youth. Listening must be affirming and nonjudgmental, however, if it is to lead to critical awareness and faithful social action. For girls, this might involve a woman's sharing from her experiences to affirm their feelings. For boys, this might mean creating space for talk during shared activities rather than conversation in a public setting where they do not feel comfortable revealing their vulnerability. In the approach to youth ministry developed at the Youth Discipleship Project, the generative themes of youth in a particular congregation and/or community are discovered through listening. The literature demonstrates, however, that this is only effective if the context for listening is safe, nonjudgmental, empathic, and affirming.[15] In such a context, through experiences of being listened to and affirmed, and of listening to adults and other youth, youth not only begin to understand the social, cultural pressures affecting their churches and communities; they also begin to understand and appreciate themselves.

In addition, listening occurs through careful observation of youth as they interact in their daily lives. About what do youth seem most passionate? Where are they pushing past apathy? This form of listening can be conducted effectively by teams of youth and adults together, such that youth experience self-reflection with critical distance as they observe other youth in their communities. Also, they can serve as translators for the adult listeners, explaining the dynamics of the youth culture in their context. This form of action-listening empowers youth to take leadership in listening for the concerns of the youth. In this way, they feel affirmed and respected by adults with whom they are partnered in the discernment process. In this process, youth may or may not share personal struggles and emotions with the adults. As the research about both girls and boys reveals, youth often feel more comfortable confiding in adults when they can come to them on their own terms rather than in an orchestrated group setting. For this reason, these informal conversations are an essential part of the listening process.

As the discernment process moves through the next stages of understanding, dreaming, and acting, listening to the voices and passions of youth remains central to the work. As adults and youth think critically together and research the generative themes in their communities, as they reflect about the resources of their faith tradition and what that tradition has to say about their particular themes, and as they collaborate to develop and implement ministries of action to address the themes, youth and adults are in constant conversation. Throughout the process, youth experience the presence of adults who take them seriously, who are willing to challenge stereotypes and the status quo, and who believe that youth can make significant contributions in the church, the surrounding community, and the larger society. While the process often takes place in groups, the research discussed above indicates that the influence of one-on-one relationships between youth and adults that develop through this work is immeasurably significant.

We also discovered that the process begins a cycle of conversion and affirmation between youth and adults. As the YDP youth came to believe in themselves—to claim their voices and their faith, name their themes, and take action to address them in their churches and communities—adults who were previously skeptical of and alienated from youth began to recognize the validity of their words and actions. In a number of congregations, the ministries initiated from listening to and thinking and dreaming with youth enriched the lives of many adults, both in the churches and in surrounding communities. The passionate voices of youth, heard in the partner churches and in the summer communities, inspired adults to take risks and get involved, speak out against the status quo, and take action to improve the quality of life for adults and youth alike.

Shared Themes, Unique Ministries

Along with the theme of alienation between youth and adults discussed earlier, the other common themes among the partner churches were stereotypes, ethnic tensions, and violence. Many congregations also found that youth longed to be of service and that spirituality was very important in their lives. These themes echo those in the summer communities, as do the themes of gender and sexuality. As with the theme of alienation between youth and adults, we discovered that all of these themes had unique forms in particular communities. The ministries developed by the diverse churches took on unique forms as well. As the following story of one congregation demonstrates, the themes of a particular community are closely related to what Paulo Freire calls a "thematic universe,"[16] such that the process of understanding one often leads to discovering others. The ministries that grow from listening, understanding, and dreaming can thus address several themes at once, as in the following story of hospitality, which addressed alienation, ethnic tensions, and violence.

The Korean American partner congregation discussed earlier is located in a lower-income neighborhood in Southern California, which has many problems with violence and vandalism. Adult church members had become concerned about the safety of the church property, and they voted to build a fence around the property that would cost $30,000. During this same period of time, the youth group began the process of discernment. They began to ask questions about the church's role in the surrounding community. While the church members are Korean and Korean American, people in the surrounding community are primarily Hispanic and African American. There was little interaction between the church community and the surrounding community.

During the dreaming process, the youth and adult leaders began to reflect upon the meaning of church. They felt that their church was "rapidly turning into a country club," rather than acting as Jesus and the early Christian church would have acted. They began to dream about how they could act differently as a church, based upon the wisdom of scripture and their United Methodist faith tradition. The dreaming process in this congregation challenged the faith of some adult church members, inspiring them to affirm that resources from their tradition do indeed speak truth. The youth and adult leaders of the discernment process described one generative theme in their congregation as: "our profound pessimism that permeated against God, saying what we could not do, what we thought to be impossible, and the massive negative caution against moving forward." In spite of alienation between youth and adults in this congregation, the adults had enough faith in the youth to support their actions. The discernment steering committee explained, "It was a long, uphill battle, but one that was eventually overcome through prayer, and kids showing adults what was possible."

The youth group decided that they needed to let community members know that their church was a safe, welcoming place for them. In their dreaming process, they envisioned bringing the diverse community together at a large, community event on the church grounds to begin to build a sense of safety and camaraderie. They decided to hold a free, community-wide barbecue on the Fourth of July. They invited community groups to have booths at the event to advertise their free services, and they solicited monetary donations to pay for food, games, and other expenses. They also invited several other churches in the area to cosponsor the event with them. To invite people from the surrounding community, they put up fliers in the neighborhood and went door-to-door to invite people to the barbecue. During their outreach, the youth experienced one of the themes of their community: they recognized that their neighbors were afraid to open their doors, fearful of the frequent violence in the area. This realization led them to explore the theme of violence as part of their discernment process.

The barbecue was a great success. The youth were completely responsible for organizing all logistics of the event, with the support of the adults in the congregation. Hispanic, African American, and European American neighbors came together with the Korean American congregation to celebrate the Fourth of July and to begin building relationships in the community.

Through their dreaming process, the youth developed a variety of other plans for reaching out and ministering with the surrounding community. The adults in the church were so impressed with the vision and commitment of the youth that they abandoned the plan to spend $30,000 on a fence. Instead, they have joined with the youth in opening the church grounds for use by community members. The money is being used to enlarge and remodel the church building that will now be used by the community-at-large.

In this particular context, the youth had to address the language barriers between many of the Korean-speaking adults and English-speaking youth, as well as cultural mores in the Korean culture that dictate against direct conversation about difficult issues. Because of these challenges, the steering committee in this congregation felt that many adult church members would not be comfortable with personal and critical conversations with youth during the discernment process. Therefore, the youth primarily experienced their youth pastor and a few other adults on the steering committee as the nonjudgmental adult listeners who listened to their concerns and dreams and guided their reflections. However, when the youth were able to articulate their plan for ministry, based on their understanding of issues that were important to them, to the church, and to the surrounding community, the adults of the congregation listened and affirmed their vision. The results were transformative for adults and youth alike.

The youth came to experience themselves as empowered leaders, affirmed and valued by the adults. They gained a deeper connection with their faith as they dared to engage in direct action and to lead the adults in transformative ministries. The adults were challenged on many levels–to affirm and follow the leadership and vision of youth, to open the doors of the church to people of different ethnic and economic backgrounds, to trust that ministries of inclusion would bring safety that a fence could never accomplish, and to trust in God's ability and will to guide and bless these faithful ministries.

Implications for Ministries with Youth

The findings from the Youth Discipleship Project, in conversation with studies about adolescent development, reveal that a combination of listening styles is needed to engage youth effectively. Group activities and discussions, geared toward eliciting the passions of youth in particular communities, are an essential part of listening to youth. These need to be conducted in an affirming, nonjudgmental environment. In addition, girls and boys need opportunities to initiate conversations with adults individually. Taken as a whole, these activities, discussions, and one-on-one conversations will reveal the complex textures of passions and concerns among youth in a particular community.

This holistic approach to ministry with youth, holding adolescents' need to be heard at its center, can be profoundly transformative for youth and adults alike. This approach pays loving attention to the uniqueness of each individual and of each faith community. Rather than relying upon prepackaged curriculum resources for youth ministry, which are often written from a European American, middle-class perspective, this approach allows faith communities to delve into the resources of the youth themselves–their passion, knowledge, experiences, and faith–to generate ministries *with* youth as opposed to *for* them. When youth are taken seriously, listened to with acceptance and care, challenged to think critically and faithfully about issues in their lives, and empowered to take action, they rise to the occasion beautifully. They find that their faith is indeed relevant to their lives and that they can be agents of that faith in healing the world. They experience the love of God for themselves and for the world as they live out God's call toward wholeness for themselves, for their communities, and for all of creation.

At the core of this transformation are relationships between adults and youth. In this approach, young people can affirm their voices, feelings, and frustrations with the pressures on them for conformity without fearing retaliation, ridicule, or rejection. In a safe space, through conversation and action with adults and other youth, they can claim their full selves, honor their gifts, express their emotions, and develop their capacity for authentic relationships. They are able to engage their faith in relation to larger social issues. They are able to say "no!" to social forces of sexism, racism, consumerism, classism, and other forms of oppression, trusting that God says "no!" alongside them.

This approach to youth ministry does the precarious and desperately needed work of helping youth grow into the fullness of who God created them to be in a society that often causes both girls and boys to sacrifice much of their full selves. To do this holy work, adults need to be willing to face themselves and the realities of their communities and society with critical and compassionate eyes. They must be willing to do the difficult work of healing old wounds within themselves, learning to be in authentic relationships, and seeking courage to take faithful action for social change. Fortunately for adults, youth are often more than willing to lead the way if given the chance.

Choosing Life Requires Action

Life-Giving Praxis with Children and Youth

ALMEDA M. WRIGHT

For this commandment that I command you today is not too hard for you, neither is it far off. It is not in heaven... Neither is it beyond the sea... But the word is very near you. It is in your mouth and in your heart, so that you can do it. See, I have set before you today life and good, death and evil... I call heaven and earth to witness against you today, that I have set before you life and death, blessing and curse. Therefore choose life, that you and your offspring may live, loving the LORD your God, obeying [God's] voice and holding fast to [God], for [God] is your life and length of days, that you may dwell in the land that the LORD swore to your fathers, to Abraham, to Isaac, and to Jacob, to give them. (Deut. 30:11–15, 19–20, ESV)

Too Hard, Too Far

Each week in my youth ministry seminar we start with a ritual of listening to the voices of adolescents. During the second week of the semester, the adolescent voice of the day was Sal. While I never met Sal in person (knowing him only from a case study about pastors working with youth in the Boston area), his story has stayed with me.[1] Sal's story is complex and troubling, because he was a "big time" drug dealer who, after being mentored by a group of concerned pastors, worked hard to change his life. Change was not easy for Sal, however, and he lived with a seemingly insurmountable tension: feeling that he was letting his family down because he was not able to provide for them the way he did when he sold drugs, and encountering challenge after challenge as he tried to find a legal means to use his intelligence and talents.[2] Sal attended a Christian college, but encountered drug abuse and dealing there also. Sal came home and worked with his mentors to find a job or internship, but the internship was slow in coming. Sal faced a choice: to wait and struggle or to go back to his "former hustle." The class paused in the case study and envisioned how they might minister with a young person like Sal.

After some discussion, we returned to the case study, to the narrative of Sal's life-altering choice:

> [Sal] borrowed $400 from his uncle and went and bought some drugs. He planned to do a quick hit—mark up the price, sell it quick, then give his family the money, to hold them over until he got the internship at the bank. What he didn't know was that his friend who had sold him the drugs had given him what are called "hot packs," which are tainted drugs... We think the boy did it on purpose, because he didn't want Sal to be back in the business. Sal was good at what he did, Sal was big time. So the kid sold him the hot packs, figured that if Sal was giving bad drugs to folks, his name would be gone. What he didn't anticipate was that Sal and his girlfriend decided to use some that night. They both OD'd. She woke up, he didn't. And the damnable thing about it was that Monday morning the internship came in. He died Saturday. And that Monday, it came in.[3]

The group of seminarians sat awestruck, feeling the weight of this story as we again envisioned how we could minister with a young man like Sal. The students felt disturbed that I did not tell them the outcome of Sal's story until after we first imagined ministry with him. The underlying sentiment was, "Why would you make us think about this case *as if* we could do something about it?" They struggled to see that, even in the tragedy of Sal's death, much *can* be learned about ministry with children and youth. Even as Sal struggled, he hoped for something better for the young people around him: "Maybe it is too late for me, Eugene, but save the kids" Sal told Azusa Christian Community pastor Eugene Rivers two days before he overdosed and died.[4]

The case of Sal, in dialogue with the class's struggle, reveals the challenge of this book. The authors here have struggled and wondered how to help children and youth choose life—to live in ways that enhance their flourishing and, for Christians, to reflect the Gospel of Jesus Christ and God's blessings for creation. People who are concerned about children and youth, and many young people themselves, fear that choosing life and the work of empowering young people to choose life are *too hard and too far* beyond our reach.

Sal's story and the chapters of this book echo the narrative of Deuteronomy 30, in which the children of Israel faced decisions about how they were going to make the transition from slavery in Egypt to liberation in an already occupied territory.[5] The Deuteronomic writers emphasized God's fidelity in providing for God's people, and the people's responsibility to choose life and act accordingly and choose blessings rather than curses (v. 19). Earlier the writers of Deuteronomy challenged the people to see that the call to choose life was not too hard nor was it beyond them: "For this commandment that I command you today is not too hard for you, neither is it far off... But the word is very near you. It is in your mouth and in your heart, so that you can do it" (30:11, 14). This text still leaves the burning question of what it means for the "word" to be very near to us or for the possibility of choosing life to be in our mouths and in our hearts. The text is a reminder to seek the powerful resources of our spiritual traditions to guide and strengthen us in ways that foster life. Yet how does it address the troubling world described by authors in this book?

My class initially responded to Sal's story by suggesting that the ministers should have worked harder or longer with Sal. They quickly remembered, however, how Sal had come to the ministers' houses at all hours of the night, and they had invested much time, energy, and reputation to get Sal into college and then to get him a job. Then, the students suggested that the ministers should have built more familial and communal forms of ministry and have worked more on the *whys* of youth drug involvement and the support of families. Sal's life situation made it almost impossible to choose life; life for his family meant death for his new life focused on God. For Sal, choosing life was complicated by struggles for family survival in a death-centered culture. Recognizing this, students moved to other questions. How can leaders recover and continue to minister in a situation like this? How can adult leaders and young people imagine a future of blessings and flourishing and then choose life? The overwhelming response was to acknowledge the need to step back and reflect critically on ministry in difficult situations, then to reshape our approaches to ministry with youth.

Similarly, the authors in this volume have called us to attend to the difficult stories of children and youth, for whom choosing life is not an easy or clear option. Josh Thomas's research called us to reflect on the hard stories of Bosnian youth struggling to rebuild their lives and imagine a future after the devastation of war. Katherine Turpin called us to the difficult task of confronting corporate systems and conglomerates (such as Disney), which seem impenetrable and indestructible, as they increase their influence in the lives of children globally. Likewise, Bonnie Miller-McLemore and Luther Smith called us to attend to how children and youth are treated in our society—within faith communities and other institutions and in the public sphere. They describe some of the systems and social trends that promote distortion and neglect of young lives. On the other hand, the authors argue that we *can* do something. Even in the face of death and destructive forces, we are called to attend carefully to the lives of children and youth and ask where and how God is calling us to be agents of transformation in the world.

Practical Theological Reflection:
Life-affirming Practices with Children and Youth

The authors of this volume have invited us to consider the troubling realities of children and youth, to consider gifts of religion and spirituality for addressing these concerns, and to take seriously the spiritual resources, worldviews, and actions that children and youth have to offer. The authors have written their chapters in conversation with children and youth, as well as with other concerned adults. They have utilized practical theology resources and methods, seeking to discover life-giving practices in a world that often espouses death. While the methodology of practical theology resists a "one-size-fits-all" recommendation for improved practice, the authors do identify promising practices and patterns for future ministries with children and youth.

Though the authors utilize quite different methods, their work exemplifies and nuances the three movements of practical theology that Mary Elizabeth Moore identifies in the Introduction: (1) originates in the world of practice, (2) moves into constructive reflection, and (3) returns to praxis as the goal. The challenge now is to extend the third movement by reflecting on the insights and proposals of the volume, taken as a whole. In this section, I discuss the authors' proposals within the frame of practical theology, emphasizing that the methods and spirit of practical theology offer an approach for ministering with children and youth.[6] This is not to say that the practice of ministry is the whole of practical theology, but that the practice of ministry is an instance of practical theology. In fact, the practices of practical theology and practices of ministry have parallels. The correspondence is exemplified throughout this volume, as in: Claire Bischoff's "story sharing theology"; David White's and Jennie Knight's accents on discernment processes (listening, interpreting, and acting); and Susanne Johnson's description of analysis and action in Youth Community Organizing. Our concluding recommendations also reflect a practical theological approach to ministry to, for, and with children and youth.

Originating in Practice: Attending to the Lives of Children and Youth

Practical theological reflection begins, as does ministry with children and youth, in the world of practice. This is a world of complex, messy, and not easily classifiable experiences. Therefore, the first challenge is to attend closely to lives of children and youth because they are often unable to articulate the details of their worlds and their voices are often silenced, even when they attempt to express themselves. (See the essays by Miles,

Wright, White, and Johnson.) The very young often require advocates to attend to their lives and listen carefully for their concerns and needs, while older youth often require opportunities and skills to observe their worlds, raise critical questions, contribute their gifts, and work to effect change.

Attending to young lives calls us to move beyond our assumptions and those of prominent theories, as the chapters by Rodger Nishioka and Joyce Mercer highlight. It also encourages young people themselves to question the norms and stereotypes of their worlds, revealed in chapters by Claire Bischoff and Susanne Johnson. Authors in this volume point to the destabilizing effects of living in a world riddled with violence and war, where terror is real. This suggests that attending to young lives requires people to attend not only to individual lives but also to the worlds in which young people live, as Josh Thomas did in his post-war interviews with young adults in Bosnia-Herzegovina.

The idea of attending to young people is not new, but it may be more difficult and complex than is usually recognized. In attending to children and youth, we must constantly balance what can be seen as placing young lives under a microscope—making them vulnerable to the scrutiny of the entire community—with investing the time and effort to open ourselves to the worlds of children and youth. At times youth say things that make us feel uncomfortable, as Jennie Knight's opening story indicates. At other times, the degree of alienation between adults and young people has grown to such proportions that adults do not know where to begin in attending to the young. (See the Introduction, and essays by Knight, Moore, Parker, and Yust.) Sometimes people attend to young lives rather easily, but only on the surface. We do not always see the deep experiences and revelations of God (Moore), the intense vulnerability (Smith), and the powerful gifts that resound in their lives (Smith).

Drawing upon the wisdom of young people and reflections in this volume, we consider five specific proposals for practice that can embody the larger practice of attending to young people and their worlds.

Listen to Children and Youth

Authors in this volume have stressed the need to listen to the young, to be aware of their deep passions and concerns, and to be alert to their worlds. This requires people to *listen deeply,* or what Luther Smith described as a move beyond celebration to being invested in the lives of children. Such listening will awaken us to the real experiences of young people that popular wisdom distorts, such as the experiences of girls who have lost their fathers (Mercer) and of boys growing up with heavy male expectations (Nishioka). Listening also requires that we *create venues for active communal listening,* as described in the discernment process of White and Knight, the story-sharing of Bischoff, and the youth testimonies advocated by Wright, Parker, and Miles.

Discern the Movements of God in the Lives of Children and Youth

Luther Smith includes in chapter 1 a reference to Mark's story of Jesus blessing the children (10:13–16). All the authors in Part Two echo this view, emphasizing that God honors and values young lives and moves in and through young people. Moore describes the yearnings for and the presence of the Holy in young lives, and Bischoff and Yust highlight the significance of young people's narratives as sources for theological reflection. All of these authors remind us that attending to what young people say and do will reveal the Divine; thus, our challenge is to *expect and seek God's movement in young people.*

Attend to Cultural Influences

The authors also stress the need to be critically aware of the ways that theorists and scholars describe youth, ways that marketers target youth, and ways that public policy is *not* designed with the best interests of children and youth in mind. To be aware of cultural influences is to attend to how the lives and actions of young people are received, ignored, celebrated, welcomed, abused, or manipulated. This requires practical theological reflections that *recognize distortions and omissions in intellectual and public discourse on the young,* as Bonnie Miller-McLemore offers in her chapter. It further requires ministries that *engage with young people as they engage with their cultures,* as Bischoff does in watching *OC* with young women, Turpin does in attending a Disney production with her daughter, and Miles does in calling adults to be co-journeyers with youth as they "mind" the worlds of hip-hop and other media.

Attend to the Influences of the Faith Community

Faith communities are also vital in the lives of young people. The authors of this volume have focused particularly on Christian communities as spiritual homes for young people: pointing beyond themselves to God, nurturing young people, growing *with* them, and advocating for them in the public square. We need to *treasure those instances when faith communities provide safe and welcoming space* for children, as when Katherine Turpin's daughter told her dad, "At least I get to go to church tomorrow." We also need to *be alert to failures of faith communities to be fully present to young people,* such as the church's difficulty in receiving youth's rage (Parker). Finally, we need to *recognize the presence, absence, and complicated influences of religion in children's lives* (Miller-McLemore), and *find ways to partner with faith communities* in ministering to and with young people (White).

Practice a Ministry of Presence

To attend to the lives of children and youth is to be present with them. Thus, we conclude this section with the need to *engage in a ministry of presence and lingering.* This practice is vividly portrayed in Karen Marie

Yust's (non)cosmetic ministry with young women in a residential treatment facility and in Miles' well-named concept of co-journeying. This practice of being physically present with youth reminds us of the need to attend to the yearnings of youth for relationship with nonjudgmental, listening adults (Knight) and to be mindful of the ongoing ways that we are called to be in communion with young lives.

Reflecting Constructively: Clarifying, Critiquing, and Re-creating

While one of the hallmarks of practical theological reflection is "originating in the world" or focusing on everyday contexts and particular experiences, practical theological reflection also requires that we step back from the streams of our lives to reflect on their meaning. Stepping back includes asking questions such as, "Where is God in this situation?" and, "What in our Christian heritage, culture, and understanding of the world is revealed in the present situation?" It also requires that we draw upon theology and other theories to help interpret the thickness of our everyday lives, placing our experiences into conversation with the experiences and reflections of others.[7]

Many authors in this volume point to the ways that a particular event, personal experience, case study, or observation served as the catalyst for deeper reflection and called them into conversation with theorists of theology, philosophy, psychology, education, or literature. Such conversation with theory sheds light upon the current realities of children and youth. For example, Mercer's description of father-loss and her understanding of this phenomenon are enlivened by her inclusion of a literary account of father-loss and its interpretive frame. Similarly, Parker's discussion of rage among African American adolescents originates in her listening to the narratives of adolescents, but is illumined by placing it in conversation with theories of historical oppression and statistical evidence of rage among African American youth today.

In critically reflecting on the world of practice with children and youth and in placing these experiences in conversation with other sources, we *clarify the complexities of our lived experiences,* even if the clarification is to be more cognizant of the messiness. We also *critique the experiences themselves and critique the religious and human science traditions that have interpreted or misinterpreted those experiences.* Critically reflecting on the lives of children and youth challenges dominant assumptions in theological systems and cultural narratives. Mercer notes how the stories of father-loss she includes challenge dominant notions that fathers do not matter in the lives of daughters because of gender differences. Parker describes how the rage of African American adolescents challenges traditional beliefs and practices of African American churches, calling them to make room for the anger of adolescents and to engage biblical accounts of transformative anger. In the opening narrative of this conclusion, Sal's story and the efforts of the ministers with him challenge commonly held assumptions about why youth are involved with drugs and what constitutes effective ministry with young people.

These moves toward clarifying and critiquing open the way to *re-create traditions of belief, values, and practices.* Looking at the big picture, Miller-McLemore advocates a re-creation of religion as important to discourse in the public square, as well as a re-creation of popular understandings of children. Susanne Johnson studies Youth Community Organizing and historical spiritual traditions to construct a picture of "subversive spirituality." Josh Thomas, in studying young adults in Bosnia-Herzegovina, discovers their strong impulses to move "beyond hate," impulses that can empower and inform theories and practices of peace-building. These are all pictures of re-creating.

The work of clarifying, critiquing, and re-creating is not only the work of scholars, but also the work of children and youth. Thus, we lift up some powerful practices for reflective ministry with children and youth that were described in this volume.

Engage in Contemplation and Prayer

Vital to this movement of practical theology are spiritual disciplines, most notably contemplation and prayer. Consider the forms of group prayer and the practice of lament that Karen Marie Yust practiced with the young women at Germaine Lawrence School, the daily sweet grass ceremonies and talking circle described by Moore at Joe Duquette School, or the subversive spirituality elaborated by Johnson. Bischoff also shares her experiences of practicing contemplative prayer with youth and describes the potential significance of this spiritual discipline for youth identity development. She describes the values of silent meditation in a world filled with technology, advertisements, and communication. Each of these authors emphasizes the ways that spiritual disciplines create the space and discipline for children and youth to reflect on their lives.

Build Communities of Reflection

In addition to offering spiritual disciplines, the authors point to the need to build communities of reflections. Such communities can take many forms, whether stirred by preaching as done by Miles in her fresh interpretation of the Numbers text about Zelophehad's daughters, or engaged through a critical pedagogy as described by White. Sometimes it simply involves being present to the questions and reflections of young people that are offered spontaneously, as in Yust's cosmetic sessions with the Germaine Lawrence girls, which she combined also with preaching and counseling. These examples point to the necessity of our intentional and ongoing efforts to carve out space and support the questions and reflections of young people, as well as the ways that this reflection is shaped by and shapes communities.

Stretch the Experiences of Young People

Constructive reflection is also stirred and enriched by new experiences, as White describes in the worship visits to diverse community churches in the Youth Discipleship Project, as Thomas describes in the interreligious encounters of young adults in Bosnia-Herzegovina, and as Bischoff describes in the delight of young women in hearing the faith stories of others. Such experiences expand horizons, serving as points of dialogue and comparison, and also help young people see the world from diverse points of view. New experiences open youth to contemplate the complexities of their previous and current experiences.

Encourage and Equip Young People to Reflect on Their Lives and Their Worlds in Dialogue with Theology, and Theology in Dialogue with Their Lives

All of the practices described thus far encourage and equip young people to reflect on their lives and on theology in dialogue. Some approaches particularly lend themselves to developing these skills, such as the pedagogical approach described by David White and Jennie Knight in which young people identify generative themes in their lives and communities and then reflect on what these mean and how they can be addressed. Susanne Johnson has found similar processes among youth in community organizing. This book reveals further that ministries of preaching can open biblical texts and theological questions that generate intense reflection among young people, especially exemplified by Miles and Yust.

Invite Imagination

We conclude this section with the practice of imagining and inviting others to imagine. This theme is persistent in the book, and is developed in some detail by Bischoff. Two bright examples are the proposals by Joyce Mercer and Josh Thomas, both of whom appeal to narrative therapy as a means of encouraging young people to reimagine their life stories and then to make choices about how they will live the next phase of their lives. Another powerful example is Nishioka's urging of young men to reimagine the "boy code" and to ponder the kinds of men they want to become. Yust also invites young women to "imagine" the Divine in ways that complement their current struggles and realities. In sum, imagination is vital to young people's emotional health, identity development, understandings of the Divine, and future formation.

Improving Praxis: Enacting Life-giving Practices

Attending to and critically reflecting upon the lives of children and youth are insufficient without "touching back down" in the world of practice—imagining and enacting proposals that can reshape the world. These are practices that support life and "make a difference" (Moore). Of course, the acts of attending and reflecting are themselves practices, but more is still needed. Practical theology, whether in the academy, religious community, or larger society, is concerned with improving young lives. This can best be done by empowering children, youth, and adults to think and act differently in response to their particular situations. The authors in this book suggest several directions for life-giving practice. We consider some of these here.

Raise Consciousness and Reimagine the Church and World as They *Can* Be

This practice is a natural extension of attending and imagining, which have already been discussed. To name the practice here is a reminder, however, that the process of awaking consciousness and critiquing the world, our lives, and our inherited religious traditions is a never-ending one. Consciousness-raising creates a breach in the normalcy of daily life and pushes children and youth to rethink their current realities. Katherine Turpin calls these practices of contestation and questioning. Knight describes opportunities to challenge the status quo, as in challenging young people to rethink the "normalcy" of sexual harassment and violence in their schools. Parker also illumines the significance of this process in challenging the normalcy of church practices with youth, such as codes of respect that limit the expression of youth rage. Such acts create spaces through which social transformation can take place.

Work with Children and Youth to Effect Change

In addition to the work that we are called to do as advocates for children and youth in the public square, the authors remind us that youth activism, and participation in transforming the world, is not something of legends or the 1960s protest movements. It is something that youth still crave and need. White and Knight both highlight the significance of nurturing a spirit of action and a sense of calling in young lives. Knight further points to the significant contributions that children and youth can make in leading their church communities to take action in their local communities. The prodding of youth, for example, stirred one Korean American church to become more involved in its community. Similarly, Johnson's subversive youth ministry is a process for empowering youth to think about the concerns of their communities, and then to move from naming "hurts and hopes" to strategizing about doable and "winnable" issues. In a different context, Thomas's interviews with Bosnian youth reveal the role youth can play in social change and reconciliation for a war-torn country.

Invite Youth to Participate in and Transform Christian Practices

All too often, the Christian community thinks of its sacred texts and practices—celebration of the sacraments, reading scripture, saying prayers, doing theology, preaching, testifying, and participating in social witness—as the "serious" work of the church, the work that children and youth must grow into. While tension will inevitably remain between the needs of young people for specialized ministry and their inclusion in the overall life of the church, the authors of this volume emphasize the inclusion of young people in the full range of Christian practices and opening to the possibility that the practices would be transformed with the influence of children and youth. Miles describes the process of including adolescents in the practice of *meaning-full* preaching as a way to empower youth to engage biblical texts in fresh ways. She argues that sermon content must reflect the realities, questions, and even cultural ethos of young people; thus, preaching will be transformed when children and youth are taken into account as a sacred source of theological reflection. Likewise, Parker and Wright seek to recover the tradition of testifying in worship and engaging youth fully in the practice, thus changing the spiritual practice to include more diverse forms (e.g., dramatic interpretations and improvisation) and content (e.g., rage). Yust also engaged young women in writing and speaking prayers of lament as a way to express despair and pain and to cry out to God.

"The Word Is Very Near You"

The team of authors who have collaborated on this book share enthusiasm for children and youth, and a sense of the large task we have undertaken. As a community, we continue to remind one another and our readers that young people often find it difficult to choose life in a world that is consumed with death. This somber note is not the final word, however; each author also calls us to reflect critically, to imagine, and to learn together how best to live in a troubling world. Collectively, the authors are committed to creating a world that loves life. The text from Deuteronomy 30 offers a reminder and reassurance, especially when the Deuteronomic authors say that the word is very near (neither far away nor hard to find) and that the community *can* and *must* choose life. As we ponder the young lives that interconnect with and shape our lives, we must remember that we, too, are called to choose life, and to choose it *with,* and sometimes *for,* these children and youth. With that challenge comes the ancient Deuteronomic reassurance that the word and resources are "very near to [us]...so that [we] can do it."

Notes

Introduction: Children and Youth Choosing Life

[1]Grace M. Jantzen, *Foundations of Violence*, Vol. One of *Death and the Displacement of Beauty* (London: Routledge, 2004), 5–6.

[2]Ibid., 6–14.

[3]Ibid., 6–11.

[4]Examples include: Donald Ng, *Asian Pacific American Youth Ministry: Planning, Helps, and Programs* (Valley Forge, Pa.: Judson Press, 1988); Charles R. Foster and Grant S. Shockley, eds., *Working with Black Youth* (Nashville: Abingdon Press, 1989); Gregory Cajete, *Look to the Mountain: An Ecology of Indigenous Education* (Durango, Colo.: Kivaki, 1994); Beverly Tatum, *Why Are All the Black Kids Sitting Together in the Cafeteria?* (New York: Basic Books, 1997); Patricia Hersch, *A Tribe Apart: A Journey into the Heart of American Adolescence* (New York: Ballantine Books, 1998); Evelyn Parker, *Trouble Don't Last Always: Emancipatory Hope among African American Adolescents* (Cleveland: Pilgrim Press, 2003); Anne E. Streaty Wimberly, ed., *Keep It Real: Working with Today's Black Youth* (Nashville: Abingdon Press, 2005); Evelyn L. Parker, ed., *The Sacred Selves of Adolescent Girls: Hard Stories of Race, Class, and Gender* (Cleveland: Pilgrim Press, 2006).

[5]Examples of works based in quantitative data include: Robert Wuthnow, *Growing Up Religious: Christians and Jews and Their Journeys of Faith* (Boston: Beacon, 1999); Hans-Günter Heimbrock, Christoph Scheilke, Peter Schreiner, eds., *Towards Religious Competence: Diversity as a Challenge for Education in Europe* (Münster: Lit Verlag, 2002); Chris A. M. Hermans, *Participatory Learning: Religious Education in a Globalizing Society* (Leiden: Brill, 2003); Christian Smith, with Melinda Lundquist Denton, *Soul Searching: The Religious and Spiritual Lives of American Teenagers* (Oxford: Oxford University, 2005). Examples of social and/or theological issue analyses include: Michael Warren, *Seeing through the Media: A Religious View of Communications and Cultural Analysis* (New York: Continuum, 1997); Anne Higonnet, *Pictures of Innocence: The History and Crisis of Ideal Childhood* (New York: Thames and Hudson, 1998); Thomas Hine, *The Rise and Fall of the American Teenager* (New York: HarperCollins, 2000); Marcia J. Bunge, ed., *The Child in Christian Thought* (Grand Rapids, Mich.: Eerdmans, 2000); Michael Warren, *Youth and the Future of the Church: Ministry with Youth and Young Adults* (Eugene, Oreg.: WIPF and Stock, 2002); Bonnie Miller-McLemore, *Let the Children Come: Reimagining Childhood from a Christian Perspective* (San Francisco: Jossey-Bass, 2003); Kenda Creasy Dean, *Practicing Passion: Youth and the Quest for a Passionate Church* (Grand Rapids, Mich.: Eerdmans, 2004); Dori Grinenko Baker, *Doing Girlfriend Theology: God-Talk with Young Women* (Cleveland: Pilgrim Press, 2005); Kristin Herzog, *Children and Our Global Future* (Cleveland: Pilgrim Press, 2005); David White, *Practicing Discernment with Youth: A Transformative Youth Ministry Approach* (Cleveland: Pilgrim Press, 2005); Bonnie Miller-McLemore, *In the Midst of Chaos: Care of Children as Religious Practice* (San Francisco: Jossey-Bass, 2006); Pamela D. Couture, *Child Poverty: Love, Justice and Social Responsibility* (St. Louis: Chalice Press, 2007).

[6]I have made this case elsewhere, as in: Mary Elizabeth Moore, "Practical Theology: Bound by a Common Center or Thin Threads?" *International Journal of Practical Theology* 10 (2006): 163–67, esp. 166–67. Practical theologians often exhibit a thin use of footnotes and other references to practical theologians. They more commonly refer to biblical, theological, and other scholars. When practical theology references do appear, they are usually limited to one or two scholars and one or two books from that person's corpus, though much writing in practical theology is generative and worthy of more significant engagement.

Chapter 1: When Celebrating Children Is Not Enough

[1]The terms "children" and "youth" are interchangeable in this essay, referring to all persons below age eighteen.

See "Kids Count 2004 Data Book Online," at www.aecf.org/kidscount/databook/essay/essay2.htm.

[3]Some who have given attention to this concern are: Pamela D. Couture, *Seeing Children, Seeing God: A Practical Theology of Children and Poverty* (Nashville: Abingdon Press, 2000); id., *Child Poverty: Love, Justice and Social Responsibility* (St. Louis: Chalice Press, 2007); Bonnie Miller-McLemore, *In the Midst of Chaos: Care of Children as Religious Practice* (San Francisco: Jossey-Bass, 2006).

[4]See, for example: Kay A. Read and Isabel Wollaston, eds., *Suffer the Little Children: Urban Violence and Sacred Space* (Edgbaston: University of Birmingham Press, 2001).

[5]Carl S. Dudley, *Effective Small Churches in the Twenty-first Century* (Nashville: Abingdon Press, 2003). Dudley insists that small churches do not have to be captive to a "caring cell" method of inclusion, but the caring cell remains a dominant feature in limiting or extending the outreach of churches to others. This discussion runs throughout Dudley's book.

[6]These 2007 estimates are based on *The World Factbook* and are found on the website of the Central Intelligence Agency of the United States. See www.cia.gov/library/publications/the-world-factbook/rankorder/2091.

[7]See "March of Dimes" Web site www.marchofdimes.com/professionals/681_1153.asp.

[8]Data from "Prevent Child Abuse Georgia" and is consistent with data from the Action Council of "The Children's Defense Fund."

[9]Children's Defense Fund Action Council, *Stand Up for Children Now!*, n.d., inside cover. The Fund attained its information from the Centers for Disease Control and prevention.

[10]Marian Wright Edelman, "Standing Up for Children," in *The Impossible Will Take a Little While: A Citizen's Guide to Hope in a Time of Fear,* ed. Paul Rogat Loeb (New York: Basic Books, 2004), 45.

[11]Ibid.

[12]For an historical interpretation of the marginality of children in society, see: Colin Heywood, *A History of Childhood: Children and Childhood in the West from Medieval to Modern Times* (Malden, Mass.: Blackwell Publishing, 2001).

[13]Others have found this text suggestive for a theology of childhood and an approach to ministry with children. See, for example: Bonnie Miller-McLemore, *Let the Children Come: Re-imagining Childhood from a Christian Perspective* (San Francisco: Jossey-Bass, 2003) and Mary Elizabeth Moore, "Walking with Children toward Hope: The Long Road to Justice and Reconciliation," in *Spirituality and Ethics in Education: Philosophical, Theological, and Radical Perspectives,* ed. Hanan Alexander (Sussex: Sussex Academic Press, 2004), 83–97.

[14]The Children's Defense Fund collects data on high school dropout rates and consequences that result from the failure to have stronger retention rates in schools. The Fund also conducts policy analyses of government programs and budgets on the well-being of children. What emerges from their publications and online studies is a pattern of government and public ineffectiveness with these problems. See their Web site for access to these publications and studies: www.childrensdefense.org..

[15]Marion Wright Edelman conveys the extent of failure to provide mental health services to juveniles charged with offences: "A recent Congressional study . . . reports that two-thirds of juvenile detention facilities in 47 states are holding children solely because they need mental health services unavailable in their communities. . . . Over a six-month period in 2003, nearly 15,000 incarcerated children waited for community mental health services in their states, some as young as seven." See *Focus Magazine: Joint Center for Political and Economic Studies,* November/December 2006.

[16]"Keeping the Faith: A Call for Collaboration Between the Faith and Child Protection Communities," *Medical, Legal & Social Science Aspects of Child Sexual Exploitation* (St. Louis: GW Medical Publishing, 2005), 948.

[17]Coretta Scott King, "Foreword," in Martin L. King, Jr., *Strength to Love* (Philadelphia: Fortress Press, 1981), 9.

[18]Two organizations that are resources for media literacy programs are the Center for Media Literacy (www.medialit.org) and the National Telemedia Council (www.nationaltelemediacouncil.org).

[19]See www.newhavencenterchurch.org/documents/chronicle/CCNH_The_Chronicle_June_2003.swf.

Chapter 2: Children and Religion in the Public Square

[1]This article first appeared as Bonnie J. Miller-McLemore, "Children and Religion in the Public Square: 'Too Dangerous and Too Safe, Too Difficult and Too Silly,'" *Journal of Religion* 86, no. 3 (Fall 2006): 385–401. It is slightly revised here to reflect significant developments in the literature on religion and children since I initiated research on this topic in 1999, presented the ideas at the Association of Practical Theology in 2002, and presented at a conference at the University of Chicago in honor of Don S. Browning in 2003. My research also informed a larger project, now published, aimed at reconstructing contemporary portraits of children, Bonnie J. Miller-McLemore, *Let the Children Come: Reimagining Childhood from a Christian Perspective* (San Francisco: Jossey-Bass, 2003).

[2]Anne Higonnet, *Pictures of Innocence: The History and Crisis of Ideal Childhood* (New York: Thames and Hudson, 1998), 13–14.

[3]Barbara Dafoe Whitehead, "Dan Quayle Was Right," *The Atlantic Monthly* (April 1993): 47. See also her *The Divorce Culture: Rethinking Our Commitments to Marriage and Family* (New York: Vintage Books, 1998).

[4]*Marriage in America: A Report to the Nation* (New York: Council on Families in America of the Institution for American Values, 1995), 1.

[5]See, e.g., Arlene Skolnick and Stacey Rosencrantz, "The New Crusade for the Old Family," *American Prospect* (Summer 1994): 59–65; Judith Stacey, "Dan Quayle's Revenge: The New Family Values Crusaders," *The Nation* (July 25/August 1, 1994): 119–22.

[6]See http://www.contemporaryfamilies.org/.

[7]Iris Marion Young, "Making Single Motherhood Normal," *Dissent* (Winter 1994): 91. See also Paul Amato and Alan Booth, *A Generation at Risk: Growing Up in an Era of Family Upheaval* (Cambridge, Mass.: Harvard University Press, 1997); Sara McLanahan and Gary Sandefur, *Growing Up with a Single Parent* (Cambridge, Mass.: Harvard University Press, 1994).

[8]Ellen Goodman, "She's Up on the Tight Wire," *Tennessean,* 27 April 2001.

[9]Jay Belsky, cited by Goodman, "She's Up on the Tight Wire."

[10]Rosalind C. Barnett and Caryl Rivers, *She Works, He Works: How Two-Income Families Are Happier, Healthier, and Better Off* (New York: HarperCollins, 1996).

[11]James Halstead and Jule D. Ward, "When Children Are Killed, What Do We Do? One Community's Response," in *Suffer the Little Children: Urban Violence and Sacred Space,* eds. Kay A. Read and Isabel Wollaston (Edgbaston, U.K.: University of Birmingham Press, 2001), 50.

[12]Sylvia Ann Hewlett and Cornel West, *The War against Parents: What We Can Do for America's Beleaguered Moms and Dads* (New York: Houghton Mifflin, 1998), xiii.

[13]Dana Mack, *The Assault on Parenthood: How Our Culture Undermines the Family* (New York: Simon & Schuster, 1997), 16.

[14]Hewlett and West, *The War against Parents,* 25.

[15]Peter L. Berger, *The Sacred Canopy: Elements in a Sociological Theory of Religion* (Garden City, N.Y.: Doubleday, 1967), 108.

[16]Cristina Traina, "Concluding Remarks" for a panel presentation on "The Child and Moral Agency," Society of Christian Ethics, Washington, D.C., January 8, 2000.

[17]Marcia J. Bunge, Introduction to *The Child in Christian Thought,* ed. Marcia J. Bunge (Grand Rapids, Mich.: Eerdmans, 2000), 4, note 12.

[18]Karl Rahner, "Ideas for a Theology of Childhood," in *Theological Investigations* (London: Darton, Longman & Todd, 1971), 8: 48, 50.

[19]Mary Ann Hinsdale, "'Infinite Openness to the Infinite': Karl Rahner's Contribution to Modern Catholic Thought on the Child," in *The Child in Christian Thought,* , 421.

[20]Rahner, "Ideas for a Theology of Childhood," 33.

[21]Douglas Sturm, "On the Suffering and Rights of Children: Toward a Theology of Childhood Liberation," *Cross Currents* (Summer 1992): 150.

[22]Ibid., 154.

[23]Adrian Thatcher, *Marriage after Modernity: Christian Marriage in Postmodern Times* (New York: New York University Press, 1999).

[24]Jürgen Moltmann, "Child and Childhood as Metaphors of Hope," *Theology Today* 56 (January 2000): 601.

[25]Ibid., 603.

²⁶For a fuller development of this argument and a look at alternative voices that do attend to children in religious education, see Bonnie J. Miller-McLemore, "Whither the Children? Childhood in Religious Education," *Journal of Religion* 86, no. 4 (October 2006): 635–57.

²⁷See, for example, Iris V. Cully, *Christian Child Development* (San Francisco: Harper & Row, 1979) and her earlier book, *Children in Church* (Philadelphia: Westminster, 1960) and, prior to Cully, the important work of Sophia Lyon Fahs, such as *Today's Children and Yesterday's Heritage: A Philosophy of Creative Religious Development* (Boston: Beacon, 1952). See also: Fahs with Elizabeth M. Manwell, *Consider the Children—How They Grow* (Boston: Beacon, 1940, 1951). See notes below for recent publications in religious education that radically reorient our attention to children.

²⁸John H. Westerhoff, *Will Our Children Have Faith?* rev. ed. (Toronto: Morehouse, 1976, 2000).

²⁹James W. Fowler, *Stages of Faith: The Psychology of Human Development and the Quest for Meaning* (San Francisco: Harper & Row, 1981) and id., *Becoming Adult, Becoming Christian* (San Francisco: Harper & Row, 1983).

³⁰Fowler, *Stages of Faith,* 5. He is following the modern distinction of Paul Tillich, H. Richard Niebuhr, and Wilfred Cantwell Smith between institutional religion and ultimate concern or between doctrinal belief and loyalty to centering values.

³¹Jerome Berryman, *Godly Play: An Imaginative Approach to Religious Education* (Minneapolis: Augsburg, 1991); Catherine Stonehouse, *Joining Children on the Spiritual Journey: Nurturing a Life of Faith* (Grand Rapids: Baker, 1998); Elizabeth F. Caldwell, *Making a Home for Faith: Nurturing the Spiritual Life of Your Children* (Cleveland: Pilgrim Press, 2000); id., *Leaving Home with Faith: Nurturing the Spiritual Life of Our Youth* (Cleveland: Pilgrim Press, 2002); J. Bradley Wigger, *The Power of God at Home: Nurturing Our Children in Love and Grace* (San Francisco: Jossey-Bass, 2003); Karen Marie Yust, *Real Kids, Real Faith* (San Francisco: Jossey-Bass, 2004); Karen Marie Yust, Aostre N. Johnson, Sandy Eisenberg Sasso, and Eugene C. Roehlkepartain, eds., *Nurturing Child and Adolescent Spirituality: Perspectives from the World's Religious Traditions* (Lanham, Md.: Rowman & Littlefield, 2006); and Joyce Ann Mercer, *Welcoming Children: A Practical Theology of Childhood* (St. Louis: Chalice Press, 2005). See also Mary Elizabeth Moore, "Walking with Children toward Hope: The Long Road to Justice and Reconciliation," in *Spirituality and Ethics in Education: Philosophical, Theological, and Radical Perspectives,* ed. Hanan Alexander (Sussex: Sussex Academic Press, 2004), 83–97.

³²Bunge, ed., *The Child in Christian Thought*; Margaret Lamberts Bendroth, *Growing Up Protestant: Parents, Children, and Mainline Churches* (New Brunswick, N.J.: Rutgers University Press, 2002); Pamela D. Couture, *Seeing Children, Seeing God: A Practical Theology of Children and Poverty* (Nashville: Abingdon Press, 2000) and *Child Poverty: Love, Justice and Social Responsibility* (St. Louis: Chalice Press, 2007); Miller-McLemore, *Let the Children Come,* and *In the Midst of Chaos: Care of Children as Religious Practice* (San Francisco: Jossey-Bass, 2006); David H. Jensen, *Graced Vulnerability: A Theology of Childhood* (Cleveland: Pilgrim Press, 2005); Susan Ridgely Bales, *When I Was a Child: Children's Interpretations of First Communion* (Chapel Hill: University of North Carolina, 2005); Christian Smith and Melinda Denton, *Soul Searching: The Religious and Spiritual Lives of American Teenagers* (Oxford: Oxford University Press, 2005); Kristin Herzog, *Children and Our Global Future* (Cleveland: Pilgrim Press, 2005); Don S. Browning and Bonnie J. Miller-McLemore, eds., *Children and Childhood in American Religions* (New Brunswick, N.J.: Rutgers University Press, forthcoming); Don S. Browning and Marcia Bunge, eds., *Children and Childhood in World Religions* (New Brunswick, N.J.: Rutgers University Press, forthcoming). John Wall and Bunge have written many articles and are working on books. Some of Bunge's articles include: "A More Vibrant Theology of Children," *Christian Reflection: A Series in Faith and Ethics* (Summer 2003): 11–19; "Retrieving a Biblically Informed View of Children: Implications for Religious Education, a Theology of Childhood, and Social Justice," *Lutheran Education* 139, no. 2 (2003): 72–87; "The Dignity and Complexity of Children: Constructing Christian Theologies of Childhood," in Yust et al., eds., *Nurturing Child and Adolescent Spirituality,* 53–68; and "The Child, Religion, and the Academy: Developing Robust Theological and Religious Understandings of Children and Childhood," *Journal of Religion* 86, no. 4 (October 2006): 549–79. Some of Wall's articles include: "Animals and Innocents: Theological Reflections on the Meaning and Purpose of Children-Rearing," *Theology Today* 59 (January 2003): 559–82; "The Christian Ethics of

Children: Emerging Questions and Possibilities," *Journal of Lutheran Ethics* 4 (January 2004); "'Let the Little Children Come': Child Rearing as Challenge to Contemporary Christian Ethics," *Horizons* 31 (Spring 2004): 64–87; "Fallen Angels: A Contemporary Christian Ethical Ontology of Childhood," *International Journal of Practical Theology* 8 (Fall 2004): 160–84; and "Childhood Studies, Hermeneutics, and Theological Ethics," *Journal of Religion* 86, no. 4 (October 2006): 523–48.

[33]For helpful reviews of this growing literature, see Bonnie J. Miller-McLemore and Don S. Browning, "Introduction: Children and Childhood in American Religions," in *Children and Childhood in American Religions;* Jerome Berryman, "Children and Christian Theology: A New/Old Genre," *Religious Studies Review* 33, no. 2, (2007); Bunge, "The Child, Religion, and the Academy," *Journal of Religion* 86; and Wall, "Childhood Studies, Hermeneutics, and Theological Ethics," *Journal of Religion* 86. Volume 86 of *Journal of Religion,* containing the latter two articles, is the most recent journal volume devoted to *children* and the first to recognize the "emergence of a new, vibrant field: childhood studies" (521). Prior journal publications with children as the theme include: *Dialog* 37 (Summer 1998); *Theology Today* 56, no. 4 (January 2000); *Interpretation: A Journal of Bible and Tradition* 55, no. 2 (April 2001); *New Theology Review: An American Catholic Journal of Ministry* 14, no. 3 (August 2001); *Christian Reflection* (July 2003); *The Living Pulpit* 12, no. 4 (2003); *Sewanee Theological Review* 48, no. 1 (2004); and *African Ecclesial Review* 46, no. 2 (2004).

[34]Andrew D. Lester, *Pastoral Care with Children in Crisis* (Philadelphia: Westminster, 1985), 15, 24.

[35]Herbert Anderson and Susan B. W. Johnson, *Regarding Children: A New Respect for Childhood and Families* (Louisville: Westminster John Knox Press, 1994), 20.

[36]Some systematic theologians have begun to do their own "practicing theology," but sometimes with little awareness or acknowledgment of previous efforts within practical theology. See, e.g., Miroslav Volf and Dorothy Bass, eds., *Practicing Theology: Beliefs and Practices in Christian Life* (Grand Rapids, Mich.: Eerdmans, 2002), or Delwin Brown, Sheila Greeve Davaney, and Kathryn Tanner, eds., *Converging on Culture: Theologians in Dialogue with Cultural Analysis and Criticism* (New York: Oxford University Press, 2001).

[37]Don S. Browning, A Fundamental Practical Theology: Descriptive and Strategic Proposals (Minneapolis: Fortress Press, 1996).

[38]See David Tracy's portrait of practical theology in *Blessed Rage for Order: The New Pluralism in Theology* (Chicago: University of Chicago Press, 1988).

[39]See Bonnie J. Miller-McLemore, "Pastoral Theology and Public Theology: Developments in the U.S.," in *Pathways to the Public Square: Practical Theology in an Age of Pluralism,* ed. Elaine Graham and Anna Rowlands (Münster, Germany: Lit-Verlag, 2005), 95–105, and "Pastoral Theology as Public Theology: Revolutions in the 'Fourth Area,'" in *Pastoral Care and Counseling: Redefining the Paradigms,* ed. Nancy Ramsay (Nashville: Abingdon Press, 2004), 44–64. See also Elaine Graham, *Transforming Practice: Pastoral Theology in an Age of Uncertainty* (London and New York: Mowbray, 1996) and Stephen Pattison with James Woodward, *A Vision of Pastoral Theology: In Search of Words that Resurrect the Dead* (Edinburgh: Contact Pastoral Limited Trust, 1994).

[40]See Robert Wuthnow's definition of practice in his own study of *Growing Up Religious: Christians and Jews and Their Journeys of Faith* (Boston: Beacon, 1999), xxxvi.

[41]Rodney J. Hunter, "The Future of Pastoral Theology," *Pastoral Psychology* 29 (Fall 1980): 67, 65.

[42]Bonnie J. Miller-McLemore, *Also a Mother: Work and Family as Theological Dilemma* (Nashville: Abingdon Press, 1994), 104–5; see also her "'Pondering All These Things': Mary and Motherhood," in *Blessed One: Protestant Perceptions of Mary,* ed. Cynthia L. Rigby and Beverly Roberts Gaventa (Louisville: Westminster John Knox Press, 2002), 97–114; *Let the Children Come*; and *In the Midst of Chaos.*

[43]Others, such as John Wall and Joyce Mercer, have tackled similar questions of method. Wall suggests a "postmodern hermeneutical circle" with the human sciences and religion that includes child and adult perspectives and the irreducibility of the other ("Childhood Studies, Hermeneutics, and Theological Ethics," 533–38). Mercer turns to a Christian feminist practical theology that draws on cultural and close ethnographic study of practices, or the habitus surrounding children and faith (*Welcoming Children,* 6–39).

[44]Sara Ruddick, "Maternal Thinking," in *Mothering: Essays in Feminist Theory,* ed. Joyce Treblicot (Totowa, N.J.: Rowman & Allanheld, 1983), 213.

[45]Ibid., 214.

[46]Sara Ruddick, *Maternal Thinking: Toward a Politics of Peace* (Boston: Beacon, 1989), 24.

[47]Valerie Saiving, "The Human Situation: A Feminine View," *Journal of Religion* 40 (April 1960): 108; reprinted in *Womanspirit Rising: A Feminist Reader in Religion,* ed. Carol P. Christ and Judith Plaskow (San Francisco: Harper & Row, 1979), 25–42.

[48]See, for example, Christine E. Gudorf, "Parenting, Mutual Love, and Sacrifice," in *Women's Consciousness and Women's Conscience: A Reader in Feminist Ethics,* ed. Barbara Hilkert Andolsen, Christine E. Gudorf and Mary D. Pellauer (San Francisco: Harper & Row, 1985), 175–91; Sally Purvis, "Mothers, Neighbors and Strangers: Another Look at Agape," *Journal of Feminist Studies in Religion* 7 (Spring 1991): 19–34; Cristina Traina, "Maternal Experience and the Boundaries of Christian Sexual Ethics," *Signs: Journal of Women in Culture and Society* 25 (Winter 2000): 369–405; id., "Passionate Mothering: Toward an Ethic of Appropriate Parent-Child Intimacy," *Annual of Christian Ethics* 18 (1998): 177–96; and Cynthia L. Rigby, "Exploring Our Hesitation: Feminist Theologies and the Nurture of Children," *Theology Today* 56 (January 2000): 540–54.

[49]See W. Bradford Wilcox, "For the Sake of the Children? Family-Related Discourse and Practice in the Mainline" in *The Quiet Hand of God: Faith-Based Activism and the Public Role of Mainline Protestantism,* ed. Robert Wuthnow and John H. Evans (Berkeley: University of California Press, 2002), 287–316. Portions of Wilcox's paper appear in "Mixed Messages: Churches' Witness on the Family," *Christian Century,* 21 February 2001, 16–19.

Chapter 3: Princess Dreams

[1]"Snow White was the first indication of what eventually became a multibillion dollar revenue for the Disney empire constructed around the copywriting of images." Stephen Kline, *Out of the Garden: Toys, TV, and Children's Culture in the Age of Marketing* (New York: Verso, 1993), 118.

[2]Janet Wasko, "Understanding the Disney Universe," in *Mass Media and Society,* 2d edition, ed. James Curran and Michael Gurevitch (New York: St. Martin's Press, 1996), 359.

[3]Ibid.

[4]Disney has published multiple storybooks that continue the princess stories after their marriages. Most often, the princesses are portrayed as benevolent members of the upper class, philanthropists helping to address the needs of those less fortunate than themselves. They throw parties for orphans, help children discover their nascent gifts, host social gatherings, and perform other classic expressions of *noblesse oblige.*

[5]Henry Giroux, "Animating Youth: The Disneyfication of Children's Culture," in his *Fugitive Cultures* (New York: Routledge, 1996), 90–91.

[6]Ibid., 113.

[7]Kline, *Out of the Garden,* 136.

[8]Susan Linn, "The Commercialization of Childhood," in *Childhood Lost: How American Culture Is Failing Our Kids,* ed. Sharna Olfman (Westport, Conn.: Praeger, 2005), 109.

[9]Norma Odom Pecora, *The Business of Children's Entertainment* (New York: The Guilford Press, 1998), 131.

[10]An estimated $14 billion in Disney products were sold around the world in 1994, and that number has only increased in recent years. See Wasko, "Understanding the Disney Universe," 355.

[11]Juliet B. Schor, *Born to Buy: The Commercialized Child and the New Consumer Culture* (New York: Scribner, 2004), 63.

[12]Pecora, *Business of Children's Entertainment,* 131–32.

[13]Schor, *Born to Buy,* 23; Linn, "Commercialization of Childhood," 110.

[14]Linn, "Commercialization of Childhood," 110.

[15]Ibid., 111.

[16]Ibid., 114.

[17]Barrie Gunter and Adrian Furnham, *Children as Consumers: A Psychological Analysis of the Young People's Market* (New York: Routledge, 1998), 171.

[18]Ibid., 173.

[19]Linn, "Commercialization of Childhood," 117.

[20]Ibid., 115.

[21]Gunter and Furnham, *Children as Consumers,* 125.

[22]Ibid., 126.

[23]Linn, "Commercialization of Childhood," 116.

[24]Joyce Mercer, *Welcoming Children: A Practical Theology of Childhood* (St. Louis: Chalice Press, 2005), 73.

[25]Ibid.

[26]Ibid.

[27]Elizabeth Chin, *Purchasing Power: Black Kids and American Consumer Culture* (Minneapolis: University of Minnesota Press, 2001), 7.

[28]Ibid., 3.

[29]Alex Kotlowitz, "False Connections," in *Consuming Desires,* ed. Roger Rosenblatt (Washington, D.C.: Island Press, 1999), 72.

[30]Schor, *Born to Buy,* 63.

[31]Mercer, *Welcoming Children,* 92.

[32]Linn, "Commercialization of Childhood," 107.

[33]Ibid., 108.

[34]Michael Warren, *Seeing through the Media: A Religious View of Communications and Cultural Analysis* (Harrisburg, Pa.: Trinity Press International, 1997), 13.

[35]Ibid., 10.

[36]Stewart M. Hoover, Lynn Schofield Clark, Diane F. Alters, *Media, Home, and Family* (New York: Routledge, 2004), 176.

[37]Chin, *Purchasing Power,* 1.

[38]Ibid., 10.

Chapter 4: Violence, Boy Code, and Schools

[1]Over the course of six months, I interviewed seventy-seven adolescent males, ages 12–19. While my fulltime vocation is as a professor, I am frequently invited to preach in churches and to speak to gatherings of young people. I took advantage of these opportunities to conduct interviews. The interviews took place in Chicago, Sarasota, San Anselmo, Calif.; Seattle; Kansas City, Mo.; Clinton, S.C.; Honolulu; Montreat, N.C.; Hunt, Tex.; and Atlanta. At each site, I gathered a group of young men and told them about my research and asked them several questions, recording their responses on tape. This is how I met Nathan and Curtis. In my group interviews, I asked Nathan and Curtis if I might follow up with them electronically or over the phone. I am grateful for their willingness to engage in further conversation and also for their parents' support. Nathan and Curtis are real people, but these are not their real names.

[2]James Garbarino, *Lost Boys: Why Our Sons Turn Violent and How We Can Save Them* (New York: The Free Press, 1999), 4.

[3]C. J. Pascoe, *Dude, You're a Fag: Masculinity and Sexuality in High School* (Berkeley, Calif.: University of California Press, 2007), 5.

[4]William Pollack, *Real Boys: Rescuing Our Sons from the Myths of Boyhood* (New York: Henry Holt, 1998).

[5]Ibid., 23.

[6]Ibid., 15.

[7]Michael Gurian and Kathy Stevens, *The Minds of Boys: Saving Our Sons from Falling behind in School and Life* (San Francisco: Jossey-Bass, 2005), 21.

[8]Ibid.

[9]Pedro A. Noguera, "The Trouble with Black Boys: The Role and Influence of Environmental Factors on the Academic Performance of African American Males" (pt. 3), *In Motion,* (May 12, 2002), cited by Gurian and Stevens, *Minds of Boys,* 22.

[10]Dan Kindlon and Michael Thompson, *Raising Cain: Protecting the Emotional Life of Boys* (New York: Random House, 1999), 72.

[11]Robert C. Dykstra, Allan Hugh Cole Jr., and Donald Capps, *Losers, Loners, and Rebels: The Spiritual Struggle of Boys* (Louisville, Ky.: Westminster/John Knox Press, 2007), 33.

[12]Kindlon and Thompson, *Raising Cain,* 241.

[13]Pollack, 396.

[14]Garbarino, *Lost Boys,* 160.

[15]Michael Gurian, *A Fine Young Man: What Parents, Mentors, and Educators Can Do to Shape Adolescent Boys into Exceptional Men* (New York: Putnam, 1999), 231.

Chapter 5: "Sometimes I Feel Like a Fatherless Child"

[1]For a discussion of portraiture as a research methodology, see Sara Lawrence-Lightfoot and Jessica Hoffmann Davis, *The Art and Science of Portraiture*, 1st ed. (San Francisco: Jossey-Bass, 1997). Portraiture provides a means of getting a close-in look at a person, community, or issue. Its goals are less oriented to generalizability than particularity. The focus on exploring a specific situation allows the construction of knowledge about it, which may or may not have bearing on parallel situations.

[2]Judy Pascoe, *Our Father Who Art in a Tree* (New York: Random House, Inc., 2004), 3.

[3]Ibid., 74.

[4]Ibid., 186.

[5]Ibid., 94.

[6]Ibid., 176–77.

[7]Ibid., 192.

[8]Ibid., 166,

[9]Niobe Way and Helena Stauber, "Are 'Absent Fathers' Really Absent? Urban Adolescent Girls Speak Out about Their Fathers," in *Urban Girls: Resisting Stereotypes, Creating Identities*, ed. Bonnie J. Ross Leadbeater and Niobe Way (New York: New York University Press, 1996), 132–48.

[10]Rachel Devlin, *Relative Intimacy: Fathers, Adolescent Daughters, and Postwar American Culture*, in Gender and American Culture series, ed. Thadious M. Davis and Linda K. Kerber (Chapel Hill: The University of North Carolina Press, 2005), 10.

[11]Ibid., 18.

[12]E. Mavis Hetherington, "Effects of Father Absence on Personality Development in Adolescent Daughters," *Developmental Psychology* 7, no. 3 (1972): 313–26.

[13]See, for example: Stanley H. Cath, Alan R. Gurwitt, and John Munder Ross, *Father and Child: Developmental and Clinical Perspectives*, 1st ed. (Boston: Little Brown, 1982); Louise J. Kaplan, *Adolescence, the Farewell to Childhood* (New York: Simon and Schuster, 1984).

[14]Jennifer A. Hodgetts, *The Influence of Fathers and Other Significant Male Figures on Girls' Well-Being and Achievement in Early Adolescence* (vol. 65 (11–B) 2005: 6070) [Dissertation Abstract] Dissertation Abstracts International, Section B: The Sciences and Engineering, ProQuest Information and Learning, 2005, http://librarycatalog.vts.edu/screens/libinfo.html (accessed Jan. 15, 2007).

[15]Michael White and David Epston, *Narrative Means to Therapeutic Ends*, 1st ed. (New York: Norton, 1990), 19.

[16]Ibid., 15. See also Christie Cozad Neuger, *Counseling Women: A Narrative/Pastoral Approach* (Minneapolis:Augsburg/Fortress Press, 2002).

[17]Gerald Monk, "How Narrative Therapy Works," in *Narrative Therapy in Practice: The Archeology of Hope*, ed. Gerald Monk, John Winslade, Kathie Crocket, and David Epston (San Francisco: Jossey-Bass, 1997), 21.

Chapter 6: Healing the Wounds of War

[1]Previously published research from these studies includes Joshua Thomas and Andrew Garrod, "Forgiveness after Genocide? Perspectives from Bosnian Youth," in *Before Forgiving: Cautionary Views of Forgiveness in Psychotherapy*, ed. Sharon Lamb and Jeffrie G. Murphy (Oxford; New York: Oxford University Press, 2002), and Andrew Garrod, et al., "Culture, Ethnic Conflict and Moral Orientation in Bosnian Children," *Journal of Moral Education* 32 (2003): 131–150.

[2]Drawing on the work of developmental psychologists Jean Piaget, Lawrence Kohlberg, and Erik Erikson, as well as the theological insights of Paul Tillich and H. Richard Niebuhr, James Fowler proposed a series of definable stages through which human faith may progress over the course of the lifespan. Fowler conceptualized faith not as a set of beliefs but as a human activity of constructing meaning out of ordinary life, in light of what is perceived to be ultimate or transcendent. In his book *Stages of Faith*, Fowler also presented a research interview protocol that can be used to discern a particular individual's faith stage. See James Fowler, *Stages of Faith: The Psychology of Human Development and the Quest for Meaning* (San Francisco: Harper & Row, 1981). Our research team developed a shorter version of the interview, due to the additional time required for translation. Because Fowler's interview

asks subjects to speak at length about their life histories and important relationships, as well as to respond to specific questions about hopes for the future, views on suffering, and attitudes to other religions, it was a valuable vehicle to test the cross-cultural validity of Fowler's theory, and also to gain wisdom from young people about how they make meaning amid traumatic life experiences and continuing inter-ethnic hostility.

[3]Names and identifying details have been changed to protect the privacy of inteview subjects.

[4]Similar findings were made by: Lynne Jones, *Then They Started Shooting: Growing Up in Wartime Bosnia* (Cambridge, Mass.: Harvard University Press, 2005). Similar conclusions have also been drawn from other modern wartime contexts: James Garbarino, Kathleen Kostelny, and Nancy Dubrow, *No Place to Be a Child: Growing Up in a War Zone* (Hoboken, N.J.: John Wiley & Sons, Inc., 1999).

[5]See similar findings in Jones, *Then They Started Shooting.*

[6]Jodi Halpern and Harvey M. Weinstein, "Empathy and Rehumanization after Mass Violence," in *My Neighbor, My Enemy: Justice and Community in the Aftermath of Mass Atrocity,* ed. Eric Stover and Harvey M. Weinstein (Cambridge, U.K.: Cambridge University Press, 2004), 303–22.

[7]Tom Gallagher, *The Balkans in the New Millennium: In the Shadow of War and Peace* (London: Routledge, 2005), 144.

[8]John Paul Lederach, *Building Peace: Sustainable Reconciliation in Divided Societies* (Washington, DC: United States Institute of Peace Press, 1997), 150.

[9]Michael White and David Epston, *Narrative Means to Therapeutic Ends* (New York: W. W. Norton & Co., Inc., 1990). See also: Jill Freedman and Gene Coombs, *Narrative Therapy: The Social Construction of Preferred Realities* (New York: W.W. Norton & Co., Inc., 1996); Christie Cozad Neuger, *Counseling Women: A Narrative/Pastoral Approach* (Minneapolis: Augsburg/Fortress Press, 2002); and chapter 5 above: Joyce Ann Mercer, "'Sometimes I Feel Like a Fatherless Child': Adolescent Girls and Father-Loss."

[10]Marc Gopin, *Between Eden and Armageddon: The Future of World Religions, Violence and Peacemaking* (Oxford: Oxford University Press, 2000), 10.

[11]Gopin, *Between Eden and Armageddon,* 6.

[12]Sharon Daloz Parks, *Big Questions, Worthy Dreams: Mentoring Young Adults in Their Search for Meaning, Purpose, and Faith* (San Francisco: Jossey-Bass, 2000), 103.

[13]An excellent survey of Christian attitudes toward other religions, including arguments for pluralism on mystical and ethical grounds, is: Paul Knitter, *Introducing Theologies of Religions* (Maryknoll, N.Y.: Orbis Books, 2002). A starting point for Muslim resources is: Farid Esack, *Qur'an, Liberation & Pluralism: An Islamic Perspective of Interreligious Solidarity Against Oppression* (Oxford: OneWorld, 1997).

Chapter 7: Yearnings, Hopes, and Visions

[1]Consider, for example, Martin E. P. Seligman, *Learned Optimism* (New York: Pocket Books, 1998).

[2]John Dewey, as quoted in James W. Garrison, *Dewey and Eros: Wisdom and Desire in the Art of Teaching* (New York: Teachers College, 1997), 22.

[3]All of the statistics in this section are available in "America's Children," www.childstats. gov(accessed September 2007). In translating these figures into living conditions, consider that, in 2001, 36 percent of U.S. households with children had one or more of the following housing problems: physically inadequate housing, crowded housing, or housing that cost more than 30 percent of the household income.

[4]Chitra Golestani, unpublished study, 2002. Golestani, a research associate with the Paulo Freire Institute, UCLA, conducts educational research on social justice and global citizenship.

[5]Anne Marie Cox, "Phoenix Ascending," *In These Times* (May 13, 2002): 10.

[6]Joseph Smith, "History A-1," Nov. 1835, LDS Historical Department, Salt Lake City, 120, cited in Church Educational System, *Church History in the Fulness of Times: The History of The Church of Jesus Christ of Latter-day Saints* (Salt Lake City: The Church of Jesus Christ of Latter-day Saints, 1993), 31, cf. 29–36. See also Milton V. Backman Jr., *Joseph Smith's First Vision: The First Vision in its Historical Context* (Salt Lake City: Bookcraft, 1971), 155–77;

Dean C. Jessee, "The Early Accounts of Joseph Smith's First Vision," B.Y.U. Studies 9 (1969): 275–94; Richard L. Bushman, *Joseph Smith and the Beginnings of Mormonism* (Urbana: University of Illinois, 1984), 53, cf. 3–8, 49–64.

[7]Church Educational System, *Church History,* 31, cf. 29–36.

[8]Ibid., 21. See also Joseph Smith, *History of the Church of Jesus Christ of Latter-day Saints,* vol. 1, ed. B. H. Roberts (Salt Lake City: Church of the Jesus Christ of Latter-day Saints, 1932), 6–7.

[9]Celia Haig-Brown, Kathy L. Hodgson-Smith, Robert Regnier, Jo-ann Archibald, *Making the Spirit Dance Within: Joe Duquette High School and an Aboriginal Community* (Toronto: James Lorimer & Co., Ltd.), 46.

[10]Evelyn L. Parker, "Hungry for Honor: Children in Violent Youth Gangs," *Interpretation: A Journal of Bible and Theology* 55, no. 2 (April 2001): 148–60.

[11]Roger Hazelton, *God's Way with Man: Variations on the Theme of Providence* (New York: Abingdon Press, 1956).

[12]James W. Fowler, Constructive Practical Theology Seminar, Emory University, 4 September 2002.

[13]James W. Fowler, *Stages of Faith: The Psychology of Human Development and the Quest for Meaning* (San Francisco: Harper & Row, 1981). This is Fowler's first and formative book on faith development.

[14]Viktor E. Frankl, *Man's Search for Meaning* (New York: Washington Square Press/ Pocket Books, 1959, 1984), 55–56.

[15]Alice (pseudonym), interview conducted in Oakland, Calif., July 2005.

[16]Patricia Hersch, *A Tribe Apart: A Journey into the Heart of American Adolescence* (New York: Ballantine Books, 1998), 3–9.

[17]Ibid., 8.

[18]Ibid., 9.

[19]See, for example http://www.lovematters.com/truelovewaits.htm and http://www.lovematters.com.

[20]This quality was present in the six congregations that participated in the Youth and Culture Project, Claremont School of Theology, Claremont, Calif., 1985–1998. The congregations were Protestant and Roman Catholic, and they represented diverse ethnicities and parts of the United States. Ethnicities included: African American and Caribbean American; mixed European American; Norwegian American; Navajo; mixed Native American; and Korean American.

[21]An ethnically mixed Protestant congregation (largely European American) located in Southern California.

[22]A Native American congregation in Southern California, with Native people from fifteen tribes and nations and from several different parts of the United States.

[23]An African American and Caribbean American Roman Catholic parish in Southern California.

[24]A Norwegian American congregation in rural Minnesota.

[25]A Navajo Roman Catholic parish in New Mexico.

[26]A Korean American congregation in Southern California in which most of the parents are first-generation immigrants, and most of the young people are 1.5 generation.

[27]Samuel Oliner and Pearl Oliner, *Embracing the Other* (New York: New York University, 1995), 375–76, 386.

[28]Research in this arena covers a wide range of variables. Some samples are Daniel P. Goleman, *Emotional Intelligence,* 10th ed. (New York: Bantam Books, 2005); Howard E. Gardner, *Frames of Mind: The Theory of Multiple Intelligences,* 2d ed. (New York: Perseus Publishing, 1993); Stephen Nowicki and Erin Carton, "The Relation of Nonverbal Processing Ability of Faces and Voice and Children's Feelings of Depression and Competence," *The Journal of Genetic Psychology* 158 (Sept. 1997): 357–63. Some evidence suggests that positive expectations about the possibility of increasing intelligence are positively correlated with classroom motivation and performance. See Lisa S. Blackwell, Kali H. Trzeniewsky, and Carol S. Dweck, "Implicit Theories of Intelligence Predict Achievement Across an Adolescent Transition: A Longitudinal Study and an Intervention," *Child Development* 78, no. 1 (Jan./ Feb. 2007): 246–63; Ying-Yi Hong, Chi-yue Chiu, and Carol S. Dweck, "Implicit Theories, Attributions, and Coping: A Meaning System Approach," *Journal of Personality and Social*

Psychology 77, no. 3 (Sept. 1999): 588–99; Dweck and Ellen L. Leggett, "A Social-Cognitive Approach to Motivation and Personality," *Psychological Review* 95 (April 1988): 256–73.

²⁹This theme is grounded in scripture, especially in Proverbs 8:22–31 and John 1:1–13. The theme is more fully developed by theologians such as Elizabeth Johnson, *She Who Is: The Mystery of God in Feminist Theological Discourse* (New York: Crossroad, 1994).

³⁰See, for example, Tom Beaudoin, *Virtual Faith: The Irreverent Spiritual Quest of Generation X* (San Francisco: Jossey-Bass, 1998).

³¹Hans-Günter Heimbrock, "Beyond Secularisation: Experiences of the Sacred in Childhood and Adolescence as a Challenge for RE Development Theory," *British Journal of Religious Education* 26, no. 2 (2004): 119–31; id., "Perceiving and Understanding Religion: A Task for RE in the Classroom," *Journal of Beliefs and Values* 22, no. 2 (October 2001): 141–54; cf. Heimbrock, Christoph Scheilke, Peter Schreiner, eds., *Towards Religious Competence: Diversity as a Challenge for Education in Europe* (Münster: Lit Verlag, 2002).

³²Fred Smith, "A Prophetic Christian Education for Black Boys: Overcoming Violence," plenary address, International Seminar on Religious Education and Values, XIII, Kristiansand, Norway, July 2002.

³³Robert Coles, David Elkind, Lorraine Monroe, Charles Shelton, Buster Soaries, et al., *The Ongoing Journey* (Boys Town, Neb.: Boys Town Press, 1997); David D. Mitchell, *Black Theology and Youths at Risk* (New York: Peter Lang, 2001); Seligman, *Learned Optimism*.

³⁴Mitchell, *Learned Optimism*, 45–75.

³⁵Gregory Cajete, *Look to the Mountain: An Ecology of Indigenous Education* (Durango, Colo.: Kivaki, 1994).

³⁶Yaacov J. Katz, "A Value Based Core Curriculum: The Case of Israel," collegial paper, International Seminar on Religious Education and Values, XIII, Kristiansand, Norway, July 2002.

³⁷Sissel Ostberg, "Religious Education in a Multicultural Society: The Quest for Identity and Dialogue," in *Crossing Boundaries: Contributions to Inter-religious and Intercultural Education*, ed. T. Andree, C. Bakker and P. Schreiner (Münster: Comenius-Institut, 1997).

³⁸Heid Leganger-Krogstad, "Dialogue among Young Citizens in a Pluralistic Religious Education Classroom," collegial paper, International Seminar on Religious Education and Values, XIII, Kristiansand, Norway, July 2002, 5.

³⁹Lissi Rasmussen, "Diapraksis og Dialog Mellom Kristne og Muslimer, http:// www.tf.uio.no/krlnett/tekster/art_diaprax_berg_nov98.htm; cited in Leganger-Krogstad, "Dialogue among Young Citizens," 5. See also C. Platt, "Civic Education and Academic Culture: Learning to Practice What We Teach," *Liberal Education* 84, no. 1 (1998): 18–25; P. R. Souza, "Values Education and Cultural Diversity," in *Systems of Education: Theories, Policies and Implicit Values*, ed. M. Leicester, C. Modgil, and S. Modgil (London: Falmer Press, 2000).

⁴⁰Sissel Ostberg, "Norwegian-Pakistani Adolescents: Negotiating Religion, Gender, Ethnicity and Social Boundaries," collegial paper, International Seminar on Religious Education and Values, XIII, Kristiansand, Norway, July 2002; id., "Cultural Diversity and Common Citizenship: Reflections on Ethnicity, Religion, Nationhood and Citizenship among Pakistani Young People in Europe," in *International Perspectives on Citizenship, Education and Religious Diversity*, ed. Robert Jackson (London: RoutledgeFalmer, 2002), 83–97.

⁴¹Donald Ng, *Asian Pacific American Youth Ministry: Planning, Helps, and Programs* (Valley Forge, Pa.: Judson, 1988).

⁴²Mualla Selcuk, "An Approach to Religious Curricula in Turkey in the Context of Peace Education," collegial paper, International Seminar on Religious Education and Values, XIII Kristiansand, Norway, July 2002, 12.

⁴³Marisa L. Crawford and Graham M. Rossiter, *Reasons for Living: Education and Young People's Search for Meaning, Identity and Spirituality* (Melbourne: ACER, 2006); Rossiter, "The Development of Identity: Implications for Religious Education," in *Echo and Silence: Contemporary issues for Australian Religious Education*, ed. M. Ryan (Wentworth Falls, NSW: Social Science Press, 2001); Rossiter, "The Shaping Influence of Film and Television on the Moral and Spiritual Development of Young People: An Educational Response," in *Developing Child, Developing Media*, ed. J. Squires (Sydney: New College Institute for Values Research, 1999).

⁴⁴Kasonga wa Kasonga, collegial paper, International Seminar on Religious Education and Values, XIII, Kristiansand, Norway, July 2002.

[45]Mualla Selcuk, "An Approach."

[46]Heid Leganger-Krogstad, "Dialogue among Young Citizens in a Pluralistic Religious Education Classroom," in *International Persrpectives on Citizenship, Education and Religious Diversity,* ed. Robert Jackson (London: RoutledgeFalmer, 2003); Leganger-Krogstad, "Religious Education in a Global Perspective: A Contextual Approach." in *Towards Religious Competence: Diversity as a Challenge for Education in Europe,* ed. Hans-Günther Heimbrock, Christoph Th. Scheilke, Peter Schreiner (Münster: LIT Verlag, 2001).

[47]Michael Warren, *Youth and the Future of the Church: Ministry with Youth and Young Adults* (Eugene, Oreg.: Wipf & Stock, 2002); Warren, *Youth, Gospel, Liberation,* rev. ed. (Dublin: Veritas, 1999).

[48]One early exemplar of this emphasis is Paul Irwin, who drew heavily upon Erik Erikson. See Paul Irwin, *The Care and Counseling of Youth in the Church* (Philadelphia: Fortress Press, 1975).

[49]James Youniss and Miranda Yates, *Community Service and Social Responsibility in Youth* (Chicago: University of Chicago, 1997). See also Miranda Yates and James Youniss, eds., *Roots of Civic Identity: International Perspectives on Community Service and Activism in Youth* (Cambridge: Cambridge University, 1999).

[50]David Halberstam, *The Children* (New York: Random House, 1999).

Chapter 8: (Non)Cosmetic Ministry

[1]These and all others names of Germaine Lawrence students and staff have been changed to protect their privacy. The event described here took place on March 21, 1999.

[2]"Services and Education: An Overview," http://germainelawrence.org/services/index.html (accessed May 4, 2006). Germaine Lawrence uses dialectical behavior therapy.

[3]Walter Brueggemann, *Praying the Psalms* (Winona, Minn.: Saint Mary's Press, 1993), 25.

[4]Ibid.

[5]Sermon preached in chapel at Germaine Lawrence on June 8, 1997.

[6]Sermon preached in chapel at Germaine Lawrence on December 14, 1997.

[7]Sermon preached in chapel at Germaine Lawrence on October 11, 1998.

[8]Brueggemann, *Praying the Psalms,* 57, 59.

[9]Ibid., 61, 63.

[10]These petitions were shared in writing during chapel at Germaine Lawrence on March 21, 1999. The second petitioner's request to "make level" refers to earning sufficient points in the treatment program's behavioral modification system to maintain current privileges or advance to new privileges.

[11]Brueggemann, *Praying the Psalms,* 27.

[12]"Cutting" is the term counselors use to describe injuries girls inflict on themselves with any instrument sharp enough to break the skin. Treatment programs frequently ban or carefully regulate the use of metal, glass, and rigid plastic objects to prevent self-mutilation.

[13]Index card submitted during Germaine Lawrence chapel service on April 11, 1999.

[14]She made this assertion in part because she was aware of the *Left Behind* book series by Tim LaHaye and Jerry Jenkins, first published by Tyndale House in 1996.

[15]James Fowler and Mary Lynn Dell, "Stages of Faith from Infancy through Adolescence: Reflections on Three Decades of Faith Development Theory," in *The Handbook of Spiritual Development in Childhood and Adolescence,* ed. Eugene Roehlkepartain, Pamela Ebstyne King, Linda Wagener, and Peter Benson (Thousand Oaks, Calif.: Sage Publications, 2006), 39.

[16]This is Fowler's term for Stage II faith development, which typically coincides with middle childhood, but can extend beyond that timeframe. For further explication, see Fowler, *Stages of Faith: The Psychology of Human Development and the Quest for Meaning* (New York: HarperCollins, 1981).

[17]Melvin Levine, as cited in Fowler and Dell, "Stages of Faith from Infancy through Adolescence," 38.

[18]Emily Crawford, Margaret O'Dougherty Wright, and Ann Masten, "Resilience and Spirituality in Youth," in *Handbook of Spiritual Development,* ed. Roehlkepartain et al., 363.

[19]Fowler and Dell, "Stages of Faith from Infancy through Adolescence," 40.

[20]"Goth," a shortened form of "Gothic," is a teen style that emphasizes black clothing, pale skin with dark eyes and lips, and body adornments with romanticized death imagery.

The classic "Goth scene" includes an affinity for punk rock music, which birthed the culture. The character Abby on the popular television series *NCIS* is a good example of a competent and engaging young adult committed to Goth style. For a sympathetic discussion of Goth culture, see Voltaire, *What Is Goth?* (Boston: Weiser Books, 2004) or Paul Hodkinson, *Goth: Identity, Style, and Subculture* (London: Berg Publishers, 2002).

[21] Index card submitted during Germaine Lawrence chapel service on April 11, 1999.

[22] Voltaire, *What Is Goth?* 2.

[23] Given the Goth fascination with death and the high incidence of suicidal ideation among the school's population, participation in Goth culture was typically limited to age-appropriate dress, makeup, and musical choices, and reserved for those in advanced stages of their treatment programs.

[24] Parker Palmer, *To Know as We Are Known* (New York: HarperSanFrancisco, 1993), xii.

[25] Ibid., 67.

[26] A description of this incident is included in a popular teen magazine article about Germaine Lawrence: Sabrina Solin, "A Home of their Own," *Seventeen* (September 1996), 256.

[27] Ronnie Blakeney and Charles Blakeney, "Delinquency: A Quest for Moral and Spiritual Integrity?" in *Handbook of Spiritual Development,* ed. Roehlkepartain et al., 317.

[28] If staff members suspect a girl might try to run away–or if she has already attempted to run–they lock her shoes in a closet until the danger of running is past. A sock-footed girl cannot run as fast or as far on city streets as a girl in shoes, and stocking feet are also a reminder to the counselors on duty to remain vigilant.

[29] "About Germaine Lawrence," http://germainelawrence.org/services/index.html (accessed May 4, 2006).

[30] Crawford, Wright, and Masten, "Resilience and Spirituality in Youth," 363.

[31] Carol Lytch, *Choosing Church: What Makes a Difference for Teens* (Louisville: Westminster John Knox Press, 2004), 25.

[32] Ibid.

[33] Rose's prayer, shared in writing during chapel at Germaine Lawrence on March 21, 1999.

Chapter 9: Living Out Loud in a World That Demands Silence

[1] I use the *good life* here as indicative of what it means to live meaningfully in the world. The *good life* is defined variously, given one's understanding of what makes life purposeful and meaningful.

[2] The gospel as *good news for the poor* and as an invitation to imagine a world in which persons are fed, clothed, and made whole is drawn from Luke 4:18–21 and Matthew 25:31–40.

[3] Daniel 1:1–21.

[4] Numbers 27:4.

[5] Numbers 27:3–4. Quoted fully: "Our father died in the wilderness; he was not among the company of those who gathered themselves together against the LORD in the company of Korah, but died for his own sin; and he had no sons. Why should the name of our father be taken away from his clan because he had no son? *Give to us a possession among our father's brothers*" (emphasis added).

[6] Numbers 27:5–7. Quoted fully: "Moses brought their case before the LORD. And the LORD spoke to Moses, saying: 'The daughters of Zelophehad are right in what they are saying; you shall indeed let them possess an inheritance among their father's brothers and pass the inheritance of their father on to them.'"

[7] An African Call for Life, "Reflections on Wholeness," in *An African Prayer Book,* ed. Desmond Tutu (New York: Doubleday, 1995), 110–13.

[8] Robert Kegan, *In Over Our Heads: The Mental Demands of Modern Life* (Cambridge: Harvard University Press, 1994), 26. Kegan characterizes this as the transition from durable categories to cross-categorical meaning-making.

[9] Charles R. Foster, *The Future of Christian Education: Educating Congregations* (Nashville: Abingdon Press, 1994), 89. Foster argues that feeling intensifies thought, and thought or knowing clarifies feeling: "Something has significance if we 'think' it is important. But its significance is enhanced if we also 'feel' it is important."

[10]Ibid.

[11]Ibid.

[12]Ibid.

[13]Robert Kegan, *The Evolving Self: Problem and Process in Human Development* (Cambridge: Harvard University Press, 1982), 11. Kegan argues: "Thus, it is not that a person makes meaning, as much as that the activity of being a person is the activity of meaning-making. There is thus no feeling, no experience, no thought, no perception independent of a meaning-making context in which it becomes a feeling, an experience, a thought, a perception, because we *are* the meaning-making context."

[14]Kegan, *In Over Our Heads,* 26.

[15]Ibid.

[16]I am primarily concerned with youth whose acts of resistance and contestation promote well-being. See Kegan, *In Over Our Heads,* for a full discussion of adolescent behavior that subverts existing social constructions.

[17]Henry Mitchell, *Celebration and Experience in Preaching* (Nashville: Abingdon Press, 1990), 24. Quoted more fully, Mitchell explains: "[The] intuition contain[s] impression gathered and stored during the flow of life. This input is not examined, adopted or organized in a *consciously* rational manner. It includes a wide variety of insights from culture, family, church, school and community, and individual experience. Intuition can be guilty of harboring prejudice, but it may also contain most if not all of our highest and most valid values and insights."

[18]Salvatore R. Maddie, *Personality Theories: A Comparative Analysis* (Homewood, Ill.: Dorsey Press, 1968), 9. Maddie argues that rational knowledge is "reflective, explicit, logical, analytical, and precise." He describes intuitive knowledge by referencing "the times you have been seized by an inarticulate, private and emotional, as well as vivid, immediate and compelling, sense of the meaning of what is happening."

[19]Maxine Greene, *The Dialectic of Freedom* (New York: Teachers College Press, 1988), 6. Greene draws from John Dewey's use of *mind*: "And, as Dewey wrote, 'mind' should be thought of as primarily a verb. 'It denotes all the ways in which we deal consciously and expressly with the situations in which we find ourselves'... Clearly this relates to the kind of critical interpretation that gives content to the idea of freedom, that reveals lacks and deficiencies, and that may open the way to surpassing and repair." See also John Dewey, *Art as Experience* (New York: Minton, Belch & Co., 1934), 263.

[20]The notion that *hard work yields success* is essentially a recapitulation of the American work ethic and the notion that persons can "pull themselves up by their own boot straps."

[21]Michael Warren, *Seeing Through the Media: A Religious View Of Communications And Cultural Analysis* (Harrisburg, Pa.: Trinity Press International, 1997).

[22]Ibid., 40. Warren argues that iconic images have mimetic power that can "move those who see them toward mimesis or imitation" (128). He also contends that "the examination of images, understanding how they function, and discerning in whose interest they are produced, are all skills that can be learned." (135)

[23]Ibid., 129.

[24]Ibid.

[25]In this volume, Katherine Turpin's investigation of the princess image in Disney movies and its influence on young girls adds credence to the idea that media representations possess latent power to create and alter our perception of the world. She suggests that these so-called innocent fantasies have great influence on the identity development and nascent social commitments of young girls.

[26]Patricia J. Williams, *Seeing a Color-Blind Future: The Paradox of Race* (New York: Farrar, Straus and Giroux, 1997), 16.

[27]Patricia Hill Collins, *Black Feminist Thought: Knowledge, Consciousness and the Politics of Empowerment* (New York: Routledge, 2000), 69.

[28]Warren, *Seeing Through the Media,* 132.

[29]M. Shawn Copeland, "The Wounds of Jesus, the Wounds of My People," in *Telling the Truth: Preaching about Sexual and Domestic Violence,* ed. John S. McClure and Nancy J. Ramsay (Cleveland: United Church Press, 1998), 39.

[30]I use *racialized* intentionally to draw attention to how nonwhite racial and ethnic groups are deemed to have race while whiteness is "exonominated" as a color or race. See

Patricia Williams' *Seeing a Color-Blind Future* for a full discussion of color-blindness and the exnomination of whiteness in the Western world.

[31]"Devaluation" refers to a diminished view of persons who are members of particular ethnic, racial, economic, or gender groups over against the cultural norms of whiteness, maleness, and affluence.

[32]Evelyn L. Parker, *Trouble Don't Last Always: Emancipatory Hope among African American Adolescents* (Cleveland: Pilgrim Press, 2003), 46–47.

[33]Ibid., 46.

[34]Ibid.

[35]Aasim, Afrika Bambaataa, *The Definition of Hip-Hop* (online source no longer accessible, from , 1996). Aasim (Kevin Donovan), a 1970s DJ from the Bronx who became one of hip-hop's foremost artists with his 1982 release *Planet Rock,* notes the crosscultural impact of hip-hop: "Hip-hop means the whole culture of the movement... Rap is part of the hip-hop culture. The emceeing,...the djaying is part of the hip-hop culture. The dressing, the languages are all part of the hip-hop culture. The break-dancing, the b-boys, b-girls,...how you act, walk, look, talk are all part of hip-hop culture;...and *the music is colorless...hip-hop music is made from Black, brown, yellow, red, white.* Whatever music that gives you the grunt... that funk...that groove or that beat,...it's all part of hip-hop."

[36]Collins, *Black Feminist Thought,* 82.

[37]Parker, *Trouble Don't Last Always,* 140.

[38]India Aire, "I'm Not My Hair," on the CD *Testimony: Vol. 1, Life and Relationship* (Universal Motown Records, 2007).

[39]Kegan, *In Over Our Heads,* 342. In his discussion of communal ideologies that promote diversity, Kegan says: "Any 'community of ideology,' whether it is a culturally embedded community, and thus less visible (such as the induction of those favored by the culture into the professions), or a community of counterdominant ideology and thus necessarily visible (such as induction into feminism or Afrocentrism), can serve as a support or a holding environment for evolving the fourth order of consciousness." Although adolescence is included in Kegan's third order of consciousness, the concept of a "holding environment" appears appropriate to my discussion of a shared communal ethos.

[40]The importance of creating connections between the biblical text and the hearers' experiences is drawn from educational theorist Anne Streaty Wimberly's story-linking pedagogy. For a full discussion of story-linking, see Anne Streaty Wimberly, *Soul Stories: African American Christian Education* (Nashville: Abingdon Press, 1994).

[41]Walter Bauer, *A Greek-English Lexicon of the New Testament and Other Early Christian Literature,* 3rd ed., rev. and ed. Frederick W. Danker (Chicago: The University of Chicago Press, 2000). This lexicon describes the Greek πληρόω (pronounced *pleroo,* fulfilled): "fulfillment of divine predictions or promises." Bauer further describes *fulfillment:* "The active *bring to fulfillment,* partly of God who brings divine prophecies to fulfillment...partly of humans who, by what they do, help to bring the divine prophecies to realization." I use *fulfillment* as indicative of divine process and as a summons for an active human response.

[42]This is akin to educational theorist Anne Streaty Wimberly's story-linking process.

[43]A reading of Matthew 25:34–40.

Chapter 10: Subversive Spirituality in Youth Ministry at the Margins

[1]For an introduction to faith-based community organizing, see Edward T. Chambers and Michael A. Cowan, *Roots for Radicals: Organizing for Power, Action, and Justice* (New York: Continuum, 2003); Michael Gecan, *Going Public: An Organizer's Guide to Citizen Action,* reprint edition (New York: Anchor, 2004); id., *Going Public: An Inside Story of Disrupting Politics as Usual* (Boston: Beacon Press, 2002); Harry C. Boyte, *Everyday Politics: Reconnecting Citizens and Public Life* (Philadelphia: University of Pennsylvania Press, 2004); Robert Fisher, *Let the People Decide: Neighborhood Organizing in America,* updated edition (New York: Twayne Publishers, 1994); Mary Beth Rogers, *Cold Anger: A Story of Faith and Power Politics* (Denton, Tex.: University of North Texas Press, 1990); Saul D. Alinsky, *Rules for Radicals,* reissue edition (New York: Vintage Books, 1989); Mark R. Warren, *Dry Bones Rattling: Community Building to Revitalize American Democracy* (Princeton, N.J.: Princeton University Press,

2001); Richard L. Wood, *Faith in Action: Religion, Race, and Democratic Organizing in America* (Chicago: University of Chicago Press, 2002); Dennis A. Jacobsen, *Doing Justice: Congregations and Community Organizing* (Minneapolis: Augsburg Fortress Press, 2001); Gregory F. Pierce, *Activism That Makes Sense: Congregations and Community Organization,* reprint edition (Calgary: ACTA Publications, 1997); Robert C. Linthicum, *Transforming Power: Biblical Strategies for Making a Difference in Your Community* (Westmont, Ill.: Intervarsity Press, 2003); http://uac. utoledo.edu/(Web site hosted by the Urban Affairs Center and Department of Sociology, Anthropology, and Social Work, University of Toledo); http://www.industrialareasfoundation. org/ (the official Web site of the national network that trains groups in the Alinsky tradition of faith-based grassroots community organizing); and "The Democratic Promise" (video documentary) that examines the history of community organizing, from the work of Saul Alinsky to the present time, focusing on two faith-based organizations in New York and Texas (available through: Chicago Video Project, CVP, 800 W. Huron, Suite 3 South, Chicago, IL 60622; tel. 312–666–0195; e-mail cvp@chicagovideo.com).

[2]Jürgen Moltmann characterizes his theological work in a similar way. See Richard Bauckham, *The Theology of Jurgen Moltmann* (Edinburgh: T & T Clark, 1985), 8.

[3]Representative works include: Henry Giroux, *Theory and Resistance in Education: Toward a Pedagogy for the Opposition,* rev. ed. (Westport, Conn.: Bergin & Garvey Paperback, 2001); id., *Teachers as Intellectuals: Toward a Critical Pedagogy of Learning* (Westport, Conn.: Bergin & Garvey Paperback, 1988); id., *Between Borders: Pedagogy and the Politics of Cultural Studies* (London: Routledge, 1993); id., *Living Dangerously: Multiculturalism and the Politics of Difference* (Berlin/New York: Peter Lang Pub. Inc., 1996); id., *Border Crossings* (London: Routledge, 1991); Paulo Freire, *Pedagogy of the Oppressed* (New York: Continuum, 1970); id., *Pedagogy of Hope: Reliving Pedagogy of the Oppressed* (New York: Continuum, 1994); id., *Pedagogy of Freedom: Ethics, Democracy, and Civic Courage* (Lanham, Md.: Rowman & Littlefield Publishers, Inc., 2000); id., *Education for Critical Consciousness* (New York: Continuum, 2005); id., with intro. by Donaldo Macedo, *Dreams and Possibilities: A New Pedagogy of Hope* (Boulder, Colo.: Paradigm Publishers, 2007); bell hooks, *Teaching to Transgress: Education as the Practice of Freedom* (London: Routledge, 1994); id., *Teaching Community: A Pedagogy of Hope* (London: Routledge, 2003); id., *Where We Stand: Class Matters* (London: Routledge, 2000); id., *Feminist Theory: From Margin to Center,* 2d ed. (Cambridge, Mass.: South End Press, 2000); Ira Shor, *Empowering Education: Critical Teaching for Social Change* (Chicago: University of Chicago Press, 1992).

[4]Such crises might be seen as analogues to "transforming moments" on the individual level, as explored in: James Loder, *The Transforming Moment: Understanding Convictional Experiences,* revised 2nd edition (Colorado Springs, Colo.: Helmers & Howard, 1990). Additional perspective on this point is supplied by Walter Brueggemann, *Hope within History* (Philadelphia: Westminster/John Knox Press, 1987).

[5]The implied theology of creation in Genesis 1 is that God's order is implicit within disorder, chaos, and "void." In theories of human development, stage transitions are seen to occur in moments of disequilibrium and disintegration of old patterns. During these passages, limitations are lost or minimized, allowing persons to accommodate further degrees of complexity into their personality development. In Loder's view, the "conflict-creativity" paradigm that supplies the inner grammar of transforming moments is the same paradigm that supplies the inner grammar of transformations in every sphere of the created order. Theologically, this is none other than the power and presence of *Spiritus Creator.*

[6]The United States Department of Housing and Urban Development defines a *colonia* as a community located within 150 miles of the U.S.–Mexico border that lacks one or more of the following: potable water supply, adequate sewage and drainage systems, safe and sanitary housing, or paved roads. Pajarito Mesa is a *colonia* that overlooks Albuquerque's South Valley and is home to several hundred families who lack basic services such as water, electricity, roads, emergency services, and school bus transportation. Many *colonias* are situated in flood plains, exposing homes to flood waters, as well as trash and raw sewage from flooded septic tanks, cesspools, and water from other areas. In addition to a lack of infrastructure and the hazards of environmentalism racism, residents of *colonias* face a host of other challenges in relation to economics, education, healthcare, and immigration. *Colonia* communities tend to be unincorporated, lacking a village or community government, compounding the difficulties that residents face in getting their needs addressed. New Mexico is home to more than one hundred *colonias.*

[7]Saul Alinsky's basic philosophy is spelled out in two works: Saul D. Alinsky, *Rules for Radicals,* reissue edition (New York: Vintage Books, 1989), and id., *Reveille for Radicals,* reissue edition (New York: Vintage Books, 1989).

[8]For a fuller discussion, see Susanne Johnson, "Christian Spiritual Formation in an Age of 'Whatever,'" *Review and Expositor* 98 (Summer 2001): 309–31.

[9]Thomas H. Groome, *Christian Religious Education: Sharing Our Story and Vision* (San Francisco: Harper and Row, 1980); id., *Sharing Faith: A Comprehensive Approach to Religious Education and Pastoral Ministry* (San Francisco: HarperSanFrancisco, 1991).

[10]From the perspective of gospel writers Luke and Matthew, *presence with the poor* is the precondition for the capacity to recognize and respond to our Living Lord. See Marianne Sawicki, "Recognizing the Risen Lord," *Theology Today* 44, 4 (January 1988): 441–49.

[11]Jürgen Moltmann, *Hope for the Church: Moltmann in Dialogue with Practical Theology,* ed. and trans. Theodore Runyon (Nashville: Abingdon Press, 1979), 26.

[12]The biblical notion of fellowship–*koinonia,* or fellowship in the Spirit–defies such compartmentalization. It is the result of two or more parties coming together and co-participating in a "third thing," which is none other than the active presence and ministry of Jesus. Experientially, youth groups know this to be the case. While they may never articulate it, they know tacitly the qualitative difference between "fellowship" that arises from a pizza party, for instance, and the "fellowship" that arises during a mission trip, where they meet "strangers" and together repair, build, or paint a house, sharing intense experiences of work, witness, and worship.

[13]Jürgen Moltmann, *The Church in the Power of the Spirit: A Contribution to Messianic Ecclesiology,* trans. Margaret Kohl. (Minneapolis: Augsburg Fortress Press, 1993), 14. The church has failed to emphasize the active presence of Jesus in a full spectrum of ways, so believers practice routine actions that leave them empty and bored. Moreover, churches often fixate on only one practice. For example, the WWJD–What Would Jesus Do?–movement of the 1990s was a popular experiment in making Jesus real in the lives of young people. Ironically, WWJD may have made Jesus seem more remote. As my colleague, theologian Joerg Rieger, points out, the implied ending of the phrase is: What would Jesus do if he were here? This suggests that Jesus is located elsewhere. The phraseology fails to affirm that Jesus is present, and his efficacy is framed simply as a moral exemplar. More theologically appropriate questions for young people are: What is Jesus doing? Where is Jesus already present in my neighborhood and city? What is he redeeming and transforming? How am I being called to participate?

[14]Jürgen Moltmann, *Theology of Hope* (London: SCM Press, 1967), 18.

[15]In his reexamination of sources of eschatological thought, Moltmann found that, rather than looking toward "the future as such" or the "hereafter," Christian eschatology looks toward the revolutionizing and transforming of the present in light of the future promised by God. See Moltmann, *Theology of Hope,* 10. As theological praxis, hope is something that Christians *do* together in the context of community; hope contests those things that thwart the full flourishing of life. See Jürgen Moltmann, *Hope for the Church: Moltmann in Dialogue with Practical Theology,* ed. and trans. Theodore Runyon (Nashville: Abingdon Press, 1979). According to Letty Russell, for whom eschatology holds the key to theology, we must learn to act eschatologically, practicing our ministry from "the other end," while at the same time working socially, economically, and politically from the "underside" of history, immersed in concrete engagement with persons who live there daily. See Letty M. Russell, *Church in the Round: Feminist Interpretation of the Church* (Louisville: Westminster/John Knox Press, 1993).

[16]Moltmann, Theology of Hope, 21.

[17]Jürgen Moltmann, *God Will Be All in All: The Eschatology of Jurgen Moltmann,* ed. Richard Bauckham (Minneapolis: Augsburg Fortress Press, 2001), 51.

[18]James Loder, *The Logic of the Spirit: Human Development in Theological Perspective* (San Francisco: Jossey-Bass, 1998), 257–58.

[19]Walter Brueggemann, *Hope within History* (Louisville: John Knox Press, 1987), 8.

[20]Ibid, 9–10.

[21]Justo Gonzalez, *Santa Biblia: The Bible through Hispanic Eyes* (Nashville: Abingdon Press, 1996), 61.

[22]A short prayer often said repeatedly. A form often used is, "Lord Jesus Christ, Son of God, have mercy on me, a sinner."

[23]Joerg Rieger, "The Word of God and the People of God: Revitalizing Theological Discourse from the Bottom Up," *Quarterly Review* 21 (Spring 2001): 33–44.

Chapter 11: With New Eyes to See

[1]*Merchants of Cool,* PBS Frontline Documentary, original airdate: February 27, 2001. Brittany Spears and Johnny Knoxville and his gang from *Jackass: The Movie* are paradigmatic examples of the "midriff" and "mook" stereotypes. The transcript of *Merchants of Cool* is available on the PBS Web site at [http://www.pbs.org/wgbh/pages/frontline/shows/cool/etc/script.html].

[2]Mary Elizabeth Mullino Moore, "Imagination at the Center: Identity on the Margins," *Process Studies* 34, no. 2 (2005): 282–300.

[3]Ibid.

[4]Maxine Greene, *Releasing the Imagination: Essays on Education, the Arts, and Social Change* (San Francisco: Jossey-Bass, 1995), 3.

[5]Maria Harris, *Teaching and the Religious Imagination: An Essay in the Theology of Teaching* (San Francisco: Harper San Francisco, 1987), 54.

[6]Greene, *Releasing the Imagination,* 123.

[7]By crisis, Erikson means a "necessary turning point, a crucial moment, when development must move one way or another, marshaling resources of growth, recovery, and further differentiation." See Erik Erikson, *Identity: Youth and Crisis* (New York: W.W. Norton and Company, 1968), 16.

[8]Erikson posits that the identity versus role confusion crisis must be resolved before a person can resolve the next developmental crisis–intimacy versus isolation. However, as Carol Gilligan points out, Erikson actually noticed another pattern of development that did not influence his normative stage theory. She writes, "Though Erikson observes that, for women, identity has as much to do with intimacy as with separation, this observation is not integrated into his developmental chart." See Carol Gilligan, *In a Different Voice: Psychological Theory and Women's Development* (Cambridge, Mass.: Harvard University Press, 1982), 98.

[9]Friedrich L. Schweitzer, *The Postmodern Life Cycle: Challenges for Church and Theology* (St. Louis: Chalice Press, 2004), 4.

[10]Kenneth Gergen, *The Saturated Self: Dilemmas of Identity in Contemporary Life* (New York: Basic Books, 1991).

[11]See Catherine Keller, *From a Broken Web: Separation, Sexism, and Self* (Boston: Beacon Press, 1986), esp. 129–136.

[12]Nancy Ammerman, "Religious Identities and Religious Institutions," in *Handbook of the Sociology of Religion,* ed. Michele Dillon (Cambridge, UK: Cambridge University Press, 2003), 207–24, esp. 213.

[13]Heinz Streib, "Mass Media, Myth, and Narrative Religious Education," *British Journal of Religious Education* 20, no. 1 (1998): 42–52, esp. 47 (italics in original).

[14]Mary Field Belenky, Blythe McVicker Clinchy, Nancy Rule Goldberger, and Jill Mattuck Tarule, *Women's Ways of Knowing: The Development of Self, Voice, and Mind* (New York: Basic Books, 1986), 5.

[15]Mary Pipher's bestseller *Reviving Ophelia: Saving the Selves of Adolescent Girls* (New York: Ballantine Books, 1994) is a well-known work that deals with the lost voices of girls. In *Young Femininity: Girlhood, Power, and Social Change,* Sinikka Aapola, Marnina Gonick, and Anita Harris discuss the increased criminalization of women of color and working-class women as the new "bad girl" becomes defined as the white, middle-class social aggressor (New York: Palgrave MacMillan, 2005).

[16]According to the American Academy of Pediatrics, 65 percent of young people age 8–18 have a television set in their bedroom. American Academy of Pediatrics, "Children, Adolescents, and Television" [*http://aappolicy.aappublications.org/cgi/content/full/pediatrics;107/2/423*], 10 May 2006. A study by the University of Michigan found that sleeping is the only thing that adolescents spend more time doing than watching television. See University of Michigan Medical School, "Television" [*http://www.med.umich.edu/1libr/yourchild/tv.htm*], 10 May 2006.

[17]Religious educator and media scholar Mary Hess draws on Douglas Kellner to define media culture as "a culture that is permeated by images, artifacts, music, and other elements

available for the creation of meaning, which are produced by commercial industries that also, for the most part, control their distribution." See Mary Hess, "From Trucks Carrying Messages to Ritualized Identities: Implications for Religious Educators of the Postmodern Paradigm Shift in Media Studies," *Religious Education* 94, no. 3 (1999): 273–88, esp. 274.

[18] Gergen, *Saturated Self,* 49.

[19] Ibid., 56.

[20] See Kathleen Engebretson, "Young People, Culture, and Spirituality: Some Implications for Ministry," *Religious Education* 98, no. 1 (2003): 5–24; Don C. Richter, Doug Magnuson, and Michael Baizerman, "Reconceiving Youth Ministry," *Religious Education* 93, no. 3 (1998): 340–58; Bert Roebben, "Do We Still Have Faith in Young People? A West-European Answer to the Evangelization of Young People in a Postmodern World," *Religious Education* 90, no. 3/4 (1995): 327–45; and id., "Shaping a Playground for Transcendence: Postmodern Youth Ministry as a Radical Challenge," *Religious Education* 92, no. 3 (1997): 332–48.

[21] Hess, "From Trucks Carrying Messages," 273.

[22] Bettina Fritzsche, "Spicy Strategies: Pop Feminism and Other Empowerments in Girl Culture," in *All About the Girl: Culture, Power, and Identity,* ed. Anita Harris (New York: Routledge, 2004), 155–62.

[23] See Stephen Crites, "The Narrative Quality of Experience," *Journal of the American Academy of Religion* 39, no. 3 (1971): 291–311.

[24] Alasdair MacIntyre, "Chapter 15–The Virtues, the Unity of a Human Life and the Concept of a Tradition," in *After Virtue: A Study in Moral Theory* (Notre Dame, Ind.: University of Notre Dame Press, 1984), 204–25, esp. 213.

[25] Aapola et al., *Young Femininity,* 36.

[26] Ibid., 39.

[27] Ibid., 61.

[28] Patricia Hersch, *A Tribe Apart: A Journey into the Heart of American Adolescence* (New York: Ballantine Books, 1998), 19.

[29] David F. White, *Practicing Discernment with Youth: A Transformative Youth Ministry Approach* (Cleveland: Pilgrim Press, 2005).

[30] Ibid., 4.

[31] Christian Smith with Melinda Lundquist Denton, *Soul Searching: The Religious and Spiritual Lives of American Teenagers* (Oxford: Oxford University Press, 2005).

[32] Pamela J. Bettis, Debra Jordan, and Diane Montgomery, "Girls in Groups: The Preps and the Sex Mob Try Out for Womanhood," in *Geographies of Girlhood: Identities In-Between,* ed. Pamela J. Bettis and Natalie G. Adams (Mahwah, N.J.: Lawrence Erlbaum Associates, 2005), 69–83.

[33] Marnina Gonick, *Between Femininities: Ambivalence, Identity, and the Education of Girls* (Albany, N.Y.: State University of New York Press, 2003), 41.

[34] See, for instance, Christie Cozad Neuger, *Counseling Women: A Narrative, Pastoral Approach* (Minneapolis: Fortress Press, 2001).

[35] Carol Lakey Hess, *Caretakers of Our Common House: Women's Development in Communities of Faith* (Nashville: Abingdon Press, 1997).

[36] Dori Grinenko Baker, *Doing Girlfriend Theology: God-Talk with Young Women* (Cleveland: Pilgrim Press, 2005). In the Stories of Gender project, I closely followed Baker's methodology, although I adapted it to deal specifically with questions of female and religious identity. In what follows I draw upon exit interviews I did with young women from two of the story sharing groups that I ran as part of Stories of Gender in 2005. Bethany, Emmy, and Lauren, three European American women, all rising sophomores who attend a Methodist church in an exurb of Atlanta, made up one group. Iesha, Idana, Alexa, Aasha, and Shantell, all African American women, ranging in ages from 14–21, who attend a Baptist church in Atlanta, made up the other group. All of the young women's names are pseudonyms, and all of the direct quotations are taken from the transcripts of the individuals' exit interviews.

[37] I want to recognize that the God-language used by Emmy, Bethany, and Lauren is primarily male language. As a researcher and not their youth minister, I did not feel it was my place to problematize their reliance on male language for God, although I struggled with this decision during the research process.

[38] Richter et al., "Reconceiving Youth Ministry."

[39]Paulo Freire argues that the first step toward transformation is "conscientization"– that is, coming to critical consciousness about the causes of oppression. Similarly, bell hooks describes conscientization as critical thinking, and she argues that critical thinking is stimulated when we realize that the way things are is not the way things have to be, a process that can be initiated either through experience or through recognizing the voice of another. See Paulo Freire, *Pedagogy of the Oppressed*, 30th anniversary edition (New York: Continuum, 2003); bell hooks, *Teaching to Transgress: Education as the Practice of Freedom* (New York: Routledge, 1994).

[40]Maxine Greene, *Releasing the Imagination,* 16.

[41]Mary Elizabeth Moore, "The Myth of Objectivity in Public Education: Intersubjective Teaching of Religion," *Religious Education* 90, no. 2 (1995): 207–25, esp. 224.

[42]*The OC* could be described as this generation's version of *Beverly Hills 90210* or *Dawson's Creek.*

[43]Robert Kegan, *The Evolving Self: Problem and Process in Human Development* (Cambridge, Mass.: Harvard University Press, 1982), 113–14.

[44]Revolutionary Brazilian educator Paulo Freire would call what I am recommending "problem-posing education." As Freire writes, "In problem-posing education, people develop their power to perceive critically *the way they exist* in the world *with which* and *in which* they find themselves; they come to see the world not as static reality, but as a reality in process, in transformation." Freire, *Pedagogy of the Oppressed,* 83 (italics in original).

[45]For instance, religious educator S. Steve Kang argues, "The media plays a crucial role in enabling the human being to encounter many diverse peoples representing different social enclaves and ethnic or religious backgrounds." S. Steve Kang, "The Socioculturally Constructed Multivoiced Self as a Framework for Christian Education of Second-Generation Korean American Young Adults," *Religious Education* 97, no. 1 (2002): 81–96, esp. 89.

[46]Richard Kearney, *On Stories* (London: Routledge, 2002), 137.

[47]I recognize that the belief that God works in "secular" culture might have the best support from the sacramental worldview of the Roman Catholic tradition in which I was reared. See Terrence Tilley, *Inventing Catholic Tradition* (Maryknoll, N.Y.: Orbis Books, 2000), 128–32. Tilley lists the sacramental universe as a second feature of the Catholic analogical imagination, one of the five principals of the Catholic intellectual tradition.

[48]Mary Hess, "Transforming Traditions: Taking Popular Culture Seriously in Religious Education," *Religious Education* 99, no. 1 (2004): 86–94, esp. 93.

[49]Schweitzer, *The Postmodern Life Cycle,* 58.

[50]Don S. Browning, "Congregational Studies as Practical Theology," in *American Congregations, Volume 2: New Perspectives in the Study of Congregations,* ed. James P. Wind and James W. Lewis (Chicago: The University of Chicago Press, 1998), 192–221, esp. 198.

[51]E. Byron Anderson, "A Constructive Task in Religious Education: Making Christian Selves," *Religious Education* 93, no. 2 (1998): 173–88, esp. 173.

Chapter 12: The Power of Testimonies

[1]I observed this youth service at a church in Atlanta, Georgia, and the reflections are drawn from field notes. The fieldwork project focused on worship practices of African American youth, part of my work in Theophus Smith's *Phenomenology of Black Religion* class. In this project, the practice of testimony sharing emerged as powerful.

[2]My understanding of voice/voicelessness among African American youth is informed by the work of feminist theorists on voice and silence. I acknowledge a nuance in my understanding of voice/voicelessness among African American female adolescents—for African American girls typically do not lose voice in adolescence. They remain boisterous and outspoken, but are often "silenced" by being criticized for being too loud or uncouth. For one explication of the complexity of the terms "voice" and "silence," see Mary Field Belenky, Blythe McVicker Clinchy, Nancy Rule Goldberger, and Jill Mattuck Tarule, *Women's Ways of Knowing: The Development of Self, Voice, and Mind* (New York: Basic Books, 1997), 17–20.

[3]Charles R. Foster and Grant S. Shockley, eds., *Working with Black Youth* (Nashville: Abingdon Press, 1989), 9.

[4]Ibid., 23. While I do not agree with his generalization that Black churches in the north and south were "squarely" behind the struggle for civil rights, I recognize that, in an era of

civil rights struggles and radicalism in Black churches (some if not all), the fact that youth education was not a more vital component of the struggle is peculiar. Note: Shockley himself recounts a study that shows the ambivalent or isolated position of many Black churches from the civil rights movement (24).

[5]Albert G. Miller, "What Jesus Christ and African American Teenagers Are Telling the African American Church," in *The Princeton Lectures on Youth, Church and Culture 1997, http:// www.ptsem.edu/iym/lectures/1997/Miller-What.pdf,* (accessed May 20, 2007), 37.

[6]Ibid. See also C. Eric Lincoln and Lawrence Mamiya, *The Black Church in the African American Experience* (Durham, N.C.: Duke University, 1990), 309–10.

[7]Miller, "What Jesus Christ and African American Teenagers Are Telling," 41.

[8]Anne E. Streaty Wimberly, ed., *Keep It Real: Working with Today's Black Youth.* (Nashville: Abingdon Press, 2005), xi–xxiii.

[9]Ibid., xiv.

[10]A.G. Miller discusses the "spiritual crisis" experienced by African American urban, poor youth. He describes the fact that this group of youth did not benefit from the gains of the civil rights movement. Given the "black flight" or exodus of Black middle class and professionals from urban areas, as well as the economic changes that came along with the closing of many urban industries, this group of urban working class has been abandoned and has morphed into a seemingly hopeless subset of the African American community.

Other scholars such as Evelyn Parker also discuss the necessity of developing "emancipatory hope" among African American adolescents. She, too, notes that these youth do not possess the same type of hope of, say, youth workers during the civil rights era to expect or affect change in their worlds.

[11]W. E. B. Du Bois, *Souls of Black Folks* (New York: First Vintage Books, Library of America Edition, 1990), 138. In his essay on "Of Faith of the Fathers," Du Bois describes his encounter of a Negro revival in Tennessee, while he was a student at Fisk University. I refer here to his text, for it is often cited as one of the first scholarly considerations of black religion in America, and it describes both the worship practices and experiences and the sociopolitical implications of the church.

[12]Drawing upon the language of legal proceedings and courtrooms, giving a testimony involves a witness of some set of events sharing the truth/details of the events as he/she perceived, remembered, and experienced them. Testimony in the African American Christian worship experience involves a similar type of sharing an event as the person perceived it, but usually involves an account of divine agency working in that event, either changing it or giving the person strength to endure it.

[13]Cheryl Townsend Gilkes, *If It Wasn't for the Women* (Maryknoll, N.Y.: Orbis, 2001), 137. Gilkes includes testimonies as a pillar of Afro-Christian worship, alongside biblical (KJV) references and imagination, preaching, prayer, and music. She discusses each from the perspective of black feminists and explores how they address issues of gender within Black churches and communities.

[14]See Thomas Hoyt, "Testimony," in *Practicing Our Faith: A Way of Life for Searching People,* ed. Dorothy C. Bass (San Francisco: Jossey-Bass, 1997), 91–103. In the preface to this work, Bass describes one of the guiding purposes of the work as offering "reflections on practices as a way of connecting our faith with our daily lives. It also opens a path of spiritual formation... The book represents a refusal to leave our beliefs in the realm of theory, insisting that they can make a difference in our lives" (p. xiii). The practice of testimony sharing is discussed in this context, demonstrating the ways for generations African Americans have been practicing their faith and always remaining hopeful that God had something to say or do or some way to be connected with their everyday lives.

[15]Hoyt, "Testimony," 102.

[16]Gilkes, *If It Wasn't for the Women,* 131. She writes, "Testimonies are priceless resources for sermons... Testimonies provide connections between the situation of biblical characters and contemporary problems and situations... Overwhelmingly, it is women who provide the testimony from which preachers are able to draw illustrations."

[17]Hoyt, "Testimony," 98.

[18]This revamping of testimony into a more formal structured practice also parallels the shift in some African American worship styles from a more "free church" tradition to a more structured order of worship. Although the worship styles evolved, the practice of sharing testimonies has persisted (in a somewhat truncated or more orchestrated form).

[19]In this section all references are drawn from my fieldwork project on worship practices of African American youth, part of my work in Theophus Smith's *Phenomenology of Black Religion* class. I observed worship at two predominately African American churches in Atlanta, Georgia, and Boston, Massachusetts. The Boston church is a congregation of about 300–500 members. Youth testimony services were a part of the whole church community celebrations, with the youth taking greater roles in worship. The Atlanta church is a larger congregation of about 2500–3000 members. The youth had bi-weekly worship services, with the youth in leadership of the youth worship service; however, the youth ministry, for the most part, remained separate from adult worship services. Note: All names are pseudonyms.

[20]All direct quotes are from "Michelle's" manuscript of her testimony and/or her e-mailed responses to my questions regarding her experience of testifying in church.

[21]See N. Lynne Westfield, *Dear Sisters: A Womanist Practice of Hospitality* (Cleveland: Pilgrim Press, 2001), 105; bell hooks, *Teaching to Transgress* (New York: Routledge, 1994), 12; Belenky, et al., *Women's Ways of Knowing*, 228.

[22]I am intentional in not foregrounding the goal of Christian formation. I believe that Christianity does not need to be sold to youth explicitly, nor do those who work with youth *need* to focus on proselytizing. In the face of myriad injustices and obstacles to adolescent survival and thriving, Christianity serves as the source from which my call to minister with youth emerges, and is not the *only* goal of that ministry.

[23]Kenda C. Dean and Ron Foster, *The Godbearing Life* (Nashville: Upper Room books, 2000), 27–39. In this section, Dean and Foster actually prefer the term "incarnational ministry," pointing toward the special relationship they desire youth to form with Christ, who becomes God in the flesh, or incarnate. Hence they look at relationships between youth ministers and young people as having the purpose of directing youth in their relationships with Christ. For my purposes here, it is sufficient to focus on relationships broadly, looking at both the relationships youth form with mentoring adults and other peers, and not be narrowly focused on guidance in the Christian faith. I see the impact of testimony sharing going much beyond what is often defined as one's spiritual life or faith walk.

[24]Ibid., 107–8.

[25]Ibid., 108–9. In regard to standards of excellence, Dean and Foster note that, even as we are open to serving God in a variety of ways, we recognize that some ways are effective and some ways are not. Dean and Foster argue that, despite the fact that a practice is part of our communal history, we can tell when it is done correctly or incorrectly (e.g., we know when there was good preaching or bad preaching, etc.). The idea is not to be punitive or judgmental in how others live out a practice. What is important is for persons to help others discern whether or not a practice is transformative for them. For example, in the practice of testimony, the community is essential in helping the adolescent discern the difference between transformative testimony and merely complaining about a bad situation or bragging about some great accomplishment.

[26]Gilkes, *If It Wasn't for the Women,* 138.

[27]Miller, "What Jesus Christ and African American Teenagers Are Telling," 35–37.

[28]My conception of identity builds upon Erik Erikson's notion of identity, succinctly described by more contemporary theorists. My understanding also emphasizes the multiple dimensions of identity and the ways both individuals and communities come to self-understanding. See James W. Fowler, *Stages of Faith: The Psychology of Human Development and the Quest for Meaning* (San Francisco: Harper San Francisco, 1981), 77. Writing in the voice of Erik Erikson, Fowler writes, "By identity I mean an accrued awareness of oneself that maintains continuity with one's past meanings to others and to oneself and that integrates the images of oneself given by significant others with one's own inner feelings of who one is and of what one can do, all in such a way as to enable one to anticipate the future without undue anxiety about "losing" oneself. Identity, thought of in this way, is by no means a fully conscious matter. But when it is present, *it gives rise to a feeling of inner firmness or of "being together" as a self.* It communicates to others a sense of personal unity or integration."

See also Michael Sadowski, ed., *Adolescents at School* (Cambridge, Mass.: Harvard Education Press, 2003), 7–8. Sadowski writes, "contrary to popular misinterpretations of [Erikson's] identity development theory, identity is not the culmination of a key event or a series of events, although key events can play an important role in the larger process. In fact, it is not the culmination of anything. It is rather, the lived experience of ongoing process–the process of integrating successes, failures, routines, habits, rituals, novelties, thrills, threats, violations, gratifications, and frustrations into a coherent and evolving interpretation of who we are. *Identity is the embodiment of self-understanding.* We are who we understand ourselves to be, as that understanding is shaped and lived out in everyday experience" (Italics added).

[29]Fowler, *Stages of Faith,* 153.

[30]This complex process of identity formation is compounded in light of an overarching view of what's acceptable in the dominant culture, articulated as a "double consciousness" by W. E. B. Du Bois over one hundred years ago. Du Bois describes the struggle of the Negro in America as "[having] two souls, two thoughts, two unreconciled strivings; two warring ideals in one dark body, whose dogged strength alone keeps it from being torn asunder."

Also see Beverly Tatum, *Why Are All the Black Kids Sitting Together in the Cafeteria?* (New York: Basic Books, 1997). Tatum discusses the developmental concerns of African American adolescents regarding the complexities of identity formation and racial identity formation. She also stresses the necessity of African American adolescents' having positive images and understandings of what it means to be Black in the U.S. reflected to them.

[31]All direct and summarized quotes from the youth minister are from my field notes and transcribed telephone interviews.

[32]Christie Neuger, *Counseling Women* (Minneapolis: Fortress Press, 2001), 143–47.

[33]Paulo Freire, *Pedagogy of the Oppressed,* 30th anniversary edition (New York: Continuum, 2000), 87. See also works by Henry Giroux and bell hooks—as they discuss the power of naming a particular reality as part of the process of reflecting upon it and then moving to action.

[34] Parker goes on to point to the ways that this type of testifying does not parallel the traditional practice/form of testifying in the Black church. She notes that, instead of looking at the purest form of the tradition, youth testimony offers us something more.

[35]Hoyt, "Testimony," 102.

Chapter 13: Sanctified Rage

[1]This is the retelling of a true event by a young woman interviewed for Evelyn Parker, *Trouble Don't Last Always: Emancipatory Hope among African American Adolescents* (Cleveland: Pilgrim Press, 2003). Allie is a pseudonym.

[2]bell hooks, *Killing Rage: Ending Racism* (New York: Henry Holt and Company, 1995), 19.

[3]Parker, *Trouble Don't Last Always,* 126–27.

[4]Michael R. McCart, "Psychosocial Needs of African American Youth Presenting to a Pediatric Emergency Department with Assault-related Injuries," *Pediatric Emergency Care* 22, no. 3 (March 2006): 154–59.

[5]Carol A. Wong, Jacquelynne S. Eccles, and Arnold Sameroff, "The Influence of Ethnic Discrimination and Ethnic Identification on African American Adolescents' School and Socioemotional Adjustment," *The Journal of Personality* 71, no. 6 (December 2003): 1197–233.

[6]See the discussion of findings in each chapter of Parker, *Trouble Don't Last Always.*

[7]Church Palahniuk, *Fight Club* (New York: W.W. Norton, 1996). The 1999 movie from Art Linson Productions was directed by David Fincher.

[8]Michael McCarthy, "Illegal, Violent Teen Fight Clubs Face Police Crackdown," *USA Today,* http://www.usatoday.com/news/nation/2006-07-31-violent-fight-clubs_x.htm (accessed October 2, 2006).

[9]William H. Grier and Price M. Cobbs*, Black Rage* (San Francisco: Basic Books, 1992).

[10]Robert Franklin, *Another Day's Journey* (Minneapolis: Fortress Press, 1997).

[11]Cornel West, *Race Matters* (Boston: Beacon Press, 1993), 14.

[12]Ibid., 18.

[13]Ibid., 15. Here I am appropriating Cornel West's argument regarding religious and civic institutions as buffers against the nihilistic threat.

[14]The African Methodist Episcopal, African Methodist Episcopal Zion, and Christian Methodist Episcopal Churches are examples of denominations that also had social creeds, which originated from the Wesleyan Methodist tradition before the Church of God in Christ.

[15]Elder C. F. Range Jr., ed., *Official Manual with the Doctrines and Discipline of the Church of God in Christ 1973* (Memphis, Tenn.: Board of Publication of the Church of God in Christ, Inc., 1991/92), 93.

[16]Ibid.

[17]Ibid., 119–20.

[18]Cheryl Townsend Gilkes, *If It Wasn't for the Women* (Maryknoll, N.Y.: Orbis Books, 2001), 49.

[19]John Storey, *Cultural Studies and the Study of Popular Culture* (Athens: The University of Georgia Press, 2003), 3. The work of John Storey is helpful in defining popular culture. I have appropriated his definition of hip-hop culture.

[20]For a comprehensive review of hip-hop culture and rap music, see Anthony Pinn, "Blues, Rap, and Nitty-Gritty Hermeneutics," in *Why Lord: Suffering and Evil in Black Theology* (New York: Continuum, 1995); Tricia Rose, *Black Noise: Rap Music and Black Culture in Contemporary America* (Middletown, Conn.: Wesleyan University Press, 1994); Anthony Pinn, *Noise and Spirit: The Religious and Spiritual Sensibilities of Rap Music* (New York: NYU Press, 2003).

[21]Pinn, "Blues, Rap, and Nitty-Gritty Hermeneutics," 122.

[22]Ibid.

[23]Ibid.

[24]Evelyn L. Parker, "Turning the World Upside Down: The Holy Spirit, Rage, and Righteousness," in *Longing for God: Youth and the Quest for a Passionate Church,* ed. Amy Scott Vaughn (Princeton, N.J.: The Princeton Lectures on Youth, Church, and Culture, 2004), 64–75.

[25]Robert W. Wall, "The Acts of the Apostles: Introduction, Commentary, and Reflections," in *The New Interpreter's Bible* (Nashville, Tenn.: Abingdon Press, 2002), 55.

[26]Evelyn L. Parker, ed., *The Sacred Selves of Adolescent Girls: Hard Stories of Race, Class, and Gender* (Cleveland: Pilgrim Press, 2006), 8.

[27]Parker, *Trouble Don't Last Always,* 141–44.

[28]Thomas Hoyt, "Testimony," in *Practicing Our Faith: A Way of Life for Searching People,* ed. Dorothy Bass (San Francisco: Jossey-Bass), 92.

[29]Ibid., 102.

[30]David White, *Practicing Discernment with Youth: A Transformative Youth Ministry Approach* (Cleveland: Pilgrim Press, 2005); Parker, *Trouble Don't Last Always.*

Chapter 14: Welcoming the Vernal Season of the Heart

[1]G. Stanley Hall, *Adolescence: Its Psychology and Its Relations to Physiology, Anthropology, Sociology, Sex, Crime, Religion and Education,* Volume 2 (New York: Appleton, 1904), 450.

[2]The Lilly Foundation, Inc., sponsored an initiative titled Theological Programs for High School Youth, in which, by its peak in 2005, forty-nine seminaries across the United States participated, exploring ways to strengthen capacities of youth and congregations for ministry with youth. The pilot program was the Youth Theological Initiative (YTI) at Emory University, which began in 1993, but the programs that have followed have taken many different forms.

[3]Parker J. Palmer, *To Know as We Are Known: A Spirituality of Education* (San Francisco: HarperCollins, 1983), 69ff.

[4]For an analysis of the abstraction of youth, see Grace Palladino's book, *Teenagers: An American History* (New York: BasicBooks, 1996). Also, for an incisive analysis of the role of technology and media in abstracting youth from their families and local communities, see Quentin Schultze, Roy Anker, James Bratt, William Romanowski, John Worst, and Lambert Zuidervaart, *Dancing in the Dark: Youth, Popular Culture and the Electronic Media* (Grand Rapids, Mich.: Eerdmans, 1990). I have included a general analysis of adolescence as an abstraction in my book, David F. White, *Practicing Discernment with Youth: A Transformative Youth Ministry Approach* (Cleveland: Pilgrim Press, 2005).

[5]See Richard Gaillardetz, *Transforming Our Days: Spirituality, Community and Liturgy in a Technological Culture* (New York: Crossroad, 2000).

[6]For a more complete description of this pedagogy and its uses, see David F. White, *Practicing Discernment with Youth*; or id., "Focusing Youth Ministry through Critical

Consciousness," in *Starting Right,* eds. Kenda Dean, Chap Clark, and Dave Rahn (El Cajon: Zondervan/Youth Specialties, 2001).

[7]The exception was the selection process, which did not remain the same. The changes in the selection process will be explained in a later section.

[8]The original model for YDP was drawn from the Youth Theological Initiative at Emory University.

[9]See Schultze, et al., *Dancing in the Dark.*

[10]See especially Henri Nouwen, *Lifesigns: Intimacy, Fecundity, and Ecstasy in Christian Perspective* (New York: Doubleday, 1986), 15ff.

[11]For a more in-depth articulation of this notion of practice, see Brian Mahan, *Forgetting Ourselves on Purpose: Vocation and the Ethics of Ambition* (San Francisco: Jossey-Bass, 2002).

[12]This theme is emphasized in Eagleton's analysis of aesthetics in the context of late capitalism. See Terry Eagleton, *The Ideology of the Aesthetic* (Cambridge: Blackwell Publishers, 1990), 366ff.

[13]The exception was the Pentecostal congregation, which had no facilities to host us. However, we did visit their worship service on the final Sunday and enjoyed one of their staff members as part of our staff throughout the month.

Chapter 15: Transformative Listening

[1]The Youth Discipleship Project spanned 1998–2001. My focus is on the first two years, whereas David White (previous chapter) focuses on the 2001 shift of locus from a summer residential program to one taking place in and with faith communities.

[2]David White describes the forms of listening, as well as the four stages of the discernment process in: *Practicing Discernment with Youth: A Transformative Youth Ministry Approach* (Cleveland: Pilgrim Press, 2005).

[3]For a thorough, helpful discussion of the preparation and use of codes, see Anne Hope and Sally Timmel's *Training for Transformation,* vol. 1 (Zimbabwe: Mambo Press, 1984), 74–82.

[4]Recent studies such as Dori Baker's *Doing Girlfriend Theology* (Cleveland: Pilgrim Press, 2005) and Evelyn Parker's *Trouble Don't Last Always: Emancipatory Hope among African American Adolescents* (Cleveland: Pilgrim Press, 2004) confirm the power of listening to the particularities of the stories of youth.

[5]Jill McLean Taylor, Carol Gilligan, and Amy M. Sullivan, *Between Voice and Silence: Women and Girls, Race and Relationship* (Cambridge: Harvard University Press, 1995), 120–21; William Pollack, *Real Boys: Rescuing Our Sons from the Myths of Boyhood* (New York: Random House, 1998), 7–9, 19.

[6]Taylor, Gilligan, and Sullivan, *Between Voice and Silence,* 203.

[7]Ibid., 23.

[8]Ibid., 25.

[9]Ibid., 26.

[10]Ibid., 120.

[11]Pollack, *Real Boys,* xx, xxi, 235. Pollack and his research team also chronicle hours of interviews with boys in the companion volume: William Pollack, with Todd Shuster, *Real Boys' Voices* (New York: Random House, 2000).

[12]Pollack, *Real Boys,* xxii.

[13]Ibid., xxiii.

[14]Pollack, with Shuster, *Real Boys' Voices,* xxv–xxxiv.

[15]See, for example, Baker, *Doing Girlfriend Theology*; Parker, *Trouble Don't Last Always*; Taylor, Gilligan, and Sullivan, *Between Voice and Silence*; Pollack, *Real Boys.*

[16]Paulo Freire, *Pedagogy of the Oppressed* (New York: Continuum, 1970), 101.

Conclusion: Choosing Life Requires Action

[1]Alexis Gendron and Kathleen McGinn, "Reverend Jeffrey Brown: Cops, Kids, and Ministers." Case Study Harvard Business School, Product Number 9–801–284, 2002.See also Joshua Cohen, *Boston Review: A Political and Literary Forum,* http://bostonreview.net/ BR18.3/BR18.3.html (accessed Sept. 27, 2007). Cohen gives an additional description of Sal: "Selven Brown ("Sal") a remarkable, complex, tragic person. He has been described by

his friends as a charming and brilliant man–interested in theology and philosophy, money and power–who worried about what he called his 'shady side.' Eugene Rivers, pastor of the Azusa Christian Community, first met Sal in 1988... Sal was a major Dorchester drug dealer–who kept his client list on a PC. After meeting Rivers, Sal struggled for five years to turn his life around. He developed a serious interest in religion, attended Concordia College for a year, and was scheduled to start as an investment broker trainee on June 7. Rivers last spoke to Sal on June 4. At the end of a conversation that extended through much of the night, Sal said, 'Maybe it is too late for me, Eugene, but save the kids.' He died two days later of a drug overdose..."

Also, the Ten Point Coalition's work with adolescents has served as the source of much critical reflection about ministry with youth. See Albert G. Miller, "What Jesus Christ and African American Teenagers are telling the African American Church," in The Princeton Lectures on Youth, Church and Culture 1997, http://www.ptsem.edu/iym/lectures/1997/Miller-What.pdf. (accessed May 20, 2007); and Eugene F. Rivers, III, "New Wineskins, New Models and New Vision for a New Century," in The Princeton Lectures on Youth, Church and Culture 1999, http://www.ptsem.edu/iym/lectures/1999/Rivers-New.pdf, (accessed Sept. 27, 2007).

[2]Sal was an older adolescent, in his early twenties, so the discussion of supporting a family is complex and we remain unclear if he was struggling to provide for an extended family, his parents, or his children (or some combination).

[3]Alexis Gendron and Kathleen McGinn, "Reverend Jeffrey Brown," 17.

[4]Cohen, *Boston Review.*

[5]Note that the biblical text is both affirming and problematic. The text emerges in the midst of a culture defined by war and even the genocide of Canaanites, a culture that held to a God of vengeance and retribution. An alternative reading and understanding of the text reminds us that, even in a culture of violence, people can make choices: choices to end violence, or choices to perpetuate it.

[6]Others have made this case as well. See Joyce Mercer, *Welcoming Children* (St. Louis: Chalice Press, 2005); Kenda Creasy Dean, et al., *Starting Right: Thinking Theologically about Youth Ministry* (Grand Rapids: Zondervan, 2001), 19–21. Dean writes, "Approaching youth ministry from the perspective of practical theology assumes that youth are called to take part in every practice of Christian ministry... All Christians are called to be practical theologians, disciples whose obedience to God in the church and world puts our truth claims into practice." Here, Dean intentionally blurs the lines between professional practical theologians and the tasks of "theologically reflecting on our Christian action" required of each Christian, but I appreciate her emphasis on the collective and intentional work of practical theology to which we must invite children and youth.

While each scholar in this volume is a practical theologian, a practical theological approach to ministry with youth has not always been the case, and reminding practitioners of practical theological methods that can and should take place in churches and other religious and public communities is significant. Along these lines are also James Fowler, *Faith Development and Pastoral Care* (Minneapolis: Fortress Press, 1987), 17; and Robert J. Schreiter, "Theology in the Congregation: Discovering and Doing," in *Studying Congregations,* ed. Nancy T. Ammerman, et al. (Nashville: Abingdon Press, 1998). These auhtors commend the task of practical theological reflection as one that should take place in a community of practice, and not simply or primarily in academia.

[7]Friedrich Schweitzer, *The Postmodern Life Cycle: Challenges for Church and Theology* (St. Louis: Chalice Press, 2004), 19.